# MARCION: ON THE RESTITUTION
# OF CHRISTIANITY

# American Academy of Religion
# Academy Series
## Edited by
## Carl A. Raschke

R. Joseph Hoffmann

# MARCION: ON THE RESTITUTION OF CHRISTIANITY
## An Essay on the Development of Radical Paulinist Theology in the Second Century

Scholars Press
Chico, California
94551

# MARCION: ON THE RESTITUTION OF CHRISTIANITY

An Essay on the Development of Radical
Paulinist Theology in the Second Century

by
R. Joseph Hoffmann
Ph.D., 1982, Oxford University

**Library of Congress Cataloging in Publication Data**

Hoffmann, R. Joseph.
    Marcion, on the restitution of Christianity.

    (AAR academy series ; no. 46)
    Thesis (Ph.D.)—St. Cross College, 1982.
Bibliography: p.
    1. Marcion, of Sinope, 2d cent. 2. Bible. N.T. Epistles
of Paul—Criticism, interpretation, etc.—History—Early
church, ca. 30–600. I. Title. II. Series: American Academy
of Religion academy series ; no. 46.
BT1415.H59   1984   230'.113'0924          83–9008
ISBN 0–89130–638–2

Printed in the United States of America

Für Leora:

Mein Schatz und meine Gehilfin

# PREFACE

Significant works of scholarship require a combination of two very different skills that do not always go naturally together. On the one hand there is need for a bold vision or hypothesis which enables the subject of study to be seen from a genuinely new perspective; but equally important is a readiness to check any such new insight by careful attention to the detailed evidence. It is the combination of these two skills in Dr. Hoffmann's work that gives it both its attractiveness and its importance as a contribution to theological scholarship.

His proposed revision of the date of Marcion's activity certainly offers an interestingly new picture of the Christian Church at the turn of the first century. And his theological assessment of Marcion's position is worked out on the basis of a full and detailed review of the evidence. How far he will succeed in convincing other scholars of the various provocative suggestions that he puts forward remains to be seen. But the process of debate to which this book ought certainly to give rise, whatever its outcome, cannot but serve to add to our understanding of this crucial, but still very obscure period in the development of the Christian Church. I warmly commend the book as one full of enlightening stimulus to anyone concerned with this very early period of Christian history.

MAURICE WILES

# CONTENTS

# FOREWORD

The present study is devoted to a consideration of the theology of
Marcion of Sinope (c. 70-150 CE). By his orthodox opponents, more than a
score ranging from Polycarp of Smyrna to Eznik de Kolb, Marcion was
known as the thief who attempted to rob the Church of its deposit of
received truth, corrupted the oracles of the Lord, and 'drove such a wedge
between the Law and the Gospel as to make two separate Gods'
(Tertullian). Depending on whose testimony one decides to credit, Marcion
was a seducer, a sailor, a wrecker of families, a hermit, a bishop, an
amanuensis of John the Evangelist, a predecessor of Simon Magus, a dabbler
in Jewish myths, an adherent of the philosophical schools, the pupil of a
Roman arch-gnostic, and a repentant heretic who in old age renounced his
error and (unbeknownst to his disciples) made peace with the Church.
According to Polycarp, whose warning to the Christians at Philippi
epitomizes the earliest view of the marcionite danger, Marcion was 'the
first-born of Satan', the anti-Christ himself. Taken together, the evidence
speaks more clearly of the seriousness of Marcion's heresy in the eyes of the
church fathers than of its substance, and church historians have attempted
with only variable success to reconstruct his teaching on the basis of the
polemic against it. In the interest of providing a background for the present
study, it is worthwhile to consider briefly the history of these attempts.

A. The reopening of Marcion's case after the Reformation had to do
with a renewed interest in the problem of the New Testament canon, and
was largely an undertaking of the German Theologen. Both Semler/1/ and
Schmidt/2/ concluded, before the end of the eighteenth century, that the
patristic accounts of Marcion's gospel were unreliable and that the heretic's
version of Luke was independent of any canonical source./3/ With the
intention of reasserting the credibility of the patristic testimonies, Hahn in

---

/1/ Semler, Proleg. in Ep. ad Galatas, 1771.

/2/ Schmidt, Henke's Magazin, 5 (1796), 3.

/3/ Cf. P. Couchoud, 'Is Marcion's Gospel One of the Synoptics?', Hibbert
Jnl. (1936), 265-77.

1823 undertook to reconstruct the text of Marcion's gospel./4/ His work was advanced in 1832 by Thilo/5/ and in 1849 by Harting./6/ Hahn's thesis was first persuasively challenged by Ritschl in 1846,/7/ followed in close train by Baur (1849)/8/ and Volckmar (1852)./9/ This formidable triumvirate supported the idea that Marcion's gospel had not been merely a falsification of Luke, but was dependent on an older prototype. Similar conclusions were put forward at Halle by Hilgenfeld in an 1880 monograph,/10/ and at Erlangen in 1892 by Zahn./11/

The textual debate was revived in 1907, when Dom Donatien de Bruyne convincingly argued that the prologues to the epistles of Paul in the most reliable MSS of the Vulgate, including the sixth-century Codex Fuldensis, originated in marcionite circles./12/ In 1927 de Bruyne attempted to show that three Latin prologues to the Gospels were anti-marcionite, the one to the Fourth Gospel naming Marcion as a contemporary of John./13/ Although

---

/4/ Hahn, Das Evangelium Marcionis in seiner ursprünglichen Gestalt, followed in the next year by his De canone Marcionis.

/5/ Thilo, 'Evangelium Marcionis ex auctoritate veterum monumentorum', Codex Apoc. NT, I, 401-86.

/6/ Harting, Quaestionem de Marcione Lucani Evangelii, ut fertur, adultere, collatis Hahnii.

/7/ Ritschl, Das Evangelium Marcions und das kanonische Evang. des Lucas.

/8 Baur, Kritische Untersuchungen über die kanonischen Evangelien.

/9/ Volckmar, Das Evangelium Markions, Texte und Kritik mit Rücksicht auf die Evangelium des Martyrers Justin, der Klementinen, und der apostolischen Väter.

/10/ Hilgenfeld, Kritische Untersuchungen über die Evangelien Justins, den clementinischen Homilien, und Markions.

/11/ Zahn, Geschichte des Ntln. Kanons (I.2, 585-718; II.2, 409-529). Zahn argued also Marcion's dependence on other gospels.

/12/ De Bruyne, 'Prologes bibliques d'origine Marcionite', Rev. Bénéd. (1907). Harnack (agreeing), cf. 'Die ältesten Evangelien-prologen und die Bildung des NTs', SBA (1928), 320f.

/13/ De Bruyne, 'Les plus anciens prologues latins des Evangiles', Rev. Bénéd. (1928), 195ff.

Harnack lent his support to de Bruyne's conclusions,/14/ the anti-marcionite character of the Gospel-prologues has been repeatedly disputed./15/

British scholarship produced no study of Marcion during the nineteenth century comparable in scope to Ritschl's, but English biblical critics were not long in responding to the German debate. In 1855, Westcott, then Regius Professor of Divinity at Cambridge, questioned the patristic evidence about Marcion's text of the gospel, suggesting that Epiphanius is all but useless for the purpose of reconstructing Marcion's sources./16/ Westcott also defended Marcion's claim to be the founder of the 'idea' of a NT canon. Twenty years later, the Oxford NT scholar William Sanday argued against Baur and Ritschl that the passages omitted by Marcion 'were indeed Lucan', though he concluded that there had been different versions of Luke available to Marcion./17/

B. An outgrowth of the interest in Marcion's text of the gospel was an interest in the practices of the Marcionites, the relationship between Marcionism and so-called early Catholicism, and the extent of the marcionite chuch. Arendzen, one of the first Catholic scholars to describe the religious practices of the gnostics in historical terms, distinguished between the doctrines of the Marcionites and the beliefs of the gnostic Christians./18/ His lead was followed by Amann in a 1927 article which broached the question of Marcion's significance for the study of christian origins./19/ The results of these early scientific descriptions are apparent

---

/14/ Above, note 12.

/15/ Most recently, J. Regul, Die antimarcionitischen Evangelien-prologe (1969).

/16/ Westcott, General Survey of the History of the NT Canon (1855/1896), 318ff.

/17/ Sanday, The Gospel in the Second Century, 204; cf. 'Marcion's Gospel', Fortnightly Review (1875).

/18/ Arendzen, CE (1910), IX, 645ff.

/19/ Amann, DCT, IX (1927), 2009ff.

in the work of Daniélou/20/ and Baus./21/ Neander/22/ and Meyboom/23/ had already called attention to Marcion's importance as a religious reformer and continuator of Paul's theology, and Barnikol in 1922 had urged that the first christian chuch, in the proper sense of the word, was that of the Marcionites. Renan had reached a similar conclusion, albeit guardedly, in his 1869 study, L' Eglise chrétienne, but preferred to say that Marcionism was the most profound 'sectarian crisis' that the Church had experienced before Arius. Loisy, in La naissance du Christianisme (1948), advanced the bold thesis that 'Marcionism was the most formidable rival and almost the only dangerous rival that Christianity had to encounter during the whole time it was in the process of being organized into a system' (ET: p. 323).

 C. It is difficult to pinpoint the beginning of interest in Marcion's religious thought. The overcoming of the patristic indictment of his exegetical methods also brought into question what his critics had said about his teachings. Hahn attempted in an ambitious 1823 work, Antitheses Marcionis gnostici, to systematize Marcion's religious opinions on the basis of the patristic evidence, but his work was little more than an anthology of citations. The same can be said about Hilgenfeld's effort to reproduce Marcion's apostolikon./24/ A number of scholars occupied themselves with the task of showing the sources of Marcion's opinions; of these, the most significant and influential was Bousset's effort to prove that Marcionism was a species of Persian dualism./25/ Other notable studies of the themes of Marcion's theology include Riviere's 1921 examination of the marcionite doctrine of redemption/26/ and Kayser's 1929 offering, 'Natur und Gott bei

---

/20/ Daniélou, Christian Centuries (1964), I, 97f.

/21/ Baus, Handbuch der Kirchengeschichte, ed. Jedin; ET: Handbook of Church History (1964), I, 190ff.

/22/ Neander, Antignostikus (1818); ET: II, 490.

/23/ Meyboom, Marcion en de Marcioniten (1888).

/24/ Cf. also Hilgenfeld, 'Das marcionitische Evangelium und seine neueste Bearbeitung', Theol. Jahrbücher, 12 (1853), 192-224; and Zeitschrift für hist. Theologie (1855).

/25/ Bousset, Hauptprobleme der Gnosis (1907); cf. Kyrios Christos (1913), 191.

/26/ Riviere, in RSR (1921), 185-207; ibid., (1925), 633ff.

Markion'./27/ One may also point to three studies written in English in the
first half of the present century: Despite its title, Wilson's Marcion: A
study of a Second Century Heretic (1933) was a fair attempt to present a
synoptic view of Marcion's religious thought. The appearance in 1942 of
Knox's Marcion and the New Testament and in 1948 of Blackman's Marcion
and His Influence helped to fill the gap in competent English-language
studies of Marcionism. Two further items can be mentioned in the same
connection: Harris's essay, 'Marcion's Book of Contradictions'/28/ and P. N.
Harrison's 1936 monograph, Polycarp's Two Epistles to the Philippians,
although the latter's use of Marcionism as a reference point for the dating of
Polycarp's letter(s) raises a number of problems./29/

D. By any reckoning, it was the appearance of Harnack's
monograph, Marcion: Das Evangelium vom fremden Gott in 1921 that
opened the modern era in Marcion-studies. Harnack stressed, like no
scholar before him (Neander is a partial exception), Marcion's significance
as an early christian reformator and disciple of Paul./30/ Harnack also
undertook to reproduce Marcion's text of the gospel, the letters of Paul, and
the Antitheses on the basis of patristic testimony, using in the process
sources that Hahn and Hilgenfeld had overlooked, or had not discovered.
The appearance of Neue Studien zu Marcion in 1923 did little to quiet the
storm of controversy that the 1921 study provoked. But despite critical
reviews by theologians as far apart as Loisy and Lietzmann,/31/ Harnack's
work remains unrivalled as a compendium of the relevant texts for the study
of Marcion's theology.

E. In the present study, I have tried to avoid approaching Marcion
on the basis of Harnack's conclusions. For reasons outlined in the course of
discussion, the amount of patristic evidence that I have felt able to credit is
much less than Harnack put forward; accordingly, there has been no attempt
to reproduce the text of Marcion's gospel. On the other hand, far greater

---

/27/ Kayser, in Th.St.K. (1929), 279ff.

/28/ Harris, in BJRL (1924).

/29/ Harrison, esp, 172-206.

/30/ 2nd ed. (1924); see further, SBA (1928); ZNTW (1925).

/31/ Loisy, in Hibbert Jnl. (1936), 378-87; Lietzmann, in ZNTW (1921),
94f. Cf. further, Lagrange, Rev. B. (1921), 602f.: Amann, RSR (1923),
111f.

emphasis has been given to the manifestations of Marcionism in the New Testament itself, and to the theological premises that determine Marcion's exegesis of the Gospel and Epistles. The relation of Marcionism to 'Ephesian orthodoxy', to hellenistic Judaism, and to the gnostic communities has been treated in greater detail than in Harnack's work, owing not only to a different approach to the sources, but also to the availability of sources discovered since the appearance of the 1921 monograph. Chief among these are the Nag Hammadi tractates, which permit for the first time a detailed comparison of Marcion's theology with that of gnostic teachers on the basis of writings emerging directly from the gnostic communities themselves.

The conclusions to be drawn from these comparisons are the primary support for the argument of this thesis: An adequate understanding of the formation of the ecclesiastical Paulusbild/32/ is possible only by examining carefully the encounter between the rival interpreters of the Apostle's teaching and authority against the background of second-century heterodoxy. From among these interpreters, Marcion emerges as the one whose teaching was the most influential in shaping the events that led to the domestication of the Apostle.

---

/32/ See the excellent discussion by Andreas Lindemann, Paulus im ältesten Christentum (1979), esp. pp. 395f.

# ABBREVIATIONS

## A. Primary Sources: Ancient Authors and Texts

| | |
|---|---|
| Act. Thom. | Acta Thomae |
| Acts Jn. | Acta Johannis |
| Adam. | Adamantius |
|    Dial. |    De recta in Deum fide |
| Augustine | Augustine of Hippo |
|    De pecc. mer. |    De peccatorum meritis et remissione |
|    Serm. |    Sermons |
| Ep. Barn. | Epistle of Barnabas |
| Can. Mur. | Muratorian Canon |
| Clem. | Clement of Alexandria |
|    Strom. |    Stromata |
| 1 Clem. | First Letter of Clement |
| 2 Clem. | Second Letter of Clement |
| Cyprian | Cyprian of Carthage |
|    Ep. |    Letters |
| Ps.-Cyprian | Pseudo-Cyprian |
|    De rebapt. |    De rebaptismate |
| Diog. Laert. | Diogenes Laertius (Lives) |
| Epiph. | Epiphanius of Salamis |
|    Panar. |    Refutation of all the Heresies |
| Eus. | Eusebius of Caesarea |
|    HE |    Ecclesiastical History |
| Eznik | Eznik de Kolb |
|    De sect. |    Confutation of the Sects |
| Hippol. | Hippolytus of Rome |

| | |
|---|---|
| Philos. | Philosophumena |
| Ref. omn. haer. | On Heresies |
| Ign. | Ignatius of Antioch |
| Eph. | Letter to the Ephesians |
| Magn. | Letter to the Magnesians |
| Philad. | Letter to the Philadelphians |
| Polyc. | Letter to Polycarp |
| Rom. | Letter to the Romans |
| Smyrn. | Letter to the Smyrneans |
| Trall. | Letter to the Trallians |
| Iren. | Irenaeus of Lyons |
| Haer. | Adversus Haereses |
| Jerome | Jerome |
| De vir. illus. | Lives of Illustrious Men |
| Josephus | Flavius Josephus |
| Antiq. | Jewish Antiquities |
| Contra ap. | Against Apion |
| Justin | Justin Martyr |
| I Apol. | First Apology |
| Tryph. | Dialogue with Trypho |
| Lucretius | Titus Lucretius Carus |
| De nat. rer. | On the Nature of Things |
| Marcion | Marcion of Sinope |
| Laod. | Epistle to the Laodiceans |
| Marc. Prol. | Marcionite Prologues |
| Ad Gal. | To the Galatians |
| Ad Phil. | To the Philippians |
| Ad Rom. | To the Romans |
| NHL | Nag Hammadi Tractates |

| | |
|---|---|
| Apoc. James | Apocryphon of James |
| Apoc. John | Apocryphon of John |
| Gos. Philip | Gospel of Philip |
| GT | Gospel of Truth |
| 2 Seth | Second Treatise of the Great Seth |
| Soph. Jes. Chr. | Sophia of Jesus Christ |
| Test. Truth | Testimony of Truth |
| Tri. Tract. | Tripartite Tractate |
| Origen | Origen of Alexandria |
| Contra Cels. | Against Celsus |
| In Luc. hom. | Homilies on the Gospel of Luke |
| De princ. | On First Principles |
| Philas. | Philastrius |
| Lib. haer. | Liber de haeresibus |
| Polyc. | Polycarp of Smyrna |
| Phil. | Letter to the Philippians |
| Recog. | Clementine Recognitions |
| Sib. or. | Christian Sibylline Oracles |
| Tert. | Tertullian of Carthage |
| Apol. | Apologeticum |
| De bapt. | De baptismo |
| De carne | De carne Christi |
| Adv. Jud. | Adversus Judaeos |
| AM | Adversus Marcionem |
| Ad nat. | Ad nationes |
| De paen. | De paenitentia |
| Praes. | De praescriptione |
| Adv. Prax. | Adversus Praxean |

| | |
|---|---|
| De pud. | De pudicitia |
| De res. | De resurrectione carnis |
| Adv. Valent. | Adversus Valentinianos |
| Ps.-Tert. | Pseudo-Tertullian |
| Omn. haer. | Against all Heresies |
| Theodoret | Theodoret of Cyrrhus |
| Eps. | Letters |

## B. Editions, Collections and Reference Works

| | |
|---|---|
| ACW | Ancient Christian Writers, ed. J. Quasten (Westminster MD, 1946ff.) |
| ANF | Ante-Nicene Fathers, ed. A. Roberts & J. Donaldson (Edinburgh, 1864ff.) |
| CBC | Century Bible Commentary, ed. W.F. Adeney (34 vols., Edinburgh, 1901-22) |
| CC | Corpus Christianorum (Turnhout, 1953ff.) |
| CE | Catholic Encyclopedia (15 vols., New York, 1907-14) |
| CSCO | Corpus scriptorum Christianorum orientalium (Paris, 1903ff.) |
| CSEL | Corpus Scriptorum Ecclesiasticorum Latinorum (Vienna, 1866ff.) |
| DAC | Dictionary of the Apostolic Church, ed. J. Hastings (2 vols., 1915-18) |
| DCB | Dictionary of Christian Biography, ed. W. Smith & H. Wace (4 vols., 1877-87) |
| DCT | Dictionnaire de théologie catholique (Paris) |
| Dict. Sp., suppl. | Dictionnaire de Spiritualité, ed. M. Viller, SJ, et al. (1937ff.) |
| EP | Encyclopedia of Philosophy, ed. P. Edwards (8 vols., New York, 1972) |

| | |
|---|---|
| GCS | Die griechischen christlichen Schriftsteller, etc. (Leipzig, 1877ff.) |
| ICB | Interpreters Commentary on the Bible, ed. C. Laymon (New York, 1971) |
| JE | Jewish Encyclopedia, ed. I. Singer, et al. (12 vols., New York, 1901-06) |
| LCC | Library of Christian Classics, ed. J. Baillie, et al. (Philadelphia, 1953ff.) |
| LThK | Lexikon für Theologie und Kirche, ed. 2 by J. Höfe & K. Rahner (13 vols., 1957ff.) |
| NCE | New Catholic Encyclopedia, (14 vols., New York, 1967) |
| NHL | Nag Hammadi Library in English, ed J.M. Robinson (Leiden, 1977) |
| NTA | New Testament Apocrypha, ed. E. Hennecke & W. Schneemelcher; ET, R.McL. Wilson (2 vols., Philadelphia, 1965) |
| OECT | Oxford Early Christian Texts, ed. H. Chadwick (Oxford, 1970ff.) |
| PG | Patrologiae cursus completus. Ser. graeca (161 vols, Paris, 1857-66) |
| PL | Patrologiae cursus completus. Ser. latina (221 vols., Paris, 1844-55) |
| PRE$^3$ | Realencyklopädie für protestantische Theologie und Kirche, ed. A. Hauck (21 vols., 1898-1908) |
| RAC | Reallexikon für Antike und Christentum (Stuttgart, 1950ff.) |
| RGG$^2$ | Die Religion in Geschichte und Gegenwart, ed. 2 by H. Gunkel (5 vols., 1927-31) |
| RGG$^3$ | Die Religion in Geschichte und Gegenwart, ed. 3 by K. Galling (6 vols., 1957-65) |
| Source chrét. | Sources chrétiennes, ed. C. Mondesert (Paris, 1941ff.) |

| TU | Texte und Untersuchungen zur Geschichte der altchristlichen Literatur (Leipzig, 1882ff.) |

## C. Secondary Sources: Periodical Literature

| BJRL | Bulletin of the John Rylands Library |
| BZ | Biblische Zeitschrift |
| CBQ | Catholic Biblical Quarterly |
| ChQ | Church Quarterly Review |
| EvTh | Evangelische Theologie |
| ExT | Expository Times |
| HTR | Harvard Theological Review |
| JAC | Jahrbuch für Antike und Christentum |
| JBL | Journal of Biblical Literature |
| JEH | Journal of Ecclesiastical History |
| JQR | Jewish Quarterly Review |
| JTC | Journal for Theology and Church |
| JTS | Journal for Theological Studies |
| NF | Neue Folge |
| NTS | New Testament Studies |
| Rev. Bénéd. | Revue Bénédictine |
| Rev. B. | Revue Biblique |
| RHPhR | Revue d'histoire et de philosophie religieuses |
| RHR | Revue de l'histoire des religions |
| RSR | Recherches de Science Religieuse |
| RThAM | Recherches de théologie ancienne et médiévale |
| ThZ | Theologische Zeitschrift |
| TLZ | Theologische Literaturzeitung |

| | |
|---|---|
| TS | Texts and Studies |
| VC | Vigiliae Christianae |
| ZKG | Zeitschrift für Kirchengeschichte |
| ZNTW | Zeitschrift für die neutestamentliche Wissenschaft |
| ZRGes | Zeitschrift für Religions- und Geistesgeschichte |
| ZTK | Zeitschrift für Theologie und Kirche |

## D. Secondary Sources: Books and Monographs

Barnikol, E.

Entstehung      Die Entstehung der Kirche im zweiten Jahrhundert und die Zeit Marcions (Kiel, 1933)

Barrett, C.K.

Documents      The New Testament Background: Selected Documents (London, 1956)

Bauer, W.

Orthodoxy and Heresy      Orthodoxy and Heresy in Earliest Christianity (Philadelphia, 1971)

Blackman, E.C.

Influence      Marcion and his Influence (London, 1948)

Bultmann, R.

ThNT      Theology of the New Testament (2 vols., New York, 1951-55)

Campenhausen, H.v.

Ecclesiastical Authority      Ecclesiastical Authority and spiritual Power in the Church of the First Three Centuries (London, 1965)

Formation      The Formation of the Christian Bible (London, 1972)

Conzelmann, H.

    ThNT                      Theology of the New Testament (London, 1969)

Hanson, R.P.C.

    Tradition               Tradition in the Early Church (London, 1962)

Harnack, A.

    Chronologie            Geschichte der altchristlichen Literatur (3 vols., Leipzig 1893-1904)

    Marcion                 Marcion: Das Evangelium vom fremden Gott, 2nd ed. TU 45 (1924)

Klijn, A.F.J.

    Introd.                  An Introduction to the New Testament (Leiden, 1967)

Köster, H.

    Einführung             Einführung in das neue Testament (Berlin, 1980)

    Trajectories           Trajectories through Early Christianity (Philadelphia, 1971)

Kümmel, W.G.

    Intro. to the NT       Introduction to the New Testament (London, 1966)

Loisy, A.

    Christian Religion     The Birth of the Christian Religion (London, 1948)

Marxsen, W.

    Introd. NT            Introduction to the New Testament (Oxford, 1968)

Souter, A.

    Text and Canon      Text and Canon of the New Testament (London, 1954)

Wilson, R.S.

    Heretic                  Marcion: A Study of a Second-Century Heretic (London, 1933)

Zahn, T.

   Forschung.                      Forschungen zur Geschichte des Ntln. Kanons (1881-1929).

[See further, pp. 313ff.]

# CHAPTER ONE

# THE HELLENISTIC MATRIX OF MARCION'S RELIGIOUS THOUGHT

## 1.1 Pontus

The significance of Marcion's religious thought for doctrinal developments in the second century is far easier to determine than the facts of his life or the sources of his opinions. /1/ According to the most ancient authorities, /2/ Marcion was a native of Pontus in Asia Minor, a region which Tertullian describes as barbarous and inhospitable:

> All is torpid here, everything stark. Savagery is there the only thing warm -- such savagery as has provided the theater with tales of Tauric sacrifices, Colchian love-affairs, and Caucasian crucifixions. Even so, the most barbarous and melancholy thing about Pontus is that Marcion was born there, more uncouth than a Scythian, more unsettled than a Wagon-dweller, more uncivilized than a Massagete, with more effrontery than an Amazon, darker than fog, colder than winter, more brittle than ice, more treacherous than the Danube, and more precipitous than Caucasus. /3/

For Tertullian, the barbarism of Marcion's unholy birthplace is matched only by the ravings of 'the Pontic mouse who has nibbled away the Gospels', 'abolished marriage', and 'torn God almight to bits with [his] blasphemies'.

---

/1/ See, for example, Loisy, La naissance du Christianisme; ET The Birth of the Christian Religion (1948), 323; J. Knox, Marcion and the NT (1942), 1ff.; J. Arendzen, CE (1910), IX, 645; R.S. Wilson, Heretic (1933), 176ff.; E.C. Blackman, Influence (1948), x, 125-27 (a response to the following); Harnack, Marcion (1921/1924); E. Barnikol, Die Entstehung der Kirche iim zweiten Jahrhundert und die Zeit Marcions (1933); B. Streeter, The Four Gospels (1924), 5; W. Bauer, Orthodoxy and Heresy (1934/1971), 128f.1A1

/2/ Justin, I Apol. 26; Tert., AM 1.1; Ps.-Tert., Omn. haer. 6 ('Ponticus genere'); Epiphanius, Panar. 42.1. Epiphanius adds the information that Marcion lived at Sinope.

/3/ AM 1.1.3f. This description appears to be based on that of Herodotus (c. BCE 484): 'Ho de Pontos ho Euxeinos ep hon estrateueto ho Dareios chōreōn paseōn parechetai exō tou Skythikou ethnea amathestata' (4.46). Tert. also recalls that certain Cimmerians from the north, pursued by Scythians, settled in Sinope (Herodotus, 4.12); but the geographical description does not comport with the ancient survey (Herodotus, 4.84).

The true picture of Pontus is somewhat less brutal than the one Tertullian paints./4/ Politically, the kingdom had represented a problem for its Roman governors in the two centuries preceding Marcion's birth./5/ In the second century BCE, the kings of Pontus controlled the considerable trade flowing between Sinope, Amius, and Trapezus. About BCE 120 the ruler, Mithridates V (Euergetes), was assassinated and the kingdom passed into the hands of his wife and eleven year-old son, Mithridates VI (Eupator). Prior to the accession of Mithridates VI, an alliance between Rome and the kings of Pergamum, Bithynia, Cappadocia, and expansion-minded Pontus had ensured a tenuous Pax Anatoliana. This peace was interrupted briefly in 179 when a coalition army of Pergamenes and Cappadocians were required to persuade Pharneces II (BCE 185-57) to withdraw his forces from the territories of neighboring Cappadocia and Galatia.

The pattern of belligerence toward Rome and toward its neighbors intensified under Mithridates VI, who had murdered his mother and brother in order to gain the throne at the age of nineteen. Initially, it would seem, Mithridates was less interested in taking on the power of Rome than in annexing the Crimea with its vast agricultural riches. As the Romans became more involved with the German problem to the north, however, Mithridates ventured to invade Cappadocia, using his son-in-law, Tigranes of Armenia, as his surrogate. In BCE 96, and again in 92, Mithridates' forces engaged the Romans, sweeping them from Anatolia and reducing the

---

/4/ Hegesippus states that after the destruction of the Temple in CE 70 there were 'many Christians living outside Jerusalem' (Eusebius, HE 3.20.6; cf. 3.32.6). The christian presence in Asia Minor is also confirmed by rabbinical sources; cf. A. Schlatter, Die Gesch. der Ersten Christenheit (1927), 363. If the ancillae mentioned by Pliny in his letter to Trajan (c. 111) were deaconesses, then the Christians of Pontus must have possessed a church order by the early decades of the second century (cf. Epp. 10.96-97 in E.T. Merrill, Essays in Early Christian History (1924), 174; F. Bruce, NT History (1971), 423f.; Ps.-Tert., Omn. haer. 6, claims, almost certainly without warrant, that Marcion's father was a Pontic bishop, but Tert. knows nothing of this.

/5/ The following section of Plutarch's Vitae are relevant: Caius Marius [346-353]; Sulla [370-382]; Sulla/Lysander [389]; Lucullus [401-418]; Crassus [445ff.]; Pompey [508-518]. Numbers in brackets indicate pagination in the Chicago (1952) edition. See also, F.E. Peters, The Harvest of Hellenism (1970), 316-24; 318-95; 517-28; W. Tarn, Hellenistic Civilization (1927), 108-41; 166-92; 266-98; Eduard Lohse, Umwelt des Neuen Testaments (ET: 1976), 15-53.

region to a heap of ruined cities./6/

Following on his successes against the imperial powers, the Pontic king urged the people of Asia to join with him in a massacre of the Romans in their midst./7/ In some fifty places, the command was carried out. One hundred fifty thousand Roman officials and functionaries were murdered. Encouraged by his apparent victory, Mithridates next proclaimed the liberation of Greece and sent armies into the province to drive out the Romans.

In BCE 87, Sulla was successful in putting down the Pontic threat in Greece,/8/ and at the same time the cities of Asia Minor began to rebel against their militant 'liberators'. But in BCE 74 Mithridates once again mustered his forces over the question of Cappadocia, this time against the Roman armies under Lucullus./9/ Reclaiming his own territory in BCE 69, Mithridates inflicted a number of humiliating defeats on the occupying Roman forces, a situation which caused the tribune Manilius to suggest that the hero of the Spanish campaign against Sertorius should be granted the imperium against the old war-lord from Pontus. It was thus left to Pompey to drive Mithridates' forces to ground,/10/ and the king into exile in the Crimea, where he died in BCE 63 while trying to raise an army for the invasion of Italy. When it was announced in Rome that Mithridates was dead at last and that his former kingdom had become a province of Rome, a celebration lasting ten days broke out in the city./11/

## 1.2 Sinope

Culturally, Sinope was far from being the barbarian enclave that Tertullian imagines. In most ways it resembled other hellenistic cities of

---

/6/ Plutarch, Vit., 404-22.

/7/ Tert. may have reference to this when he complains of the crucibus Caucasorum, AM 1.1.4.

/8/ Plutarch, Vit., 370-82.

/9/ Plutarch, Vit., 401-18.

/10/ Plutarch, Vit., 508-18.

/11/ After the death of Mithridates VI, his son Pharnaces attempted to regain the ancestral domain. He was unsuccessful against the superior forces of Rome under Julius Caesar. Plutarch, Vit., 597.

the oikoumene, although its pattern of unruliness detracted somewhat from its cultural virtues as a client of Rome.

Epiphanius tells us that Aquila, a relative of the Emperor Hadrian and a Jewish-Christian convert, was a native of Sinope./12/ His literalist rendering of the OT, produced after his reconversion to Judaism, was intended to replace the Septuagint which by CE 130 had become the Bible of the Christians./13/ It is likely that the (hellenistic) rabbinical tradition was strong in Sinope and that Aquila was merely one in a succession of Jewish teachers who flourished there. We learn from Cicero, for example,/14/ that more than a century before the time of Marcion and Aquila, Jews from the south had settled in the region. And Josephus, citing a passage from Strabo (d. CE 21) concerning the wealth of the Temple in the time of Sulla (BCE 178-138) reports that 'when Sulla crossed over into Greece to make war on Mithridates, the habitable world was filled with Jews'./15/ This information is the more valuable because Strabo was himself a native of the region.

If Sinope followed the pattern of other hellenistic cities of the period, the Jews would have occupied a class in society beneath the citizens, the farmers, and the metics. There is evidence to suggest that in some respects Sinopean Jews were more thoroughly hellenized than those of Antioch and Alexandria./16/ It is certain that the Jews in Asia Minor and Syria went beyond the mere imitation of Greek forms in religion. The eastern Jews had long been receptive to hellenistic syncretism: women had learned to wail for Tammuz and make cakes for the Queen of Heaven; Jews had taken Babylonian names which implied an identification of YHWH with Bel-Merodach and Nebo, and a Persian demon figures in Tobit. As the

---

/12/ Epiphanius, De mens. et pond., 14f.

/13/ Cf. Jerome, Com. in Isa. 7.14. By legend Aquila became a convert to Christianity, but was excommunicated and returned again to Judaism. His translation of the OT was formerly known only through extracts preserved in Origen's Hexapla. In 1897, some fragments were found in Caira Geniza in Cairo. See S. Sandmel, 'Aquila', JE 2, 34-8; 'Onkeles the Convert', JE 9, 405.

/14/ Cicero, Pro flac., 28.

/15/ Josephus, Antiq., 14.110-18.

/16/ D.M. Robinson, 'Ancient Sinope', Am. Jnl. of Philology, 27 (1906), 125-153; 245-79.

inscriptions from the synagogue at Delos show, YHWH took the Greek name Theos Hypsistos, a name later used by Philo./17/

    The Irano-Babylonian mythology has a special bearing on the development of Christianity in Pontus. An original Jewish diaspora had emigrated from Babylonia well before the loss of the Seleucid Empire in BCE 188, settling in a region dominated by semitic peoples originally from Persia. The confluence of these traditions in Pontus -- the Irano-Babylonian and Jewish -- created a religious climate of a distinctly pluralistic variety. Marcion's 'Aquilane' literalism in the interpretation of the OT, his doctrine of the greater and lesser gods, and his doctrinal heterodoxy may derive specifically from these circles, as Harnack tried to suggest./18/ It is beyond question however that his opinions originated in a syncretistic environment/19/ in which the christian orthodoxy assumed by the heresiologists of later times was completely unknown./20/

---

/17/ Cf. Tarn, Hellenistic Civilization, 180f.

/18/ Harnack, Neue Studien zu Marcion (1923), 15.

/19/ Hengel writes as follows: 'From the middle of the third century BC all Judaism must really be designated "Hellenistic Judiasm" in the strict sense, and a better differentiation could be made between the Greek-speaking Judaism of the western diaspora and the Aramaic/Hebrew-speaking Judaism of Palestine and Babylonia. . . . [The] differentiation between "Palestinian" and "Hellenistic" Judaism, which is one of the fundamental heuristic principles of NT scholarship [becomes thus] much more difficult; indeed, on the whole it proves to be no longer adequate' (Judaism and Hellenism, I, 104, 105; cf. 311). Hengel argues (Judaism and Hellenism, I, 308) that in Judaea itself a 'brake was put on the manifest syncretistic tendencies which led to an assimilation of Judaism to paganism'. According to Aboth 1.1., an attempt was made to 'put a hedge around the law' (cf. Barrett, Documents, 139, no. 127). Braun has described this process as the concept of 'sharpening the Torah' (Spätjudischhäretiker und frühchristlicher Radikalismus [1957], 155f.). 'The fixation [on the Torah] meant that no fundamental theological criticism of the cult and law could develop fully within Judaism' (Hengel, Judaism and Hellenism, I, 309). Hence the charge of apostasy to Hellenism, levelled at Paul by observant Jews: 'The apostle appears as a diaspora Jew who had become alienated from the faith of the fathers' (H.J. Schoeps, Paul, 261). The same characterization can fairly be applied to Marcion.

/20/ Enslin remarks (Christian Beginnings, 183) that 'any attempt to understand the development of early Christianity must recognize the fact that it is largely the story of the transformation and modification of . . . Judaism under the influence of the thought and practice of the Graeco-Oriental world'. See further, O. Linton, Das Problem der Urkirche in der neueren Forschung (1932); Harnack, Die Mission und Ausbreitung des Christentums in der ersten drei Jahrhunderten (1902); R. Sohm Wesen und Ursprung des Katholizismus (1909); K.L. Schmidt, Die Kirche des Urchristentums: Eine Lexikographische und biblisch-theologische Studie, in Festg. A. Deissmann (1927); M. Goguel, The Primitive Church (1947).

Reports of the Jewish insurrections of CE 66-70, 116-17, and 132-35 must have reverberated throughout Pontus but the effects in Sinope are difficult to assess. We learn from Dio Cassius that at the time of Hadrian's foundation of the Aelia Capitolina on the Temple-site in Jerusalem, 'All Judaea was stirred up, and Jews everywhere were showing signs of disturbance, gathering together and showing great hostility toward the Romans. Many outside nations were joining with them'./21/ Pontic Jews are almost certainly to be counted among the ones from outside Judaea who joined in the disturbances.

At the end of Tiberius' reign, Pontus was still a client kingdom, as it had been since the defeat of Mithridates VI by Pompey in BCE 64. The educated citizens of Sinope would have been familiar with Josephus' apologetic in the Jewish Wars,/22/ to the effect that unruly and reckless rebels had brought the abomination upon themselves. But the apologetic was of limited appeal, and to zealous Jews of the dispersion of no appeal at all. As Hengel has argued,/23/ the Jewish rebellions had the universal effect of sharpening suspicions among gentile citizens that the Jews considered hellenism a form of national apostasy. The extent of the anti-semitism and the Jewish reaction can be inferred from Josephus' arguments in the treatise, Contra Apionem:

> I have, I think, made sufficiently clear . . . the extreme antiquity of our Jewish race, the purity of the original stock, and the manner in which it established itself in the country which we occupy today. . . . Since, however, I observe that a considerable number of persons, influenced by the malicious calumnies of certain individuals, discredit the statements . . . concerning our antiquity . . . I consider it my duty to devote a brief treatise to all these points. . . . [The law was appointed] to be the most excellent and necessary form of instruction. . . . Should anyone of our nation be questioned about the laws, he would repeat them all more readily than his own name. The result then of our thorough grounding in the laws from the first dawn of intelligence is that we have them, as it were, engraven on our souls . . . . To this cause . . . we owe our admirable harmony. Unity and identity of religious belief, perfect uniformity in habits and customs . . . . Among [the Jews] alone will be heard no contradictory statements

---

/21/ Dio Cassius, Hist. Rom. 49.12ff.

/22/ Josephus, bel. Jud. 5.362-74; 6.392f., 399-403.

/23/ Hengel, Judaism and Hellenism, I, 306.

about God, such as are common among other nations./24/
While it might be thought that Pontic Jews, being more susceptible to
assimilation than Antiochene or Ionian Jews,/25/ would have been rather
vaguer targets for the kind of calumny that Josephus describes, and hence
less prone to the anti-hellenistic reaction implied by his insistence on the
unity and uniformity of Jewish belief and custom, we have only the case of
Aquila -- Marcion's contemporary -- from which to judge. Aquila's biblical
literalism, however, is quite clearly reactionary and unhellenistic in design,
manifesting growing Jewish disdain for the Septuagint./26/ Doubtless
Sinope had its share of hellenizing Jews as well, whose devotion to the
religion of the fathers was somewhat less perfect than Josephus indicates.

---

/24/ Josephus, contra Apionem, (Loeb ed.) 1.1-3; 2.175, 178-80.

/25/ There is substantial evidence for the existence of Jewish-pagan mixed
cults in Asia Minor from about the time of Augustus onwards: inscriptions
on the Sambatheion in Thyatira; the worship of the god Sabbatistēs in
Cilicia, and the Hypsistos-cult in Bosporus and elsewhere; the 'synhodos
Sambathike' in Egyptian Naucritus, etc. The ambiguity of the evidence
makes it difficult to distinguish between judaizing pagans and hellenizing
Jews. Tcherikover argued for the existence of pagan groups who imitated
Jewish customs (Corp. papyrorum Jud., III, 45ff.), while Goodenough
thought the Hypsistos-worshippers in Bosporus were Jews (JQR, 47 [1956],
221-44; cf. Tarn, Hellenistic Civilization, 179-80). Cf. Hengel, Judaism
and Hellenism, II, 200-01, notes 265-66; p. 205, n. 309. It is significant
that the oldest dated inscription from a christian place of worship comes
from a marcionite meeting place in Lebaba (Deir-Ali), three miles to the
south of Damascus: Synagoge Markioniston kom(es) Lebabon tou k(yrio)u kai
s(ote)r(os) Ie(sou) Kristou pronoia Paulou presb(yterou) - tou LX etous LX
(630 Seleucid = CE 318). The use of the word 'synagogue' as a designation
for a marcionite meeting place has perplexed scholars. It may be due to the
translation of keneseth as both synagogue and ecclesia (thus, e.g., James
2.2) in reference to a christian place of worship. But synagogue was also
the preferred designation of Jewish-Christians (Wilson, Heretic, 69). It is
likely that the survival of the usage in the marcionite community points back
to the origins of the marcionite church in the syncretistic milieu of second-
century Pontus. Hengel (Judaism and Hellenism, I, 308) believes that
gnosticism sprang from the same climate among Jewish-Samaritan groups,
but that 'having the law as its center prevented Judaism, even in Asia
Minor, from betraying its original trust'.

/26/ Hengel, Judaism and Hellenism, I, 102. Sandmel has suggested that
Aquila's translation was designed to provide a version of the OT which did
not lend itself to the prooftexting for which the Christians used the LXX
(Judaism and Christian Beginnings, 261) and thus represents Judaism's
'turning in upon itself after the destruction of Jerusalem'. Cf. Enslin,
Christian Beginnings, 84: The successive Greek versions of Aquila,
Symmachus, and Theodotion were produced 'by an outraged Jewry,
nominally to provide more accurate translations; actually because the LXX
had become essentially a christian book'.

But the existence of teachers such as Aquila points to the beginnings of a rigorist strain in Pontic Judiasm and a 'sharpening of the Torah' as a response to the destruction of the Temple. This being so, anti-Jewish sentiment can hardly have been less intense in Pontus than elsewhere between the years 70 and 140 CE./27/ What is perhaps of more significance is that it is precisely such a 'reactionary strain' of biblical exegesis that seems to stand behind Marcion's interpretation of the law and prophets as literal (i.e., purely historical) accounts of God's convenant with the Jews. Like Aquila -- though obviously for a very different reason -- Marcion opposed the spiritual and allegorical exegesis of the OT, which christian interpreters themselves derived from the hellenistic rabbis./28/ Marcion's attitude toward the law thus seems to have been informed both by the (anti-hellenist) literalism with which some Jews in Pontus were construing the Torah,/29/ and by the anti-Jewish sentiment which caused Judaism to turn in upon itself in the first place. Indeed, it is highly improbable that Marcion's theological development is not to some degree a reflection of this tension.

---

/27/ Fresh in the minds of many Jews would have been the words of I Macc. 1.56-57 concerning the Jewish persecution under Antiochus IV (BCE 175-63): 'And they rent in pieces the books of the law which they found, and set them on fire. And wheresoever was found any with a book of the convenant and if they consented to the law, the king's sentence delivered him unto death'.

/28/ Cf. Harnack, Marcion, 115 (on Marcion's use of the OT). Marcion was insistent that the prophecies of the OT had predictive value only with reference to the history and people of Israel (cf. AM 3.13-14). Cf. Daniélou, Gospel Message and Hellenistic Culture (1973/1980), 211-20. A similar disdain for allegory is expressed in the Clementine Recognitions, 10.42; and cf. Tert. de res. 20(!).

/29/ 'The enemies of the Jews were quick to recognize the reliance which they put on the Torah and the enthusiasm with which they rallied to its defense. And so the written Torah became the focus of their attack upon Judaism . . . . To attack the Torah was to attack Judaism itself; to defend the Torah was to defend the faith of their fathers', D.S. Russell, Between the Testaments (1960), 45; cf. T. Herford, Talmud and Apocrypha (1933), 80.

## 1.3 Diogenes

Philosophically, Sinope had long been associated with the name of Diogenes (fl. BCE 360), whose Greek nickname, 'the dog', is the butt of a withering chiasmus in Tertullian's AM: 'The dog-worshipper Diogenes carried a lamp about at midday looking to find a man, whereas Marcion, by putting out the light of his own faith has lost the God whom once he had found'./30/ Here again Tertullian's words are meant for ridicule, but point to the interesting fact that there are certain similarities between Marcion and his Sinopean predecessor./31/

In the tradition preserved by Diogenes Laertius (BCE 200),/32/ Diogenes came to Athens as an exile from Sinope and there sat at the feet of the famous proto-cynic Antisthenes./33/ Thereafter he began to preach an eccentric form of the Socratic philosophy (Plato calls him Sōkratēs mainomenos)/34/ in which he excoriated wealth, marriage,/35/ private property, and Platonism./36/ According to Laertius, 'he saw no impropriety either in stealing anything from a temple or in eating the flesh of any animal; nor even anything impious in touching human flesh, this, he said being clear from the custom of some foreign nations . . . . He held that we should neglect music, geometry, astronomy, and like studies, as useless and unnecessary'./37/ Both Diogenes and Antisthenes/38/ seem to have been

---

/30/ AM 1.1.6. This rhetorical flourish serves as an introduction to Tert.'s claim (therafter repeated) that Marcion was at first an 'orthodox' Christian: 'Non negabunt discipuli eius primam illius fidem nobiscum fuisse'; cf. Praes. 30; AM 4.4.3.

/31/ This is evident from the fact that later writers, such as Hippolytus, seem to conflate the biographies of Marcion and Diogenes.

/32/ Lives of the Philosophers, 6.20-81.

/33/ Cf. Clem. Alex., Strom. 1.66.

/34/ Diog. Laertius, Lives, 6.54.

/35/ He did not advocate continence, but 'recognized no other marriage than the union of a man who asks and a woman who consents'; Diog. Laertius, Lives, 6.72.

/36/ E.g., Lives, 6.53.

/37/ Lives, 6.73.

/38/ Lives, 6.1-21.

interested in <u>practical</u> ethics rather than in developing a theory of moral virtue. Like the Socratics, Antisthenes stressed the importance of self-control/39/ and advocated hostility toward sensual pleasures, the paradigm of which praxis was the toil of Heracles. Diogenes himself believed that virtue is revealed in action rather than in analysis and argument. He was a man of essentially practical aims, who 'in disillusioned protest against a corrupt society and a hostile world, advocated happiness as self-realization and self-mastery in an inner spiritual freedom'./40/

It would be far-fetched to imagine that the teaching of Diogenes served as a model for the ascetic ethic developed by Marcion centuries later. But Marcion may well have been familiar with stories about the famous Sinopean teacher. Whether the local philosophical tradition had been colored to any degree by its historical links with fourth-century cynicism is questionable. Tertullian tells us -- incredibly -- that Marcion was a zealous student of stoicism,/41/ and while stoicism (itself a creation of the oikoumene)/42/ and cynicism are far from being ethically incompatible, Marcion's contempt for allegorical exegesis/43/ and his disavowal of the active pursuit of virtue through good works (duty) are rooted in a pre-stoical belief in the passive virtue of renunciation. Moreover, Marcion makes a primary theological distinction between God and the world which is entirely absent from the philosophy of the stoics. If in some respects Marcion's ascetic ethic/44/ and his contempt for the philosophical construction of religious faith harken back to the beggar-preacher of

---

/39/ Cf. Xenophon, <u>Memorabilia</u>, 4.7.

/40/ I.G. Kidd, 'Diogenes', EP, II, 409.

/41/ Tert., <u>Praes</u>. 30. Elsewhere, however, he associates Marcion's theology with the philosophy of Epicurus (AM 1.25.3): 'Si aliquem de Epicuri schola deum affectavit Christi nomine titulare, etc.'; cf. 2.16.2; 4.15.2; 5.19.7; and Hippolytus, <u>Ref</u>. <u>omn</u>. <u>haer</u>., 7.17ff. (Marcion and Empedocles).

/42/ P. Hallie, 'Stoicism', EP, VIII, 19b. The standard work on the subject is still that of Eduard Zeller, <u>The Stoics</u>, <u>Epicureans</u>, <u>and Sceptics</u> (London 1870/NY 1962); cf. Tarn, <u>Hellenistic Civilization</u>, 266.

/43/ Hengel has questioned the extent to which allegorical exegesis can be traced to Alexandria and to the stoa (<u>Judaism</u> <u>and</u> <u>Hellenism</u>, I, 246; cf. Peters, <u>The Harvest of Hellenism</u>, 450f.).

/44/ <u>Lives</u>, 6.77.

Athens, his philosophical mentor was not Diogenes but Paul, and the patristic effort to find philosophical analogues for marcionite doctrines is characterized by contradiction and inconsistency. (See further pp. 228ff.)

## 1.4 Religious Syncretism in Pontus

Tertullian depicts the inhabitants of Pontus as a race of savages given to strange religious practices: 'Nihil illic nisi feritas calet, illa scilicet quae fabulas scenis dedit de sacrificiis Taurorum et amoribus Colchorum et crucibus Caucasorum'./45/ To be sure, this description is more intriguing than accurate. But it is not an altogether uninformed comment on the religious situation in Sinope during the early second century. Rather, it is a polemical way of expressing the syncretistic climate of Asia Minor from the standpoint of the christian orthodoxy of a century later.

Located at the trading axis of the upper-Mediterranean, with the Crimea to the north and Syria-Palestine to the south, Sinope was uniquely positioned to experience the religious and intellectual cross-currents of the oikoumene. In Pontus, where the Asiatic influence was especially strong owing to the Iranian-Babylonian provenance of the inhabitants, this religious syncretism naturally assumed the character of a theogonic dualism. Thus in addition to the worship of the prevalent hellenistic deities -- to Theion, Ananke, and the Sol Invictus -- the Sinopeans knew the cults of Mithra, Ahura Mazdas, and YHWH, each of which presented this dualism in its own way.

The background of the religious situation in Pontus is the explanation of its complexity. The sizeable Iranian diaspora in Anatolia and northern Syria had introduced the cult of Mithra to the area during the days of the Achaemenian Empire, some three hundred years before the time of Marcion. According to F. E. Peters, Mithraism was actually the product of the Iranian diaspora of Parthian times, and remained untouched by and large both by the Zoroastrian reform and political meddling. Anatolian Mithraism, with its hereditary priesthood (the maguaei) found political sustenance in Cappadocia and Commagene as well, but it was in Pontus that Mithra was linked, from a very early period, to dynastic fortunes; hence, the frequency of the dynastic name 'Mithridates'. Yet another member of

---

/45/ AM 1.1.3.

the Iranian pantheon, Anahita, reigned as the Great Mother at (Pontic) Comana. It was the savior-god Mithra who presided over the victories of Eupator in BCE 96 and 92.

In the earlier (Vedic and Avestan) forms, Mithra was known as a companion of the high-god Ahura. The Mithraists worshipped him in the context of a well-defined dualistic cosmogony, wherein he served as the intermediary between the god of the heavens (Ormazd) and the lord of the underworld (Ahrihman). The Mithra of the Iranian diaspora was also a savior-god -- the 'spirit of light born into this world' in a cave, where the primordial soteriological act, the slaughter of a cosmic bull, had taken place. This belief accounts for Tertullian's snide reference to the sacrificiis taurorum (AM 1.1.3). Mithra's slaughter of the bull was also apprehended as the guarantee of the fertility of the earth, the organs and blood of the animal being the source of all animal and vegetable life. Hence, as Bultmann has remarked, 'salvation' in Mithraism was perceived to have a physical as well as a spiritual dimension./46/

It has been suggested that the Mithraism of the Iranian diaspora differed from the primitive Vedic and Avestan forms of the cult. Peters believes that the religion came to Pontus by way of semitic Babylonia, since the later (Anatolian) cult betrays 'marks of an astral theology foreign to the Iranian type'./47/ Moreover, Mithraist liturgies in Anatolia were in Aramaic, the semitic lingua franca of the Achaemenians. In a yet later and transmogrified form, Mithra is drawn into the cult of the Sol Invictus, doubtless in recognition of his record in the Mithridatic Wars, and after a period of quiescence becomes under Diocletian and Augustus Galerius (CE 307) the official protector of the Roman Empire.

Anatolian Mithraism was limited in its appeal, and attracted chiefly members of the military class. Bultmann has argued/48/ that its austerity

---

/46/ Bultmann, Primitive Christianity (1956), 161. Although Mithra was not responsible for the creation of the world, he nevertheless provided for its good and for the sustenance of mankind, pledging in the sacrificial act man's freedom from the dark powers of Ahriman and survival beyond death. There is obviously an echo of this soteriology in Marcion's teaching of the distinction between the good and just Gods; but it is wrong to assume that Marcion derived his theogonic dualism from the Mithraists. In terms of its qualified world-renunciation, however, Marcionism is closer to the Mithraists than to the gnostic sects.

/47/ Peters, The Harvest of Hellenism, 477.

/48/ Primitive Christianity, 157.

made it 'alien to the Greek world', but this may only mean that the cult appealed mainly to men of a non-philosophical cast of mind. It cannot mean that there was anything foreign or questionable in the ethical or religious practice of Mithraism which would have made it inherently unacceptable to men of the oikoumene, and indeed this was not the case. Moreover, the austerity of Mithraism was practical rather than ritual; members of the cult practiced the self-denial of the athlete in training rather than that of the mystic. Their participation in the life of the god was understood to be symbolized by physical well-being, such that the virtues of strength and courage acquired an almost sacramental nuance within the cult.

With respect to liturgy, the Mithraists followed the elaborate pattern of other Asian mysteries, with the exception that women were never permitted to become initiates. The rite (teletē) was held in a chapel intended to simulate Mithra's underground birthplace. It was preceded by a ceremony of purification which included fasting, castigation, and baptism. After the performance of the lustrations, the initiate was delivered (paradosis) of the sacred formula (synthema; symbolon) the execution of which effected a vision of the deity (epopteia). In the course of this vision, the initiate was endowed with immortality and salvation (sōtēria) was imparted./49/ Thereafter the political and sacramental life of the initiate was highly ordered, within the structure of a military hierarchy. Apparently, the sacraments included baptism, confirmation, and a communal sacred meal./50/

The cosmogony of Mithraism is obscure, but it bears some resemblance in its Anatolian variety to that of Zoroastrianism. Its dualism was graduated, like that of the gnostic systems. It projected a seven-storeyed cosmos, corresponding to (e.g.) the seven stoles of Isis, the seven gates of hell, and the 'seventh heaven' in analogous cosmogonies of the oikoumene./51/ The powers associated with the number seven derived from the ancient astral theology, which Mithraism had acquired from its

---

/49/ But cf. Bultmann, Primitive Christianity, 158.

/50/ See F. Cumont, The Oriental Religions in Roman Paganism (1911), and Die Mysterien des Mithras (1923). An older but still valuable survey is that by R. Reitzenstein, Die hellenistischen Mysterien religionen (1901); S. Angus, The Mystery Religions and Christianity (1925).

/51/ Tarn, Hellenistic Civilization, 286.

engagement with Babylonian religion./52/ The seven planets were regarded as both the interpreters of fate (Tyche) and the imperium of the evil powers who threaten man's well-being./53/ 'Salvation' from these powers consists in strategic avoidance of the fate decreed by the Cosmocrater ab origine. This is accomplished in the mystery itself by partaking of the pharmakon tēs zoēs, the 'medicine of immortality',/54/ whereby the believer shares in the power of the savior who is able to transcend the evil powers and rise to immortal life:

> Be gracious unto me Providence and Fate, as I write down these first traditional mysteries [granting] immortality to my only child, a worthy initiate into this our power, which the great god Helios Mithras commanded to be imparted to me by his archangel, in order that I alone, an eagle, might tread heaven and behold all things. . . . I who was born mortal from a mortal womb, but transformed by mighty power and an incorruptible right hand./55/

The inducement to be faithful to the moral regimen and teaching of the cult was the belief that Mithra's warriors would be called upon to answer for their deeds in a final judgment, and that only those who had satisfactorily maintained the regula would attain to the light./56/ Thus in Mithraism, the assault on the powers of darkness was pursued more militantly than in the other mysteries. By the rite of confirmation Mithra's warriors were prepared to fight beside their god for the victory of the light: self-denial and moral rigor were merely the ethical corollaries of the training

---

/52/ Peters, The Harvest of Hellenism, 477.

/53/ Writes Bultmann, 'There is a sense in which this world is a very untoward place, with hostile demonic powers at work in it. The presuppositions for a dualistic interpretation of the world are present here, and the logical conclusion is drawn in mysticism, which grows up out of the mystery religions. Where that conlusion is drawn, we are already in the presence of gnosticism' (Primitive Christianity, 161).

/54/ Cf. Ign., Eph. 20.2, 'hos estin pharmakon athanasias'; Act. Thom., 135. On the derivation of the term, see W. Bauer, Handb. zum NT, suppl., II: Bultmann (Primitive Christianity, 277, n. 46) suggests the phrase is taken over from the mystery religions.

/55/ In A. Dieterich, Eine Mithrasliturgie ([3]1923), 2f.; Barrett, Documents, 102, no. 96 (edited); A.S. Geden, Select Passages Illustrating Mithraism (1925); on the subject of 'rebirth', consult H.R. Willoughby, Pagan Regeneration (1929). Interpretation of the mithraist rites is supplied by F. Cumont, Les mysteres de Mithra (1913).

/56/ Lohse, Umwelt des Neues Testaments: ET (1971), 241.

process./57/

The affinities between the religious praxis of the Marcionites and Mithraism will be examined further in this chapter. Here it suffices to point out the predominance of the cult in Pontus and Asia Minor during Marcion's lifetime./58/ Mithraism stood beside Judaism and the cults of the city-gods of the oikoumene and was thus influential in determining the shape and texture of Sinopean Christianity in the last decades of the first century.

## 1.5 Christianity in Pontus

The existence of a christian community in Pontus by the turn of the century is attested in the NT./59/ The Letter of James (c. 100), addressed to 'the twelve tribes of the dispersion', envisages the church in Asia Minor as heir to the Jewish diaspora, and I Peter (c. 110), addressed to the elect who are sojourning in the dispersion of Pontus, Galatia, Cappadocia, Asia, and Bithynia (1.1), makes the connection explicit.

The wave of anti-Jewish feeling that swept through the oikoumene following the rebellion of CE 66-70 was preceded in 64 by the great fire at Rome, which Nero is alleged to have blamed on the Christians./60/ Whether Nero could distinguish between Jews and Christians is unclear. The famous passage in the Annals of Tacitus implies that he could, but also that he associated the crime of the Christians -- evidently their rejection of the state-approved cults -- with the rebelliousness of the Jews./61/ Tertullian tells us that after the events of CE 64, Nero made the admission of

---

/57/ For the use of similar imagery in the New Testament cf. 1 Thess 5.8; Rom 13.12f.; 2 Cor 6.7; 10.4; Eph 6.13-17. Marcion apparently thought that the Creator's Christ (still to come) would be a warrior; but this was in contrast to the Christ of the unknown God, who came only to reveal the purposes of his father: AM 3.13.1: 'Aeque et sono nominum duceris, cum virtutem Damasci et spolia Samariae et regem Assyriorum sic accipis quasi bellatorem portendant Christum creatoris, etc.'; cf. 3.14.1.

/58/ Justin evidences the currency of Mithraism in his first Apology (66).

/59/ See note 4, above.

/60/ Tacitus, Annals, 15.44; but it should be noted that no other contemporary suggests that Nero used the Christians as scapegoats. Cf. however Sulpicius Severus, Chron., 2.29; Suetonius, Nero, 16; Claud., 25.4.

/61/ Tacitus, Annals, 15.44.

Christianity a capital offense./62/ His statement is contradicted by two letters which, while they do not date from Nero's time,/63/ provide important information about the religious situation of Christianity in Pontus in the early decades of the second century. During the period when Marcion was probably still resident in Sinope, the younger Pliny was appointed proconsul of Bithynia and Pontus (CE 111-12). Pliny had at first taken summary action against a number of Christians whom he found in the province, exercising the wide discretionary powers that belonged to his proconsular imperium./64/ As further cases were brought to his attention, however, he began to wonder whether a precedent existed for his dealings, and finding none he addressed his doubts to Trajan./65/ From this correspondence we learn, among other things, that Pliny's measures to contain the growth of the movement in Pontus had been unsuccessful: 'As usually happens', he complains, 'the trouble spread by the very treatment of it, and further varieties came to my notice'./66/ It is also clear from Pliny's letter that many of the Christians brought before him had professed the faith for as much as twenty years, some apparently having renounced it in the meantime and reverted to it at a later date. These, Pliny claims, were willing to 'invoke the gods and to do reverence with incense and wine before an image of the emperor'. Based on this evidence, one may conclude that there was a christian population in Pontus-Bithynia at least as early as Domitian's time (CE 91).

---

/62/ Ter., ad Nat. 1.7; Apol. 5; and Sulpicius Severus, Chron., 2.29.15 (c. 410?), who repeats the legend that at the time of the reaction 'Peter and Paul were condemned to death'.

/63/ Not until the beginning of the third century was there an enactment binding throughout the Empire proscribing Christianity. In the second century, the profession of Christianity fell extra ordinem, and was dealt with by the procedure called cognitio, in which provincial magistrates such as Pliny had unlimited discretionary powers. Pliny's letter thus concerns procedure and precedent rather than authority. See A.N. Sherwin-White, 'The Early Persecution and the Roman Law Again', JTS, 3 (1952), 199ff.; and C. Saumagne, 'Tertullien et l'institutum Neronianum', ThZ, 17 (1961), 334-36.

/64/ Bruce, New Testament History, 422.

/65/ Cf. E.T. Merrill, Essays in Early Christian History (1924), 174f.

/66/ Pliny, Epp. 10.96. Cf. Tert., Apol. 50.

Pliny provides valuable information about the practice of the Christians in Pontus, remarking that the cult consists of men and women of every age and class

> [who are] in the habit of meeting on a certain day before sunrise and reciting an antiphonal hymn to Christ as to a god, and binding themselves with an oath: not to commit any crime, but to abstain from all acts of theft, robbery, and licentiousness, from breaches of faith, from denying a trust when called upon to honor it. After this (they went on) it was their custom to separate and then meet again to partake of food, but food of an ordinary and innocent kind./67/

He notes as well the arraignment of two female slaves whom he calls ancillae of the cult. This is of special interest, inasmuch as the high place accorded women in the christian community of Pontus conforms to marcionite policy. Tertullian reproaches the Marcionites for allowing women to exorcise, lay hands on the sick, and baptize./68/ And we know from a complaint of Eznik de Kolb (fl. 453) that marcionite deaconesses were to be found in fifth-century Syria, 'though Marcion would not permit them to be priests'./69/ While it is not certain that the Christians whom Pliny discusses in this letter were Marcionites, there is nothing in his description to rule it out./70/

Moreover, we learn from Eusebius/71/ and by implication from other

---

/67/ Epp. 10.96; Trajan's reply (10.97) that no general edict can be issued provides that a retraction of the earlier profession, accompanied by the invocation of the gods as proof, is sufficient for the acquittal of anyone accused of being a Christian.

/68/ Praes. 41.

/69/ De sectis, 4; cf. Epiphanius, Panar. 42.4.

/70/ See, e.g., Justin, 1 Apol. 26 who testifies to the strength of the movement in CE 150. If the chronology provided in chapter 2 is substantially accurate, Marcion would have been about forty years old during the proconsulate of Pliny in 111-12. Cf. Bauer, Orthodoxy and Heresy, 90-91: 'We have no reason to conclude that Pliny was opposing a Christianity of an indubitably ecclesiastical orientation'; but Harnack (Marcion, 23) argues that orthodox belief predominated in Pontus.

/71/ HE, 5.16.21: 'Kai prōtoi ge hoi apo tēs Markiōnos haireseōs Markianistai kaloumenoi pleistous hosous echein Christou martyras legousin alla ton ge Christon auton kat' alētheian ouch homologousin'. 'More from the Marcionites than . . . orthodoxy would like to admit' (Bauer, Orthodoxy and Heresy, 91); cf. Harnack, Marcion, 150, note 4; 154, note 1: 315*f; 340*; 348*.

writers that marcionite churches of the period produced 'a multitude of martyrs'. Eusebius also records that the Smyrnean persecution of 156, in which Polycarp suffered, affected the Marcionites as well, and that a marcionite presbyter named Metrodorus suffered death by fire./72/ Under the Valerian persecution of CE 257 a marcionite woman of Caesarea was martyred in the arena alongside three others,/73/ while the successive edicts of 23 February 303 - January 304, ordering the arrest of the heads of christian churches, resulted in the death by burning of the marcionite bishop Asclepius./74/ Eusebius points out that Asclepius was burned on the same pyre as the orthodox bishop, Apselamus. Thus there is no lack of evidence to suggest that until at least the fourth century, the designation 'christian' was willingly and competitively embraced by 'orthodox' and marcionite confessors alike. Indeed this is precisely the issue when Justin complains (c. 150) that 'all those who take their opinions from these men are . . . called Christians . . . . And this man [Marcion] many have believed, as if he alone knew the truth, and laugh at us, though they have no proof of what they say'./75/

## 1.6 Marcionite and Orthodox Christianity in Pontus: Principles of Differentiation

The task of differentiating marcionite and 'orthodox' Christianity belonged properly to apologists such as Justin. The differences were far from clear to Pliny, who speaks in the passage above of 'varieties' coming to

---

/72/ HE, 4.15.46: ' . . . meth hōn kai Mētrodōros tēs kata Markiōna planēs presbyteros dē einai dokōn pyri paradotheis hanērētai'. On the date of this persecution and Eusebius' dating of the martyrdom of Polycarp, see Light-foot, Apostolic Fathers, I.2, 622f. Lightfoot argues that the Marcionite was martyred in the Decian persecution of CE 250.

/73/ HE, 7.12.1f.: 'Tēs de Markiōnos autēn haireseōs genesthai katechei logos'.

/74/ Eusebius, Mart. Pal., 10. The arrest of heads of churches was provided for in the second edict. The third led to the release of those who agreed to make libations and offer sacrifice to the Emperor. H. Marrou, 'The Last Persecution and the Peace of the Church', in Christian Centuries, I, 332-33.

/75/ Justin, 1 Apol.26:58. The Marcionites' refusal to engage in argument or to provide 'proofs' for their doctrine is also mentioned by Rhodo, Eus., HE, 5.13.4-7.

his attention. Unfortunately he gives no indication of what these varieties might have been, and seems to think that all Christians in his province follow the same liturgical practice, 'gathering before dawn [antelucanum] to sing a hymn to Christ as to a god [Christo quasi deo]'./76/ This may mean that the 'varieties' were distinguished by doctrine rather than by ritual, since we know from other sources that marcionite liturgical forms were similar to those in use in the other christian churches. Tertullian reveals that the Marcionites made use of the 'sign on the foreheads and the sacraments and sacrifices of the church in their purity',/77/ and that the church possessed a (rotating) hierarchical structure composed of bishops, presbyters, deacons/deaconesses, and a catechumenate for beginners in the faith./78/ So close apparently was the resemblance between 'orthodox' and marcionite practice that Cyril of Jerusalem felt it necessary to warn his own catechumens against wandering into a marcionite place of worship by mistake; upon arriving in a new city, he advised, 'inquire after the catholic church'./79/

Confusion of this sort is also evident in Theodoret's effort to wrest Christians in the See of Cyrrhus in Syria from the doctrines of Marcion. Writing to the consul Nomus in 443, he claims to have led 'eight villages of Marcionites . . . into the way of truth'./80/ Addressing Leo, bishop of Rome, Theodoret boasts of having delivered over a thousand souls from the 'plague of Marcion'/81/ and to the presbyter Renatus of having written over thirty books against the heretics, including the Marcionites (Ep. 116).

---

/76/ On this see H. Köster, Einführung in das NT (1980), 12., 774ff.

/77/ AM 3.22.7 Harnack (Marcion, 52) suggests with some probability that Marcion's insistence on 'purity' of form in worship may have had the effect of standardizing catholic practice. Blackman (Influence, 4) thinks that 'mutual imitation' was quite unlikely.

/78/ Praes., 41. Adamantius (De rectum in deum fide. 1.8) suggests that the Marcionites claimed an orderly succession of bishops from Marcion onwards; the marcionite Megethius there speaks of 'Markion episkopos'.

/79/ Cyril, Cat., 18.26: ' . . . kai gar hai loipai tōn asebōn haireseis 'kyriaka' ta heautōn spēlaia kalein epicheirousi'. Blackman (Influence, 4) has suggested that many small towns in Cyril's diocese would have possessed only a marcionite building.

/80/ Theodoret of Cyrrhus, Ep. 81.

/81/ Ep. 113; cf. 145, 151.

Hence the confusion of names which writers such as Justin and Tertullian found so intolerable continued into the fifth century. Although Constantine's ban on heretical buildings inevitably spelled the decline of Marcionism in the west,/82/ Eznik de Kolb writes of the strength of marcionite churches in Syria and Armenia as late as 445./83/

Even Marcion's severest critics were obliged to admit that no clear-cut distinction could be made between their own sacramental practice and ecclesiastical organization and that of the Marcionites: 'Wasps make combs and Marcionites build churches'./84/ Tertullian nevertheless provides some basis for contrast between the two communities, in the course of establishing the connections between the rites of the Marcionites and those of the mystery cults. Thus in the Praes. he makes an explicit association of Marcionism and Mithraism, alleging that the pagan rites 'vie in form with the essential portions of the sacraments of God':

> [The devil], too, baptizes some--that is, his own believers and faithful followers; he [too] promises the putting away of sins by a washing of his own . . . . Mithra there, in the kingdom of Satan, sets his marks on the foreheads of his soldiers; celebrates also the oblation of bread, and introduces an image of a resurrection, and before a sword wreathes a crown . . . . He too has his virgins, he too has his experts in continence./85/

What Tertullian imports is that a strictly formal resemblance between rites and sacraments/86/ is not a guarantee of their catholicity or genuineness. Marcionite rites may indeed appear similar to catholic ritual; but so also do the rites of the Mithraists. And yet who would dare to call such practices

---

/82/ Eusebius, Vit. Const., 3.64.

/83/ Eznik, De sectis, 4. On the persistence of Marcionism in Syria, cf. Amann, DCT 9 (1927), 2027-8.

/84/ AM 4.5.3; but cf. Irenaeus, Haer. 3.4.2: 'Neque enim congregatio fuit apud eos neque doctrina instituta' (if Marcion is envisaged).

/85/ Tert., Praes., 40.

/86/ Tert., AM 3.22.7: 'Quae omnia cum in te quoque deprehendantur, et signaculum frontium et ecclesiarum sacramenta et munditiae sacrificiorum, etc.'

'christian'?/87/ Tertullian is not the only one to use this line of attack. As early as 150 Justin had observed with evident dismay the parallels between the christian eucharist and mithraist oblation. There could, he said, be but one conclusion: 'These wicked devils [the Mithraists] have imitated [us] in their mysteries . . . commanding the same thing to be done. For that bread and a cup of water are placed with certain incantations in the mystic rites of one who is being initiated [into the cult]'./88/ Both writers try to show that Marcionism bears no more resemblance to christian practice than does Mithraism, and that the proof of sacramental authenticity is not <u>form</u> but <u>doctrine</u>. Hence Justin cautions that 'no man is allowed to partake of the eucharist unless he believes that the things which we teach are true'./89/ On this reckoning, the sacraments of the Marcionites are 'imitations' in virtue of being based on perversion of catholic truth. Catholicity of practice is no proof right-teaching; rather, right-teaching validates the sacramental practice.

For Tertullian, the essential difference between the sacramental life of the two churches centered on the question of ethos and doctrinal coherence. He understood the ethos of the marcionite christians as a world-renouncing ascetic idealism the sacramental forms of which proved the inconsistency and hypocrisy of their teaching./90/ Marcion's insistence on celibacy as a prerequisite to baptism reminded Tertullian of the ritual ascesis of the Mithraists: 'Why does he impose upon the flesh, so utterly weak and unworthy, the great burden of . . . chastity? Or what shall I say of the folly of a moral requirement by which he sanctifies an object already holy? If it is weak, why lay a burden on it? Or if [it is] unworthy, why

---

/87/ Cf. Cyprian to Jubianus, 72.4 (ANF = Oxford ed. 73.4); to Pompey, 73.7-8 (ANF = Oxford ed. 74.7-8). Augustine made a distinction between the schismatic baptism of the Donatists and the integrity of marcionite baptism on the basis of intention (<u>De bapt. c. Donat.</u>, 7.14.31): 'In Marcione agnoscenda est baptismi integritas'; cf. 3.15.20. Cf. Harnack, <u>Marcion</u>, 390*, n. 4.

/88/ 1 <u>Apol.</u> 66.

/89/ 1 <u>Apol.</u>, <u>loc. cit.</u>

/90/ On the dietary practices of the Marcionites, consult Wilson, <u>Heretic</u>, 168f. Hippolytus inveighs against these observances, <u>Ref. omn. haer.</u> 7.18.

embellish it?'/91/ If Epiphanius is to be credited, Marcion seems to have regarded baptism as a kind of lustration: 'You forbid marriage . . . [while] enjoining the purifactory rites of Empedocles'./92/ This testimony comports with Tertullian's statement to the effect that Marcionites refused baptism to anyone who was not 'widowed, virgin, unmarried, or divorc[ed]'./93/

The vow of continence which seems to have been associated with the baptismal rite implied abstinence of another sort as well. There is evidence that Marcion, for all his disdain for the Jewish law, prescribed strict dietary observances for members of the community, and it is known that marcionite presbyters abjured the use of wine in celebrating the eucharist.

Marcionite baptism was not a washing away of sin but a sacramental rejection of the cellula creatoris./94/ As man's situation in the world reflects the cruelty and wantonness of the creator-God, the world itself must be rejected. The rite of baptism made effective the separation between man and the things of the creator, and was thus the supreme symbolon of marcionite belief. Tertullian and later writers found this theology of baptism one of the most vexing parts of Marcion's teaching: Marcion did not reject the Creator's water, 'for in it he washes his own: nor the oil with which he anoints them'./95/ Commenting on marcionite practice in Syria, Eznik writes some two centuries later that Marcion urges men to be baptized in place of catechumens who have died, 'And he has the boldness to ask women to administer baptism -- which no one from the other sects has taken it upon himself to do'./96/ Because Marcion prescribed continence for all members of the church, the catechumenate could only

---

/91/ AM 1.28.4f. Tert.'s defense of matrimony (AM 1.29.2f.) is a correlate of his defense of the goodness of the Creator (cf. 4.34; 1.14).

/92/ Hippol. Ref. omn. haer. 7.18; cf. Epiphanius, Panar., 42.3; Eznik, De sectis, 4.

/93/ According to Tert. (AM 1.29.1f.) the Marcionites refused baptism to anyone who was not strictly continent. A man who was married was kept a catechumen of the church until he had given up relations with his wife (AM 4.34.5). Cf. Hippol. Ref. omn. haer. 7.18.

/94/ Cf. H. Jonas, The Gnostic Religion (1958), 55.

/95/ Am 1.14.2-3.

/96/ De sectis, 4. (Harnack, Marcion, 372*-80*, 176f.). Eznik's testimony is perhaps an exaggeration of Epiphanius' (Panar. 42.3f.); but see Blackman, Influence, 8.

consist of adults who by the rite of baptism had been 'born' into the cult.

The evidence suggests that Marcion's understanding of baptism was not altogether unlike that which obtained in the hellenistic mysteries, and especially in the cult of Mithra, a fact acknowledged by Tertullian when he warns that in the mithraist rite 'even the devil baptizes'./97/    The significance of water as a symbol of world-opposition is pronounced both in the mithraist rite and in Marcionism.  The evidence of the liturgy preserved in Paris Papyrus 574 is conclusive on this point:/98/

> Water of water, first-fruit of water within me . . . in a world unilluminated yet bright, with no living soul, yet with a living soul: if it seem good to you to give me, held as I am by my underlying nature, to immortal birth, in order that, after the present need which presses sore upon me, I may behold by deathless spirit the deathless Beginning, by deathless water, . . . that I may be born anew by Thought, that I may be initiated and that a sacred spirit may breathe in me, . . . I who was born mortal from a mortal womb, but transformed by a mighty power and an incorruptible right hand . . . . Lord if it please thee, announce me to the Greatest God [Helios Mithras ] . . . who is good beyond measure./99/

Ascesis and world-renunciation do not here involve a capitulation with the elements of the demiurge, as Tertullian asserted of Marcion's teaching; rather the whole sense of the rite is that the initiate is born out of the

---

/97/ Praes., 40.    Tert. himself preferred that baptism should not be administered to children (De bapt. 18), since it was unrepeatable except in the case of heretics who had never received true baptism (De pud. 19).  Its effects included remission of sin, liberation from death, rebirth, and the light of the Spirit (De bapt. 18;  AM 1.28).  Marcion's closest known contemporary, Justin Martyr, relates that the christian practice of the mid-second century involved 'baptism in the name of God the father and master of all things' (1 Apol. 61.3) and of 'Jesus Christ who was crucified under Pontius Pilate' and 'of the Holy Spirit who foretold [by] the prophets the whole story of Jesus'.    Cf. Irenaeus (Demonstr. 3, 7).    According to Cyprian (Ep. 73.4) Marcion baptized 'in nomine Jesu Christi', apparently in accordance with Romans 6.3 and Ps.-Cyprian mentions heretical teachers who baptize 'in nomine Christi' (De rebapt. 13).  It is possible at least that these heretics were marcionite Christians.  However Augustine attributes the three-fold formula to the Marcionites of his day (De bapt. 3.15.20), and would not have admitted the integrity of their rite if they had abjured the trinal invocation.  Chrysostom (cited in Harnack, Marcion, 176) makes the unlikely claim that Marcionites practiced baptism for the dead.

/98/ The Iranian symbolism underlying this rite is discussed in Jonas, The Gnostic Religion, 58ff. (cf. esp., Turfan Frag. M7).

/99/ Given in A. Dieterich, Eine Mithrasliturgie (1923), 2-15; Barrett, Documents (edited), 102-3.

world. Hippolytus suggests that this is Marcion's purpose when he writes
that '[Marcion] believes he vexes the demiurge [by] abstaining from what he
has made or instituted'./100/ He refers specifically to the fact that
Marcionites abstain from certain foods in order to symbolize their general
opposition to the things of this world. Hence the Marcionites must not have
viewed baptism as the 'use of the creator's water' as Tertullian wants to
suggest, but on the contrary, as an effective means of rejecting the world
by subverting the use of one of its primary elements. The doctrine may
have affinities with the Iranian doctrine of 'mixture' which Jonas defines as a
belief in 'two original and opposite entities [as the basis] for the formation
of the world'./101/ The mixture is, however, an uneven one, and the term
essentially denotes the tragedy of the portions of Light separated from its
main body and immersed in the foreign element. Baptism in the mithraist
rite as in later gnostic usage is understood as a repetition of the primordial
mixture. A passage from the mandaen Book of John serves to illustrate the
point:

> They brought living water and poured it into the turbid
> water; they brought shining light and cast it into the dense
> darkness. They brought the refreshing wind and cast it
> into scorching wind. They brought the living fire, and
> cast it into the devouring fire. They brought the soul, the
> pure Mana, and cast it into the worthless body. . . . As it
> entered the turbid water, the living water lamented and
> wept . . . . As he mingled the living water with the
> turbid, darkness entered the light./102/

As an heir to the Iranian cosmogony, Marcion may well have seen baptism in
a similar way, though he would have rejected the more elaborate soteriology
which the mandaen rite presupposes. According to Clement of Alexandria,
himself no stranger to gnosticism, Marcion rejected the use of the things of
this world in order to oppose the demiurge: 'Thus they are in opposition to
their Maker and hasten towards him who is called the good God'./103/
Marcion's rejection of the world was not therefore a matter of ethics but of

---

/100/ Ref. omn. haer. 10.15; cf. Clem., Strom. 3.3.12f.; 3.4.25.

/101/ Jonas, The Gnostic Religion, 57f.

/102/ Book of John, 56; 216. Given in Jonas, The Gnostic Religion, 58f.

/103/ Strom. 3.3.12 (Oulton's transl. Alexandrian Christianity [1954], 46).

metaphysical alignment./104/ It rests on the belief that the world, not being good, must be reduced to a bare minimum, and has nothing to do with sanctification in the here and now or the remediation of past wrongs./105/ This is also the philosophy underlying the mithraist baptismal liturgy just cited: the initiate asks for deathless water in exchange for the water of creation in which he is immersed, and to be delivered from 'present need unto deathless spirit'. There is nothing in such a liturgy that Marcion would have found unacceptable, and the possibility that the Marcionites understood the sacrament in a comparably dualistic way is strongly suggested by the evidence.

### 1.7 Conclusions

Pontic Christianity, including the marcionite variety, was affected by a number of socio-political and religious circumstances: the Mithridatic Wars, which resulted in the expropriation of the kingdom by Rome in CE 64; the large Jewish population, with its ambivalent attitude toward helleniza-tion and the Law; the predominance of Irano-Babylonian dualism as exem-plified by the cult of Mithra; anti-Jewish reaction to the rebellions of CE 66-135; the tradition of ascesis and world-rejection going back several hundred years to the time of the cynic philosopher, Diogenes.

The term 'syncretism', however, is an unenlightening one. It connotes religious diversity and random mixing rather than substantive points of contact between one religious system and another. Unfortunately Marcion was permitted to leave no writings which would allow us to speak about such points of contact in greater detail, and we are therefore dependent for our knowledge of his doctrines on the writings of men who not only disagreed with his teachings, but misunderstood the provenance and intellectual matrix of his religious ideas as well.

A significant exception to this rule is the existence of the so-called 'Marcionite' Prologues to the epistles of Paul, which date from as early as

---

/104/ Jonas, The Gnostic Religion, 144.

/105/ Jonas believes that Marcion's asceticism is genuinely and 'typically' gnostic in conception, finding parallels in Manichaeism. But the suggestion that Marcion regarded the reproductive scheme as 'a clever archontic device for the indefinite retention of souls in the world' (The Gnostic Religion, 145) cannot be shown from the patristic evidence.

the end of the second century./106/ These paragraphs of introduction to the letters of the 'true Apostle' make it clear that Marcionism was very much a product of the east. The prologue-writer regards only Philippi (significantly, the recipient-church of Polycarp's heresiological epistle), Laodicea, and Thessalonica secure in the faith of Paul ('Hi accepto verbo veritatis perstituerunt in fide nec receperunt falsos apostolos', ad Phil.). All other beneficiaries of Paul's teaching, and Rome soonest of all, have been corrupted by the doctrines of pseudo-apostles preaching the law and prophets. In short, one thing about which we can be reasonably certain, on the basis of writings stemming from his own circle, is that Marcion regarded the locus of normative teaching to be outside Rome and in the east ('Hi [Romani] praeventi a pseudo-apostolis, sub nomine domini nostri Jesu Christi in lege et prophetis erant inducti', ad Rom.). No doubt the belief that Philippi and Laodicea rather than Rome and Ephesus possessed the true faith accounts at least in part for the early significance of Polycarp in anti-marcionite polemic.

The Pontic Christianity of Marcion's day occupied an intermediate position between Judaism and the cults; sharing features of both, it was really neither. But if Sinope followed the pattern of other hellenistic cities in the east, it was the synagogue that represented the greatest obstacle to the process which A. D. Nock has termed 'conversion', a 'turning away from a sense of present wrongness . . . [and] a turning toward a positive ideal'./107/ Conservative Judaism understood this process in terms of adherence to the law./108/ The eastern Jews, by the same token,

---

/106/ Given in Harnack, Marcion, 127ff.; Knox, Marcion and the NT, 169-71; Souter, Text and Canon, 188ff. Studies include, De Bruyne, 'Prologues bibliques d'origine Marcionite', Rev. Bénéd. (1907), 1-16; W. Mundel, 'Der Herkunft der Marcionitischen Prologe zu den Paulinischen Briefen' ZNTW, 24 (1925), 56ff.: Harnack, 'Der Marcionitische Ursprung der ältesten Vulgata-Prologe zu den Paulus-briefen' ZNTW, 24 (1925), 204ff.; M.J. Lagrange, 'Les Prologues prétendu Marcionites', Rev. biblique, 35 (1926), 161ff.

/107/ Nock, Conversion, 8.

/108/ Bruce remarks (New Testament History, 135f.) however that in Phrygia the Jews were 'reputed to be exceptionally lax in their devotion to the law and prone to assimilation by their neighbors; the barriers between Judaism and paganism there were not impenetrable'. The evidence for assimilation in Phrygia and the surrounding area is discussed by W.M. Ramsay, Cities and Bishoprics of Phrygia, II (1897), 649f; 673f.

particularly those who saw God's judgment in the fate of the unsuccessful nationalists, perceived conversion as a turning away from the rigor of the law, and -- as the case of Marcion may illustrate -- as an outright rejection of the law. What Christianity required was an even more dramatic reversal: the putting aside of the old man. In Pontus as elsewhere, the Jews were hampered by an exclusivistic theology which remained essentially closed even to those gentile cosmopolites who dabbled in Jewish customs and respected the Sabbath observance./109/ Christianity was open to Jew and gentile alike, *'Ou gar estin diastolē Ioudaiou te kai Hellēnos; ho gar autos kurios pantōn, ploutōn eis pantas tous epikaloumenous auton'* (Rom 10.12).

The Book of Acts charges that wherever Paul went he encountered 'Jewish' opposition./110/ At Lystra 'because of Jews' (Acts 16.3) he circumcized Timothy as a concession to Jewish sensibilities; at Thessalonica the Jews 'out of jealousy' stirred up the people against him, and during his second journey (c. CE 54-7) he encountered sharp opposition from Jewish Christians in Asia (Acts 19.33). On the occasion of the apostolic council in Jerusalem, he was confronted by a group of pharisaic Jewish Christians who 'believed it was necessary to circumcize [proselytes] and to command them to keep the law of Moses' (Acts 15.5). Luke interprets the rift between Jewish Christians and the synagogue as being originally an internal struggle centering on the denial of Jesus by fellow Jews; the gentile mission, as Luke depicts it, is the result of this denial: the Sons of the Prophets, the intended beneficiaries of the covenant, have forsaken it. By the time of Marcion, however, the author of the Apocalypse of John (c. 100+) is able to argue that the synagogue has nothing at all to do with Christianity: *'Ouk eisin alla synagōgē tou Satana'* (Rev 2.9)./111/

Despite the natural antagonism which existed between the (Jewish) christian converts and the adherents of the law, the process of conversion was at high pitch in the generation immediately preceding Marcion's birth.

---

/109/ Nock, Conversion, 63.

/110/ Cf. Acts 9.23-25; 13.6, 8; 13.44-50; 14.2-6, 19.

/111/ Cf. Peter's speech in Solomon's portico, Acts 3.11-26; 4.1-4. In the passage from Revelation the offer of salvation which Luke presupposes has been withdrawn, since the writer denies the identity of the Jews: *' . . . tōn legontōn Ioudaious einai heautous, kai ouk eisin'* ('those that say they are Jews but are not'), i.e., because they have spoken out against the sonship of Jesus.

What Nock says of Antioch can reasonably be applied to the situation in Sinope: 'In the life of that city, where Greek and Semitic elements blended freely . . . there grew up a full self-consciousness of the new movement [i.e., Christianity]. While there may be an accentuated conservatism in a group living under these conditions, the inward pressure of Jewish loyalty on reformers was weaker here'./112/ With the further reduction of this 'inward pressure', provoked by the razing of the Temple (an event which Jewish Christians could interpret ex eventu as the verdict of God foretold by Jesus)/113/ and with the psychological crisis brought on by the destruction of what was for many Jews their most tangible link with the religion of the fathers, the stage was set for an aggressive christian preaching. In Pontus, where the numerical strength of the movement was substantial, apparently from a very early date, this preaching took the form of provocative statements about the law, statements directed at the recalcitrant who had replaced the Temple with the Torah and insisted on its rigorous and literal interpretation./114/ In countries where Christians were fewer, the preaching seems to have taken a different form./115/

By the third century, Pontus had experienced mass conversions, owing to the efforts of the Origenist, Gregory the Thaumaturge./116/ Tradition has it that he preached the Gospel with such zeal and persuasion that at his death only a few pagans remained in all of Pontus. But this is tradition

---

/112/ Nock, Conversion, 190.

/113/ Luke 21.20-24; Mark 13.14-20; Mt. 24.15-20. Note that the 'desolating sacrilege' (Bdelygma tēs erēmōseōs) spoken of by Mark and set in prophetic context by Matthew becomes in the words of Luke, (Marcion's Gospel) the verdict of Jesus on the Temple. For Luke, the destruction of Jerusalem means the coming of the 'time of the gentiles' (21.24) -- specifically a time of conversion prior to the time of redemption (21.28) when the Son of Man will come in power and glory. Doubtless Marcion interpreted this to mean that conversion had been mandated in the verdict of God. Cf. Hengel, Acts and the History of Earliest Christianity, 59-65.

/114/ Cf. Nock, Conversion, 202.

/115/ The 'prophet' Alexander Abonuteichus (fl. c. 160) claimed that his teaching was rejected because 'Pontus is full of Christians and atheists' (Lucian, Alex., 25; given in R.M. Grant, Early Christianity and Society [1977], 3-4).

/116/ Born at Neocaesarea in Pontus c. 213. Latin biography in A. Poncelet, 'La vie Latine de s. Gregoire Thaumaturge', RSR 1 (1910), 132-60. S.D.F. Salmond, ANF 6, 21-39; Address to Origen, ed. M. Metcalfe (1920). Cf. Daniélou, Christian Centuries, 1, 284.

only. The movement away from paganism had begun in force more than a century before, and among the earliest missionaries was Marcion of Sinope, himself a convert from the Jewish community in Pontus. As Bauer has observed, the speed with which the doctrine and ideology of Marcion spread can only be explained if it had found the ground already prepared:

> Apparently a great number of the baptized, especially in the east, inclined toward this view of Christianity and joined Marcion without hesitation as soon as he appeared, finding in him the classic embodiment of their own belief. What had dwelt in their own inner consciousness in a more or less undefined form until then, acquired through Marcion the definite form that satisfied head and heart. No one can call that a falling away from orthodoxy to heresy./117/

---

/117/ Bauer, Orthodoxy and Heresy, 194.

# CHAPTER TWO

# TRADITION AND INVENTION: THE GENEALOGY OF RIGHT-TEACHING

## 2.1 Marcionites and 'Christians'

We know nothing of Marcion's teaching-career in Pontus and next to nothing about his activity after leaving Sinope for Rome./1/ Tertullian claims at several junctures that Marcion originally professed an orthodox Christianity ('Non negabunt discipuli eius primam illius fidem nobiscum fuisse')/2/ and that he knows of a letter in which Marcion confesses as much ('ipsius litteris testibus'). Justin, writing about 150, is unaware of such a letter and of Marcion's erstwhile orthodoxy./3/ Indeed Justin's testimony presupposes a very different situation from that known to Tertullian.

In his first Apology, Justin complains that 'all those who take their opinions from [the Heretics] are called Christians, just as also those who do not agree with the philosophers in their doctrines are yet called philosophers'. He continues,

> Whether they perpetrate those fabulous and shameful deeds -- the upsetting of the lamp, and promiscuous intercourse, and eating human flesh -- we know not. But we do know that they are neither persecuted nor put to death by you, at least on account of their opinions./4/

This attempt to distinguish the Marcionites from other Christians envisages no drift into heresy by the former, but rather a state of confusion in which two contemporary groups, each calling itself 'Christian' and claiming to represent the true faith, are competing for the title on the basis of different doctrines. This state of affairs lies behind Justin's complaint about the arrogance of the Marcionites: '[They] laugh at us, though they have no proof

---

/1/ The evidence supplied in the anti-marcionite Prologue to the Fourth Gospel has been considered most recently by J. Regul, Die antimarcion-itischen Evangelienprologe (Freiburg, 1969). See also the works cited by knox, Marcion and the NT (1942), 9ff.

/2/ AM 1.1.6.

/3/ 1 Apol. 26; cf. 58. On the credibility of Tert.'s report, see further, note 108 p. 226f.

/4/ 1 Apol. 26.

of what they say'./5/ Thus he is willing that the allegations of moral turpitude -- ritual prostitution, incest, and cannibalism -- should be substantiated by examining the practices of false teachers, such as the Marcionites. But Justin is probably too well aware of their reputation for moral ascesis to do more than implicate them in the slander by a profession of ignorance.

Justin's principle of discrimination is doctrinal: Marcion teaches men to deny that God is the creator; that the Christ predicted by the prophets is his son; and he affirms that there is a God above the creator who accomplishes greater works./6/ He also discloses that 'the Marcionites are neither persecuted nor put to death [by the authorities] on account of their opinions'. This is a puzzling accusation since as we have seen (pp. 18f.) the Marcionites suffered alongside other Christians during the persecutions of the second and third centuries./7/ What Justin appears to mean is that the Marcionites, inasmuch as they die for false doctrine, are not to be accounted true martyrs. The true christian martyrs are those that suffer for the true faith. Nevertheless, Justin does not attempt to disguise the severity of the threat posed by Marcion's teaching. He is the first (named) witness to the extent and success of Marcionism during the middle decade of the second century: 'By the aid of devils, he has caused many of every nation to speak blasphemies and to deny that God is the maker of this universe'./8/ Indeed, Justin's attempt to distinguish marcionite Christianity from his own, his profession of ignorance concerning their liturgical practices, and his complaint that they are not persecuted for their opinions amount really to a suggestion that the imperial legislation be enforced to impede their remarkable progress.

---

/5/ 1 Apol. 58. There is an echo of this criticism in Rhodo's remarks on the theology of the marcionite teacher, Apelles (Eusebius, HE 5.13.6f.).

/6/ 1 Apol. 58.

/7/ According to Apollinarius of Hierapolis, the Marcionites were in the habit of boasting about the number of their martyrs; 'Kai prōtoi ge hoi apo tēs Markiōnos hairesoēs Markianistai kaloumenoi pleistous hosous echein Christou martyras legousin, alla ton ge Christon auton kat alētheian ouch homologousin'; ('The so-called Marcionites following the heresy of Marcion say that they have numberless Martyrs to Christ, but Christ himself they do not confess in truth'), Eusebius, HE 5.16.21.

/8/ 1 Apol. 26.

The success of Marcion's teaching is attested persuasively by the volume and distribution of the polemic against it: Justin in Rome (c. 150); Theophilus of Antioch (160); Dionysius and Modestus in Greece (c. 170); Irenaeus in Lyons (176); Rhodon in Rome (c. 180); Clement of Alexandria (c. 200); Tertullian at Carthage (200 seqq.); Bardesanes in Armenia (c. 200); Commodianus in Gaul (c. 300); 'Adamantius' in Greece (320); Ephraem in Syria (370); Philastruius in Brescia (385); Eznik de Kolb at Bagrevand (445), and scattered references in the works of these and other writers to lost works against the heresy of Marcion. As late as the middle of the fifth century we find Theodoret, bishop of Cyrrhus in Syria, waging an assault on marcionite teachers in his diocese:

> Against the victims of the corruption of Marcion, I have never ceased to struggle; trying to convince the heathen that the Eternal Son of the ever-living God is himself creator of the universe . . . [and] Marcion's mad adherents that he is not only good but just; and savior, not as they fable, of another's works, but of his own . . . It is only right that I should point out from what sources they have derived this impiety: Simon, Menander, Cerdo, and Marcion absolutely deny the Incarnation and call the birth from a virgin fable./9/

Theodoret's association of Marcion with the gnostic teachers before him has a long history, but one of doubtful credibility. Justin himself mentions Simon Magus, Menander, and Marcion (but not Cerdo) within a few lines of each other in the twenty-sixth chapter of the first Apology. But he does not attempt to prove that they have more in common than a spurious claim to the designation 'Christian', and he says nothing of theological connections between them. By Theodoret's time, some three centuries later, the connections, in particular the association of Marcion with the teaching of Cerdo, had become a commonplace of anti-marcionite polemical writing. Here we shall try to ascertain how this genealogy of heresy arose, and how it has to do with the idea of tradition in the early church.

## 2.2 Irenaeus on the Morphology of Heresy

Irenaeus is the first writer to specify the connections among the heretics and to provide a chronological structure for the discussion of the various heresies. In the Haer., Marcion is named as a follower of Cerdo at

---

/9/ Theodoret, Eps., 145.

Rome in the reign of Anicetus (154-66)./10/ Marcion's dates are thus arranged to coincide with the conference of Polycarp and Anicetus in Rome (c. 155), thereby creating a mise en scène for the famous sentence occurring in Polycarp's Epistle to the Philippians: *'Houtos prōtotokos esti tou Satana'* ('Cognosco te primogenitum Satanae')./11/

Unfortunately, however, Irenaeus' account creates far more difficulties than it obviates. In the first place, his approach to the problem of heresy -- to defend 'the only true and life-giving faith which the church has received from the apostles and imparted to her sons'/12/ -- requires him to produce a genealogy of the true faith as a proof of its pedigree. This he does by arguing that the apostles, having founded the church,/13/ committed to Linus and to his successor-bishops a deposit of right-teaching./14/ The guarantee of this teaching corresponds to that which Luke affords at the beginning of his Gospel (1.1-2): 'To set forth those things which are believed among us, even as they delivered [paredosan] them unto us'.

According to Irenaeus, Clement and the first bishops were not only conversant with the apostles, but they 'might be said to have the preaching of the apostles still echoing in [their] ears and the tradition before [their] eyes'./15/ Thus when Clement of Rome, as one 'who had spoken with them', was confronted with dissension in the church at Corinth,

> [He] dispatched a most powerful letter . . . declaring the tradition which it had lately received from the apostles, proclaiming the one God omnipotent, the maker of heaven and earth, the creator of man, who brought on the deluge

---

/10/ Irenaeus, Haer., 3.4.3. Cerdo is said to have flourished under Hyginus, c. 136-40.

/11/ Haer., 3.3.4; cf. Eusebius, HE 4.14.7f.

/12/ Haer., 3, praef.

/13/ Haer., 3.3.3; 'Fundantes igitur et instruentes beati apostoli ecclesiam . . .'

/14/ On the use of this term in patristic literature, see G.L. Prestige, 'Tradition: or, the Scriptural Basis of Theology', in Fathers and Heretics (1940), 1-22. B. Reynders, 'Paradosis: Le progres de l'idée de tradition jusque s. Irenée', RThAM, 5 (1933), 155-91; H. Holstein, 'La tradition des apôtres chez s. Irenée', RSR, 36 (1949), 229-70; and A. Benoit, 'Ecriture et tradition chez s. Irenée', RHPhR, 40 (1950), 36ff.

/15/ Haer., 3.3.3: Irenaeus refers in the passage cited to Clement.

> and called Abraham, who led the people from the land of
> Egypt, spoke with Moses, set forth the Law, sent the
> prophets . . . From this document whoever chooses to do
> so may learn that He, the Father of our Lord Jesus
> Christ, was preached by the churches and may also
> understand the apostolical tradition of the church, since
> this epistle is of older date than these men who are now
> propagating falsehood and who conjure into existence
> another God beyond the creator and maker of all existing
> things./16/

It seems not to have concerned Irenaeus that in stressing the antiquity of the
letter of Clement to the Corinthians, he was at the same time asserting the
antiquity of the situation which occasioned it. Moreover, there can be very
little doubt that as construed in this credal synopsis, the teaching of the
letter is perceived as an antidote to Marcionism.

This is not to say that Irenaeus' synopsis is an accurate representation
of the views of the third bishop of Rome. As defined by the author of 1
Clement, the Corinthian heresy is oblique. It involves men who are 'double-
minded' and have 'doubts concerning the power' and judgment of God./17/
The writer beckons them to the love and fear of 'the Creator and Father of
all ages' ('ho dēmiourgos kai patēr tōn aiōnōn')/18/ who rejoices in his works
('autos gar ho dēmiourgos kai despotēs tōn hapantōn epi tois ergois autou
agalliatai')./19/ He also acknowledges the extent of the schism, which, he
laments, has turned many aside and caused many others to doubt ('To
schisma hymōn pollous diestrepsen')./20/ Finally, he invokes against the
spirit of sedition the 'unity' of catholic teaching:

> Have we not one God, and one Christ, and one Spirit of
> grace poured out upon us?/21/

> The Apostles received the Gospel for us from the Lord
> Jesus Christ; Jesus the Christ was sent from God. The
> Christ therefore is from God and the Apostles from the

---

/16/ Haer., loc. cit.: on the use of the argument from antiquity, see
Osborn, The Beginnings of Christian Philosophy (1981), 2; Andresen, Logos
und Nomos (1955), 146f.

/17/ 1 Clement 11.2.

/18/ 1 Clement 35.3.

/19/ 1 Clement 33.2.

/20/ 1 Clement 46.9.

/21/ 1 Clement, loc. cit.; cf. Irenaeus, Haer., 1.10.2.

Christ. In both ways then they were in accordance with
the appointed order of God's will./22/

There are a number of indications that the Corinthian heresy of CE 98
corresponds to Marcionism. One notes, for example, the stress placed on
marriage and family life (1.3); the disquisitions on the nature of God as
creator, judge, savior, and father (61.2; 59.3; 27.1; 35.1; 19.2; 18.4;
23.1): the strong anti-docetic tincture of the phrase Iesous Christous ho pais
sou (59.4; 16.3, etc.); the pedagogical use of the OT as a christian book,
together with references to the 'commandments' of Christ and the
ordinances of the Lord ('Ta prostagmata kai ta dikaiōmata tou kyriou', 2.8;
cf. 3.4); and finally, the emphasis on judgment and resurrection (24.1f.;
25.1f.; 27.1, etc.)./23/

Taken together, however, these motifs do not add up to the existence
of a marcionite 'error' as early as CE 98, and the most specific reference,
to 'those who have doubts concerning the power of God', may imply nothing
more than the waning of eschatological fervor in the Corinthian church,
following on the wave of enthusiasm for which they were reproached by Paul
some fifty years before.

Irenaeus' point is that the false doctrines of Marcion were anticipated
and peremptorily countered in the Clementine synopsis of right-teaching.
That heresy (as opposed to dissent) lay behind the writing was the furthest
thing from Irenaeus' mind; indeed he would have balked at any suggestion
that the opinions of Marcion dated from the time of Clement: 'Cum sit
vetustior epistola his qui nunc false docent et alterum deum super
demiurgum et factorem horum omnium quae sunt commentiuntur'./24/ He
appeals, therefore, to a preexisting body of catholic truth which, in virtue
of its antiquity and faithful transmission, excludes whatever doctrines
cannot be shown to possess the same origin. Moreover, in making this
separation effective, Irenaeus provides not only a genealogy of right

---

/22/ 1 Clement 42.1-2: 'Ho Christos oun apo tou Theou kai hoi apostoloi apo
tou Christou'; cf. 7.2.

/23/ On 1 Clement, see K. Beyschlag, Clement Romanus und der
Fruhkatholizismus: Untersuchungen zu 1 Clemens 1-7 (1966); L. Sanders, Le
hellenisme de s. Clement de Rome et le paulinisme (1943). On the ancient
authorship-tradition, cf. Eusebius, HE 4.23.11; Hermas, Past. vis.,
2.4.3.

/24/ Haer., 3.3.3.

teaching (traditio ab apostolis),/25/ but a genealogy of heretical inventions (haereticis adinventa) as well. The positive value of his historical assertions concerning Marcion's life and work must be understood within this larger heresiological context.

## 2.3 Polycarp: Contra Marcionem

For Irenaeus it is Polycarp ('ab apostolis in Asia constitutus episcopus') who first refutes Marcion face to face./26/ Irenaeus interprets this encounter (occurring by implication at Rome)/27/ as a condemnation pronounced by someone who received the teaching of the church directly from the apostles. Polycarp is not only the guarantor of the apostolic tradition in Asia, but a symbol of the unity of catholic teaching east and west,/28/ a central theme for Irenaeus:

> The Church, . . . although scattered throughout the whole world, yet, as if occupying but one house, carefully preserves [its teaching]. She also believes these points just as if she had but one soul, and one and the same heart, and she proclaims them, and teaches them, and hands them down [paradidōsin], with perfect harmony, as

---

/25/ On the distinction between traditio apostolorum and the traditio ab Apostolis, cf. J. Daniélou, Hellenistic Culture, II, 144ff.: 'Emphasis on the link between the tradition and the Apostles is a primary characteristic of Irenaeus, and implies a sharp differentiation of tradition, in the sense of the transmission of true doctrine, from traditions which are merely material going back to apostolic times [traditio apostolorum]'. Reynders maintains that for Irenaeus 'the apostles are in the strictest sense of the word transmitters and only transmitters' ('Paradosis', 188); and Holstein has shown ('La tradition . . . chez s. Irenée', 238) that the verb paradidonai (= tradere) is almost exclusively used with the apostles as subject by Irenaeus (e.g., Haer., 2.9.1; 3.2.2; 3.3.2; 3.3.3; 3.5.1). Hence, concludes Holstein, the tradition comes from the apostles, but it is received by the church; it is apostolic as regards its source, and ecclesiastical as regards its destination, that is to say, it is a traditio ab apostolis ad ecclesiam. Daniélou (ibid., 146) submits that 'the thing Irenaeus threw into bold relief was the prëeminent role of the Apostles, since it was to them that Christ officially entrusted his message'.

/26/ Haer., 3.3.4.

/27/ Cf. on the 'use' of Rome, W. Bauer, 'Rome's Persuasive and Polemical Tactics', Orthodoxy and Heresy, 111-29.

/28/ Haer., 3.3.2; Jer., De vir, illus. 17: 'princeps totius asiae'; and see Bauer, Orthodoxy and Heresy, 70ff.; v. Campenhausen, 'Polycarp von Smyrna und die Pastoralbriefe', Aus der Frühzeit des Christentums (1963), 214ff.

> if she possessed only one mouth. For, although the
> languages of the world are dissimilar, yet the import of
> the tradition [dynamis tēs paradōseōs] is one and the
> same. (Haer. 1.10.2)

In every sense, then, it is an official condemnation, the tradition adduced in
its favor being the warning of Paul to Titus: 'A man who is a heretic, after
the first and second times reject, knowing that he stands condemned in
himself' (3.10f.)./29/ In this way Irenaeus brings to bear against the heresy
of Marcion the words of the very Apostle whose authority serves as the basis
of his teaching. Besides this, in invoking the authority of Paul by
retrojecting into his lifetime the concept of right-teaching (didaskalia),
Irenaeus purports to uphold the written tradition which Marcion, in
'rejecting' the Pastoral Epistles, had corrupted./30/

Whatever kernel of historicity may underlie Irenaeus' account of the
meeting of Polycarp and Marcion sub Aniceto/31/ the chief purpose of
recounting the incident is to underscore the opposition between truth and
error by providing an authoritative witness to the rejection of heresy by a
faithful teacher who had conversed with the disciples of the Lord. In
Irenaeus' account, this opposition is so constructed that the representatives
of apostolic tradition and false teaching never really enter into dialogue (cf.
Haer. 3.4.2)./32/ Polycarp merely 'recognizes' ( cognoscere) Marcion as a
corrupter of the truth, and in the act of recognition condemns him. Within
this mise en scène, the figures of Marcion and Polycarp function as symbols
of Irenaeus' conviction that truth and error do not mix and are historically
separate, the purity of the former being guaranteed by 'recourse to the most

---

/29/ This sanction grew up specifically out of the encounter between the
catholics and the orthodox, Polycarp being the first writer to appeal to the
authority of the Pastoral Epistles. On the heretics' aversion to the Pastorals, cf. Clement, Strom., 3.

/30/ Haer., 1.27.4.

/31/ And not in Asia, sic. Harnack, 'Die ältesten Evangelien-Prologe und
die Bildung des Neuen Testaments', Sb. Berlin Akad. (1928), 16f.; cf.
Wilson, Heretic, 48; G. Pelland, Dict. Sp., suppl., 312f.; Bauer,
Orthodoxy and Heresy, 70; E. Barnikol, Entstehung, 1-33; Harrison,
Polycarp's Two Epistles to the Philippians (1936), 199f. Further, B.W.
Bacon, 'Marcion, Papias, and the Elders' JTS 23 (1922), 134ff.; G. Krüger,
'Marcion', PRE 12 (1903), 266ff. Eus. HE 4.14.1.

/32/ Cf. Eusebius, HE 4.14.7.

ancient churches with which the apostles held constant discussion'./33/ Marcion stands outside this conversation and hence outside the received tratition: thus he has no claim to the traditio veritatis, itself derived from the traditio ab apostolis. Irenaeus resorts to the banking simile to make his point. The apostles deposited their teaching in the church, just as a rich man deposits his money in a bank. The bank has an obligation to its investors to guard the deposit against thieves; consequently the deposited wealth must be locked away. Indeed, it has always been locked away, and the deposit remains always the same: 'Propter quod oportet devitare quidem illos quae autem sunt Ecclesiae cum summa diligentia diligere et apprehendere veritatis traditionem'./34/

### 2.4 Marcion at Rome: The Genealogy of Error

While Irenaeus' mise en scène is a valuable commentary on the idea of tradition, it is less reliable as a source for dating Marcion's activity in Rome. The sentence which he attributes to Polycarp first appears in that writer's letter to the Philippians, dating in part from around CE 130./35/ That Polycarp used the same words in rebuking Marcion at Rome in the reign of Anicetus a generation later (155) may reasonably be doubted,/36/ inasmuch as the choice of Rome as the scene of the encounter between the two rivals is probably to be explained on theological grounds: As the See associated with the two great Apostles, Rome represents the locus of the traditio veritatis./37/ Polycarp, 'who always taught the things he had

---

/33/ Haer., 3.4.1.

/34/ Haer., 3.4.1. Perhaps suggested by 1 Tim 6.20.

/35/ Thus P. N. Harrison, Polycarp's Two Epistles. Harrison's theory that the thirteenth and (possibly) fourteenth chapters of the Epistle date from around 115 is supported by J. Quasten, Patrol., 1, 80; cf. A.C. Gloucester, 'The Epistle of Polycarp to the Philippians', ChQ, 141 (1945), 1-25; and W.M. Ramsay, 'The Date of Polycarp's Martyrdom', Jahreshefte des Oesterreichischen Archaeologischen Institutes, 27 (1932), 245-48.

/36/ But see K. Lake, The Apostolic Fathers, 1, 293, n. 1.

/37/ P. Nautin, 'Église de Rome ou Église universelle', RHR, 151 (1957), 37-78.

learned from the apostles',/38/ is the (eastern) custodian of this tradition in territory which has fallen prey to Marcion's error. But in Rome Marcion is out of place; he is clearly the intruder come to take the kingdom by storm./39/

In the interest of underscoring the difference between apostolic tradition and its later corruptions, Irenaeus stresses the historical distance between the heretical inventions and the truth received by the church./40/ He does so in the form of a genealogy of false-teaching which stands alongside but in point of origin postdates the traditio ab apostolis and its transmission./41/ This genealogy begins with Simon the Magician,/42/ whom Irenaeus regards as the source 'from whom all sorts of heresies derive their origin',/43/ and who is reckoned to have been rejected by Peter himself./44/ Standing in direct succession to Simon are Menander, Saturninus, Basilides, Carpocrates, Marcellina, Cerinthus, and Nicolas. With the introduction of Cerdo (1.26.1), Irenaeus begins to date the heresies with greater precision: These are of recent memory; but the complexity and variety of their teaching (in sharp contrast to the unity of catholic

---

/38/ Haer., 3.3.4.

/39/ That the meeting is legendary is suggested by J. Regul, 'Die Antimarcionitischen Evangelien-Prologe', in Geschichte der lateinischen Bibel, 6 (1969), 164-77; and G. Pelland, Dict. Sp., suppl., 313.

/40/ Haer., 3.4.2.

/41/ Irenaeus speaks in terms of a family tree: 'Cum sit igitur adversus omnes haereticos detectio atque convictio varia et multifaria et nobis propositum est omnibus his secundum ipsorum charactera contradicere, necessarium arbitrati sumus prius referre fontem et radicem eorum, uti sublimissimum ipsorum Bythum cognoscens, intellegas arborem de qua defluxerunt tales fructus', Haer., 1.22.1-2.

/42/ Acts 8.9-24. Justin, 1 Apol. 26, 56; Acts of Peter, 3-6; 8; Ps.-Clementines, H II, 22.2-H III, 29.1-58.2. (NTA II, 546-552). Streeter (Primitive Church, 10) posits the existence of an older Ebionite work about Simon which has been incorporated in the Clementine literature.

/43/ Haer., 1.23.2: 'ex quo universae haereses substiterunt'.

/44/ Acts 8.20ff. The early association of Marcion with Simon is doubtless the source of the legend of Marcion's simony in Rome. The story is first recounted by Tertullian, AM 4.4.3. The Ps.- Clementines perhaps contain references to the teaching of Marcion which have been retrojected into the heresy of Simon; thus, 'The content of the law [Simon] interprets according to personal arbitrariness. He speaks of a future judgment, but he does not reckon it in earnest' (Hom. II, 22.2).

tradition)/45/ betray their links with the false teachings rejected by the apostles. It might even be said that Irenaeus regards the contemporary rejection of heretics as a prerogative of the catholics precisely because this historical connection exists, i.e., because it can be shown that the progenitors of wrong teaching had been denied by the fathers of orthodox faith.

Irenaeus calls Cerdo 'one who took his system from the followers of Simon and came to live at Rome in the time of Hyginus'./46/ This would place Cerdo's activity somewhere in the range of CE136-40, the same period to which Irenaeus assigns the teaching-activity of Valentinus in Rome. Unfortunately, there is no contemporary evidence that would confirm or belie Irenaeus' report. Almost nothing is known about Cerdo beyond what can be gleaned from the Haer., and most of what later writers have to tell comes largely from this work./47/ According to Irenaeus' report Cerdo taught a distinction between the OT God and the God proclaimed by Jesus, 'the former being known (cognosci), the other unknown (ignorari); the one righteous (justum), the other benevolent (bonum)'./48/ Irenaeus considers Marcion not merely a follower of Cerdo, but the developer of his ideas. This is significant since in no other case is the relationship between two teachers stated in such unequivocal language./49/ The claim vexed Harnack: If Irenaeus is correct, then Marcion becomes merely the retailer of another's ideas, and he forfeits his claim to originality. Indeed, this conclusion had already been drawn, with maximum polemic advantage, by the third-century author of the adversus omnes haereses: '[Marcion] tried to approve the heresy of Cerdo, so that his assertions are identical with those of the former heretic before him' (Omn. haer. 6).

---

/45/ Cf. Haer., 3.4.1f.; 5.20.1.

/46/ Irenaeus makes Hyginus ninth in succession from the apostles, Linus being accounted the first. Haer. 1.27.1.

/47/ Haer. 1.27.1; 3.4.3; cf. Hippolytus, Ref. omn. haer., 10.15; Tertullian, AM 1.2.3; 1.22.10; 4.17.11; Philastrius, lib. haer., 44; Ps.-Tertullian, Omn, haer., 6; Epiphanius, Panar., 41. See the discussion in Hilgenfeld, Ketzergeschichte, 316-32.

/48/ Haer., 1.27.1; cf. Hippol. Ref. omn. haer. 10.15.

/49/ Haer., 1.27.2: 'Marcion adampliavit doctrinam'.

It has often been pointed out, however, that Irenaeus really provides no more than a caption of Cerdo's thought, and may in fact have derived this much from his knowledge of Marcion's teachings, after having determined on other grounds (not known to us, unfortunately) that the two men were active in Rome at the same time. Thus while there can be no doubt that Marcion's career was linked by tradition from a very early date with that of Cerdo, there is no solid basis for adducing an historical relationship between the teaching of the two men from the tradition which Irenaeus has inherited./50/ Irenaeus presupposes the connection between Cerdo and Marcion; he is not concerned to establish it by the laws of historical evidence. And for later writers, the prooftext of the connection was to be found in the Haer./51/ The association, therefore, must be seen as a

---

/50/ On the question of Cerdo's influence, see F. Legge, 'Marcion', in Forerunners and Rivals of Christianity (1915), II, 203f.: 'The inference is unavoidable that Marcion's views were original and that they were formed by a sort of centrifugal process; after rejecting in turn all heathen and Jewish elements, as well as most of the traditions which had already grown up in the Catholic church'. Harnack has argued the same case for Marcion's originality and independence of Cerdo's influence: 'Die Kircheväter von Irenäus an haben diesen Einfluss [i.e., Cerdo's] masslos übertrieben, um M.s Originalität herabzudrücken und ihn dem landläufigen Gnostizismus unterzuordnen; aber das Haupstück der Lehre M.s, die Entegegensetzung des guten und gerechten Gottes, stammt nicht von Cerdo, der vielmehr den Gegensatz des guten und des schlechten Gottes, wie andere Gnostiker verkündigte' (Marcion, 26; cf. 38*, and Beilage II, 'Cerdo und Marcion'). Harrison (Polycarp's Two Epistles, 183; 195) argues however for Cerdo's influence on the grounds that Polycarp's letter to the Philippians lacks any clear reference to the ditheism which Marcion must have learned in Rome; it was there, Harrison submits, that Marcion finally gave up the monotheism he had previously defended 'as the only way out of his theological dilemma' (p. 195). Cf. Salmon, DCB, 818a; Hilgenfeld, Ketzergeschichte, 316ff.

/51/ According to Haer., 1.26.1, Cerinthus taught all of the doctrines ascribed to Cerdo, and not a few of those attributed to Marcion: (a) that the God who made the world is other than the God who reigns above all; (b) that the creator-God is ignorant of the supreme and unknown God; (c) that Jesus, being endowed with the spirit of God at baptism, proclaimed the unknown Father. Unlike Marcion, however, Cerinthus taught also the human generation of Jesus and made a sharp separation of Jesus and the Christ (= the Spirit of God), the latter remaining impassible while the former 'truly suffers'. But the emphasis on the reality of the passion is also a feature of Marcionism (cf. Harnack, Marcion, 125; Chronologie II, 187). It is Cerinthus whom John is supposed to have rejected at Ephesus (Haer., 3.3.4; Eusebius, HE 3.28.6) and against whom John is said to have written his Gospel (Haer., 3.11.1; but cf. Epiphanius, Panar., 51 [the 'Alogoi']); while Philastrius and the anti-marcionite prologist confuse Cerinthus and Marcion, possibly because they knew of a connection between them, or because they were unable to distinguish their teachings.

corollary of the heresiological enterprise -- that is to say, Irenaeus' intention in establishing links among the various heretical schools. Thus, following a synopsis of Marcion's view, he writes:

> I have been led to mention this in order that you may know that all who in any way corrupt the truth and injuriously affect the preaching of the church are the disciples and successors of Simon Magus of Samaria. Although they do not confess the name of their master, in order all the more to seduce others, yet they do teach his doctrines./52/

Even though Irenaeus presupposes this generic relation among the heresies, his chief proof of their status as offenses against catholic truth is not their relation as such, but their multiplicity. There is, to be sure, a heretical 'tradition' of sorts, but this tradition lacks unity. Each heretic invents his own teaching, which is nothing less than a development, modification, or elaboration of the original (Simonian) aberration. Marcion's 'development' of Cerdo's ideas is a part of this tradition. Writes Irenaeus, 'This wisdom each one of them alleges to be the fiction of his own inventing . . . , so that according to their idea, the truth properly resides at one time in Valentinus, at another in Marcion, at another in Cerinthus . . . . For every one of these men, being altogether of a perverse disposition, depraving the system of truth, is not ashamed to preach himself'./53/

At one point, Irenaeus seems to suggest that the gnostics derive from Simon's successor Menander,/54/ and in another place that Cerdo took his teaching from Simon's followers, while Marcion developed these ideas further./55/ Here the genealogy falls short, since Marcion's doctrines as related in the Haer. can scarcely be called a development of the speculative systems catalogued in Book 1 and which Irenaeus specifically associates with the gnostic heresy of Valentinus (1.11.1f.). Irenaeus is not unaware of the

---

/52/ Haer., 1.27.4.

/53/ Haer., 3.2.1; cf. 5.20.1: '[They] are all very much later than the bishops to whom the apostles handed over (tradiderunt) the churches. . . . Hence the aforesaid heretics, being blind to the truth, are bound to wander out of the way, taking now one road and now the other, scattering their teaching abroad without any harmony or sequence' (my translation).

/54/ Haer., 3.4.3; cf. 1.23.5.

/55/ Haer., 1.27.1.

difficulties posed by his undertaking, in view of 'the numbers and offshoots'/56/ of the heresies. He compares the gnostic sects to 'so many mushrooms springing up out of the ground'./57/ But in the process of relating the heretical branches to each other and to the ancestral false teacher at the same time, he makes an ambiguous distinction between the more speculative teachers (e.g., Valentinus, Menander), whom he knows as gnostics, and teachers such as Cerdo and Marcion, whom he knows only as 'Simonians': 'Super hos autem ex his qui praedicti sunt Simoniani, multitudo gnosticorum exsurrexit'./58/ But the distinction remains obscure, owing largely to the structure which Irenaeus seeks to superimpose upon the heretical systems. As all of the heresies have Simon as their source, the gnostic disciples of Menander must also be Simonians. Nevertheless, it is significant that Irenaeus nowhere expressly refers to Marcion as a gnostic,/59/ but rather as Cerdo's successor and as the impetus behind the Encratite movement./60/

## 2.5 The Biographical Problem

The question of the terminus a quo of Marcion's activity is tied to Irenaeus' report that Marcion came to Rome during the reign of Anicetus, that is, not earlier than 150, and that there he learned and developed the

---

/56/ Haer., 1.28.1.

/57/ Haer., 1.29.1.

/58/ Haer., loc. cit.

/59/ Cf. Haer., 3.4.3.

/60/ Haer., 1.28.1: According to Irenaeus, the Encratites preached self-control, continence, and abstinence from certain foods. That he identifies Marcion with this movement speaks decisively against later stories designed to cast doubts on Marcion's personal code of conduct (e.g., Ps.-Tert., Omn. haer., 6; cf. Clement of Alex., Strom. 3.4; Epiphanius, Panar. 42.1). The marcionite position on marriage and the use of certain meats and wine parallels that of the Encratites, but the connection probably stops there. Cf. Hippol. Ref. omn. haer. 7.18; 8.13; AM 1.27.5. On the stuprum cuiusdam virginis (Ps.-Tert., Omn. haer. 6), see Regul's discussion, Evangelienprologe, 183-185. Regul quite correctly stresses the unreliability of the tradition.

doctrines of Cerdo./61/ We have suggested that a significant reason for Irenaeus' selection of this period and location was to provide a mise en scène for the encounter with Polycarp, whom Irenaeus knows as Marcion's traditional rival, and whose presence in Rome to consult with Anicetus on the Quartodeciman practice was well-attested. Inserted into this historical scene is a bit of dialogue taken from Polycarp's letter to the church at Philippi, significant nonetheless because Irenaeus identifies the teaching proscribed in this letter as being that of Marcion.

The historicity of the encounter comes into question as soon as we attempt to correlate Irenaeus' testimony with that of Justin,/62/ who remarks around 150 that Marcion's teaching had spread 'to every nation', and (what is more significant) records his surprise that the famous heretic is 'even until now alive [kai nun eti] and teaching his disciples to believe in some other God greater than the Creator'./63/ This indicates that for some years prior to the date given by Irenaeus for Marcion's encounter with Cerdo, Marcion had been teaching his ditheistic doctrines throughout Asia Minor. As Knox interprets Justin's statement, it indicates that Marcion's influence was more widespread than one would suppose possible if his career as a christian teacher had begun only a few years earlier. Moreover, the phrase kai nun eti suggests a longer period of heretical activity than is allowed for by the usual theory that Marcion became an influential teacher only after he reached the west./64/ Inasmuch as Justin had sojourned in Samaria and Ephesus before coming to Rome, he was obviously in a position to know the extent of marcionite influence in the east./65/

It is therefore impossible to correlate Justin's testimony with Irenaeus' assertion that Marcion came to Rome around 150, became a disciple of Cerdo, and thereafter (having been definitively denounced by Polycarp) began to teach what he had learned. If however we assume the connection with Cerdo to be legendary, as it almost certainly is, we may conclude that

---

/61/ Haer., 3.4.3.

/62/ 1 Apol., 26.

/63/ 1 Apol., 26; cf. 58.

/64/ Knox, Marcion and the NT, 8.

/65/ Writing half a century later, Tert. suggests that Marcion's heresy has filled the whole world ('cum totum impleverit mundum'), AM 5.19.2, though he records this as a supposition.

the presence of Marcion in Rome during the reign of Anicetus does not exclude the possibility of a long period of teaching in the east. But how reliable is the tradition which places Marcion in Rome at the time of Polycarp's visit? Are there grounds for assuming the historicity of his presence there, or is it more likely that he had been led hither only for the sake of the encounter with Polycarp?

The direct evidence for the tradition is scant and contradictory. Ephraem Syrus speaks of Marcion as 'wandering like Cain',/66/ and Rhodo, punning on Tertullian's use of the term nauclerus in reference to Marcion's profession, calls him nautēs ('sailor')./67/ Both of these allusions point ambiguously to missionary activity in Asia Minor, but not to Rome as Marcion's destination.

Far more troublesome is Philastrius' assertion that 'Marcion was driven out of Ephesus by the blessed John the Evangelist and the presbyters, and spread his heresy in Rome'./68/ This tradition, apparently an early one, is also known by the author of the anti-marcionite Prologue to the Gospel of John. In this case we would seem to have a clear indication of Marcion's whereabouts after leaving Pontus and travelling in Asia, and indeed a motive for the latter journey, namely to vindicate teachings which the church at Ephesus considered heretical./69/ But the problem with this information is self-evident. Even if one accepts Harnack's claim that the words 'proiectus est a Iohanne' (Prologue) have been interpolated,/70/ thereby substituting

---

/66/ Cited in Wilson, Heretic, 48.

/67/ Eusebius, HE 5.13.3.

/68/ Lib. haer., 45.72 (Harnack, Marcion, 13*; Regul, Evangelienprologe, 196f.).

/69/ But cf. G. Pelland, Dict. Sp., suppl., 313.

/70/ Harnack, Marcion, 11*-15*. Following de Bruyne, Harnack (Sb. der preussischen Akad. [1928], 322-41) argued that the prologues were originally composed in Greek (the Gk. form of the Lucan prol. still being extant) and that the so-called Monarchian and Priscillianist prologues are later expansions of these. Harnack dated the Greek versions soon after Marcion's death (i.e., 160+), but before the composition of the Adversus Haereses. Haenchen (Acts of the Apostles [1970], 10) finds no evidence of an anti-marcionite intention in the prologues to Mark and Luke; but such an intention is almost impossible to overlook in the case of the johannine prologue, and it is chiefly on this evidence that de Bruyne based his argument: 'Marcion haereticus, cum ab eo [i.e., Papias] fuisset improbatus eo quod contraria sentiebat abjectus est ab Iohanne. Is vero scripta vel

for the name of the relatively unknown bishop the authority of John, we are left with the curious suggestion that Marcion expected to receive a fairer hearing for his views in Rome than he had in Ephesus./71/ Apparently, both Philastrius and the author of the anti-marcionite Prologue know a different version of the story of the meeting between Cerinthus and the disciple John at a bath-house in Ephesus./72/ In their accounts, it is Marcion who

---

epistulas ad eum pertulerat a fratribus qui in Ponto fuerunt' (text in W.F. Howard, ExT [1936], 534-38; cf. emendation in J. Regul, Evangelienprologe, 35 [= II.20]). Writes Wilson, 'Whatever difficulties there may be on historical grounds about this reference to an excommunication of Marcion by the Apostle, after a previous expostulation and exposure of his heretical views by the faithful Papias, there can be no doubt that the prologue-writer considered Marcion a dangerous deceiver who had to be dealt with peremptorily' (Heretic, 55). Harnack would resolve the historical difficulties by removing the phrase 'abjectus est ab Iohanne' on the reckoning that the name of John has been substituted for that of some less significant bishop; de Bruyne was similarly inclined to this view. But such a conclusion is scarcely more probable than that the incident preserves a belief prevalent among the marcionite Christians: that their founder was Paul's successor in Asia Minor, and not John. That John could pass judgment on Marcion by ejecting him from the church at Ephesus is no more than a romantic way of illustrating his authority as the true compatriot of Paul. It therefore seems unlikely that John's name has been interpolated; the scene is a double of that which takes place in Rome between Marcion and Polycarp, the continuator of the apostolic tradition in the east. On the suggestion that Marcion set out from Pontus bearing letters of recommendation, see B. Bacon, JBL, 49, 43-54; R. Grant, Angl. Theol. Rev., 23 (1941), 231ff. Pelland has argued (Dict. Sp., suppl., 313) that the prologue to John is not earlier than the fourth century. But R. Brown (The Gospel of John [1966], I, xcix) dates it around 200, claiming however that the tradition associating Marcion with John is not earlier than the fourth century. J. Quasten accepts the dating of Harnack and de Bruyne (viz., 160-80) (Patrol. II, 210); but cf. E. Gutwenger, 'The Anti-Marcionite Prologues', TS 7 (1946), 393-409; and R. Eisler, 'La ponctuation du prologue anti-marcionite a l'Evangile selon Jean', RHPhR, 4 (1930), 350-71.

/71/ Cf. Pelland, Dict. Sp., suppl. 313: 'It is difficult to believe that an individual excommunicated by the church in Asia should have been accepted with favor by the Church at Rome'.

/72/ But cf. R. Eisler, The Enigma of the Fourth Gospel (1938): Marcion was John's amanuensis and was dismissed by the Evangelist when he was discovered to have made heretical interpolations in the Gospel. The relation of Marcion to the Fourth Gospel is no less problematical than the question of his knowledge of canonical Luke. Standing behind the story of Marcion's rejection by John is the legend of Cerinthus' repudiation by the same Apostle; thus there is the difficulty of explaining the connection between Philastrius' statements concerning the association of John and Marcion with those of Epiphanius (Panar., 42.1) and Irenaeus (Haer. 3.11.1). See further, Krüger, art., 'Marcion', PRE³ (1903), 12, 267f. The source of the legends later associated with Marcion is the lost Syntagma of Hippolytus; so Harnack, Marcion, 17*-22*.

encounters John and not Cerinthus, whose doctrines are curiously similar to those assigned to Cerdo and Marcion. Irenaeus' report comes as a short digression in the third book of the Haer., just after a claim that Polycarp had caused many in Rome to turn away from Marcion and Cerdo: 'Et sunt qui audierunt eum quoniam Iohannes domini discipulus in Epheso iens lavari, cum vidisset intus Cerinthum, exsilierit de balneo non lotus, dicens quod timeat ne balneum concidat, cum intus esset Cerinthus inimicus veritatis'./73/

The story is associated with the one immediately following: that of Marcion's rejection by Polycarp;/74/ the report of John's reaction to the presence of Cerinthus is linked further to the matter following the Marcion-Polycarp encounter, namely the warning of Paul to Titus concerning the proper handling of heretics (Titus 3.10)./75/

Accordingly, Irenaeus' logic in the passage runs something like this:

(a) Polycarp has his authority from the apostolic church in Ephesus, whose custodian is John, the disciple of the Lord; Polycarp was himself constituted bishop of Smyrna by 'apostles in Asia'.

(b) The immediate precedent for Polycarp's handling of Marcion is the story of John's fleeing from the bath-house in Ephesus upon hearing of Cerinthus' presence within; moreover,

(c) John acts in accordance with a practice for which there is also a warrant in the letters of Paul, the founder of the church at Ephesus.

By this logic, the digression on Cerinthus becomes a step in an argument. Polycarp has acted toward Marcion in a way consistent with John's dealings with an earlier heretic; John has demonstrated the proper handling of schismatic men who 'stand condemned in themselves'. Significantly, therefore, it is the eastern phalanx of the tradition which Irenaeus brings to bear against the doctrines of Marcion: Paul the founder of the church in Asia; John, 'who remained [in Ephesus] until the times of Trajan'; Polycarp, the student of John and bishop of Smyrna by the design of the apostles. There is not only an apostolic tradition of right-teaching, but also a tradition which specifies the way in which false teachers are to be handled: 'Such was the horror', writes Irenaeus, 'which the apostles and their disciples

---

/73/ Haer., 3.3.4.

/74/ Haer., 3.3.4/84-87 v. 3.3.4/88-92.

/75/ Haer., 3.3.4/92-96.

had at holding even verbal communication with any corrupters of the truth'.

This argument is a step beyond the legend known to the Prologue-writer and Philastrius, who have it that Marcion was rejected by John on his home soil, Ephesus. In all probability, Irenaeus also knew the story of Marcion's rejection by John, but substituted Cerinthus' name for Marcion's in the Ephesus-account. As in the case of Cerdo, nothing is known of 'Cerinthus' beyond what Irenaeus has to offer./76/ The information that John wrote his gospel to refute Cerinthus (Haer. 3.11.1) may also have belonged originally to the Marcion-tradition, here corrected by Irenaeus in the interest of his argument. Although Irenaeus' account antedates at least the story Philastrius tells, we need not discredit the latter's testimony or that supplied in the anti-marcionite Prologue to John strictly on the basis of Irenaeus' version of Marcion's biography. There is a high probability that they preserve the memory of Marcion's teaching activity in Asia Minor before coming to Rome. Whether this activity involved an attempt to preach the gospel in Ephesus is uncertain (see ch. 8 pp. 244f.) but far from unlikely, and the 'evidence' supplied by the Pastoral Epistles (cf. ch. 9) would appear to indicate a heretical (marcionite?) missionary endeavor in Ephesus before 120. Marcion's canon possessed no pauline epistle entitled Ephesians and there is no marcionite prologue to Ephesians, suggesting that the Marcionites either did not know or did not wish to preserve the memory of Paul's activity -- or perhaps their own -- in that city. We know only that the marcionite prologist considered Philippi, Laodicea, and Thessalonica strong in the faith of the true Apostle. In any event, the testimony of Philastrius and the anti-marcionite prologist evidence another line of attack against Marcionism, one which depends not on the historical breach between Marcion and the apostles, but on the reckoning that Marcion's teaching is an aberration of Ephesian orthodoxy (see further pp. 253ff.).

## 2.6 The Dating of Marcion's Heresy

Knox finds more dependable criteria for dating the start of Marcion's teaching career in the letter of Polycarp to the church at Philippi. As a source for establishing the substance of Marcion's religious thought prior to

---

/76/ Cf. Hippol., Ref. Omn. haer., 7.21; G. Bardy, 'Cerinthe' in Rev. B., 30 (1921), 344-73.

CE 140, the letter is of questionable value,/77/ since despite Harrison's attempt to show that Marcion's ditheism emerges fully-fledged only after the encounter with Cerdo in Rome, the absence of any reference to such a teaching in Polycarp's letter need not point to an earlier stratum of marcionite doctrine./78/ The less historical value one assigns to the association between Cerdo and Marcion in Rome sub Aniceto, the less likely it is that the date CE 154 (i.e., the first year of Anicetus' episcopate) can be used as the time of a theological 'turning point' in Marcion's career. As we have seen, Marcion's ditheism must have surfaced in the east at least by the time of Justin's first Apology, as Justin has first-hand knowledge of the teaching./79/

---

/77/ But cf. Harrison, Polycarp's Two Epistles, 191f. Harrison takes seriously Tert's report that Marcion was at first a member of the 'orthodox' church and that he was converted to heresy by Cerdo. He bases his conclusions on the reckoning that 'Sinope was a hotbed of literalism [as] indicated by the existence of . . . his contemporary, Aquila'. Hence for Marcion to have 'learned' the doctrine of two Gods represented a complete reversal of his earlier and necessarily monotheistic thinking; according to Harnack, 'This utter turnabout in his ideology as to the value of the OT involved in its rejection . . . the deepest dismay and the hottest pain' (Marcion, 31). Unfortunately, this view of Marcion's background and of the religious situation in Sinope is unhistorical; Marcion would have had ample opportunity within the religiously pluralistic culture of Pontus to have developed an unfavorable view of the Law and the Prophets, as well as a ditheistic theology. Cf. pp. 3ff., above, chapter 1.

/78/ Harrison, Polycarp's Two Epistles, 190: 'We have no evidence that Marcion held or taught the doctrine of two Gods before he got to Rome. . . . That the doctrine of two Gods was imparted to Marcion by Cerdo is stated by our most ancient authorities, from Irenaeus onwards' (p. 196). Harrison implies a consensus of these authorities with respect to Cerdo's doctrine and the extent of his influence on Marcion. In fact, however, only Hippolytus seems to have access to a source of information other than Irenaeus, and where he differs from Irenaeus he differs also from the doctrine taught by Marcion; thus, according to the account preserved in the Omn. haer. (6), Cerdo taught the existence of two Gods, 'unum bonum et alterum saevum'. This characterization is repeated by Epiphanius (Panar., 41.1) and Philastrius (lib. haer., 44: 'Unum deum bonum et unum malum'). These accounts however expressly contradict Irenaeus' caption of Cerdo's teaching (Haer., 1.27.1): 'et alterum justum et alterum autem bonum esse'. This caption, moreover, is clearly an inference from Marcion's teaching, as can be seen from the information which Tert. provides: 'Quam ob rem . . . alium deum lucis ostendisse debueras, alium vero tenebrarum, quo facilius alium bonitatis, alium severitatis persuasisses' (AM 2.29.4). Nor has Harrison acknowledged that Justin, the most ancient of our witnesses, knows nothing of Cerdo's influence.

/79/ This is not to reject the substance of Harrison's argument regarding the date of Polycarp's letter. That the false teacher at Philippi is Marcion has

Polycarp does not specify the false-teacher against whom he warns the Philippian church, but it is now widely agreed that Marcion's teaching is envisaged in chapter seven and elsewhere in the letter. Moreover, Irenaeus, who claims to have seen Polycarp 'in early youth', makes it quite clear that Marcion is the target of Polycarp's warning.

As to the date of the letter, Harrison proposed in 1936 a 'two-document' hypothesis which has since gained wide support. According to this theory, chapters 1-12 of the letter were written c. 130. At the core of this section is a proscription of Marcion which provides irrefragable evidence of Marcion's enterprise in Asia Minor about this time. Chapter thirteen (and possibly also fourteen) was written as early as CE 117, and represents a covering letter to accompany the Ignatian correspondence, which had been requested by the church at Philippi (Phil. 13.2)./80/ At a later time, Harrison reasons, the two originally discrete documents were fused to become a single letter, and it is in this form that the epistle has come down to us.

Harrison's theory is not without its shortcomings, the most obvious of which is the assumption that Marcion could not have been active as early as CE 117, when the so-called covering letter was composed. But if at least the identification of Marcion with the false teacher at Philippi is correct, we can conclude that Marcion was active in the east about 130, that is to say a generation prior to the date given for his coming to Rome by Irenaeus./81/

If this conclusion is accepted, however, a further question must be raised: 'Why may not Marcion's activity have begun much earlier [than 130]? On what grounds do we conclude that it may not have begun by 120 or 110? Certainly nothing we know about the time of Marcion's death precludes

now been widely accepted; cf. Quasten, Patrol., I, 80. It is less certain that the teachings therein proscribed belong to an early stage of Marcion's teaching; and insofar as this belief is introduced as a criterion for dating Polycarp's leter, the argument is hardly compelling. Nor is Harrison's suggestion that Irenaeus had access to 'official church reports' which would have established the link between Marcion and Cerdo (p. 190) convincing, much less the conclusion that 'It is certain that the two men were in Rome at the same time . . . . There is hardly any doubt that [Marcion] attended Cerdo's school and that he was impressed and influenced by what he heard there'.

/80/ Cf. Eusebius, HE 3.36; discussion in Streeter, The Primitive Church, 273ff.

/81/ And cf. Tert., AM 1.19.3.

the possibility. And is it not natural to suppose that he worked in western Asia Minor before entering Macedonia?'/82/ Thus, while Harrison's argument frees us from the supposition that Marcion's career begins in Rome at a relatively late date, it also involves the possibility that Marcion was a mature and influential teacher in the opening decades of the second century.

The proviso is a sticking point here: the false teacher at Philippi remains an unknown quantity in the equation, and we are therefore obliged to base our conclusions as to Marcion's whereabouts (not to mention the date of the letter itself) on the correlation between the doctrines of a known teacher and the description of a rather vaguer heresy which threatens to undermine the orthodox faith of the Philippian church. Just how 'orthodox' this faith may have been can be inferred from the praise of the marcionite prologist:

> Philippenses sunt Machedones. Hi accepto verbo veritatis perstiterunt in fide, nec receperunt falsos apostolos. Hos apostolus (i.e., Paulus) conlaudat scribens eis a Roma de carcere per Epaphraditum (ad Phil.).

Polycarp writes to a church which almost alone in the east (Thessalonica and Laodicea stand beside it) is considered 'orthodox' by the Marcionites.

Harrison failed to weigh certain factors adequately in reaching his conclusions. There is for example no way to explain the absence of references to the most conspicuous of Marcion's doctrines -- namely, the doctrine of two gods and the rejection of the OT -- except as a case against construing the false teaching as Marcion's. There is no warrant, other than a too-credulous reading of Irenaeus with regard to Marcion's dependence on Cerdo, for saying that Polycarp's failure to mention these offenses is due to the fact that Marcion had not yet committed them./83/ If the most characteristic of Marcion's opinions had still to be formulated, how can we be certain that the proscribed teaching is Marcionism?/84/ Moreover, as Harnack has shown, Marcion denied neither the significance of the cross, nor the reality of judgment, the errors which stand out in boldest relief in Polycarp's letter./85/ To this objection, Harrison replies that Marcion's

---

/82/ Marcion and the NT, 11.

/83/ Harrison, Polycarp's Two Epistles, 172-74.

/84/ But cf. Knox, Marcion and the NT, 11.

/85/ As Harnack suggests, 'It is totally incorrect to think that according to Marcion Christ suffered only in appearance . . . . That was the judgment

enemies would have interpreted his doctrine as denial, and this is all that is necessary to prove the case.

Some of these difficulties can be overcome by a closer reading of the Epistle itself, leaving aside the question which preoccupied Harrison -- namely, the unity of the document. When this is done, there remain an impressive number of similarities between the doctrine which Polycarp attacks and that espoused by Marcion.

The false teacher is portrayed as a docetist who rejects the testimony of the cross, twists the logia of the Lord, and denies the resurrection and judgment: *'Pas gar hos an mē homologē Iēsoun Christoun en sarki elēluthenai, antichristos estin. Kai hos an mē homologē to martyrion tou staurou, ek tou diabolou estin. Kai hos an methodeuē ta logia tou kyriou pros tas idias epithymias kai legē mēte anastasin mēte krisin, houtos prōtotokos esti tou satana'.*/86/ As a remedy to this heresy, Polycarp enjoins the Philippians to 'persevere in the pattern of true love [agapēs ]'/87/ and to serve God in fear and certainty of judgment. Perhaps most significant of all are the references to the authority of Paul. Polycarp emphasizes the duty of wives, widows, deacons and presbyters in a series of exhortations to virtue that echoes the language of the Pastoral Epistles./88/ Like Paul, moreover, Polycarp stresses the importance of harmonious church order as an impediment to the 'false brethren who bear the name of the Lord in hypocrisy and who deceive empty-minded men'./89/ This allusion would seem to indicate the existence of a rival group of Christians who claim Paul's authority as the basis of their doctrine. Against them, Polycarp

---

of his opponents' (Chronologie II, 125; cf. Marcion, 124; 137f.; Knox, Marcion and the NT, 18; Harrison, Polycarp's Two Epistles, 175.

/86/ Polycarp, Phil., 7.1.

/87/ Phil. 1.1; cf. 2.1.

/88/ Cf. Phil. 4.1f./ 1 Tim 6.10; 6.7; 5.5; Phil. 5.1ff./1 Tim 3.8; 2 Tim 2.12; Phil. 8.1ff./1 Tim 1.1; Phil. 9.2/2 Tim 4.10; Phil. 11.4/2 Tim 2.25; Phil. 12.3/1 Tim 2.1. See Harrison, Polycarp's Two Epistles, 203f. Harrison suggests that in chapter three, Polycarp has set himself up as the defender of Paul; more precisely, he is attempting to dissuade those who claim Paul as their authority. Cf. on this von Campenhausen, 'Polykarp von Smyrna und die Pastoralbriefe' in Aus der Frühzeit des Christentums (1963), 197-252.

/89/ The reference here ('tōn en hypokrisei pherontōn to onoma tou kyriou', 6.3) parallels Justin's complaint against 'false' Christians in the first Apology (1.26); and cf. Bauer, Orthodoxy and Heresy, 24 and n. 52.

declares that 'neither I nor anyone like me can follow in the footsteps of the blessed and glorious Paul, who taught you the word of truth [alētheias logon ] accurately and constantly when he was with you, in the presence of men of that time' (3.1). The picture of the false teacher that emerges is therefore of someone who has preached in Paul's name. He has persuaded some that marriage is an evil (4.1); that the God who raised Jesus from the dead is not the judge of the world (2.1f.; 6.2); that the OT prophecies did not foretell the coming of Jesus (6.3); that Jesus came only in the likeness of the flesh (7.1);/90/ and that there is neither resurrection nor judgment (7.1)./91/ Further, the false teacher has mutilated the words of the Lord,/92/ on the pretext that he is following the 'wisdom of the blessed and glorious Paul' (3.2). Finally, we learn that the followers of this teacher bear the name Christian in 'hypocrisy' (6.3); in reality they are false brethren (pseudadelphoi) who have no right to the word delivered in the beginning (7.2).

The case for identifying the false teacher as Marcion is thus exceedingly strong, even though there seem to be no explicit references to ditheism or to a repudiation of the OT./93/ This does not mean, however, that such doctrines cannot be inferred from what Polycarp tells us about the heresy. For example, the reference in chapter six (6.3) to the predictive character of prophecy (*kathōs autos eneteilato kai hoi evangelisamenoi hēmas apostoloi kai hoi prophētai, hoi prokēryxantes tēn eleusin tou kyriou hēmōn*), and more distinctly, the reference in chapter seven (7.1) to persevering in the logia of the Lord, taken together with the emphasis on the fear and righteousness of God (e.g., 5.2; 2.1f), may well presuppose Marcion's rejection of the OT. Moreover, in chapter two Polycarp speaks plainly about a 'vulgar error' which seems to consist in the belief that the God who raised Jesus from the dead is other than the maker of the world and is (therefore) not to be feared:

> Putting aside empty vanity and vulgar error, believing on him who raised our Lord Jesus Christ from the dead and gave him glory and a throne at his right hand, to whom all

---

/90/ Cf. Am 3.8.

/91/ Cf. AM 3.8; 5.10; Epiph., Panar., 42.3, etc.

/92/ Haer., 1.27.4; cf. AM 4.2.4.

/93/ Harrison, Polycarp's Two Epistles, 172.

> things are subject in heaven and upon earth [and whom]
> all breath serves, who is coming as the judge of the living
> and the dead, whose blood God will require from them
> who disobey him: [Believe that] he who raised him from
> the dead will also raise us up. (Phil. 2.1f.)

That Marcion's ditheism is envisaged here is also indicated by the fact that what follows is Polycarp's disquisition on the authority of Paul as a champion of orthodoxy (3.1). The passage is a conflation of biblical texts which Polycarp seems to think are relevant to the error at hand. He finds it sufficient to counter the problem by insisting on three points: (a) the reality of both resurrection and judgment; (b) the subjection of creation to the power and authority of God; and (c) the importance of the law. Marcion could be brought to task on all three counts, and Polycarp does so by invoking the authority of Paul against those who claim to represent his teachings. Among these indictments, the one concerning judgment is especially important. We know from Tertullian not only that Marcion's supreme God does not judge, but that his failure to exercise judgment is what distinguishes him from the creator; it is precisely this distinction that occupies Tertullian for the first two books of the adversus Marcionem:

> These facts [which I have expounded] show how God's
> whole activity as judge is the artificer and, to put it more
> correctly, the protector of his all-embracing and supreme
> goodness. The Marcionites refuse to admit in this same
> God the presence of this goodness, clear of judicial
> sentiments, and in its own state unadulterated . . ./94/
>
> Therefore, most thoughtless Marcion, you ought rather to
> have shown that there is one God of light and another of
> darkness; after that you would have found it easier to
> persuade us that there is one God of kindness and another
> of severity . . ./95/
>
> With what confidence should I hope for goodness from such
> a [God as yours], if goodness is all he is capable of? . . .
> Justice [is] the plenitude of divinity itself, in that it
> reveals God in his perfection both as father and Lord: as
> father in clemency, as Lord in discipline; as father in
> kindly authority, as Lord in that which is stern; as father
> to be loved from affection, as Lord to be necessarily
> feared./96/

Polycarp has undertaken to defend the same principle on the basis of

---

/94/ AM 2.17.1.

/95/ AM 2.29.4.

/96/ AM 2.13.5. (slightly altered from Evans' trans.).

scripture rather than argument, but in both cases the defense relates to the doctrine of the unity of God in his dispensations as creator, father, judge, and redeemer. Neither Marcion nor Polycarp appears to have understood these dispensations with any degree of exactness. Tertullian goes so far as to make justitia an ontological category, 'the plenitude of divinity itself'. In Marcion's theology, justitia is an inferior and essentially negative attribute, characteristic of the lesser God, goodness being the essence of the God who saves.

Polycarp's appeal to the Philippian church is not a reasoned polemic, but this is so because of its pastoral focus. Phil. 2 may well presuppose Marcion's depreciation of the judgment, and if this is the case, then his theology was ditheistic before 130 at latest. That Polycarp does not mention the doctrine of two gods specifically points to the fact that he considered scriptural refutation -- the repeated assertion of the creative, judicial, and beneficient aspects of diety (6.2-3; 12.2, etc.) -- sufficient for his pastoral intentions (cf. ch. 9, pp. 285ff.; 287).

### 2.7 Marcionite Teaching in the Polemic Before Polycarp

If one accepts Knox's suggestion that Marcion may have been active in Asia Minor well before 130,/97/ the question arises, How long before? To be sure there are references in both NT and patristic literature dating from before the 'thirties which, on the surface, seem to indicate the existence of marcionite or proto-marcionite activity in the east. The letter of the church at Rome to the christian community at Corinth has already been discussed in this connection. Writing around the close of the first century, the author refers to 'disputed questions', 'unholy sedition', and 'abominable jealousy'/98/ which have resulted in the dissolution of marriages (6.3) and doubts about the judgment of God./99/ So too, the writer of the homily known as 2 Clement (c. 150) admonishes his fellow believers to 'leave off saying that this flesh is not judged and does not rise again' (9.1). Within

---

/97/ Marcion and the NT, 12. Knox puts to rest the theory that 'Marcion's heretical activity could not have begun very long before he came to Rome, since otherwise the Roman church would have been aware of his heresy and would not have admitted him to membership, even for a little while'.

/98/ 1 Clement 14.1; cf. 46.5.

/99/ Cf. 1 Clement 11.2; 13.1; 27.1.

the NT canon, the letter designated 2 Peter (c. 130?)/100/ bears witness to false teachers who deny the Lord Christ, lead dissolute lives, despise the angelic powers, and speak in high-handed fashion (2 Peter, 2.1-18; cf. Jude 4-16). But one is hard pressed to say that the heresies envisaged in these letters are related to the doctrines of Marcion. In almost every case, the proscribed teaching is too nebulous to permit anything more than guesswork about its provenance./101/ Moreover, docetism was 'heretical' during this period only in its more radical manifestations, and these, apparently, the Marcionites abjured almost as much as the catholics. If docetism was characteristic of Marcion's teaching, it was by no means the identifying birthmark of his theology. Accordingly, fugitive references to those who 'deny that Christ has come in the flesh', taken by themselves, might refer to a whole range of heresies, from 'judaizing' Christianity to gnosticism. What is more, it is not at all clear that Marcionism belongs within that range. Far less helpful are the complaints about sedition, jealousy, and factionalism within the church. Our earliest references to Marcionism do not give the picture of merely internecine strife, as for example seems to characterize the Corinthian heresy of CE 98. Rather, Marcionism is a factionalism with a clearly defined doctrinal structure, and in putting a name to any particular manifestation of what was for the orthodox of 'Clement's' day 'unholy sedition', it is the presence or absence of this structure that must guide us.

With this provision in mind, we turn to consider the letters of Ignatius, written from Smyrna and Troas in Asia Minor probably before CE 115.

Ignatius is confronted with a multiform heresy/102/ which is already widespread, and which involves among other things a denial of the humanity

---

/100/ c. 125; Marxsen, Introd. to the NT, (1968), 244; cf. Kümmel, Introd. to the NT, 31.434: citing Käsemann 'as late as 150'; Jer., de vir. illus., 1.

/101/ On the problem of identification, see H. Köster, 'Haretiker im Urchristentaum als Theologisches Problem', in Zeit und Geschichte: Dankesgabe an R. Bultmann zum 80. Geburtstag, ed. E. Dinkler (Tübingen, 1964); idem., 'GNOMAI DIAPHOROI: The Origin and Nature of Diversification in the History of Early Christianity', HTR, 58 (1965), 279-318.

/102/ Daniélou would argue that 'The letters [Ignatius] addressed to the churches show the persistence of Judaising tendencies [and] seek to curtail their excessive growth' (Christian Centuries, 1, 42). But Bauer has pointed out the difficulties in assuming that only one 'heresy' lay behind Ignatius' teaching, Orthodoxy and Heresy, 65; cf. p. 88.

of true suffering of Jesus. Ignatius counters this denial by speaking of the 'blood of God' (Eph. 11), and elsewhere of the 'flesh and blood of Jesus by his passion and resurrection both of flesh and spirit in the union of God', the last phrase becoming a central motif of his theology./103/ He admonishes the Trallians to be deaf to anyone who speaks to them apart from Jesus Christ 'who was of the family of David and Mary, who was truly born, both ate and drank [Lk. 24.41ff.], and was truly persecuted under Pontius Pilate; was truly crucified and died in the sight of those in heaven and on earth and under the earth, who was also truly raised from the dead when his father raised him up'./104/

A significant and characteristic feature of this heresy, therefore, is the denial of the humanity of Jesus, the reality of the crucifixion, and the resurrection of the dead. But the error involves more than a conventional docetism. Ignatius identifies his enemies as 'advocates of death' who are persuaded of the truth 'neither by the law of Moses nor by the prophecies'./105/ This is evidence against assuming that the proscribed teaching is merely a 'judaizing' tendency./106/ Apparently Ignatius knows of an attack on the relevance of the law and the prophets similar to that which Marcion is known to have made./107/ The same error lies at the heart of Ignatius' warning to the christian community at Philadelphia: 'If anyone interpret Judaism to you, do not listen to him, for it is better to hear Christianity from the circumcized than Judaism from the [un]circumcized. But both of them, unless they speak of Jesus Christ are to me tombstones and sepulchres of the dead'./108/

---

/103/ Smyrn. 12.2: 'Kai anastasei sarkikē te kai pneumatikē, en henotēti Theou', cf. Smyrn. 13.2; Polyc., 1.2; 2.2; Magn. 13.2.

/104/ Trall. 9.1-2; cf. Magn. 11.1; Smyrn. 5.2.

/105/ Smyrn. 5.1: 'Hous ouk epeisan hai prophēteiai oude ho nomos Mōuseōs, all oude mechri nun to evangelion, oude ta hēmetera tōn kat andra pathēmata'.

/106/ But cf. Daniélou, Christian Centuries, 1, 42f.

/107/ E.g., Am 1.19.5: 'Igitur cum ea separatio legis et evangelii ipsa sit quae alium deum evangelii insinuaverit adversus deum legis, apparet ante eam separationem deum in notitia non fuisse, etc.'; cf. 1.21.5: 'Probatio nostra munita est, qua ostendimus notitiam dei haeretici ex evangelii et legis separatione coepisse', and Irenaeus, Haer., 1.27.2, 4.

/108/ Ign. Philad. 6.1.

It has often been suggested that a Jewish 'heresy' is envisaged in Philad. 6.1/109/ but if this is so, of what kind? Ignatius speaks of the interpretation of Judaism being rendered by the false teacher; he does not specify a Jewish 'error'./110/ It is more likely, in conjunction with Smyrn. 5.1, that Ignatius points to an 'interpretation' of Judaism which includes a radical separation of law and gospel. The advocates of this interpretation call themselves 'Christians', though they may represent an alienated hellenistic Judaism which understands Paul's theology as its charter. Against their view, Ignatius stresses that Jesus 'was of the family of David according to the flesh';/111/ that 'even the prophets were disciples in the Spirit';/112/ and that Jesus Christ is the door through which the patriarchs and prophets enter the church./113/ Ignatius emphasizes that while the OT is the praeparatio christianismi (Magn. 8.1; 10.3), it is no longer possible to 'live according to Judaism'. What is of immediate concern to him, however, is that 'Judaism', by which he means the spiritual understanding of the law and the prophets, should not be surrendered to those who interpret scripture in a different (i.e., literal) way. Ignatius opposes any view of the Gospel which ignores the fact that 'Christianity did not base its faith on Judaism but Judaism on Christianity' (Magn. 10.2). Such a view is entailed by Marcion's belief that the God of Jesus Christ is 'discontinuous' with the God of Israel, and that Judaism could not be a preparation for what is not foretold in the prophets or anticipated in the law. The revelation of the unknown God in Jesus Christ is not merely the crisis of history, but an event wholly unprecedented and unexpected. Marcion therefore rejected the orthodox use of the past in the form of a spiritual reevaluation of the OT. This historical emphasis on God's dealings with man is overturned in Ignatius' spiritual construction of the relationship between the covenants; and there is little doubt that behind Ignatius' argument is a threat to the relationship

---

/109/ Thus, e.g., Daniélou, Christian Centuries, I, 42.

/110/ Nor (pace Daniélou) in Magn. 11.1; Trall. 8.2; 10.1; or Philad. 6.3 (cf. Christian Centuries, I, 42). Daniélou dismisses the more nearly accurate suggestion of E. Molland (JEH, 5 [1954], 1-6) that the heretics are gnostics.

/111/ Eph. 20.2; cf. Rom. 7.3; Smyrn. 1.1.

/112/ Magn. 9.2; cf. 8.2.

/113/ Philad. 9.1.

itself. He insists on the right teaching of the law and prophets according to Jesus Christ (Philad. 6.1). It is precisely this attempt to overcome the literal contradiction between the law and the gospel by spiritual exegesis that Marcion found unacceptable.

The heretics against whom Ignatius writes are also accused of being 'corrupters of families' (oikophthoroi), who preach continence,/114/ deride the doing of good works,/115/ and lay claim unworthily to the name 'Christian'./116/ Besides these patently marcionite themes, it is at least arguable that Ignatius' repeated references to 'Jesus Christ our God'/117/ presuppose Marcion's ditheism and are, in fact, a theological reaction based on the faulty understanding of that central marcionite doctrine. Ignatius thinks of the unity of God as a model for the unity of the church and the uniformity of catholic teaching. A christocentric (or Christ-mystical) monotheism is his ultimate point of reference in deciding what belongs to the church and what to those who speak apart from the church./118/ Jesus Christ is the will of the Father,'just as the bishops are appointed by the will of Jesus Christ', he holds./119/ To be in unity with the bishop -- the hereditary right-teacher (Eph. 6.1) -- is to commune with Christ and to know God: 'We ought to regard the bishop', Ignatius implores, 'as the Lord himself',/120/

> For as many as belong to God and Jesus Christ, these are with the bishop, and as many as repent and come to the unity of the church, these also shall be of God, to be living according to Jesus Christ. Be not deceived my

---

/114/ Polyc. 5.2.

/115/ Polyc. 6.2; 7.3; Eph. 4.2; 8.2; 10.1; 14.2, etc.

/116/ Eph. 7.1; Trall. 6.2.

/117/ Eph., prol.; Rom. prol.; 3.3; 6.3

/118/ Trall. 9.1. See further, E. v. Goltz, Ignatius von Antiochien als Christ und Theologe (TU, 12/3 [1894]); H. Schlier, Religionsgeschichtliche Untersuchungen zu den Ignatiusbriefen, suppl. to ZNTW, 8 (1929); C.C. Richardson, The Christianity of Ignatius of Antioch (Yale Pub. in Religion, 1, 1960); and H.W. Bartsch, Gnostisches Gut und Gemeindetradition bei Ignatius von Antiochien (1940).

/119/ Eph. 3.2.

/120/ Eph. 6.1. Cf. 3.2; Trall. 3.1.

> brethren, if anyone follow a maker of schism [schizonti]
> he does not inherit the kingdom of God; if any man walk in
> strange doctrines [allotriā gnōmē] he has no part in the
> passion./121/

Put in its simplest form, Ignatius' teaching centers on the theme that
divisions within the church, caused in every case by a failure to heed the
authority of the bishop, are denials of the unity of God, who manifests his
unity in the uniformity of the church order and teaching. Do nothing
without unity, he enjoins the Philadelphians: 'Love unity and flee from
divisions . . . . I did my best as a man who is set on unity. For where there
is division and anger, God does not dwell. The Lord then forgives all who
repent, if repentance lead to the unity of God and the council of the
bishop'./122/ For Ignatius, the life of the Christian is an apprehension of
the perfect coalition of flesh and spirit, God and Jesus Christ, old and new
dispensations, Christ and the church, the bishop and the congregation. 'All
these things', he writes, 'are held in the unity of God'./123/

Considering Ignatius' christocentric monotheism, and his repeated
attempts to link the themes of unity and right-teaching ('Egō men oun to
idion epoioun hōs anthrōpos eis henōsin katērtismenos', Philad. 8.1), there is
little reason to doubt that the heresy he is combatting in the churches of
Asia Minor involves an attack on the unity of God. In addition, the heresy is
characterized by assaults on marriage, the reality of the suffering and
resurrection of Jesus, the authority of the law and the prophets, and the
moral laxity of the catholics. In short, the doctrinal structure of
Marcionism is presupposed in Ignatius' counsel to the churches of Asia
Minor. Like Polycarp, however, Ignatius writes first and foremost as a
pastor, albeit one of a mystical bent, and his expository method is
determined by a desire to teach what is true rather than refute what he
believes to be false. His purpose is to offer a remedy for 'the bites of the
wild dogs who roam about secretly' (Eph. 7.1).

What we gather from the Ignatian correspondence, despite the
persistence of a number of ambiguities, is that a doctrine morphologically
similar to Marcion's was widespread in Asia Minor before CE 117. Unfor-

---

/121/ Philad. 3.3.

/122/ Philad. 7.2; 8.1; cf. Smyrn. 9.1.

/123/ Philad. 9.1.

tunately, Ignatius refuses to put a name to the heretics, 'that I might not even remember them until they repent concerning the passion, which is our resurrection' (Smyrn. 5.3). Nevertheless, there is a distinct possibility that marcionite teachers are among those envisaged in the letters, even though they need not be the only ones. As Molland has ventured, a 'gnostic' heresy may lie in the background as well, and it is possible that this gnosticism arose in Jewish-Christian circles. But a highly speculative gnosticism is not indicated. The 'heretics' in question still lay claim to the designation 'Christian',/124/ though they interpret Judaism in a way which large proportion of Syrian Christians have rejected. Both of these considerations would seem to suggest a provenance for the error close to the heart of the christian mainstream in Asia Minor. Nor can a marcionite source for the error be rejected on chronological grounds. As we have seen, the only reliable point of reference for establishing the course and duration of Marcion's career is the date of Justin's first Apology,/125/ where it is revealed that Marcion's teaching had gained a wide currency over the breadth of the eastern Empire. Leaving aside the legend of Marcion's dependence on Cerdo, we are left with Irenaeus' suggestion that Marcion was a contemporary of Polycarp./126/ On this evidence, there is good reason to think that Marcion, like Polycarp,/127/ was a teacher of advanced

---

/124/ Eph. 7.1; cf. Trall. 6.2.

/125/ Cf. 1 Apol. 46: 'Christ was born 150 years ago under Quirinus'; thus H. Colson, 'Notes on Justin Martyr's Apology 1', JTS, 23 (1922), 161-71; Blackman, Influence, 21; but cf. E. Barnikol, Entstehung, 1-33, who argues a date of 138-39 for the Apology, against Harnack's dating of 150-53 (Chronologie, 284). The case for an earlier date is based on Justin's use of the term verissimus instead of Caesar in referring to Aurelius (I.1), who received the title in the year 139; and the reference to the Jewish war as 'recent' ('en tō nun gegenemēno chronō' 1 Apol. 31), which would seem to suggest a date not long after 135. Neither of these considerations is decisive, however. Quasten (Patrol. 1, 199) believes the first Apology to have been written between 148 and 161. C. Andresen's opinion that the work dates from as late as 180 (RGG 3/3, 891) is not generally accepted.

/126/ Haer., 3.3.4.

/127/ According to the Mart. Polycarpi 9.3, Polycarp declared in front of the proconsul that he had served Christ loyally for eighty-six years. On the date of his execution, see C.H. Turner, Stud. Bibl. et Eccles., 2 (1890), 105-55, where the date 155 is defended; cf. H. Gregoire-P. Orgels, 'La veritable date du martyre de Polycarp: 23 Fevr. 177', Annal Boll., 49 (1951), 1-38 (based on Eusebius' information that the execution took place during the reign of Marcus Aurelius, CE 161-80); H.I. Marrou, 'La date du

years in the 'fifties, and that his teaching activity had begun before 115, by which date Ignatius would have completed his letters to the churches. Thus the year CE 70, generally accepted as the date of Polycarp's birth, and one which comports with Irenaeus' statement that Polycarp had 'conversed with many who had seen Christ',/128/ approximates the date of Marcion's birth in Sinope. This would mean that Marcion was a man of about forty-eight at the time of Ignatius' martyrdom, and almost certainly would have begun teaching in Asia Minor by that age.

## 2.8 Clement of Alexandria

A confused but intriguing notice in the seventh book of Clement of Alexandria's Stromateis runs as follows:

> Likewise, they allege that Valentinus was a hearer of Theudas. And he was a pupil of Paul. For Marcion, who arose at the same time with them, lived as an old man with the younger [heretics]. And after him, Simon [Magus] heard for a little while the preaching of Peter./129/

As usually interpreted, this report seems to show that Clement mistakenly believed that Marcion was a predecessor not only of Valentinus, but also of Simon Magus. Were it not that Clement's intention is to prove the lateness of the heresies as compared to the apostolic faith, it might be possible to dismiss his statement as being historically uninformed. But clearly Clement's purpose, like that of Irenaeus and Tertullian,/130/ is to show that the tradition of the church is prior to even the earliest of the heretics; thus,

> The teaching of the Lord at his advent, beginning with Augustus and Tiberius, was completed in the middle-times of Tiberius. And that of the Apostles, embracing the ministry of Paul, ends with Nero. It was later, in the

martyre de s. Polycarp' in ibid., 71 (1953), 1-20. A defense of the historical value of Pionus' Life of Polycarp is given in Streeter, Primitive Church, Appendix A, 265-72; neither Lightfoot (Ignatius and Polycarp, 435ff.; with text) nor Delehaye (Les passions des martyres et les genres litteraires) assign any such value to the work. Textanhänge by von Campenhausen, 'Bearbeitung und Interpolationen des Polykarpmartyrium', Frühzeit, 254-92; text 293-301.

/128/ Haer., 3.3.4: 'Polycarpus . . . conversatus cum multis eis qui dominum nostrum viderunt'.

/129/ Strom., 7.17.105f. (ANF trans.).

/130/ Cf. AM 1.1.5f.; 4.4; Praes. 20; Irenaeus, Haer., 3.2.2, etc.

times of Hadrian the king, that those who invented the
heresies arose; and they extended to the age of Antoninus
the elder -- as for example Basilides./131/

How can we reconcile Clement's intention as evidenced in this passage with
the eccentric chronology of heresy which follows and which makes Marcion
the predecessor of the arch-heretic, Simon Magus?

If we examine Clement's report carefully, we find that he considers
the lateness of the heresies proof that they are falsifications of the truth of
the church./132/ Clement goes further than the other heresiologists by
making a clear distinction between the time of truth and the time of heresy,
the former being subdivided between a 'time of the Lord's teaching', which
ends in CE 30, and a time of the apostles, which ends in CE 68. The time
of the heresies, however, does not begin until the reign of Hadrian, that is,
not until 117. Within this scheme, the church seems to have been heresy-
free for nearly fifty years, or until the time of Marcion who 'lived as an old
man with the younger heretics'.

What has generally been overlooked is that in the supposedly confused
passage following the divisions of time, Clement is not proposing a second
chronology; he is merely reporting with intent to slight the claims of the
heretics, who are first introduced at 7.17.106: 'Those who adhere to
impious words and dictate them to others'. Clement has already shown the
impossibility of heresy arising in the sanctified time of the Lord and his
apostles; he means to show the absurdity of the suggestions made by the
heretics themselves that their teachings are as old as the time of Tiberius
(i.e., of the apostles). Hence the passage must be read with the allegations
of the heretics in mind: 'They [the heretics] allege that Valentinus heard
Theudas, and that he was Paul's pupil. [The heretics] allege that Marcion
[arose in the apostolic age] and lived as an old man with the [apostles].
And they allege that later on Simon [Magus] heard the preaching of Peter'.
The nucleus of Clement's argument is contained in the assertion that 'the

---

/131/ Strom. 7.17.106 (ANF trans.).

/132/ Clement echoes Ignatius in saying 'The church that is really ancient is
one, and those who are enrolled in it according to God's design: for from this
very reason -- that God is one, and the Lord is one . . . .In the nature of
the one is associated in a joint heritage the one church, which [heretics]
strive to cut asunder into many sects' (Strom. 7.17). Cf. Tert., AM
5.19.1ff.

human assemblies which these [heretics] held were posterior to the catholic church', an assertion which he repeats after his disquisition on the claims of the heretics.

Admittedly, even when the passage is read as a series of allegations which the writer means to ridicule, the reference to Simon Magus is puzzling: what did Clement make of the tradition that made Simon the magician the contemporary of Peter the Apostle? The inescapable answer is that Clement treats the tradition as heretical invention rather than as a piece of canonical belief. Whether he knows the story of Simon in the Book of Acts or not is unclear;/133/ but in any event he does not treat is as history./134/ What information he provides elsewhere about Luke -- 'that Luke translated into Greek Paul's Epistle to the Hebrews'/135/ -- may call into question Clement's knowledge of Acts. However that may be, he clearly does not feel bound to accept the legend, and his preestablished chronology, in which the time of the apostles stands unadulterated by false teaching, will not permit him to do so./136/ This correction notwithstanding, we are left with the suggestion that Marcion, as being one of the older heretics, was among those to arise during the early years of Hadrian's reign./137/ Apparently this is the story which the Marcionites themselves credited.

---

/133/ A. de le Barre, DCT, 3 (1908), 137ff.; M. Spannuet, NCE (1967), 943f.

/134/ Justin appears to be the first writer to demonstrate a working knowledge of Acts (1 Apol. 49.5). Thus Haenchen, Acts (1970), 8. Haenchen has argued that until the middle of the second century, Acts was not considered an authoritative book to which one might appeal (p. 9).

/135/ Adumbr. in 1 Ptr. [GCS, 17, 206]. Haenchen calls this 'a learned attempt to explain the un-Pauline style of this allegedly Pauline letter' (Acts, 12; cf. K. Lake, Beginnings of Christianity II. 222).

/136/ Clement's strategy differs markedly from that of Irenaeus. Clement wants to show how improbable are all suggestions that heresy might have arisen in an age of truth; in effect, he has sanctified the time of Jesus and the Apostles. Irenaeus wants merely to show that the heresies developed later in point of time, but nevertheless in relation to the tradition of the church.

/137/ Both Irenaeus and Tert. assume Marcion's heresy to have emerged in Rome; Clement provides no information as to the first flowering of Marcion's teaching.

## 2.9 Later Testimony

Tertullian, Epiphanius, and the Chronicler of Edessa all know of dates earlier than that given by Irenaeus for the starting point of Marcion's career. In the fifth book of the AM, Tertullian reports that Marcion's error 'began in the days of Antoninus' ('nedum Antoniniani Marcionis');/138/ but what is more telling, in view of Clement's report, is the information supplied in the Praes., that Marcion and Valentinus were contemporaries ('believers')/139/ in Rome 'under the episcopate of the blessed Telesforus' (c. 125-36). Irenaeus places Valentinus in Rome in the time of Hyginus, and Marcion not until the time of Anicetus. Tertullian's information accords with Clement's notice that 'Marcion arose at the same time [as Valentinus]', but was the elder statesman of the heretics. What Tertullian wants to suggest is that Marcion joined the church of Rome between 125-36 (i.e., the reign of Telesforus), Valentinus being a member of the church at the same time; and that he was later -- during the reign of Hyginus (136-40) -- excommunicated for his opinions. This chronology agrees with the information supplied in the first (1.19.3), fourth (4.4.5), and fifth (5.19.2) books of the AM, according to which Marcion's heresy emerged in Rome during the imperial reign of Antoninus Pius -- that is to say, somewhere between 138 and 161./140/ Tertullian calls Marcion an 'Antoninian heretic, impious under Pius', and goes on to offer the following calculation:

> Now from Tiberius to Antoninus there are a matter of a hundred and fifteen years and a half years and half a month. This length of time do they [the Marcionites] posit between Christ and Marcion. Since therefore it was under Antoninus that, as I have proved, Marcion first brought this God on the scene . . . the fact is clear. The dates themselves put it beyond argument that which first came to light under Antoninus did not come to light under Tiberius: that is, the god of Antoninus' reign was not the god of the reign of Tiberius, and therefore, he who it is

/138/ Am 5.19.2.

/139/ Harnack's correction; given in Wilson, Heretic, 54, n. 4. The older and much-disputed reading made Marcion and Valentinus 'believers under . . . Eleutherus' (c. 174-89); but Justin's reference to Marcion in 150, and the fact that Irenaeus, who himself flourished under Eleutherus, knows Marcion as a historical figure, make such a reading impossible. Cf. Eusebius, HE 5.4.2; and see G. Salmon, DCB, 818f.

/140/ AM 1.19.3: "Cum igitur sub Antonino primus Marcion hunc deum induxerit'.

admitted was first reported to exist by Marcion had not
been revealed by Christ./141/

Like Clement, Tertullian posits a historical breach between the true
'revelation' of the apostolic era (= the reign of Tiberius) and the false
'revelations' which emerged only later, during the Antoninian period.
Clement presents his chronology as a false one dreamt up by the heretics
themselves. But the elusive tradition underlying the reports of Philastrius
and the author of the anti-marcionite Prologue to the Gospel of John,
concerning Marcion's association with the Evangelist, signals the existence
of a belief -- perhaps widespread among Marcion's disciples -- that the
founder of this church had himself been a contemporary of the
apostles./142/ Philastrius and the prologist accept this tradition as
authentic, but argue that Marcion was turned away by John at Ephesus,
later to be rejected in Rome as well. Clement, Irenaeus, and Tertullian
refuse to accept a tradition that locates Marcion's heresy in the apostolic
age. Tertullian's elaborate calculation like Irenaeus' genealogy and
Clement's ambiguous chronology must be seen in this light. It is an attempt
to counteract the effects of a tradition according to which Marcionism had
developed much earlier than in the times of Antoninus. But the attempt
leads to no consensus. Certain they are that Marcion did not converse with
apostles: but they are far from certain about the facts of his life. Did his

/141/ AM, loc. cit.

/142/ Philastrius, lib. haer., 45. On the so-called anti-Marcionite Pro-
logues, see de Bruyne, 'Les plus anciens prologues latins des Evangiles',
Rev. bénéd. 40, 195-214; and J. Regul, Evangelienprologe (1979). Both de
Bruyne and Harnack assumed that Marcion had issued his version of the NT
(Luke or proto-Luke with ten Pauline letters) with prologues for the epistles,
whereupon Rome riposted with a 'Catholic' edition containing four Gospels
(including anti-marcionite prologues) and thirteen epistles (including the
Pastorals). In doing so however, the marcionite prologues to the epistles
were taken over without noticing. Regul, inter alia, argues that if Rome
did publish a 'counter-edition' of the NT, the editors would scarcely have
failed to notice the provenance of the prologues which precipitated their
endeavor in the first place. Moreover, in the prologues to Mark and Luke
(de Bruyne failed to find a comparable prologue for Matthew in the MSS he
examined), there is no specific mention of Marcion. Cf. M.J. LaGrange
(Rev. B., 38 [1929], 115-21; B.W. Bacon, JBL, 49 (1930) 43-64, and JTS,
23; (1922), 134-60; W.F. Howard, ExT, 47 (1936), 534-38; R.M. Grant,
Angl. Theol. Rev., 23 (1941), 231-45; and R.G. Heard, JTS, 45 (1955), 1-
16.

heresy erupt under Hadrian (Clement) or under Antoninus (Tertullian)? Was he a member of the church at Rome under Telesforus and a heretic under Hyginus (Tertullian), or a follower of Cerdo under the reign of Anicetus (Irenaeus)? Tertullian is determined in the passage just quoted to put all doubts to rest: 'It was first under Antoninus that Marcion [first] brought forth this god; [it did] not come to light under Tiberius' (AM 1.19.3; cf. 5.19.2,etc). But Tertullian's argumentative ploy leaves doubts remaining. His insistence on locating the beginning of the heresy within the twenty-year span of Antoninus' reign is, by his own admission, a response to just such a tradition as is evidenced in the Liber de Haeresibus of Philastrius, the anti-marcionite Prologue to John, and the allegations recorded by Clement in the Stromateis:

> So we must pull away at the rope of contention, swaying with equal effort to the one side or the other. I say that mine is true: Marcion makes that claim for his. I say that Marcion's is falsified: Marcion says the same of mine. Who shall decide between us? Only such a reckoning of dates, as will assume that authority belongs to that which is found to be older, [ei praescribens auctoritatem quod antiquis reperietur] and will prejudge as corrupt that which is convicted of having come later. For insofar as the false is a corruption of the true, to that extent must the truth have preceded that which is false. . . . [That] has the priority which has been so since the beginning . . .that was handed down by the apostles which is held sacred and inviolate in the churches the apostles founded./143/

Some scholars, Harnack among them, have reckoned that the reference to 115 years (1.19) provides the only clue for establishing a 'certain' date in Marcion's life. Significantly, Tertullian refers the reckoning to the Marcionites ('Tantundem temporis ponunt'), and those prepared to take him at his word have speculated that the calculation must represent some important event in Marcion's life which his followers commemorated, perhaps as a festival-day in the church. Harnack believed that Marcion's excommunication from the church at Rome was insinuated, inasmuch as the sentence immediately following the calculation has to do with the emergence of Marcion's heresy under Antoninus ('Cum igitur sub Antonino primus Marcion hunc deum induxerit')./144/ In his 1911 study of the first

---

/143/ AM 4.4.1f; 4.5.1; cf. Praes., 21-22, passim; Irenaeus, Haer., 3.4.3.

/144/ Am 1.19.3; Marcion, 21*f.; Chronologie 1, 297ff.; 306ff.

book of the AM, Bill surmised that the date of Marcion's departure from Pontus was indicated,/145/ while Barnikol understood the statement to refer to the time of Marcion's death in Rome./146/ Wilson was confident enough of Tertullian's arithmetic to conclude that CE 144 (= 29, the year of the death of Tiberius, + 115, the number of years between Tiberius and Marcion), 'is the one date in Marcion's life which we can fix with any precision'./147/

In weighing the value of Tertullian's calculation, however, it is important to bear in mind that his purpose is to show that the Marcionites themselves bear witness to his own assertion that their founder flourished under Antoninus Pius, which the resulting date of 144 clearly does. But is the calculation attributable to the Marcionites or is it a juristic prop introduced by Tertullian in order to strengthen his argument?/148/ Is the date 144 one which we can fix with precision, or merely one which ensures the safe remove of Marcion's doctrine from that earlier and pristine age in which his disciples believed him to have flourished?/149/

---

/145/ A Bill, Zur Erklärung und Textkritik des Ersten Buch Adversus Marcionem (TU 38/2, 1911), 66-72.

/146/ Barnikol, Entstehung. Barnikol also tried to prove an earlier date for Marcion's teaching in Rome, c. 128-44. He based his reckoning on a passage attributed to the Marcionites by Eznik de Kolb (cf. Harnack, Marcion, 23*, note 1) according to which 2900 years had elapsed from the fall to the coming of Christ, and almost 3000 years until the coming of Marcion. Taken literally, this yields an approximate date of 129 for the beginning of Marcion's work. Unfortunately, Barnikol's estimate of Eznik's testimony is too high, and Harnack's relegation of the material to a footnote is certainly defensible. See further, Blackman, Influence, Appendix II, 20f.

/147/ Wilson, Heretic, 56. Wilson agrees with Harnack that the date refers to Marcion's expulsion from the Roman church, 'the date when Christ gained a true disciple after the gap caused by Paul's death'.

/148/ Salmon has called atention to the fact that the entire structure of 1.19.1f. is in the form of an argument, DCB. 818f.

/149/ Corroborating evidence is contradictory: Epiphanius and Hippolytus (Philos. 7.29 = PG 16, col. 3323-35) locate Marcion in Rome just after the death of Hyginus in 140 (Epiph., Panar. 42.1), while the Chronicle of Edessa gives 137/8 as the date of Marcion's expulsion from the Catholic Church (ed. J. Guidi, Chronica Minora [CSCO, Scriptoris Syris, ser. 3/4, 1903], 1-11; L. Hallier, Untersuchungen über die Edessenische Chronik [TU 9/1, 1893; ET JSL, 1864], 28ff.). Bauer was inclined to the view that the Marcionites were the first Christians to settle in Edessa (Orthodoxy and Heresy, 27-29). He is answered by H. Köster (Trajectories, 127f.). The

Inasmuch as Tertullian expressly introduces the calculation as support for the prescription, one may doubt not only the resulting date, but also his attribution of the figure to the Marcionites. Thus he writes, 'In what year of Antoninus . . . [Marcion] breathed out from his own Pontus, I do not care to inquire ('non curavi investigare')' but of this I am sure ('De quo tamen constat') that he is an Antoninian heretic'./150/ Tertullian's calculation is not offered, therefore, in the interest of supplying biographical information, but rather in order to prove that Marcion's teaching did not arise before the middle decades of the second century. Obviously, however, if the Marcionites had accepted this reckoning, as Tertullian claims, there would be no need for such proof. The only possible conclusion is that the Marcionites themselves posited a much earlier date for the founding of their church and, accordingly, for the teaching of Marcion.

## 2.10 Summary

In appraising the testimony of the fathers concerning Marcion's career, it is important to keep in mind that they were fundamentally concerned to show that the teaching of heretics is historically discontinuous with the apostolic faith delivered to the church. Already before the close of the first century, the author of 1 Clement invokes the 'venerable rule of our tradition' (paradosis)/151/ as the cure for sedition. Ignatius finds the true Christians of Ephesus 'ever of one mind with the apostles'/152/ and 'fellow-initiates (symmystai) with Paul',/153/ but the heretics 'wicked offshoots which bear deadly fruit'./154/ Polycarp enjoins the Philippians to repudiate those who 'mutilate the logia of the Lord' and to 'turn back to the word

---

Fihrist of Mohammed ben Ishak contains the following sentence: 'A hundred years before Mani, who appeared in the second year of the reign of Gallus, Marcion came forward in the reign of Antoninus, and in fact in the first year of his reign. Bardesanes appeared about thirty years after Marcion'. Given in Flügel, Mani, 160; 85. Cf. Regul, Evangelien-prologe, 192f.

/150/ AM 1.19.2f.

/151/ 1 Clement 7.2.

/152/ Ign., Eph. 11.2.

/153/ Ign., Eph. 12.2.

/154/ Ign., Trall. 11.1: 'Pheugete oun tas kakas paraphyadas tas gennōsas karpon thanatēphoron hou ean geusētai tis, par auta apothnēskei'.

delivered from the beginning'./155/ Irenaeus considers it self-evident that heresy arose 'much later -- during the intermediate period of the church',/156/ and Clement of Alexandria thinks it not difficult to show that the 'human assemblies which the heretics held were posterior to the universal church'./157/ Tertullian offers as a short cut for dealing with the problem of erroneous doctrine the following prescription: '[Regard] that which is of later importation heresy, precisely because that has to be considered truth which was delivered of old and from the beginning'./158/ Even within the New Testament canon, the anti-heretical author of the Epistles to Timothy and Titus speaks of the sound teaching (didaskalia/ didache) 'manifested through preaching committed unto [Paul] according to the commandment of God our savior',/159/ and warns against those who have erred concerning the faith ('peri tēn pistin ēstochēsan')./160/

Even though the historical statements of the fathers regarding the facts of Marcion's life are determined by dogmatic and apologetic concerns which evolve out of the struggle with Marcionism, certain conclusions can be drawn from their testimony. The nature of the evidence requires, however, that these conclusions be framed in fairly general terms:
(1) The earliest datable reference to Marcion by name (Justin, 1 Apol.26; 58) makes it clear that by the year 150 Marcion was a teacher of advanced years and that his doctrines had been widely disseminated. Justin's testimony is the more reliable because (a) it is almost certainly a contemporary account based on first-hand knowledge of Marcion's activity in Asia Minor, rather than a systematic refutation of the Marcionism of a later period; and (b) as an apology written to the Emperor on behalf of Christians, it represents a different stratum in the struggle with heresy, one in which

---

/155/ Polyc., Phil. 7.2: 'epi ton ex archēs hēmin paradothenta logon epistrepsōmen'.

/156/ Irenaeus, Haer., 3.4.3: 'Omnes autem hi multo posterius, mediantibus iam ecclesiae temporibus'.

/157/ Clement of Alexandria, Strom., 7.17.107.

/158/ Tertullian, AM 1.1.6: 'In tantum enim haeresis deputabitur quod postea inducitur, in quantum veritas habebitur quod retro et a primordio traditum est'.

/159/ Titus 1.3, 9; 1 Tim 1.10b-11.

/160/ 1 Tim 6.21.

the question of martyrdom and the encounter with pagan culture loom larger
than the task of refuting false teachers. Heresy is introduced in the interest
of providing a point of reference for the apostolic teaching, the defense of
which alone is an entitlement to martyrdom (1 Apol. 2-7). Hence we can
think of CE 150 as a date approaching the end of Marcion's work. The
reference to 'many of every nation' having been converted to Marcion's
teaching indicates that his evangelistic work in Asia Minor had been carried
out by that date.

(2) The similarity between the teaching of Marcion and that proscribed by
Polycarp in his letter to the christian community at Philippi (c. 130) invites
the conclusion that the false teacher is Marcion himself. This conclusion, in
turn, presupposes a period of heretical activity antedating 130. Further,
the mise en scène supplied by Irenaeus in the third book of the Haer.
(3.3.4) shows (a) that Irenaeus knew Marcion and Polycarp to be
contemporaries; and (b) that Irenaeus associated the heresy condemned in
Polycarp's letter with the teaching of Marcion. The Martyrium Polycarpi
makes Polycarp 86 at the time of his execution in Smyrna. Irenaeus
acknowledges that he came to Rome in the time of Anicetus and that he had
been instructed by apostles in Asia; and Eusebius (HE 3.34.1f.) knows
Polycarp to have been flourishing in Asia during Trajan's reign (98-
117)./161/ Marcion's career may be thought to parallel this. Moreover,
such information as is provided by the anti-marcionite Prologue to John and
the Liber de Haeresibus of Philastrius, while not to be relied upon
overmuch, points to the existence of a (marcionite?) tradition according to
which Marcion, like Polycarp himself, had been a companion of John at

/161/ This is evidence against the accuracy of Eusebius' statement (HE
4.14.10) to the effect that Polycarp was martyred under Marcus Aurelius.
Eusebius introduces the imperium of Aurelius twice: at 4.12.2 and again at
4.14.10. At 4.14.5f., he refers to the episcopal conference of Polycarp
and Anicetus, for which his source is Irenaeus (Haer., 3.3.4 = 4.14.1f.).
Upon leaving this source, Eusebius returns to the imperial succession, citing
the death of Antoninus Pius (CE 161) and the accession of Marcus Aurelius
and Lucius. Anicetus was bishop of Rome during the first four years of
Aurelius' reign; but Eusebius (HE 4.14.1) expresses surprise that Polycarp
was still living at the time of Anicetus' episcopate: 'Polykarpon eti perionta
tō biō genesthai . . .' It may well be that Eusebius records his confusion
over the time of Polycarp's martyrdom when he writes, 'Antōninon men dē
ton Eusebē klēthenta eikoston kai deuteron etos tēs archēs dianysanta,
Markos Aurēlios ouēros, ho kai Antōninos, hyios autou, syn kai Loukiō adelphō
diadechetai' (HE 4.14.10). Apparently, Eusebius' source contained only the
name Antoninus, and obliged to chose between Pius and Aurelius, Eusebius
chose the later of the two.

Ephesus.

(3) References in the Ignatian correspondence seem to indicate that Marcion was active in Asia Minor during Trajan's reign. We are prevented from knowing the name(s) of the false teacher(s) by Ignatius' own design (Smyrn. 7.2; 5.3); but the correlation between the condemned doctrine and that of Marcion is substantial. If Eusebius' statement concerning the activity of Polycarp between 98 and 117 is accepted as an approximation of Marcion's teaching-activity in Pontus,/162/ then Marcion will have begun his mission in Asia Minor prior to the (generally agreed) date of Ignatius' martyrdom in 117./163/

(4) Scarcely to be ignored is the evidence for Marcion's activity supplied in the Pastoral Epistles (c. 120?)./164/ Because this evidence is controversial and the dangers of circular argument correspondingly greater, it has been thought best to treat the matter in detail (ch. 9). If, however, we accept Bauer's conclusion that the reference in 1 Timothy 6.20/165/ to antitheses envisages Marcion's work by that name, then it is likely that Marcion had formulated his distinctive theological doctrines by the 'twenties of the second century, since Polycarp feels able to appeal to the authority of the letters, or at least replicates their language, in his own struggle against the Marcionite error./166/ On this view, there is also good reason to believe that the earliest anti-marcionite polemic emanated from a particular circle of orthodoxy, in which Polycarp, Ignatius, and the author of the Pastorals, played key roles (see further, p. 286)./167/

---

/162/ HE 3.36.1: 'Dieprepen ge men kata toutous epi tes Asias ton apostolon homiletes Polykarpos'; cf. HE 3.34.1.

/163/ P. Batiffol in J. Hastings, DAC, I (1916), 594f.; H. Lietzmann, Beginnings of the Christian Church (1937), 315-32.

/164/ Time of composition: 'very beginning of the second century' (Kümmel, Introd. NT, 25.387); 'at the end of the first century' (Klijn, Introd., 134; 'well into the second century' (Marxsen, Introd. NT, 215); 'between 120 and 160' (Köster, Einführung, 12.744); and cf. v. Campenhausen, Aus der Frühzeit des Christentums, 197ff.; 'between 90 and 95' (Wilson, Luke and the Past. Eps., 140); 'during Paul's lifetime' (Moule, BJRL [1965], 434).

/165/ Cf. Bauer, Orthodoxy and Heresy, 226.

/166/ E.g., Polyc., Phil. 4.1/1 Tim 6.10; Phil. 4.3/1 Tim 5.5; Phil. 5.2/1 Tim 3.8, 2 Tim 2.12, etc.

/167/ Cf. H. v. Campenhausen, Aus der Frühzeit des Christentums (1963), 197f.

(5) The schism condemned in 1 Clement does not seem to correspond closely to Marcion's teaching, but involves rather a factional dispute in the Corinthian church over the time of the judgment. We thus have no literary evidence for the existence of a marcionite error earlier than the Ignatian correspondence and the roughly contemporary Epistles to Timothy and Titus.

(6) After carrying out successful missions in Asia Minor and converting large numbers to his version of the christian faith, Marcion is said to have ventured to Rome. The journey is well-attested by the fathers, but it cannot be pinpointed with any accuracy and Justin appears to know nothing about it. If the journey is held to be historical, then Tertullian's claim that Marcion was a 'believer under Telesforus' c. 125 and a heretic during the imperial reign of Antoninus Pius (138-161) would entail a span of about thirty-five years in the capital. The Chronicle of Edessa and the Fihrist of Muhammed ben Ishak specify the early days of Hyginus as bishop of Rome (138), while Irenaeus makes the date much later (after 154) and Epiphanius avers that Marcion arrived in Rome just after the death of Hyginus. For all this confusion, it seems doubtful that Marcion ventured to Rome at all and in any event not with the intention of achieving approval for his doctrine by the authorities there. The tradition that he first learned his doctrine at Cerdo's feet is even more implausible.

(7) Irenaeus' assertion that Marcion flourished under Anicetus may preserve the memory of continued teaching activity in the 'fifties. Harnack dates Marcion's death at the end of Anicetus' episcopate, but there is no reason to make it quite as late as 160. Again we must fall back on the point fixée of Justin's testimony that Marcion is 'even yet teaching men to deny that God is the maker of all things' (1 Apol. 58). The date which Irenaeus gives for the arrival of Marcion in Rome seems the most plausible date for his death.

On the basis of this summary, the following sketch of Marcion's career emerges:

> Born in Sinope: c. CE 70
> Active in Asia Minor: c. 110-150
> Died: c. 154

CHAPTER THREE


APOSTOLIC LEGITIMACY: THE PAULINE BACKGROUND OF
MARCION'S REFORM


3.1  Introduction

We learn from Tertullian that Paul's letter to the Galatians was given
pride of place in the marcionite apostolikon, followed by the Corinthian
letters and Romans./1/   Tertullian claims to agree with Marcion in
understanding Galatians as 'the primary epistle against Judaism':
'Amplectimur etenim omnem illam legis veteris abolitionem . . .'/2/ But we
must here take Tertullian's comment with a grain of salt.  While the anti-
legalist theme of Galatians was probably influential in Marcion's decision to
put the epistle first in his collection of Paul's letters, it is less certain that
the Marcionites understood the letter as being directed against the Jews.
Furthermore, it is doubtful that the polemical features of Gal in themselves
would have warranted its priority in the pauline canon.   A more plausible
explanation is that the Marcionites regarded Gal as a kind of introduction to
Paul's theology, the letter which most clearly represented the Apostle's own
claims for the singularity of his gospel.   The Corinthian epistles may have
been seen as essential girding for this claim.   On such a premise, the
assertion of Paul's apostolic authority emerges as the ordering principle of
the marcionite corpus paulinum, a conclusion consistent with Marcion's
understanding of Paul as the only true apostle./3/
     Yet even if one accepts that Marcion employed a positive criterion
(Paul's defense of the gospel and the assertion of his apostolic authority)
rather than the negative criterion of anti-legalism in his arrangement of the
letters, we are left with the question of whether Marcion comprehended
Paul's own situation.   Given the historical distance between Paul and
Marcion and the fact that Marcion was dealing with the literary remains of
controversies that had been resolved (often in ways contrary to Paul's

---

/1/  Cf. Souter, Text and Canon, 152.

/2/  AM 5.2.1.

/3/  Cf. Haer. 3.13.1; AM 5.1.2.

hopes)/4/ two generations earlier, is there a case to be made for the continuity which Marcion perceived between Paul's mission and his own -- broadly defined as the restoration of the verbum veritatis/5/ delivered to the christian churches and variously subverted by falsifiers thereafter? To answer this question it is necessary to examine briefly the situation as it existed in Paul's lifetime.

### 3.2 Paul and Galatia

The marcionite prologist offers this description of the Galatians:

> Galatae sunt Graeci. Hi verbum veritatis primum ab apostolo acceperunt, sed post discessum eius temptati sunt a falsis apostolis ut in lege et circumcisione verterentur. Hos apostolus revocat ad fidem veritatis, scribens eis ab Epheso./6/

The prologist regards the Galatian community as gentile Christians/7/ who first learned the word of truth from the Apostle, but were subsequently tempted away from his gospel by false apostles. These apostles are specifically indicted as being advocates of the law and circumcision; or to use the word that has become an unavoidable signalement of the opponents-debate, as 'judaizers'. The prologist appears to identify them as a single front waging an assault on Paul's gospel of freedom. Put the other way around, there is no evidence that he sees a variety of groups at work in Galatia, a reckoning made more important by the fact that he holds a different view of the opponents in Corinth. Here, however, we must pause

---

/4/ Weiss offers the following assessment: 'His lifework was to some extent uneven, and that not only in a geographical sense. A church such as that at Corinth leaves an impression of incompleteness, both in its organization and in its moral progress and enlightenment. Up to the last his work was threatened by dangers and by enemies, and his missionary churches did not, generally speaking, develop after his death according to his intentions'. Earliest Christianity (1959), I, 394. Further, nn. 46, 89, below; ch.4, pp. 113; 131.

/5/ Cf. the marcionite prologues to Galatians, Corinthians, Thessalonians, and Laodiceans: the verbum veritatis (cf.2 Cor 6.7), a technical term for the prologist, is the word of the gospel delivered by Paul to the churches. Cf. AM 1.20.1 (Marcion's refurbishing of the regula).

/6/ Text in Souter, Text and Canon, 188; cf. de Bruyne, Rev. Bénéd. 24 (1907), 1ff.; Corssen, ZNTW 10 (1909), 37-9.

/7/ On the identity of the Galatians, cf. Kümmel's survey, Intro. to the NT, 296f.

to consider whether the prologist's (thus the marcionite) view of the Galatian problem will bear testing against the situation which Paul describes.

The historical situation is plain from Gal 1.6. Soon after his arrival in Ephesus, after having visited the Galatian Christians, Paul receives word that they are beginning to abandon his teaching and turning to 'another gospel'. Paul qualifies his meaning in the next clause: not another gospel, but a perverted version of the evangelion tou Christou (1.7). It is clear that the gospel being proclaimed by these missionaries is persuasive and attractive (1.10). And it is implicit (1.8a) that it carries the weight, if not the direct support, of a higher authority. Paul must therefore argue both for his gospel (1.11) and for the legitimacy of his apostolate, which like the gospel has its source in the revelation of Jesus Christ: *'Ouk ap anthrōpōn oude di' anthrōpou alla dia Iesou Christou'* (1.1a). As Schütz explains the argument in ch 1, Paul has asserted that 'there is no other gospel in the sense of any other proclamation which can lay claim to the same status as the preaching the Galatians have already heard'./8/ The Ersatzevangelium being preached by the opponents/9/ is a negation of the very essence of the gospel as Paul understands it (2.19ff.).

Underlying and qualifying this understanding of the gospel, however, is the question of apostolic legitimacy, in Schlatter's words, the question, 'What gave Paul the right to call himself an apostle at all?'/10/ It is this question that threads its way through Gal 1-2, Paul making his defense of his right to preach the gospel (2.9, 14ff.) the occasion for an exposition of its content (2.16ff.). The issue 'Which came first: the gospel or Paul's preaching of it?' (i.e., the content of the proclamation or Paul's claim to represent it in an authoritative way) is excluded by the idea (2.2) that both have their immediate origin in the act of revelation (1.12, 15f.). The gospel is what the apostle says it is because he is an apostle. Thus, the matter of legitimacy -- or in Schütz's more precise language, apostolic

---

/8/ Paul and the Anatomy of Apostolic Authority (1975), 120.

/9/ Thus Schlier, Galaterbrief, ([13]1965), 40ff.

/10/ Church in the NT Period, trans., P. Levertoff, (1961), 171.

authority/11/ -- determines the argument in favor of the true gospel./12/ As evangelizing (evangelesthai) is the primary apostolic activity,/13/ Paul's defense of his preaching in Gal (1.9, 11, 16, 23; 4.13, etc.) is coextensive with the defense of his apostolate. He was 'separated from the womb' specifically for the task of preaching to the gentiles (1.15; cf. Rom 1.1). We can also turn the issue around: Any preaching of an Ersatzevangelium such as that envisaged at 1.6 is also an attack on Paul's apostolate. This is not to deny the existence of an ad hominem attack on Paul (1.11) which causes him to stress his independence of those 'who were apostles before him' (1.17ff.). But the personal assault on Paul is closely tied to the content of his gospel: 'Oude gar egō para anthrōpou parelabon auto oute edidachthēn alla di apokalypseōs Iesou Christou' (1.12)./14/ This brings us to the question, What did the opponents' gospel look like, and in what sense was it an indictment of Paul's apostolate?

If we take Gal 5.1 as the kernel of the message that Paul preached to the Christians at Galatia (cf. 2.16ff.), we have at least a touchstone against which to measure the preaching of the opponents. Two charges are levelled against them: stirring up the congregation (1.7) and perverting the gospel of Christ. Entailed in Paul's argument for the evangelion tou Christou is the teaching (of which Marcion would make a great deal) that the gospel is singular (1.6-9) and that both Paul (1.8a) and the community (1.9b) are subordinate to it. As Schütz observes, 'Paul can preach only what he has already preached and the community can receive only what it has already received. The gospel is thus a double-sided norm -- for preaching

---

/11/ Apost. Auth., 7; 204f; 184: 'For Paul the gospel warrants apostolic authority; it does not define apostolic legitimacy'.

/12/ Cf. J.B. Lightfoot, 'The Name and Office of an Apostle', in Galatians (Commentary) (1865; rpt., 1962), 92-101. Schütz opposes v. Campenhausen's reduction of the idea of authority to authorization alone (cf. Ecclesiastical Authority and Spiritual Power [1969], 29), and further: W. Schmithals, The Office of the Apostle in the Early Church (1969), 98-110. For a view opposed to that of Schütz, see K.H. Rengstorf, art. 'Apostolos', Theological Dict. of the NT (1965), I, 407-47, who equates the notions of legitimacy and authority, linking the apostolate with the schaliach-institution of later Judaism.

/13/ 'The terms "apostle" and "gospel" are more than just intimately connected; they are functionally related', Schütz, Apost. Auth., 36.

/14/ Cf. Schütz, Apost. Auth., 112.

and for receiving. It is a norm for faith and for apostleship'./15/
Nevertheless, the actual content of the gospel (which remains fugitive in
Schütz's analysis of the problem/16/ is not sufficiently well defined to
permit us to say precisely at what points it clashed with the gospel preached
by the opponents. Schlatter tried to show that the opponents did not reject
Paul's gospel at all: 'Their opposition to Paul did not arise from his
christology or from his teaching about the Holy Spirit . . . . The new
evangelists left a considerable portion of the gospel as preached by Paul
unimpaired. Yet their gospel was in fact another gospel, since their ideal
was the union of Jews and gentiles in the messiah under the law'./17/ But
Schlatter's view is difficult to maintain since there is no evidence in the
epistle which permits us to say that the opponents left most of what Paul
had preached intact. Indeed, Paul's polemic turns on the charge that the
opponents had preached another gospel entirely, and it is a justifiable
inference that Paul himself assumed few points of contact between the
teaching of his opponents and his own.

Schlatter begins with the assumption that the opponents were judaizers, then concludes that the law must have been the only (because it was
surely the most conspicuous) point of contention. But the problem of the
content of the Ersatzevangelium, and (contingently) the identification of
opponents themselves, is by no means so simple as Schlatter would lead us to
believe. Do we have to do here with advocates of the law and circumcision,
as the marcionite prologist suggests, or with a 'double-front' of judaizers and
pneumatics, groups at odds with each other as well as with Paul's
gospel?/18/ We shall take up these proposals in turn. The more traditional
view of the opponents is that they are judaizers whose aim it was 'to bring
the Galatian churches into an alliance with the synagogue [since] the only
way to avoid a breach between Judaism and Christianity was to bring all the
churches, including the pauline foundations, into subjection to the

---

/15/ Schütz, Apost. Auth., 123.

/16/ Cf. Apost. Auth., 53ff.

/17/ Church in the NT Period, 170f.

/18/ Thus, e.g., W. Lütgert, Gesetz und Geist (1919); J.H. Ropes, The
Singular Problem of Galatians (1929).

law'./19/ This view can be defended on the basis of such passages as 5.2, 6.12f., where the opponents seem to be encouraging the churches to accept circumcision, and 3.2 and 5.4, where it can be inferred that they preach obedience to the Jewish law. From 4.9f., it appears that some have already forsaken Paul's gospel and observe Jewish festivals.

Paul accuses the opponents of being insincere, specifically of glorying in the fact that they can bring others under their control by demanding circumcision while not keeping the law themselves (6.13). What this means is not quite clear: it may refer to the opponents' interpretation of the law, which is almost certainly at variance with Paul's pharisaic belief (5.3) that circumcision requires strict observance of the whole law. Klijn's opinion that from 6.13 it can be inferred 'that the advocates of circumcision were of heathen origin'/20/ is difficult to square with the evidence of the rest of the epistle. Paul himself seems to have understood the opponents as judaizers (which is not quite the same thing as saying they are Jews); but the polemic of 4.22f. points in the direction of identifying the corrupters of the gospel as Jewish or Jewish-Christian advocates of circumcision, themselves lax in observing the law, rather than as gentile insurgents who have affected Jewish customs in the syncretistic climate of Galatia.

In Gal 1.14-2.21, Paul drives a wedge between himself and 'those who were apostles before [him]' (1.17; cf. 2.5ff.), while insisting at the same time (1.14) that he had been every bit as zealous a Jew as they. In ch 2, he introduces his controversy with the pillars -- who evidently in spite of Paul require Titus to be circumcized (2.3)/21/ -- as a precedent for the kind of judaizing activity going on in Galatia. The discursus on the apostles (2.1ff.) thus adumbrates the opposition in the Galatian church, but does not actually establish a link between the opponents and the pillars. If such a link exists,

---

/19/ Thus Schlatter, Church in the NT Period, 168; and with variations, Grant, Historical Introd. to the NT (1963), 185; and esp Kümmel, Intro. to the NT, 300; Barrett, Essays on Paul (1982), 95f.

/20/ Introd., 97f.; J. Munck calls them 'judaizing gentile Christians', Paul and the Salvation of Mankind (1959), 87f.

/21/ Cf. Furnish, ICB, 827: 'The jumbled syntax of vv. 4-5 seems to reflect Paul's embarrassment at having made a concession', i.e., Titus agreed to circumcision out of respect for Paul's total relationship with the community. A more extreme view is set forth by Enslin, Christian Beginnings, 222: 2.1-5 means that Paul had circumcized Titus, but this appears to be warranted only by reading the incident as a muddled doublet of Acts 16.3 (which involves Timothy, not Titus).

Paul is unprepared to make it explicit, although we cannot on that account conclude that he does not suspect such a connection (cf. 1.8). As it is, he seems only to be recounting a past episode, in which the pseudadelphoi (2.4) have engaged in spying -- perhaps at the behest of the Jerusalem authorities./22/ The connection between this reminiscence and the activity in Galatia is (deliberately?) oblique. Paul strives to demonstrate in his polemic that in view of his independence as an apostle he is able to rebuke even Peter to his face (2.11, 14). More specifically, he seems to regard Peter's dissimulation in Antioch (2.12) as a model of the hypocrisy which now infects the congregation in Galatia. Peter is in some sense blameable: but why? For eating with the gentiles, in defiance of the concord reached in Jerusalem (2.7, 9b), or because he and Barnabas bowed before the pressure of the tines apo Iakobou, who evidently found such a practice intolerable?/23/ There is a link between the accusation levelled at Peter and the Jewish-Christians at Antioch, and that directed against the opponents in Galatia (6.13); one might say that the disturbance at Antioch serves in some way as a prototype for the later disturbances in Galatia. As to the former, Paul does not seem to mean that Peter's accommodation to the gentiles was of itself unacceptable; rather, it was unacceptable because it was prudential. 'Peter is rebuked not for a breach of agreement but for inconsistency of behavior'./24/ And it is precisely this inconsistency that Paul finds awash now in Galatia: a return to the 'weak and beggarly elements' (4.9) from which his gospel has freed them. It is important to emphasize, however, that an involvement of Peter and the Jerusalem authorities in the Galatian disturbances is not made explicit. We have no direct evidence of a 'Petrine agitation' (Lietzmann). To resort to the psychological jargon of a later

---

/22/ On the relation between this episode and the account given in Acts 15.1, cf. Weiss, Earliest Christianity, 263ff.

/23/ As Barrett notes, Peter's hypocrisy (synupekrithēsan, tē hypokrisei) consists in having 'fallen into an attitude inconsistent with the gospel', 'Pseudapostoloi', in Essays, 96; and in accommodating truth to his own ends: '[Peter's] attitude is fundamentally insincere. He is expecting of the gentiles the Jewish kind of life that in the recent past he himself has not been living'.

/24/ Marxsen, Introd. NT, 52.

time, Paul's argument works associatively,/25/ the happenings in Galatia triggering the recollection of his encounter with Peter (2.11), with the agents of James (2.12), with the pillar apostles (2.3, 9), and with the pseudadelphoi (2.4f.) about whose identity even Paul seems uncertain. These discrete episodes nonetheless add up to the kind of error with which the Galatians are threatened: hypocrisy and a loss of liberty (3.3; 5.1ff.). Thus the polemic of 6.13 concerning the opponents is associated, in a psychological but perhaps not in a historical sense, with the material in 2.12ff.

The parallelism between chs 2 and 3 becomes even clearer if we take 2.16ff. to be a continuation of Paul's admonition to Peter, beginning in 2.14, Paul having in mind both the particular events that have transpired at Antioch as well as those of more recent occurrence in Galatia. Peter is certainly the addressee in 2.15; but thereafter the address becomes hortatory and Antioch slips into the background. With 3.1, there is a change of narrative perspective (viz., from events at Antioch the focus shifts to Galatia); but beginning in 3.10ff., the exhortation of 2.16ff. is resumed, or reiterated. Paul repeats for the benefit of the wayward community the explanation of the effect of the cross, just as he had previously explained it to a dissimulating Peter. In so doing, Paul is also asserting his apostolic authority in the community, since he is (implicitly) calling upon them to recognize his right to determine the limitations of the evangelion tēs peritomēs (2.7ff.) entrusted to Peter by the Jerusalem authorities.

If it is assumed that ch 2 functions 'associatively', that is, as a kind of narrative parallel to Paul's exhortation to the Galatians beginning in ch 3, one must be less certain that there is any historical connection between Paul's opponents in the community and those captioned in ch 2 as pseudadelphoi, and much less of any connection between the opponents and the dokountes styloi (2.9). The question of their identity has been shoved further into the margins. It is arguable that Paul himself was unaware of their provenance,/26/ even if we assume that ch 2 can also be read as evidence of Paul's strong suspicion that the opponents were agents of

---

/25/ The classic expression remains Locke's, Essay Concerning Human Understanding, 2.33, esp. 5-19 (Chicago ed., [1952], 248-250); and see E.G. Boring, Sensation and Perception in the History of Experimental Psychology (1942).

/26/ Cf. Marxsen, Introd. NT, 53ff.

James. As Enslin has commented,/27/ however, the idea that the men from James who appeared in Antioch dogged Paul's steps into Galatia is not warranted by the evidence in the epistle. Such a reckoning is usually supported by reference to Acts 15.1ff., where 'certain men coming down from Judaea' *(tines katelthontes apo tēs Ioudaias)* are said to have preached circumcision as a prerequisite of salvation. Not the least troublesome thing about the account in Acts is that James is regarded as the arbiter in the dispute occasioned by the gospel of circumcision (Acts 15.13ff.; cf. Gal 2.9) but plays no role in dispatching the 'men from Judaea' in the first place (cf. Gal 2.12: *tines apo Iakōbou).* In the account given in Acts, James and the pillars act directly in accrediting Paul (Acts 15.13, 23f.), whereas in Gal (2.6) Paul declares, *'emoi hoi dokountes ouden prosanethento'.* In any case, the dissension at Galatia cannot be explained as a continuation of the troubles in Antioch; Paul himself voices uncertainty about the identity of the opponents: *'O anoētoi Galatai tis hymas ebaskanen'* (3.1f.). This uncertainty does not belie the suspicion that the preachers are the pseudadelphoi who on another occasion 'slipped in to spy out our freedom . . . and to bring us into bondage' (2.4), but the biographical point does not establish a continuity between the two episodes.

Paul vigorously defends the independence of his apostolate (1.16ff.; 2.1-9), specifically, his freedom from the constraints imposed on others by the pillar apostles (2.7)./28/ It is sometimes thought that his insistence on the independence of his apostolate points away from the conclusion that the opponents were judaizers: Would judaizers have accused Paul of being of too close kin with the men from whom they derived their authority?/29/ Paul's argument, on this reckoning, makes better sense if we imagine the opponents to have been non-Jewish (pneumatic?), hellenizing Christians who had asserted that Paul's gospel of freedom was neutralized by the distinctly Jewish elements on which he still insisted. On these terms, Paul is answering (1.10-2.21) that his contacts with Jerusalem were slight; that he received nothing from the Jewish apostles (who only consider themselves important, anyway, 2.9); that even when brought under pressure by them

/27/ Enslin, Christian Beginnings, 221.

/28/ The apostles act as witnesses, not as accreditors; but cf. Acts 15.22ff.

/29/ Cf. Enslin's discussion, Christian Beginnings, 270.

(2.3) and by their agents (2.4), he refused to accept circumcision; and finally, that even the apostles were obliged to recognize his gosepl of freedom (2.7f.). Accordingly, Paul is able to bring Peter's gospel to the test on the basis of the truth of his own gospel *(pros tēn alētheian tou evangeliou,* 2.14). The biographical allusion in 1.14, on this premise, does not amount to boasting (cf. 2 Cor 11.22), but is contravened by 1.15. Unfortunately, this reading of chs 1-2 does not fit very well with the polemic of chs 5-6, and the not too thinly veiled allusion to the opponents in 4.30, which even considering the thrust of the argument in ch 4 (viz., that the opponents are not children of the promise) requires us to see them as sons of Abraham (4.22). Moreover, Paul's argument in ch 1.10-2.21 seems to arise in response to a direct challenge to his authority (cf. 4.13) and not merely in response to the charge that he is too dependent on the Jerusalem authorities./30/ The need to substantiate that authority over and against the dokountes styloi is sufficient to explain the thrust of the argument in chs 1-2, especially if it is thought that the pillars are somehow, although not directly instrumental in the perverting of the gospel, a charge Paul does not hesitate to lay at Peter's feet (2.14). One need not assume therefore that Paul's distancing himself from the Jerusalem authorities points in the direction of a group of opponents who are not judaizers, and who have charged Paul with inconsistency and judaizing. It is just as plausible that he is attempting to distance himself from men who claim the authority of Jerusalem, and that his uncertainty about the truth of that claim, combined with past experience, determines the run of his argument.

Nonetheless, in addition to passages which indicate a judaizing opposition (4.21; 5.4)/31/ are references which appear to suggest another faction. Gal 6.1 has repeatedly been offered as evidence of a group of pneumatic Christians who stand in opposition both to Paul (or at least to Paul's diplomatic efforts) and to the Jewish faction within the community; hence Paul's irony toward the pneumatikoi. The theory put forward by Lütgert in 1919 and adapted by Ropes ten years later provides the following: Many of the Galatians, although gentile in origin, had become

---

/30/ Thus, e.g., Schmithals, 'Die Häretiker in Galatien', ZNTW 47 (1956); rpt. in Paulus und Gnostiker (1965), 9-46, here pp. 13-22.

/31/ Cf. Barrett, Essays, 85, n. 66: 'In Galatia the judaizers were able to state their own terms in their own way and we have an example of "pure judaizing" '.

devoted to Jewish observances (cf. 4.10) (a phenomenon widely attested in Antioch as well)/32/ and perhaps saw no contradiction between these practices and the faith of Paul, 'who not improbably appeared to their uncritical eyes far closer to Judaism than he himself would have admitted'./33/ The judaizers may have been representatives of local synagogues (a permissible assumption if the idea of outside infiltration is given up)/34/ who attempted to introduce circumcision among the syncretistic christian converts. Gal 4.9 seems to point to a domestic crisis which involves a return to the bondage of the law, and may indicate either Jewish Christians who had accepted Paul's gospel of freedom and subsequently returned to their old ways (*epistrephete palin* connotes a relapse), or gentile Christians who have resumed certain Jewish practices which Paul, in his missionary effort, had temporarily deterred (cf. 4.11). Ropes argued for the internal nature of the conflict on the premise that 'a missionary enterprise at such a distance [from Jerusalem] would in itself be hard to handle'./35/

If one accepts the idea of a domestic-judaizing element in the christian churches, then it becomes possible to interpret such passages as 5.13b, 16; 6.1, 8 as addressing a separate group of Christians, who emphasize the libertarian aspects of Paul's gospel and find themselves threatened by the judaizing party. Enslin finds 5.15 a pointed rejoinder to two groups, locked in conflict over the meaning of the gospel. On the basis of what must be accounted very little evidence, he describes these anti-legalists as 'perfectionists'/36/ whose 'mystic experience of Christ had made them free from all restraints. . . . To them the demands of their judaizing fellow-Christians

---

/32/ See Tarn, Hellenistic Civilization, 179-181.

/33/ Enslin, Christian Beginnings, 221.

/34/ Paul says nothing to indicate the perverters of the gospel are from outside; and 1.7 does not point to outside agitation.

/35/ The Singular Problem, 45, n. 14.

/36/ Christian Beginnings, 222.

were not only absurd but a negation of their new confidence'/37/ According
to the Lütgert-Ropes hypothesis, the letter to the Galatians is an attack on
two groups divided in their interpretation of the gospel: 3.1-5.10 being
directed against those who dabble in Jewish practices; 1.11 against the
pneumatics; and 1.13-2.14 forming a counter-polemic against the spiritual-
ists' charge that Paul had violated his own provisions and catered to the
Jerusalem leaders (thus, 2.3) many years after his conversion. So regarded,
Paul's defense becomes a defense against the accusation that he was a quasi-
apostle, for all his protests inferior to the pillars from whom he claims to
have received nothing (2.6b).

Unfortunately, the theory that Paul is up against two discrete groups
in Galatia requires an inference from polemic that reveals nothing so clearly
as that Paul himself is uncertain about the provenance of his enemies
(3.1). His (apparent) fighting on more than one front may signal nothing
more than an attempt to cover all fronts./38/ Moreover, the conclusion
that the opponents include a group of 'pneumatic Christian perfectionists'
depends on our viewing chs 1 and 2 as apology rather than polemic, and
there is no internal evidence to justify such a reading. As Schütz observes,
'Whether or not the opponents accused Paul of denigrating tradtion and thus
having an unanchored apostolic status must remain an open question . . . .
It is at least likely and less clumsy to assume that Paul is on the offensive in
attacking their attachment to tradition (i.e., the gospel as the law) and
arguing over against this the case of the one gospel which is illustrated
through the apostolic person'./39/ This interpretation of Gal 1.10-12 is
provisionally satisfying: the opponents have tried to equate the gospel with
tradition; Paul must therefore attempt to show that it transcends tradition
-- just as his apostolic office transcends historical legitimation (1.1; 1.15;
2.5f.). He does this by opposing the true gospel to what is now passing as

/37/ Enslin, loc. cit.; far less convincing is Schmithals' contention that the
opponents are gnostics who had incorporated into their scheme elements of
the Torah-observance; cf. 'Die Häretiker in Galatien', ZNTW 47 (1956), 25-
67. Schütz notes (Apost. Auth., 125), that 'Schmithals can scarcely
account for the central concerns of chs 3 and 4 by direct appeal to any
known gnostic phenomenon, and certain indices of gnosticism seem missing
throughout Galatians'.

/38/ Cf. Marxsen, Introd. NT, 50ff.

/39/ Apost. Auth., 128; cf. D. Georgi, Die Geschichte der Kollekte des
Paulus für Jerusalem (1965), 36, n. 113.

the gospel among the Galatians, such that 'even if we or an angel from heaven preach another gospel to you than the one we have already preached, let him be accursed' (1.8).

As to the opponents themselves, there is little to suggest a polemic 'alternating between two fronts'./40/ Schlier,/41/ Stählin,/42/ and Schmithals/43/ are correct in pointing to the syncretistic and 'gnostic' elements in the opponents' teaching (which parallels in some respects the heresy attacked in Col); but the idea of the opponents as 'Jewish-christian-gnostics' or syncretistic Jews is so vague as to be uninformative. Marxsen has provided a more adequate solution, even though its effect is to shift the weight from the identity of the opponents to Paul's understanding of their goals. Given that Paul did not fully comprehend what was causing the agitation in the Galatian churches, and does not apparently encounter the subversion first-hand, what can be the significance of his focussing on circumcision (5.1ff.)? Paul seems to think (6.12) that it is being used as a device to escape persecution, and further, that it has become a symbol of the control of the opponents over the community (6.13). But this is Paul's view of the matter: 'Paul knows that [escaping persecution] is an important motive for circumcision in Jewish-christian circles [cf. 2.3] and in this way he explains to himself the practice that has been introduced'./44/ For Paul at least, this motive is inextricably tied to the opponents' desire to win esteem, and hence to the issue of authority. He struggles to understand the meaning of circumcision in Galatia (thus the discursive and 'associational' structure of the argument), but in the end is unable to understand it other than in the categories of pharisaic Judaism: to be circumcized means above all to be a debtor to the law (5.3; cf. 3.10; 4.9b, 21). This return to bondage -- this relapse -- is intolerable to Paul (4.30f.; 5.1f.). Moreover,

---

/40/ Kümmel, Intro. to the NT, 299f.: 'The opponents were without doubt Jewish Christians who preached first of all circumcision, but fulfillment of the law as well'. Lietzmann's idea (The Beginnings of the Christian Church [1953] I, 109ff.), that the opponents represent a Petrine agitation against Paul has not won much favor.

/41/ Schlier, Der Brief an die Galater (1952), 204.

/42/ Stählin, 'Galaterbrief', in RGG$^2$, 1188.

/43/ Schmithals, 'Die Häretiker in Galatien', ZNTW 47 (1956), 25ff.

/44/ Marxsen, Introd. NT, 55.

it is a violation of his gospel and an affront to his office (4.11f.; 1.6; 5.11). Writes Marxsen, 'The various difficulties are best solved by assuming that Paul did not fully understand the position of his opponents'./45/ He is perplexed (4.20) because the practice they introduce is foreign to his idea of what circumcision is supposed to be. To venture no more than a guess about the opponents' view of circumcision, we can refer to Schmithals' opinion that it edged toward a 'gnosticizing' of Jewish practice, though even this depends on reading an understanding out of Paul's confusion.

To conclude: Paul is probably fighting on only one front in Galatia. But the traditional notion that this front is composed of 'garden variety Pharisees' (Barrett) perhaps having links with the 'men from James' mentioned in the reminiscence of 2.12, is difficult to maintain in view of Paul's own perplexity and the associative turns in his argument (2.11ff.; 3.2ff.). The most tolerable assumption about the identity of the opponents is that they are local, hellenized Jewish Christians who in Paul's absence have reverted to familiar practices, encouraging gentile members of the congregation to accept their version of the gospel.

## 3.3 Paul and Corinth

The crisis in Galatia provides important evidence of the evanescence of Paul's authority/46/ in the churches he regards as being indebted to his teaching. Further evidence comes from the Corinthian letters, which formed the second (and third?) part of the marcionite corpus paulinum.

The marcionite prologist knows the Corinthians as Achaeans who

> heard the word of truth from the apostle and were perverted variously by false apostles, some by the verbal eloquence of philosophy, others led on by the sect of the Jewish law./47/

Here we would seem to have a surprisingly 'modern' recognition that Paul is up against a variety of opponents in Corinth: the evidence of the letters

---

/45/ Introd. NT, 55.

/46/ So too, in Antioch: Dunn (Unity and Diversity in the NT [1977], 254) argues that Gal 2.7-13 points to the fact that Paul was defeated at Antioch, and that the church there sided with Peter: 'it is probable that Paul was much more isolated in the strong line he maintained at Antioch than his own version of the episode admits'; cf. Loisy, Christian Religion, 161.

/47/ Latin text in Souter, Text and Canon, 188.

strongly supports the view that a distinction can and should be made between the advocates of the law (Jewish missionaries or hellenistic Jewish Christians?) and teachers of philosophy (pneumatics, gnostics?). Although the prologist does not distinguish between 1 and 2 Cor, he seems to point to a more advanced stage in the Corinthian crisis than the internal dissension created by the 'enthusiasts' at the time of the writing of 1 Cor./48/ Tertullian's discussion of the marcionite version of 2 Cor is not of much help (AM 5.11.1f.), though it does seem to be the case that Marcion emphasized the reference in 2 Cor 11.13 to pseudapostoloi (AM 5.12.6) and charged them with corrupting the faith. The epithet is employed universally by the prologist to refer to all those who have caused the churches to stray from Paul's gospel, and as a designation for false teachers of various stripes. It might therefore be assumed that 2 Cor 11.13ff. was seen by the Marcionites as an especially important indication of the kind and degree of opposition Paul was obliged to overcome. But in generalizing the opposition to Paul's gospel, in terms congenial to his view of the pauline mission, the prologist has glossed over the particulars of the struggle between Paul and his opponents. Thus, some sorting out is necessary if we are to get behind the prologist's interpretation of the Corinthian situation, concentrating on the section of the letters/49/ that provided the polemical Schlagwort for Marcion's appraisal of Paul's opposition, namely 2 Cor 10-13.

We are concerned with two problems: first, who does Paul have in mind when he refers to 'false apostles' in Corinth, and in what way does their activity determine his own understanding and definition of his apostolate. As Schütz characterizes the situation in chs 10-13:

> Paul struggles against sharp attacks on his person and on his apostolic claim, attacks which he seeks to rebuff by counter-argument but which also lead him to anticipate a

/48/ See my discussion, 'Memē ristai ho Christos? Anti-Enthusiast Polemic from Paul to Augustine', Studia Theologica 33 (1979), 149-164.

/49/ On the literary unity of the letter, see A. Hausrath, Die Vierkapitelbrief an die Korinther (1870) and Georgi, Die Gegner des Paulus im 2. Korintherbrief (1964), also Bornkamm, Die Vorgeschichte des sogennanten 2. Korintherbriefs (1961). I accept Hausrath's argument that the tone of chs 10-13 does not fit well coming after 1-7, and that 10-13 may represent a different (though not necessarily earlier) stage of correspondence. Schütz adopts the view that 2.14-6.13 and 7.2-4 is another fragment, related to 10-13 in theme but different in tone. The sections are separated by chs 8 and 9 (appeals by Paul for the collection). Cf. Apost. Auth., 166, n. 1.

lively confrontation face to face one day (cf.10.2; 12.14;
13.1ff., 10). In such a confrontation, Paul will face
people who claim their own apostolic status in part at his
expense  They deny that he belongs to Christ (10.7); they
rebuke him because he does not draw financial support
from the community (11.7; 12.1, 16); and they delight in
contrasting his impression by letter with that he makes in
person (10.1, 10). All of this is apparently negative
evidence for their identification if they are scorning Paul
for lacking their own virtues or characteristics./50/

Their presence in Corinth appears to mark a different stage in the
propagandizing of the community from that represented in 1 Cor./51/ As
Barrett suggests, '2 Cor deals no longer with the various charismata insisted
on by the "spiritual" opponents of 1 Cor, and Paul no longer has to combat

---

/50/ Apost. Auth., 166.

/51/ Barrett argues on the basis of very little evidence ('Cephas and Corinth'
in Essays, 37) that 1 Cor shows 'the certain influence and probable presence
of Peter in Corinth'; thus the references to the various  factions in 1 Cor
1.10ff.: a Paul-group, a Cephas-group, an Apollos-group, and perhaps a
group that knows itself as a Christ-group ('Christianity at Corinth', Essays,
5f.), the last being perhaps 'Christians of a gnostic type, who laid stress on
charismatic and spiritual phenomena against whom Paul found himself
obliged to defend his apostleship' (ibid., 14). With justice, however,
Barrett rejects the view that the polemic in 2 Cor reflects a simple
continuation of the crisis attested by the earlier letter: 'It was probably only
after the deterioration of the Corinthian situation, after the writing of 1
Cor . . . that Paul saw how serious the effects of the intervention of Jewish
Christian emissaries were likely to prove, or were proving' ('Cephas and
Corinth', Essays, 37). Nonetheless, the factionalism presupposed in 1 Cor
clearly forms a backdrop for the reception of the pseudapostoloi proscribed
in 2 Cor 11.13, despite the fact that we know very little about the groups
(cf. Munck, Paulus und die Heilsgeschichte (1964), 134, 141). Marxsen
argues that the opponents of Paul in 1 Cor 'can certainly -- though
indirectly, by the kind of inquiry that is made and the scandals that have
arisen -- be identified as gnostics' (Introd. NT, 75) though the evidence he
cites in ch 15 would more properly warrant retaining the term 'pneumatics'
(cf. 14.1ff). So too Kümmel (Intro. to the NT, 274): 'There is nothing in 1
Cor by way of a polemic against "Judaistic", that is, radically Jewish-
Christian views [cf. Schoeps, Paul (1961), 76f.]. Rather the whole letter
manifests a front against a gnostic perversion of the christian message which
attributes to the pneumatics, as those liberated from the sarx, a perfect
redemptive state and an unconditional moral freedom'. Kümmel rejects the
older view (cf. Hurd's discussion, The Origin of 1 Cor [1965] and Kümmel,
TLZ 91 [1966], 505ff.) that Paul is fighting on different fronts and that the
polemic of the letter can accordingly be apportioned to correlate with the
different parties. Kümmel takes note of the fact that it cannot be shown
that Paul turns his attention in later chapters of the letter to one or another
of the hypothetical 'groups' and that 3.4f.; 3.22; and 4.6 (refs. to Apollos,
Paul and Cephas) vary for no perceptible reason. Further, 'from chapter 5
on, there is no mention of groups forming' (273).

the libertinism apparent in 1 Cor'./52/ Schütz, on the other hand, finds that the difference between the opponents in the two letters turns on conflicting understandings of history: 'In 1 Cor, the opponents were appealing to a future which they regarded as already present. In order to counteract this, Paul must appeal to a past and appeals to his past to show the real, the contingent quality of the present'./53/

Given the 'evident development [in the opposition to Paul] when the letters are viewed side by side'/54/ is it possible to identify the pseudapostoloi of 2 Cor with any degree of precision? The older view, represented by F.C. Baur is that they acted as agents of the radical Jewish wing associated with Peter:

> Diese pseudapostoloi in Corinth sich namentlich auf die Auctorität des Apostels Petrus beriefen, aus Palästina nach Corinth gekommen waren, und ohne Zweifel mit den Palästinenischen Judenaposteln in irgend einem Zusammenhang stunden, so sind wohl die hyperlian apostoloi, die Apostel selbst, deren Schüler und Abgeordnete zu sein, die pseudapostoloi vorgaben./55/

Käsemann regards them, however, as representatives of Palestinian Jewish-Christianity who have claimed the authority of the Jerusalem apostles,/56/ while Kümmel has taken the position that although they are certainly Palestinian in origin, they are not necessarily connected with Jerusalem, and seem to have affinities with the more 'gnostic' opponents of 1 Cor./57/ Following Lütgert's suggestions,/58/ Bultmann/59/ and Schmithals/60/ identified the opponents as Jewish-gnostic-pneumatics, and Windisch

---

/52/ Comm. on the Second Epistle to the Corinthians (1973), 29.

/53/ Apost. Auth., 173; cf. Klijn, Introd., 91.

/54/ Klijn, Introd., 89.

/55/ Paulus, der Apostel Jesu Christi (1845), 294.

/56/ 'Die Legitimität des Apostels', ZNTW 41 (1942), 33-71; cf. Manson, 'St. Paul in Ephesus [3]: The Corinthian Correspondence', BJRL 26 (1941/2), 101ff.

/57/ In H. Lietzmann, 'An die Korinther, I, II' (Handbuch zum Neuen Testament [⁵1969], 9, suppl., 211 [Kümmel]).

/58/ Lütgert, Freiheitspredigt und Schwarmgeister in Korinth (1908).

/59/ Exegetische Probleme des zweiten Korintherbriefes (1963).

/60/ Die Gnosis in Korinth (1956).

emphasized that although they were 'fundamentally Jewish', their Judaism had been modified by an alliance that prides itself on its inspiration./61/ The 'judaizing'-view of the opponents has been defended more recently by Barrett: 'The intruders were Jews, Jerusalem Jews, judaising Jews and as such constituted a rival apostolate to Paul's backed by all the prestige of the mother church'./62/ Barrett sees the Corinthian church as engaging in the business of 'testing' apostles (cf. 2 Cor 13.5) and employing essentially hellenistic criteria in their judgments: 'The Corinthians have been con- fronted by two rival apostolates. Not improperly, they wish to determine which is true and which is false but [according to Paul] they have employed the wrong criteria. They have looked for written commendations from high authority and for ecstatic phenomena'./63/ For Barrett, the identity hinges on recognizing that the opponents must have accepted the criteria proposed by the Corinthians, an assumption strengthened if one sees the enthusiasm of 1 Cor as typifying the religious climate within which the intruders are required to justify their claims./64/ Consequently it is necessary for Paul to broaden his line of attack in 2 Cor. At the same time he must endeavor to show that the criteria accepted by the intruders are false criteria by a strategic acceptance/rejection of their 'proofs' (11.16ff.)

While there is something to be said for each of these efforts to color in the identity of the opponents on the basis of Paul's outline, none has proven wholly successful, not least because 'we have too little agreement on char- acteristics of the "Jewish-Christian" and "gnostic" './65/ Moreover, there remains the vexing problem of the relation between the pseudapostoloi mentioned in 11.13 ('crooked in their practices, masquerading as apostles of Christ') and the hyperlian apostoloi of 11.5: with the latter, Paul is able to compare himself, while the former he unequivocally condemns (11.15). The

---

/61/ Windisch, Der Zweite Korintherbrief (Komm. über das Neue Testament) (1924).

/62/ 'Paul's Opponents in 2 Cor', in Essays, 80. Barrett (Comm. on 2 Cor, 30) acknowledges however that 'a gnostic element enters into the make-up of the new opponents'.

/63/ Barrett, Essays, 78; Comm. on 2 Cor, 30.

/64/ Schmithals, Die Gnosis in Korinth (1956), includes the situation in 1 Cor in his analysis.

/65/ Schütz, Apost. Auth., 167.

problem is compounded by the fact that in 11.16ff., Paul proceeds to compare his own powers with those of the intruders. Does this mean that he is speaking ironically in 11.5, but of the same group? Käsemann proposed a way out of the difficulty by pointing to a so-called sprunghaft-transition from 11.4 to 11.5./66/ The hyperlian apostoloi are the primitive apostles, Peter and his colleagues; the pseudapostoloi of 11.13, claimants of the authority of the Jerusalem apostles. In 11.4, Paul is talking about those who preach another Jesus, another spirit, and another gospel than the one the Corinthians have received from him (cf. Gal 1.6ff.); in 11.5 he speaks of the apostles whose authority he shares./67/ 2 Cor 11.5 thus belongs to the 'boasting' that accelerates at 11.6, and to the list of proofs which Paul adduces in favor of his legitimacy (11.22ff.), culminating in the account of the visions and revelations (12.1) and the reiteration of 11.5 at 12.11f., where its meaning is reinforced by a further claim: *'Ta men sēmeia tou apostolou kateirgasthē en hymin en pasē hypomonē sēmeiois te kai terasin kai dynamesin'*. That Paul's argument turns on pneumatic proofs may be taken as evidence that 'the situation with which Paul had to deal contained both judaizing and hellenizing elements'./68/

---

/66/ Käsemann, 'Legitimität', 44; cf. Bultmann, Exegetische Probleme des Zweiten Korintherbriefes (1947), 26ff.

/67/ But cf. Bultmann, Exegetische Probleme, 26f.

/68/ Thus Barrett, 'Paul's Opponents', in Essays, 80. But Barrett's typology of 'conservative, liberal, and revolutionary Judaism' (p. 82) is overrefined: How are we to understand Paul's Judaism as defining the 'revolutionary' type if it is reckoned to be formulated in opposition to opponents whose central theme was 'We are free to do anything' (Klijn, Introd., 89). 2 Cor 9.20f. points to accomodation as much as to indifference about the external features of religion. Moreover, the ghost of Baur and the idea of a Petrine agitation against Paul still looms large in Barrett's analysis. Any typology of the sort proposed by Barrett should be weighed against the cautions put forward by W.D. Davies, Paul and Rabbinic Judaism (²1958), esp. 1-16 and in revised form by Schoeps, Paul: The Theology of the Apostle in the Light of Jewish Religious History (1961), 88-112. See further the excellent discussion by E.P. Sanders, Paul and Palestinian Judaism (1977), esp. 549ff., where solid groundwork for Paul's originality is provided.

Perhaps the most satisfying modern attempt to specify the hellenistic background of Paul's opposition is that provided by Dieter Georgi./69/ According to Georgi's appraisal, the opponents belong to a diffuse tradition of wandering preachers; specifically they are Jewish-pneumatics whose missionary efforts have been appropriated by the christian community. Their christology is based on an interpretation of Old Testament luminaries (especially Abraham and Moses) as divine men, and their apostolic 'self-consciousness' (Schütz) depends on their understanding of themselves as wandering wonder-workers whose true identity is outwardly confirmed in their ability to manifest the spirit. Georgi finds that in 2 Cor 2.14-7.4 and especially in chs 10-13 (originally discrete letters, but reflecting stages in the same controversy)/70/ Paul responds to these itinerants by lambasting their denigration of him and their own claim to represent high Jerusalem authorities: 'Die Gegner versuchten durch den Rückblick auf die Vergangenheit, die Demonstrationen der Macht des Geistes in der Gegenwart und durch den ekstatischen Ausbruch ins Jenseits und in die Zukunft die gegenwärtige Existenz zu überhöhen'./71/ What Georgi has to say about the motives and perspective of these missionaries, especially concerning their use of the Old Testament typology, correlates with what Käsemann has offered by way of explaining the derogatory language of 11.13ff. Paul (so Käsemann) had been accused by these opponents of being deficient in spiritual gifts; in view of this deficiency, Paul was not an apostle at all, but a sham apostle (hence Paul's use of the term in relation to the intruders). Moreover, the missionaries have put forward their own criteria for judging an apostle, thus challenging Paul's authority in the Corinthian church, in particular his self-designation as apostolos Christou Iesou. At Paul's expense, they have invoked a legitimation-principle (Traditionsprinzip), advanced certain requirements for the public evidence of a true apostle (12.12), and offered letters of commendation at least

---

/69/ Die Gegner des Paulus im 2. Korintherbrief (1964); cf. the general discussion by G. Friedrich, 'Die Gegner des Paulus im 2. Korintherbrief', in Abraham unser Vater, ed. O. Betz, et al. (1963), 181-215. Friedrich looks to Acts 6-7 (the Stephen-circle) for the provenance of the opponents (hellenistic visionaries, inspired preachers).

/70/ Gegner, 24.

/71/ Gegner, 301.

purported to come from Jerusalem./72/ Käsemann concludes that the intruders have tried their case against Paul 'under the eyes and banner of the original apostles':/73/

> [Paulus'] Apostolat fehlt die nachprüfbare Eindeutigkeit. Seine Autorität ist nicht 'legitim'. Sie ist es insofern nicht, als ihr die Verbindung zu der Autorität der Urapostel und der Urgemeinde fehlt, und insofern auch die Beziehung zu dem Jesus, der diese gesetzt und entsandt hat./74/

Against this Traditionsprinzip, Paul must attempt to establish his own apostolic claim./75/ As Schütz summarizes the situation, 'Paul's opponents stress continuity with the past (Old Testament, Moses) and perfection in the present, while he stresses discontinuity with the past . . . and a culmination in the future'./76/ But the situation is complicated by the additional criterion -- proof of pneumatic endowment -- which the congregation in Corinth also seems to have invoked against Paul (cf. 12.2ff.). Based on their interpretation of the OT as the 'archive of the spirit'/77/ they regard Moses as a theios anēr, a prefiguration of the christian pneumatic who is being changed from one degree of glory to another and is thus also theios anēr./78/ Paul's understanding of the spirit, not to mention of the OT (cf.

---

/72/ 'Legitimatät, 45.

/73/ 'Legitimität, 47.

/74/ 'Legitimität, 50.

/75/ Though it is argued by Georgi (Gegner, 229, n. 3; and cf. Schütz, Apost. Auth., 171) that a Traditionsprinzip in a legal sense cannot be found among the opponents, at least 'as a worldly tangible, fleshly principle over against which Paul has no appeal except to himself' (Schütz, 171). But Schütz is less persuasive in arguing that authority rather than legitimacy is the issue in chs 10-13.

/76/ Apost. Auth., 175.

/77/ Thus Georgi, Gegner, 265ff.

/78/ Georgi, Gegner, 265-82; cf. 2 Cor 3.14-18, esp. the parallelism between vv. 13 and 14; and Philo, Mos. 2.69f. According to Georgi, the kalynma-metaphor (vv. 14-16; cf. Exod 34.29ff.) is used negatively by Paul (v. 13b) but positively by the opponents who see it as the device which separates the true pneumatic (= Moses) from the people and the device the removal of which (unveiling, anakalyptomenon, 14b) is effected by the preaching of the pneumatic apostle who is responsible for the process of theosis and spiritual endowment that follows on the unveiling (Gegner, 270f.) It does not seem to be the case that the opponents had accused Paul's gospel of being veiled; the claim is rather 'Paul's own appropriation of the

3.13ff.) is so radically different from that of the intruders, that he accuses them of having another spirit (11.4, cf. 3.17) and another gospel (11.14, cf. 4.3). He cannot reject the legitimation-principle out of hand; but he regards the situation that reduces him to self-defensive 'boasting' (12.11) as a falsification of the gospel, having its roots in satanic deception (11.3).

Paul's use of the term pseudapostoloi arises in specific connection with this falsification of the gospel, an act which Paul represents in the phrase metaschēmatizomenoi eis apostolous Christou (11.13). But the term does not arise without provocation, since the polemic of 11.12ff. is really counterpolemic: Paul himself has been accused of duplicity/79/ and of being a sham apostle. He has encountered a similar charge at Corinth before, if we can take 1 Cor 9.1 as adumbrating the charge reflected in 2 Cor 11.22ff./80/ The opponents also seem to have accused Paul of being hypocritical:/81/ he has curried favor by telling the congregation what they want to hear. Further, he is evidently accused of betraying his own people (11.22ff.), and of not being a true minister of Christ. His preaching about the law has raised questions about his ancestry, giving his opponents the chance to boast of a superior Jewish pedigree (11.18, 22).

Paul's response to these charges is vitriolic: He calls the intruders to task for hawking the word of God (2.17); for spurious self-commendation (10.12, 18) and conceit (5.12; 11.12, 18; 12.1, 7); for unrightfully laying claim to an apostolic office that belongs to him (11.5, 13; 12.11); for glorying in their Jewish ancestry, kata sarka (11.22; cf. 3.4ff.); and, not

---

opponents' terminology' (Schütz, Apost. Auth., 174), and does not anticipate the polemic of 2 Ptr 3.16, which marks a different stratum in the understanding of Paul's theology.

/79/ So Barrett, 'Pseudapostoloi', Essays, 98.

/80/ Cf. Gal 1.1, 10; 5.11; 1 Cor 15.8f. According to Kümmel, 'these opponents first came into the community after the writing of 1 Cor [cf. 2 Cor 3.1; 10.15f.; 11.4]', but to all appearances 'have joined with the gnostic opposition of Paul recognizable from 1 Cor, or even before they reached Corinth adopted gnostic and pneumatic features' (Kümmel, Intro. to the NT, 285f.). But Kümmel's ideas that the opponents are Palestinian insurgents against apostolic authority cannot be maintained in view of Paul's polemic at 11.13, which is crucial to any estimate of how Paul saw the motives of the intruders. The term pseudapostoloi would be senseless unless a prior claim of true apostleship had been advanced.

/81/ 2 Cor 11.31b; cf. Rom 9.1; Gal 1.20; God as martus: Rom 1.9; 2 Cor 1.23; Phil 1.8; 1 Thess 2.5, 10. Based on this distribution Barrett rightly concludes that such passages 'are too numerous to be a mere trick of style' (Essays, 98f.).

least, for treading on his own territory (10.15f.). The severity of this attack strongly suggests that Paul's legitimacy has been questioned in the community (10.2); as Schütz characterizes the thrust of 2.14-7.4 and chs 10-13, the opponents are supplying the terms; they style themselves diakonoi Christou (11.23)/82/ and it is difficult for Paul to rise above the terms set by the opposition./83/ His own definition of apostolic authority is ultimately a contrecoup to the claims advanced by the false apostles, and this involves, apropos the Traditionsprinzip (continuity with the Jerusalem apostles) which they have put forward, Paul's emphasis on the discontinuity between old and new, as embodied in his gospel and in his understanding of apostleship (5.16; so too 3.1ff., 5.12, 17b)./84/ The tirades against self-commendation and pedigree (11.18f.; 11.22; 3.1f.) suggest that the Corinthians find the opponents' emphasis on continuity and tradition compelling, and Paul's autobiographical attempts to neutralize their claims trail off into self-defense (12.11f.) and self-pity (12.15f.).

## 3.4 Conclusion

The marcionite prologist points to a pattern of disloyalty to Paul's memory, after the intrusion of 'false apostles' in the churches of Galatia, Corinth, Rome, and Colossae. He says nothing to indicate that Paul had succeeded in restoring his gospel to these congregations. But he knows another pattern as well: churches that have remained more or less steadfast in the verbum veritatis. The Thessalonians are thought to have remained faithful to the gospel 'even under persecution from their own citizens, not having accepted what was said to them by false apostles'; and the Philippians, to have 'persevered in the faith' and 'not [to have] received the false apostles', though it would appear an attempt had been made to pull them away from Paul's gospel. Significantly, the prologist does not acknowledge

---

/82/ This may be 'as close as we come in 2 Cor to a titular self-reference, though the opponents must have called themselves apostoloi as well to elicit Paul's sarcasm' (Schütz, Apost. Auth., 179).

/83/ Schütz, Apost. Auth., 181: 'It is obvious that in manipulating the diakonoi-theme Paul contradicts his opponents' polemic. But he is also trying to set up an offensive operation and restructure the argument in terms he finds more congenial'.

/84/ If Georgi is correct, 'Iēsous' is the primary term of opposition for the opponents (cf. 11.4), kyrios for Paul (cf. 4.5f.; Gegner, 282ff.).

Paul's influence at Colossae, only that Paul writes to correct the congregation in that city after their subversion by the pseudapostoloi: 'Nec ad hos accessit ipse apostolus, sed et hos per epistulam recorrigit: audierant enim verbum ab Archippo, qui et ministerium in eos accepit'./85/ Similarly, he does not acknowledge Paul's influence at Rome (cf. Rom 1.10f. [probably unknown to Marcion]; Acts 28.14-31 [unknown or rejected]), and regards the Romans as having been 'reached beforehand by false apostles and under the name of our Lord Jesus Christ . . . led on to the law and the prophets' (cf. Rom 1.2ff.). Only the Laodiceans are credited with having remained unconditionally true to the apostle's faith: 'Hi accepto verbo veritatis perstiterunt in fide. Hos conlaudat apostolus'.

With small exception the marcionite prologues are not testimonies to Paul's success, but just the reverse: only a remnant of the churches of Asia have persevered, and of these, only one has been untroubled by the corrupters of Paul's gospel. Although there is little to suggest that this distinction between 'faithful' and 'unfaithful' churches was based on an adequate understanding of the opposition Paul had encountered in his own lifetime, the prologues provide important evidence of the fact that these troubles persisted and survived Paul's attempts to remedy them. Thus, even at Corinth, where the prologist can make a provisional distinction between those who preach the Jewish law and those who lead the community astray 'by the eloquence of philosophy', the distinction is finally unimportant, since both errors are instances of false apostleship. Paul calls the community to return to the truth and wisdom of the gospel, which the prologist (presumably) equates with the 'singular' gospel announced in 2 Cor 11.4f. (cf. Gal 1.7f.; Rom 2.16b). The legitimacy of Paul's claim to represent the evangelium veritatis, the foundation of his apostolic authority, is in each case the presupposition of the prologist's verdict.

In accepting Paul's arguments in favor of his apostolic office, the Marcionites proved themselves more receptive than many of the churches to which Paul looked for a hearing. As Käsemann succinctly puts the case:

> Almost all of [Paul's] letters show that hellenistic enthusiasm rebelled against the authority of the apostle already in his lifetime; alien missionaries were continually breaking into his field and easily establishing themselves there: rival groups hindered discipline, stability, and Paul's attempt to leave a lasting imprint on his converts.

---

/85/ Prologue to Col, in Souter, Text and Canon, 189.

> Paul bent every effort to maintain his position in Corinth,
> but it is unlikely that his influence continued even to this
> death./86/

Both as a missionary and a a theologian, Käsemann asserts,/87/ Paul had little direct and lasting influence on subsequent developments in the churches, though this recognition stands in flagrant contradiction of his own claims.

The extent to which Paul's gospel had fallen into disrepute would have been apparent to any collector and editor of his letters; and it would not have been difficult for Marcion to link the opposition he himself encountered in his effort to reassert pauline teaching with the opposition that had greeted Paul's gospel of freedom. If we take Polycarp's words in his letter to the Philippian church to refer to a marcionite missionary endeavor in that city, then we get some notion of what form the opposition must have taken, on a larger scale, throughout Asia Minor: *'Oute gar egō oute allos homoios emoi dynatai katakolouthēsai tē sophia tou makariou kai endoxou Paulou'* (Phil. 3.1). And if Thompson is right in saying that the heretics envisaged in 2 Ptr 3.16 (those who twist the words of Paul and the scriptures 'to their own destruction') are Marcionites,/88/ then we possess a relatively firm indication that by c. 130, Marcion was confronted with a situation in which not only Paul's stature in the churches was threatened, but even the ability of the churches to understand the rudiments of his theology: *'en hais estin dysnoeta tina'.*/89/ Against this background, Marcion's own version of a pauline renaissance unfolds: that is to say, against the historical record of churches that had played the Apostle false even in his own lifetime.

---

/86/ 'Paul and Early Catholicism', in New Testament Questions of Today (1969), 239.

/87/ 'Paul and Early Catholicism', 249.

/88/ C.H. Thompson, art., 'The Second Letter of Peter', ICB, 931.

/89/ Cf. Käsemann, 'Paul and Early Catholicism', 249: '[The real Paul] remains confined in seven letters and for the most part unintelligible to posterity'. Despite the appeal to Paul's 'endurance' in 1 Clement 5.5, there is no evidence that Paul's gospel is the standard against which the author is measuring the faithfulness of the Corinthian community at the end of the first century: cf. 47.1ff. On the date of the epistle, see Fischer, Die Apostolischen Väter (1964), 16ff.; further, Andresen, Geschichte des Christentums I (1975), 3ff., re: the geographical matrix of paulinism.

## CHAPTER FOUR

## THE DOCTRINE OF FALSE APOSTLESHIP
## AS THE BASIS OF MARCION'S THEOLOGICAL REFORM

### 4.1  Introduction

The failure of Paul's mission is the presupposition of Marcion's reform.  The silence of the so-called Epistle of Barnabas and the Didache concerning Paul's activity, the eclipse of his influence that seems to underlie such passages as Rev 2.2, 9, 14-15, 20-24; 3.9; 21.14; 2 Peter 3.16; James 2.17, and the negligible use made of the epistles by Justin Martyr/1/ point to the conclusion that by Marcion's day the gospel of Paul was in clear danger of being forsaken altogether./2/

Because Marcion made the reëstablishment of Paul's teaching the basis of his theological reform, he was early identified as a claimant to the authority of the Apostle./3/  The raison d'etre of his own mission was the

---

/1/ For a recent discussion, see A. Lindemann, Paulus im ältesten Christentum (1979) esp. 102-113.  Lindemann suggests (p. 102) that among Jewish Christians, Paul was generally rejected as an apostle.  His stature among heretical sects, especially the Ebionites and Encratites, was also far from secure: Epiph., Panar. 30.16.8; 30.25.1 (survey in ibid., 103ff.).  Further, Käsemann, 'Paulus und der Frühkatholizismus', ZTK 60 (1963), 75-95; rpt., 'Paul and Early Catholicism, NT Questions of Today (1969), 239 (on 2 Peter 3.16).

/2/ Lindemann rather underrates Bauer's thesis (Orthodoxy and Heresy, 225) that the appreciation of Paul by heretical groups was directly responsible for the decline of his prestige among the orthodox.  Cf. Paulus, 102f.; 113; and on the theological problem of Paul's reception, Lindemann, ibid., 401f.

/3/ We can assume this from the sometimes biting irony used by Marcion's opponents against his claim to represent Paul's gospel.  Irenaeus remarks (Haer. 3.13.1) that "Our Lord never came to save Paul alone, nor is God so limited in means that he should have but one apostle who knew the dispensation of his son'; it is clear that Irenaeus is here attempting to bring Paul's authority to bear against those who would lay exclusive claim to it, viz., the Marcionites.  So too Tertullian, who promises to refute Marcion from 'the apostle you claim as your own' (AM 1.15.1) and essays (AM 5.1.2) (asking who gave Paul into Marcion's charge) to dislodge Marcion from his claim by means of prophecy and the Acts of the Apostles (AM 5.1.6: 'inde te a defensione eius expello').  From the same passage, we gather that the Marcionites, perhaps Marcion himself, accused the orthodox of denying Paul's apostleship: 'nec timeo dicentem, Tu ergo negas apostolum Paulum? Non blasphemo quem tueor.  Nego, ut te probare compellam' (AM

101

belief that the church had received a gospel other than Paul's (Gal 1.6; cf. 1.23b), one teeming with the errors and misunderstandings of falsifiers,/4/ rather than the gospel announced by Paul in his letters./5/ Moreover, because he regarded the orthodox interpretation of the gospel as being, on his own terms, heretical,/6/ Marcion's effort also involved the quest for the ancient pauline gospel, which he seems to have understood as a simple proclamation of man's redemption.

These tasks entailed measures which in turn offended the orthodox bishops of Marcion's day -- not least the harkening back to a form of congregational polity which the passage of time had rendered obsolete -- but also the restitution of an archaic form of Paul's theology, and the delimitation of the 'gospel' according to criteria derived exclusively from his epistles.

No less radical than Marcion's insistence on the indivisibility of the teaching of Paul and the true gospel was his emphasis on the separation of the law and the gospel, and its theological corollary: that the Creator and the God revealed by Jesus Christ are two different gods. This, Marcion believed, was the meaning of the gospel, and this had been Paul's message to the Jews and gentiles. His orthodox opponents countered that Marcion had mutilated the epistles, just as he had the Gospel of Luke:/7/ If a wedge were driven between the old testament and new, law and gospel, and if one saw different gods presiding over each, then Christianity ceased to be a

---

5.1.6f.). Origen records in his commentary on Luke (in Luc. hom. 25) that in the belief of some Marcionites, Paul stood in heaven at the right hand of Christ, and Marcion at the left. Thus the degree to which Marcion was seen as the continuator of Paul's work is widely attested, even by his opponents.

/4/ AM 4.4.1f.; cf. Haer. 1.27.2, 4; and the discursus on the apostles, 3.5.1, which seems to envisage marcionite doctrine.

/5/ Cf. 1 Cor 15.1; Tert., Praes. 23.

/6/ Iren. Haer. 3.12.12: Marcion evidently made the claim that only his version of the gospel was authentic; this information is beneath Tertullian's argument at AM 4.3.2. Marcionite attitudes toward the orthodox gospels also seem to be envisaged in Irenaeus' complaint (Haer. 3.2.1) that the heretics accuse the scriptures 'as if they were not correct'; and cf. Justin, I Apol. 58.

/7/ Iren. Haer. 1.27.2; 3.11.7; 3.12.12; Tert. AM 5.1.9; 4.2.4.

religion of fulfillment, rooted in history and prophecy, and became, in the strictest sense, a mystery religion. /8/

It was essential to Maricon's theological reform that, whatever the loss to those who continued to need the ministrations of the law, the wedge must be driven. Christianity was not about fulfillment, but about salvation. As such, it was not based on history and prophecy, but on what in the theological idiom of another generation would be called the 'otherness' of its proclamation. For the historically-minded and scripturally-based Church of Irenaeus' day, it was sufficient to proscribe Marcionism as heresy by asserting that the heretics do not follow tradition:

> When we refer them to that tradition which originates from the apostles, [and] which is preserved by means of the successions of presbyters in the Churches, they object to tradition, saying that they themselves are wiser not merely than the presbyters, but even than the apostles, because they have discovered the unadulterated truth. For [they maintain] that the apostles intermingled the things of the law with the words of the Saviour. /9/

Tertullian writes, in a similar vein,

> If Marcion's complaint is that the apostles are held suspect of dissimulation or pretence, even to the debasing of the gospel, he is now accusing Christ, by thus accusing those whom Christ has chosen. /10/

> That which was first delivered is of the Lord and is true, whilst that is strange and false which was afterwards introduced. /11/

In defining the nature and grounds of christian truth, against the background of Marcion's claim that the gospel was a radical innovation, the author of the letters to Rome, Corinth, and Galatia could be of little use: if Paul had not driven a wedge between the covenants, he had at least provided the hammer. It remained for the orthodox author of the Pastoral Epistles to soften the blow in the interest of the argument from tradition, fixed Church order, and the parallelism of the covenants. But by this time (c. 120) Marcion's heresy had almost certainly become fully-fledged: belief in the

---

/8/ Cf. discussion in Harnack, Mission and Expansion, 31ff.

/9/ Iren. Haer. 3.2.2.

/10/ AM 4.3.4.

/11/ Praes. 31; cf. H. Dörrie, Gnomon 29 (1957), 195: 'Der Logos ist alt, weil er wahr ist'; Osborn, The Beginning of Christian Philosophy (1981), 2f.

antithesis of the covenants had gained wide currency throughout the East./12/

If the Church were to be recalled to the truth of the gospel, it was necessary to make Paul's message the focus of christian belief. This Marcion attempted to do by turning Paul's discursive defense of the gospel into a dialectical theology. The sole surviving sentence from Marcion's Antitheses gives some idea of the lines along which this dialectic was developed: 'Oh wealth of riches! Folly, power and ecstasy! seeing that there can be nothing to say about it, or to imagine about it; or to compare it to!'/13/ The correlates of this primary contradiction, that between the gospel and the law, were abstracted from Paul's letters as well: faith and works, justice and mercy, sin and salvation. Above all was the Supreme God, the Father of Jesus Christ and the Lord of the Gospel; infinitely below him in degree and attributes was the Creator of this world,/14/ whose law was death and whose justice blinded men to the truth of the gospel.

Besides these more specifically theological correlates Marcion postulated a 'pragmatic' antithesis for which the mission and intention of Paul, rather than his religious ideas, served as a basis. The thrust of this antithesis, the doctrine of true and false apostleship, put Paul in the right and made his gospel alone -- 'neither of men nor by man' -- the sole normative source for christian teaching. Conversely, it put the apostles of Jesus -- by implication, those who opposed Paul's mission and misunderstood his intention -- together with their bishop-successors in the wrong./15/ This antithesis was the warrant for the whole of Marcion's doctrine; it was for Marcionism what the tradition was for the orthodox, and stands over and against the traditio apostolica as a rationale for its development./16/ That

---

/12/ On the outreach of Marcionism in the first three centuries, cf. Harnack, Marcion, 238*ff.

/13/ Burkitt's trans., JTS (1929), 279f.; cf. S. Schäefers, Eine altsyrische antimarcionitische Erklärung von Parabeln des Herrn, usw. (1917), 3f. Harnack, Marcion, 81; 354*; Neue Studien, 17f. Cf. Rom 11.33: 'O bathos ploutou kai sophias kai gnōseōs Theou'.

/14/ Iren. Haer. 4.33.2.

/15/ Iren. Haer. 3.2.2; 3.5.1; 3.12.2: 'Sic non alium Deum nec aliam Plenitudinem adnuntiabant apostoli' (apparently v. Marcion).

/16/ Tert. accuses Marcion himself of being a false apostle by Paul's criterion: 'quia aliter evangelizavit'; he bases his argument on the priority of

there were true and false apostles was as self-evident to Marcion from Paul's letters as the recognition that there were two distinct Gods./17/

## 4.2   The 'Canonical' Reaction to Marcion's Theory: Introduction

As we have seen, the distinction between true and false apostleship is present in the letters of Paul himself, and was not superimposed on Paul's religious thought by Marcion (cf. 2 Cor 11.13). Nevertheless, Paul envisaged neither a 'tradition' of false apostleship nor an apostolic succession of right teaching. Marcion on the other hand understood the latter doctrine as evidence of a corrosive process that had begun in Paul's lifetime, and continued into his own. The medium by which the tradition is delivered is also the means by which error is perpetuated./18/

Paul himself understood 'bondage to the truth' rather than allegiance to a prior authority as the mark of true apostleship, although this way of thinking was in large part determined by his own unwillingness to submit his gospel for the approval of the Twelve./19/ But it is Paul's claim to have been faithful to the gospel of Jesus Christ that forms the nucleus of Marcion's systematic elaboration of the dualistic themes in Paul's theology./20/ Thus, while the distinction between true and false apostleship is certainly present in Paul's letters, only in Marcion's <u>Antitheses</u> does it become programmatic for distinguishing the truth of the gospel from the false accretions of the <u>pseudapostoloi</u>. This fact more than any other

---

the 'orthodox' gospel: 'et nostrum anterius [alterius] id emendans quod invenit, et id posterius quod de nostri emendatione constituens suum et novum fecit' (AM 4.4.5). The same rationale permits Ignatius to claim that the congregation at Ephesus has 'ever been of one mind with the Apostles of Jesus Christ' (11.2), making only token reference to Paul (12.2), and not as being an apostle.

/17/ Harnack argued that the Marcionites knew of 'degrees of false apostleship, though the Twelve 'nonetheless play a quite deplorable part in the corruption of the Lord's words and are thus to blame for the judaistic perversion of the Gospel' (<u>Marcion</u>, 34-37; 256*f.; 130, n. 2).

/18/ Cf. Harnack, <u>Marcion</u>, 230f.   Thus Irenaeus' treatment of the preaching of the apostles (<u>Haer</u>. 3.12.2-3, 13) is framed in distinctly anti-marcionite terms.

/19/ Gal 2.5f.; cf. AM 5.1.2f.; Iren. <u>Haer</u>. 3.13.3.

/20/ <u>Haer</u>. 3.13.1.

explains Marcion's delimitation of the corpus paulinum itself. 'Curtailing the Gospel according to Luke and the Epistles of Paul, they assert that these are alone authentic, which they have themselves thus shortened'./21/

In orthodox circles a parallel development occurred in the attempt to relativize Paul's authority vis à vis the Twelve. This development took place along two lines: (a) an appeal to the consensus fidei/22/ in terms of which the role of Paul grew increasingly derivative; (b) an appeal to the perfection of the 'original' apostolate and the closure of the gap between the message of Jesus and the teaching of the Twelve./23/ The secondary elaboration of these appeals was the doctrine of 'delivery' itself,/24/ which the author of the Epistle to Titus knows as a deposit of faith or 'sound doctrine' (didaskalia)/25/ delivered into the hands of church officers from the beginning -- that is, from the time of the apostles./26/

These lines of development are not confined to heresiological polemic, however. As Knox attempted to show in his study of Marcion's influence on the formation of the canon, the reaction to the doctrine of false apostleship is represented within the NT itself,/27/ both generally, as regards the orthodox of doctrine of canonicity,/28/ and specifically, with respect to the ecclesiastical 'history' of Luke and the expansion of the orthodox apostolikon

---

/21/ Haer. 3.12.12. Cf. 1.27.4.

/22/ Ign. Magn. 7.1; 13.1; Eph. 11.2: 'hoi kai tois apostolois pantote synēsan en dynamei Iesou Christou'. Cf. Acts 2.44f.; 4.31f.; 6.6f.

/23/ Luke 24.45, 49, 31ff.; Acts 1.4, etc.; cf. Iren. Haer. 3.12.2, 5; Tert. Praes. 23.

/24/ On this see G.L. Prestige, 'Tradition: or, The Scriptural Basis of Theology', in Fathers and Heretics (1940), 1-22, and H.E.W. Turner, The Pattern of Christian Truth (1954), passim.

/25/ Titus 2.1f.

/26/ Cf. Tert. AM 1.1.6; 4.5.1; Iren. Haer. 3.2.2f.; 3.4.1; 3.5.1, etc. And cf. Lk 1.2: 'Kathōs paredosan hēmin hoi ap archēs autoptai kai hypēretai genomenoi tou logou'; 'Ho ēn ap archēs, ho akēkoamen, ho heōrakamen tois ophthalomois hēmōn, etc.', 1 Jn 1.1; and Acts 1.2-3; 2 Ptr 3.2; 2. Clement 14.2.

/27/ Knox, Marcion and the NT, 36.

/28/ Knox, Marcion and the NT, 36; 139f.

to include non-pauline matter. As to the more general reaction: the influence of Marcion on the formation of the NT canon remains a subject for educated conjecture. That no canon would have emerged in the absence of the marcionite challenge is obviously false, since the trend in orthodox circles was in the direction of specifying the books 'appointed to be read' even before Marcion's time./29/ But that the existence of Marcion's apostolikon and evangelion forced the question early on and thus accelerated the process of canonization is scarcely to be overlooked.

Less obvious, however, is Knox's suggestion that Marcion's canon 'provided the structural principle and [became the] organizing idea of the Catholic New Testament'./30/ Knox would argue that Marcion forced the

---

/29/ W.G. Kümmel, Einleitung in das NT[17] (= Introduction, 1975), s. 35, p. 480. Harnack argues that Marcion was the first to promote the idea of a new 'Holy Scripture' as well as its divisions into two parts; though he assumed that Marcion found the four-gospel canon already in existence, on the basis of Tert.'s statement in AM 4.5.4 (cf. 4.2.2) where Tertullian implies that Marcion did not extend his 'expurgations' to the gospels of Matthew, John, and Mark: 'Itaque et de his Marcion flagitandus quod omissis eis Lucae potius institerit, etc.' Harnack thought that Johannine passages were treated in the Antitheses (Marcion, 81, 249*; cf. 40f.; 78, 79 n. 1; Neue Studien, 21f.). Von Campenhausen points out, however, that Marcion's criticisms of the four-gospel canon are 'not to be found in the tradition' (Formation, 157): 'It can no longer be determined with certainty why Marcion thought to find his original gospel behind Luke . . . That Luke was associated with Paul cannot have been a factor, since Marcion did not regard the text of his hypothetical gospel as Lucan'. The evidence seems to suggest not that the four gospels were 'already in existence [in Marcion's day] as an authoritative collection' (Marcion, 79), but rather that such a collection was still in the making (cf. Knox, Marcion and the NT, 156 n. 42). Both Kümmel and Hanson (Tradition, 188) correctly observe that it is doubtful that Marcion knew of a collection of four gospels: Marcion did not provide the occasion for the Church's formation of its canon, 'but the fact that Marcion has already established the canonical authority of Paul . . . strengthened the tendency which already existed within the Church for evaluating the apostolic writings on a level with the gospel writings' (Kümmel, Introd., 487f.). However, this evaluation cannot be shown to have existed prior to Marcion's delimitation of the corpus paulinum" and there is no reason to suppose that the Church did not simply establish the collection of thirteen letters in order to supersede Marcion's collection of ten such letters (thus, e.g., von Campenhausen, Formation, 148ff.; 184ff.; 159).

/30/ Knox, Marcion and the NT, 31. Against Kümmel's references to Justin (e.g., 1 Apol. 66.3; 67.7, Introd., s. 35, p. 486), it should be emphasized that Justin does not quote Paul, and there is no evidence that he 'envisaged a bipartite canon alongside the NT', even though he includes Mark and Luke among the 'apostolic memoirs': 'ta apomnēmoneumata tōn apostolōn ē ta syngrammata tōn prophētōn', 1 Apol. 66.3; cf. Tryph. 103.8. And see Campenhausen, Formation, 169 n. 101.

Church almost against its will to distinguish between scriptures 'old' and 'new', and while he does not blink the existence of other factors 'contributing to the creation of a distinctively Christian canon of scripture',/31/ he urges that Marcion be seen as providing the 'decisive occasion of . . . the creation of the New Testament'./32/

In appraising Knox's argument, it is essential to keep in view the theological motive behind Marcion's delimitation of christian scripture, namely, the pragmatic antithesis of true and false apostleship./33/ For Marcion, the primary confidence in the church's message had been destroyed. The true meaning and message of Jesus had been lost along the way; the ancient witness had been poisoned by 'mixing lime with the milk of God',/34/ and it was this libation that the successors of the false apostles offered to the christian faithful./35/ Accordingly, Marcion arranged his canon to emphasize the witness of the true Apostle, an arrangement which is only explicable in terms of his radical paulinism./36/ Everything hinged

---

/31/ Knox, Marcion and the NT, 161.

/32/ Knox, loc. cit.; R.M. Grant would argue that Marcion should not be credited with the idea of the NT, since we find before Marcion's time 'Christian interest in the origins of the NT books' (Historical Introduction to the NT, 28). Grant would, however, give Marcion credit for the 'inclusiveness of the canon which the Church did produce'. But Grant fails to distinguish between the intention of Papias, 'with his rather simple notion of the work of the evangelists as recorders or compilers', and that of Marcion, whose motive for delimitation became the guiding principle of the orthodox: i.e., to differentiate 'false' and 'true' scripture. Cf. further, von Campenhausen, Formation, 148ff.: idem., 'Marcion et les origines du canon neutestamentaire', RHPhR (1966), 213-66; C.F.D. Moule, The Birth of the NT (1962); and K.L. Carroll, 'The Creation of the Four-fold Gospel', BJRL, 37 (1954), 68-77.

/33/ 'The stimulus to set up the new canon did not come to Marcion from an analysis of what the uncertain state of church tradition in general might suggest or require, much less from any neutral, scientific examination of its elements, but was theologically conditioned. It followed from the conflict in which Marcion's fundamental conviction found itself with the whole christian preaching to date, and from the uncompromising determination with which he took up the fight and waged it to the end' (von Campenhausen, Formation, 149).

/34/ Papias cited in Iren. Haer. 3.17.4.

/35/ Cf. Harnack, Marcion, 37ff.; 256*f.; 130 n. 2.

/36/ Harnack, Marcion, 230ff.; von Campenhausen, Formation, 154f.

on Paul's gospel, and this too had been betrayed. It was no longer to be found in the great Church, devoted as it was to rationalizing the contradiction between law and gospel which Marcion believed lay at the heart of Paul's teaching. This point of departure marks the essential difference between Marcion's paulinism and that of his opponents. For while his opponents considered the gospel a fulfillment of scripture, Marcion saw it as fundamentally opposed to every revelation of the known God. In stressing this contradiction, Marcion threatened to deprive the church of its historical witness and to render invalid 'her proud claims to be the religion of the most ancient wisdom and the religion of historical fulfillment'./37/

## 4.3 The 'Canonical' Reaction (Cont.)

Marcion seems to have used his version of 'Luke' only as evidence for the separation of the gospel and the law./38/ It is highly doubtful that he was consciously interested in establishing a canon of scripture at all, since at no time does he appear to have attributed to his text of the gospel the high authority suggested, for example, in 2 Timothy 3.16. The editing out of offensive passages, that is to say verses that could not be reconciled with what was taken to be the 'intention' of Paul, had improved the text./39/ But such a procedure had not made the written text inerrant. It bore the internal marks of its own corruption in passages such as Luke 9.19ff. (cf. 9.40-45; 22.24), where the deficiency of the apostles is palpably evident.

Thus there is a fundamental distinction to be made between Marcion's appraisal of the gospel and that which would characterize the position of the Great Church: Marcion does not use his gospel for the purpose of replicating the words of the Lord, nor as a basis 'for reproof, doctrine, and correction'./40/ On the contrary, the gospel bears witness within itself that the

---

/37/ Von Campenhausen, Formation, 151.

/38/ Tert. AM 4.6.1 (Antitheses); cf. Harnack, Marcion, 81ff.

/39/ Cf. Haer. 3.12.12; AM 4.5.6f. The Marcionites perhaps saw themselves as 'improvers of the apostles' (i.e., the gospel) Haer. 3.1.1; cf. 3.2.1.

/40/ Cf. H. Köster, Synoptische Uberlieferung bei den apostolischen Vätern (1957), 6f. Harnack's suggestion (Marcion, 39, 306*) that 'Marcion understood this [original] gospel to have been at Paul's disposal' cannot be demonstrated, though he acknowledges (ibid., 66f.) that 'the Marcionites words of the Lord were beyond the comprehension of the original apostles, and that no teaching-consensus, let alone a teaching 'authority', had been established in their lifetime. Even the reduced or prototype-version of 'Luke' which supported this contention was not to be equated with the true evangelion, the 'gospel of Christ'/41/ which Paul had proclaimed./42/ Underlying Irenaeus' complaint that Marcion has mutilated the gospel 'which is according to Luke', is the strong suggestion that Marcion regarded even his own text of the gospel as imperfect: 'If any man set Luke aside as one who did not know the truth, he will [in so doing] manifestly reject that gospel of which he claims to be a disciple'./43/ It is true that this reduced version of Luke is in some sense the 'gospel', but it is not considered by Marcion to be self-authenticating; it does not stand apart from the Apostle/44/ but becomes a witness to the truth only as subjoined to the epistles of Paul. Thus the evangelion as written text stands in need of constant correction./45/ It is the inferior vehicle for the transmission of the truth, not, as among the orthodox, the primary vehicle. The main source of revelation is the gospel of Christ revealed only to Paul and

---

made no claim for the certainty of their text'. See further: Knox, Marcion and the NT, 19f.; Blackman, Influence, 23-7; and von Campenhausen, Formation, 163f.

/41/ Gal 1.7; Rom 15.20.

/42/ 'Kata to evangelion mou', Rom 16.25.

/43/ Iren. Haer. 3.14.3. Cf. Tert. AM 4.5.5f: 'He did correct the one he thought was corrupt'.

/44/ Cf. Tert. AM 4.5.4.

/45/ AM 4.4.5; 4.5.7; Marcion seems also to be envisaged by Irenaeus (3 Praef. 1) who speaks of improvers of the apostles; and at 3.2.1 (the heretics who allege the scriptures are incorrect and without authority). Importantly, Irenaeus knows Marcion as 'the only one who has dared openly to mutilate the scriptures' (Haer. 1.27.4), which suggests a rationale for the marcionite editorial revisions. In setting aside Luke (i.e., in denying the titulus of the gospel: Haer. 3.14.3), they have apparently made the claim that Paul alone knew the truth (Haer. 3.13.1) Irenaeus attempts to show that Luke's inseparability from Paul Haer. 3.14.1 bestows credit on Luke's gospel. So too Tertullian, who understands the denial of the titulus by the Marcionites to be an attempt to confer credit on their shortened gospel (AM 4.3.2), i.e., to show that it derives more immediately from Paul than the opponents would concede.

available only through faith, and this gospel is not to be identified with the written text. It is the gospel in this latter sense that Marcion hymns at the beginning of the Antitheses./46/ Strictly speaking, the gospel is nothing less than the act of revelation itself. In a less precise sense, the dialectic creation by Paul's witness and the narrative of Jesus' life which (as Marcion believed) corresponded most nearly to that witness mirrors this 'gospel'; and in a merely technical sense, this narrative could be called the gospel. But it could not be compared to the 'wealth of riches' and 'folly' which belong to the evangelion tou Christou, and Marcion's antithetical method was designed to ensure that the distinction remained clear./47/

Marcion obviously considered certain sayings of Jesus 'authentic' however, and there is no evidence that he attempted to account for the existence of such logia./48/ He believed that while the teaching of the apostles was wrong, the testimony to their ignorance was accurately recorded in the gospel. Scripture remained first and foremost a record which testified to the falsification of Jesus' teaching about himself -- the forfeiture of the 'wealth of riches' by unworthy pupils:

> [If] false apostles have falsified the truth of their gospels, and from them our copies are derived, what can have become of that genuine apostle's document which has suffered from adulterators -- that document which gave light to Paul and from him to Luke. Or if it has been completely destroyed, so wiped out by a flood of falsifiers . . . then not even Marcion has a true one./49/

---

/46/ Harnack, Marcion, 354; Neue Studien, 17f.; Burkitt, JTS (1929), 279f.

/47/ Harnack, Marcion, 35f.; Blackman, Influence, 42ff. But Blackman's suggestion that Marcion's choice of Luke 'was doubtless influenced by the tradition that Luke was the companion of Paul' (p. 43) cannot be accepted in light of the fact that Marcion did not know his evangelion as Luke: 'nullum adscribit auctorem', AM 4.2.3.

/48/ Tert. AM 1.2.1f.; re: Lk 6.43f.

/49/ Tert. AM 4.3.4. Von Campenhausen takes Tert. to mean that Marcion postulated the existence of an unadulterated written gospel to which Paul had had access. But this does not seem to be the thrust of Tert.'s invective. Tert. merely introduces the premise for purposes of argument. Cf. Harnack, Marcion, 39; 306*f. Tert.'s method obliges him to premise an original and unadulterated 'source' of teaching; Marcion does not seem to have envisaged such a source: From what quarter would it have come?

From this we can see that there was nothing inevitable about Marcion's division of his NT into an apostolikon and evangelion. The division was dictated by his belief that the true gospel could not be known except in conjunction with the True Apostle, and that the elevation of the letters of Paul to canonical status would prevent Christianity from reverting to 'another gospel'. The epistles serve as a criterion by which to measure the gospel./50/ This means that although there is a technical (structural) similarity between the marcionite and orthodox canon, the division of the canon into two parts was prompted in each case by different concerns, reflecting different theological motives. Marcion did not propose to establish Paul as an authority next to the gospel, as did the orthodox in appropriating his letters, but to make the gospel explicable exclusively in terms of Paul's teaching. It was Paul who had lifted the veil which had hidden the truth since the time of Moses./51/ This difference in motives and emphasis explains the preeminence of Paul in Marcion's canon, while among the orthodox, Paul took his place after the four-fold gospel and after Acts (which served as the transition) as the latter-day apostle and outrider to the gentiles.

We must therefore conclude that 'the structural principle of Marcion's canon' (Knox) is not as such the 'organizing idea of the Catholic NT', but rather the very idea which the expansion and subsequent closure of the canon by the orthodox sought to bring under control./52/ As Marcion had driven a wedge between the Old and New Testaments, so the orthodox required, if nothing so radical, at least leverage between the gospels and Paul. They

---

/50/ Harnack is probably correct that Marcion began with the epistles and thereby obtained a criterion by which to judge the gospel, cf. Marcion, 35ff.; 42f. It is important to note that the existence of a bipartite canon is not attested in the tradition prior to Marcion. See further, Kümmel, Introd., 485-494; Harnack, Die Briefsammlung des Apostels Paulus (1926); L. Mowry, 'The Early Circulation of Paul's Letters', JBL 63 (1944), 73ff.; C. H. Buck, 'The Early Order of the Pauline Corpus', JBL 68 (1949), 151ff.; K.L. Carroll, 'The Expansion of the Pauline Corpus', JBL 72 (1953), 230ff.; J. Knox, 'Acts and the Pauline Letter Corpus', in Studies in Luke-Acts: Festschr. P. Schubert (1966), 279f.; W. Schmithals, 'Zur Abfassung und ältesten Sammlung der paulinischen Hauptbriefe', ZNTW 51 (1960), 225f.; and H. Gamble, 'The Redaction of the Pauline Letters and the Formation of the Pauline Corpus', JBL 94 (1975), 403-18.

/51/ Cf. Harnack, Marcion, 308*; cf. AM 5.11.6ff.

/52/ Iren. Haer. 3.11.8: 'neque autem plura numero quam haec sunt neque rursus pauciora capit esse Evangelia'.

found this leverage in the Book of Acts./53/ It is thus preferable to think of Marcion's canon as having supplied not the structural principle but the theological stimulus for the creation of the orthodox canon./54/ But it is important to understand this stimulus in terms of the problem of true and false apostleship, to which Marcion's definition of the gospel was designed to provide a decisive answer./55/

**4.4 The 'Lucan' Reaction to Marcion's Doctrine of False Apostleship**

Marcion's theory of false apostleship finds specific refutation in the NT as well, both in the expanded edition of his gospel ('Luke'), and in the work by the same writer which has come down in the tradition as the Acts of the Apostles./56/ In these works, Marcion's theory is countered by a correction

---

/53/ E.G., AM 5.1.6: 'Certe acta apostolorum hunc mihi ordinem Pauli tradiderunt'; Praes. 23.

/54/ Cf. von Campenhausen's appraisal, Formation, 149.

/55/ See Blackman, Influence, 34-5: though Blackman finds it 'not altogether fortunate that it was pressure from heretics which accelerated and conditioned the delimiting of the Church's canon', and acknowledges that 'if some of the books (e.g., the Apocalypse) could have had a longer trial, the contents of the NT would have been slightly different. Cf. Harnack, Die Entstehung des Neuen Testaments und die wichtigsten Folgen der neuen Schöpfung (1914/1925), 22 n. 3: 'The NT was not composed as a weapon of attack, but of defense.'

/56/ Knox is correct in stating that 'there is virtually no evidence for the existence of Acts prior to 150' (Marcion and the NT, 139), which leads him to regard the work as 'an early apologetic response to Marcionism'. Kümmel on the other hand finds the apologetic element in Acts 'secondary but not unimportant' (Introd., 163), dating it somewhere in the 90's of the first century (p. 186); thus also, Fuller, Goodspeed, Marxsen, and Vötgle. The attempts to date the works before the death of Paul (c. 70) are now generally regarded as untenable (but cf. P. Parker, 'The Former Treatise and the Date of Acts', JBL 84 (1965), 52f.; O. Michel, Calwer Bibellexikon [1959³], 71f.). G. Klein, Die Zwölf Aposteln(1961), 115; idem., ZNTW 62 (1971), 42ff. J.C. O'Neill, The Theology of Acts in its Historical Setting (1961/1970), 42, argues (against the idea that Justin used Lk) that Luke used Justin's special source. (v. O'Neill, cf. H.F.D. Sparks, JTS 14 [1963], 457f.). The argument against late dating on the basis of the assumption that the author did not know the letters of Paul is not persuasive, since it fails to responses to the Marcionite over-valuation of Paul's apostolate. On this, see M.S. Enslin, 'Once Again, Luke and Paul', ZNTW 61 (1970), 253-71.
    E. Haenchen rejects the idea that 1 Clement (e.g., 5.4 v. Acts 1.25; 1 Clem. 2.2 v. Acts 2.17; 1 Clem. 18.1 v. Acts 13.22) makes use of Acts, and finds attempts to locate echoes of Luke's work in Ignatius of Antioch

of the apostolic witness read back into the life of Jesus himself, and certified by the gift of the Holy Spirit in Acts 2.1ff. The post-resurrection appearances of Jesus and the further teaching-activity associated with these appearances respond, on this reckoning, to Marcion's belief that the earliest disciples of Jesus had misunderstood his message and the revelation granted to them./57/ This conclusion rests on the following considerations:

(A) In the final chapter of Luke (24.33), the risen Lord appears to the Eleven in Jerusalem, the center of apostolic activity. Both Paul and Marcion reject the primacy of this original apostolate. In the same chapter of the gospel, Luke asserts (24.44) a recapitulation of the Lord's teaching *('Eipen de pros autous, houtoi hoi logoi mou hous elalēsa pros hymas eti ōn syn hymin')*, which effectively mitigates another stratum of passages averring the disbelief and misunderstanding of the apostles (8.9; 8.25; 9.19ff.; 9.40; 22.24, 34; 9.45-6; 24.25). While the recapitulation is

---

(e.g., Magn. 5.1 v. Acts 1.25), 2 Timothy (e.g., 3.11 v. Acts 13.50; 14.5, 19); Ep. of Barnabas (e.g., 5.9 v. Acts 1.2; and 7.2 v. Acts 10.42) unconvincing (Acts of the Apostles, 4-6). On the other hand, Haenchen concludes that Polycarp of Smyrna, while he did not use Acts as a source, 'worked with a stock of formulae held largely in common' (e.g., Phil. 2.3 v. Acts 20.35; Phil. 12.2 v. Acts 2.5; 4.12, etc.). On the basis of his examination of the evidence, Haenchen concludes that 'not until Justin Martyr (c. 150-160: Harnack vs. C. Andresen, RGG[3], III, 891 [CE 180! ]), can a knowledge and use of Luke's two works be established' (1 Apol. 50.12 v. Luke 23.29a; 24.25; Acts 1.8; 2 Apol. 10.6 v. Acts 17.23). Haenchen asserts also that 'until the middle of the second century, Acts was not yet considered an authoritative book to which one might appeal' (p. 9), and was only admitted to the canon a generation after Justin because it proved immediately useful in the struggle with gnosticism: 'From it one could prove the unity of the apostolic message'. See further, M. Dibelius, Aufsätze zur Apostelgeschichte, ed. H. Greeven (1951), 127ff. (= ET, Studies in the Acts of the Apostles [1956], 147f.). Harnack concluded that 'so far as we know, Acts was hidden in obscurity up to the time of Irenaeus -- even taking into account the writings of Justin and the gnostics' (TLZ 53 [1928], 126).

Preliminary mention is made here of S.G. Wilson's challenging thesis that 'the author of Luks-Acts also wrote the Pastoral Epistles' (Luke and the Pastoral Epistles [1979], 1f.). Wilson's study is intended to supplement and correct the previous attempts to attribute the Pastoral Epistles to Luke: See C.F.D. Moule, 'The Problem of the Pastoral Epistles: A Reappraisal', BJRL 47 (1965), 430-52; A. Stroebel, 'Schreiben des Lukas? Zum sprachlichen Problem der Pastoralbriefe', NTS 15 (1969), 191-210; and cf. N. Brox, 'Lukas als Verfasser der Pastoralbriefe?', JAC 13 (1970), 62-77. Unfortunately, neither Wilson's nor any of the earlier studies solves the problem presumed to exist, largely because the companion-tradition is adduced as proof of an early date for this expanded Lucan corpus. See further, ch. 9.

/57/ AM 4.3.2ff.; cf. Iren. Haer. 3.5.1 (assuming Marcion among those Irenaeus envisages).

unparalleled in the other Synoptics, the more primitive stratum concerning the ignorance of the apostles is perhaps present in Luke's source (Mk 4.10f.; 4.40; 8.29; 9.18; 14.29ff; 9.32ff.)./58/

(B) In the Book of Acts, the title 'apostle' is denied to Paul and there is an attempt (which need not be ascribed to the author's unfamiliarity with Paul's letters) to bring Paul's mission and teaching into line with the consensus fidei originating on Pentecost. (Acts 2.3, cf. 2.42, 46; 15.4, 23 [!] v. 2 Cor 3.1ff.). These considerations will be taken up here in sequence.

(A) Polemical Features in the Third Gospel:

The centerpiece of Marcion's gospel is Luke 6.43, which he interpreted allegorically to refer to the two gods and the consequent separation of the covenants./59/ In this logion, culminating in the warning at 6.49, Marcion found the definitive expression of Jesus' verdict on the law together with his judgment concerning the blindness of the apostles./60/ Further instances of false apostleship were highlighted in Lk 8.9; 9.40; 22.24, with Peter's 'confession' (9.20) forming the paradigm for the misunderstanding of the apostles./61/ A passage in the Haer. of Irenaeus indicates the severity of Marcion's attack on the apostolic teaching: 'To allege that these men did not know the truth is to act the part of false witnesses, and of those who have been alienated from the doctrine of Christ. For why did the Lord send the twelve apostles to the lost sheep of the house of Israel, if these men did not know the truth?'/62/

We may assume therefore that Marcion's was an attack on apostolic authority ab origine: that is, a specific indictment of the reception of the gospel by the Twelve which went to the heart of orthodox arguments in favor of a primitive consensus fidei./63/

---

/58/ Cf. T. Schramm, Der Markusstoff bei Lukas (1971), 70ff.

/59/ AM 1.2.1. Cf. 4.1.1; 4.6.1f.

/60/ Lk 6.39: 'Mēti dynatai typhlos typhlon hodēgein?'; v. AM 4.17.11 (Marcion's denial of judgment).

/61/ AM 4.22.6; 4.34.,6. Tertullian defends Peter's confession from prophecy, which Marcion of course rejected.

/62/ Iren. Haer. 3.13.2; cf. Tert. AM 4.3.4f.

/63/ AM 4.5.7; cf. Harnack, Marcion, 37f.; 256*f. Tert. Praes. 25;21.

In the last chapter of Luke's gospel, however, which Marcion seems to have used in conjunction with Phil 2.7 as a foundation for his docetic christology,/64/ a number of passages occur which affect to alter the picture of the unapprehending apostles given shape in chs. 4-9 of the gospel. There the risen Jesus appears to the Eleven, assembled in Jerusalem, and 'reiterates' his teaching: *'Houtoi hoi logoi mou hous elalēsa pros hymas eti ōn syn hymin'* (Lk 24.44a)./65/ Following this he 'opens their understanding' (*'diēnoixen autōn ton noun'* 24.45; cf. 24.32, *'diēnoigen hēmin tas graphas'*) 'that they might understand the scriptures' (cf. 24.25); and finally, he commands them to remain in Jerusalem until they are 'endowed with power from on high' (*'heōs hou endysēsthe ex hypsous dynamin'*: 24.49).

What use Marcion made of this chapter is difficult to ascertain on the basis of the remaining evidence. On the one hand, we can be sure that he would have rejected any suggestion of a post-resurrection 'enlightenment' of the apostles, particularly since such an idea would undermine the foundation of his religious theory, viz., the unreliability of the apostolic witness. Nor is it likely that the implication of Luke's resurrection-narrative would have escaped his notice: that even if the apostles had misunderstood the meaning of the Lord's words during his lifetime, they had nonetheless been certified by the risen Lord to preach the gospel with clear understanding. In short, in accepting 'Luke's' resurrection-narrative, Marcion would have been obliged to accept the theory that their misperceptions had been cleared away in the Easter-experience and that by the ongoing intervention of the power promised them on this occasion (Lk 24.48) they were protected against misunderstanding and error.

We have no direct word from Tertullian to suggest that Marcion accepted these verses; rather we find the remarkable claim that 'Marcion, on purpose, I believe, has abstained from crossing out of his gospel certain matters opposed to him, hoping that in view of those which he might have crossed out and has not, he may be thought not to have crossed out those which he has crossed out, or even to have crossed them out with good reason'./66/ We have no way of judging whether this imputation of motive corresponds to Marcion's exegetical principles. But there is good reason to

---

/64/ AM 4.43.6.

/65/ Iren. <u>Haer</u>. 3.12.15; cf. 3.13.2.

/66/ AM 4.43.7.

think that the only basis for Tertullian's charge is his wish to explain the existence of passages in Marcion's evangelion which seem to support an 'orthodox' christology. Moreover, Tertullian takes it for granted that Marcion's gospel corresponded in every detail to his own version of Luke, or more precisely, that Marcion had subtracted his gospel from one of those 'belonging to the church'.

What passages Marcion 'deleted' cannot be determined in the absence of knowledge about the text of his gospel; nor is it always possible to know whether a passage cited by way of refutation belonged to Marcion's text, or only occurred in that of his opponent./67/ Thus, assertions concerning what survived or what perished under Marcion's knife must be weighed against the possibility that Marcion's gospel lacked a critical verse, or that the heresiologists possessed only second-hand knowledge of his text (cf. below, pp. 232f.). Consequently, neither Tertullian's baroque explanation of Marcion's methods, nor more modern interpretations -- e.g., that Marcion was inconsistent in his editing -- help us to understand the anomalies in Marcion's gospel. There is a risk in accepting either argument, ancient or modern, since both lead to the same conclusion: viz., that Marcion must have left untouched a large number of passages which occurred in his version of Luke's gospel, even though they contradicted his teaching;/68/ and, even more improbably, that what is not specified by his opponents as having been deleted must therefore have remained. For this latter notion, the charge that Marcion 'mutilated' the gospel is too inspecific to allow us to determine what he may have omitted; but the thrust of the charge seems to point away from the idea of 'inconsistent' editing, which Harnack presupposed, and which permitted him to reconstruct Marcion's evangelion virtually verse by verse. The notion of 'inconsistent editing', moreover, begins from the premise that Marcion found canonical Luke largely in the form in which it was known to his opponents; in short, it depends on widegoing agreement with the patristic allegations that Marcion made random alterations in the ('orthodox') text in accordance with his own theological principles. It is

---

/67/ Cf. on this question H. von Soden's review of Harnack, ZKG 40 (1922), 204; cf. E. Muehlenberg, 'Marcion's Jealous God', who challenges Harnack's working principles: 'We are not furnished with a list of omissions, so that the argumentum e silentio cannot be admitted' (in Disciplina Nostra, ed. D. Winslow [Philadelphia, 1979], 98).

/68/ Cf. B. Aland, 'Marcion: Versuch einer neuen Interpretation', ZTK 70 (1973), 420f.

highly unlikely that the patristic viewpoint governing the reconstruction of Marcion's evangelion carries us very far in the direction of answering the central question, What did Marcion's gospel look like?

Rhetorician that he is, Tertullian is anxious to seize on the slightest eccentricity in Marcion's use of scripture. Such is the case, for example, with his discussion of Luke 24. If consistency were a guide, then one would suppose that Luke 24.11, or alternatively 24.26, marked the end of Marcion's evangelion. The references to the ultimate faithlessness of the apostles ('Kai ephanēsan enōpion autōn hōsei lēros ta hrēmata tauta, kai ēpistoun autais': 24.11) reinforce dramatically the controlling theme of false apostleship that Marcion saw at the center of the gospel. Beginning with the Emmaus-narrative (24.13-53; viz., 24.27), a number of aporiai appear, i.e., verses which mitigate the previous references in the gospel to the apostles' lack of understanding. The first of these comes at 24.27, in which Jesus is given to expound from scripture 'all the things concerning himself' from Moses onwards ('Kai arxamenos apo Mōyseōs kai apo pantōn tōn prophētōn. . .'). This is repeated and elaborated in the Jerusalem-section of the narrative (24.44), where the words of the Lord are treated specifically as a recapitulation of his earthly teaching: 'Houtoi hoi logoi mou hous elalēsa pros hymas eti ōn syn hymin'./69/ The sense of this passage is that the teaching of Jesus, having been fulfilled in accordance with 'the law of Moses and the prophets' is identical in substance with his previous teaching, though the perfection of the apostles (that is, their knowledge of this fulfillment) can date only from the resurrection. Following the recapitulation itself, we find the words, 'tote diēnoixen autōn ton noun tou synienai tas graphas'. This opening of the understanding is adumbrated in the Emmaus-narrative: 'autōn de diēnoichthēsan hoi ophthalmoi' (24.31a) and reiterated with respect to the comprehension of the scriptures by the Twelve: 'diēnoigen hēmin tas graphas' (24.32b). In similar language, the verse which may have formed the narrative climax of Marcion's gospel (24.11) is offset by declarations that the apostles' eyes had been opened up (diēnoichthēsan: cf. 24.16, 'Hoi de ophthalmoi autōn ekratounto . . .').

The thrust of these passages, in line with the general purpose of the gospel itself, is 'to arouse full confidence in the content of christian

---

/69/ Lk 24.44a.

teaching'./70/ The resurrection-narrative is hence the denouement of a narrative problem, created by the apostles' lack of understanding. This theme Luke found in his source and has taken pains to layer over in the course of an 'eyewitness' account: a history 'based on perfect understanding' of the things 'delivered from the beginning' ('paredosan hēmin hoi ap archēs') for the purpose of knowing the 'reliability of the words used for instruction'. The eyewitness is certified by the logion recorded in the resurrection-narrative at 24.48 ('Hymeis martyres toutōn'), and recalled in the first chapter of Acts (1.2-3), where Jesus is said to have given 'infallible proofs' to the apostles after his resurrection.

The recapitulation of the Lord's teaching is put forward by Luke as one such 'proof'. By it the teaching of the apostles who had heard the news of the resurrection 'as it were an idle tale' (24.11) is perfected and legitimated. For Luke this legitimation involves a 'linking' of the historical and post-resurrection experience of the disciples. That is to say, the 'opening of the scriptures' is considered to be possible because the Twelve were 'eyewitnesses from the beginning' (24.32b/24.45f.). Hence, the resurrection brings not a new revelation but a new understanding.

The Lucan theme of recapitulation counteracts the tradition, still obvious in Luke's source, and doubtless also in Marcion's, that the apostles had not believed in the resurrection, even when confronted by the risen Lord: 'kai epistoun autais' (24.11). Luke therefore adds to his source a second variety of proof, which involves an alternation of the spiritual view of the resurrection found in the early part of the chapter. These anti-docetic passages (24.30, 37, 39-43) advance the linking-process which connects the teaching of the earthly Jesus and the revealer who 'stands among them in Jerusalem' (24.30/22.14f.) such that after the resurrection, Jesus is pictured as having merely resumed the table-fellowship and instruction that characterized his former relation with his disciples. But beyond this, Luke strives to underscore the reality of the risen Lord and to overcome the 'docetic supposition' recorded in 24.37. Accordingly Jesus

---

/70/ Kümmel, Introd., 129; Haenchen, Acts of the Apostles, 91f. Haenchen disputes Klein's view (Zeit und Gesch., Dankesgabe an Rudolf Bultmann zum 80. Geburtstag [1964], 193ff.) that 'Luke had to rescue Paul from gnosticism': It would be wrong maintains Haenchen 'to attempt to ascribe to Luke a consciously manipulated method' (p. 127). Klein's view has also been challenged by M. Hengel (Acts and the History of Earliest Christianity [ET, 1979], 60): 'Luke's historiography has precious little to do with cheap apologetic'.

assuages fear by inviting the apostles to touch him, and then, to leave no doubt in their minds, proceeds to 'eat a broiled fish and a honey-comb . . . before them' (24.42-3; cf. Jn 21.13).

What use, if any, did Marcion make of the offending sections of the resurrection-narrative employed by Luke? In order to answer this question, we must refer back to Tertullian's proposition that 'Marcion abstained from crossing out of his gospel certain matters opposed to him'./71/ It is significant that Tertullian makes this assertion in specific reference to passages designed to establish the perfection of the original apostles. We cannot assume from what Tertullian says, however, that Marcion contrived to accept the whole of the chapter. It is true that Tertullian gives the impression that Marcion excised very little; but he may merely be expressing a rhetorician's delight in observing that Marcion had failed to omit certain passages which for the sake of his theology he ought to have omitted. That Marcion was deliberately inconsistent in his editing is hardly a satisfying explanation, and hardly permits us to decide the contents of his text: The major portion of the Lucan resurrection-narrative following 24.11, and nearly every verse following 24.26, is not merely uncogenial but positively antipathetic to Marcion's christology. We have thus to weigh Tertullian's claim against the certainty that for Marcion to have left such material as he found it would have undermined the very basis of his theological system: the doctrine of false apostleship.

A close reading of Tertullian's critique offers another explanation. It seems probable that Marcion retained (or knew) only three contiguous verses following 24.26, namely 24.39-41. But he did not accept these verses (if he knew them as such) in the Lucan redaction. Tertullian points to these verses as evidence that Marcion's gospel 'proved' the verity of Christ's body/72/ in spite of Marcion's professed denial of the physical resurrection of Jesus. Tertullian's statement has prompted generations of scholars to conclude that Marcion's docetism must have been of a very moderate variety. But this conclusion depends on our taking Tertullian's point other than in the ironic sense in which it is intended: the thrust of his argument is that Marcion had purposely declined to cross out of his gospel 'matters opposed to him'. Yet one is obliged to wonder why Marcion saw fit to leave intact verses under-

---

/71/ AM 4.43.7.

/72/ AM 4.43.6.

stood by Tertullian to contradict the 'phantasmic Christ', when he might just as well have omitted them, and been none the worse from the standpoint of Tertullian's expectations. Insofar as it is possible to reconstruct Marcion's intention from Tertullian's argument, the reason for the 'survival' of 24.39-41a seems to have had nothing to do with Marcion's christological theory. But as a statement of Jesus' final revelation to the apostles in Jerusalem, Marcion could scarcely have ignored or deleted the verse: 'Videte manus meas et pedes, quia ego ipse sum; palpate et videte, quia spiritus carnem et ossa non habet, sicut me videtis habere'./73/

Despite Tertullian's depreciation of Marcion's motives, it is equally clear from what he says that Marcion did not understand this passage as a contradiction of the spiritual resurrection, or as proving that the apostles had been moved from disbelief to belief by a post-resurrection 'correction' of their witness:

> He will have it that the words 'spirit hath not bones as ye see me having' were so spoken as to be referred to the spirit, 'as ye see me having' meaning not having bones, even as a spirit has not./74/

That Marcion permitted the passage to stand can thus be explained by the reckoning that in marcionite interpretation the passage was construed docetically, bearing implications for the doctrine of false apostleship as well. The risen Jesus is no other than the Christ who 'came down into Caphernaum in the fifteenth year of the principate of Tiberius',/75/ and whose identity the apostles consistently got wrong. His final appearance in Jerusalem -- the sedes pseudapostolorum -- is, as it were, yet another case of mistaken identity. Thus, the second of the passages following 24.26 which Marcion, on Tertullian's testimony, is known to have let stand: 'Incredulitas disciplorum perseverabat' (cf. AM 4.43.3 v. Lk 24.41: 'Eti de apistountōn autōn'; cf. 24.11). Marcion eliminated the psychological explanation for this persistence of the apostles' faithlessness.

Moreover, this reading of the evidence regarding Marcion's interpretation of 24.39-41a comports with the fact that he is known to have emphasized Jesus' rebuke of the disciples at 24.25: 'Plane invectus est in illos: O insensati et tardi corde in non credendo omnibus quae locutus est ad

---

/73/ Vulg.; cf. AM 4.43.6.

/74/ AM 4.43.7.

/75/ AM 4.7.1.

vos'./76/ Marcion, it would appear, knew nothing of a reading of this verse which referred to the teaching of the prophets as the object of the apostles' misunderstanding; and since Tertullian does not combat him by challenging his text, it seems certain that Tertullian's gospel also lacked the reference. In any case, it is the teaching of the oracles of Jesus that have been misconstrued: 'Oh fools and slow of heart in not believing everything that has been spoken to you'./77/ Tertullian explains that Jesus rebuked his disciples for being offended by his passion ('ut de sola passione scandalizantos') and for being 'doubtful in the faith of the resurrection reported to them by the women' ('ut dubios de fide resurrectionis'). Marcion, we may assume, interpreted this admonition as Jesus' final -- or penultimate -- verdict on the faithlessness of the Twelve: Judas was merely the most irrepressible of the group.

To this we may add the verses already discussed concerning the Jerusalem appearance to the Eleven, which serve to reinforce the pattern of revelation/rejection that characterized Marcion's gospel throughout. The 'minor revelation' at Emmaus parallels the major revelation at Jerusalem in terms of its outcome; both refer back to the annunciatio at 24.11. On all three occasions the disciples of the Lord are challenged to accept Jesus as the revealer of the True God; in every case they fail to understand the significance of the revelation (cf. 9.20; 9.32f.). Marcion would have had no difficulty in accepting these verses, since they supplied further evidence of a pattern of false apostleship that extended from the beginning of Jesus' ministry until after the crucifixion.

In the last chapter of Luke's gospel, this pattern of faithlessness is obscured by the proclamation that after the resurrection, the apostles were perfected in the gospel by the risen Lord (24.27, 32, 44); but in Marcion's source, the pattern would have been clearly visible:

1. On being told the news of Jesus' resurrection from the dead by the women, the apostles respond with disbelief: *'Kai ephanēsan enōpion autōn hōsei lēros ta hrēmata tauta'* (24.11).

---

/76/ Vulg.: 'O stulti et tardi corde ad credendum in omnibus, quae locuti sunt prophetae'; cf. AM 4.43.4 v. *'O anoētoi kai bradeis tē kardia tou pisteuein epi pasin hois elalēsan hoi prophētai'*, Lk 24.25 (!). Cf. Note in Aland, et al., Greek NT, 316.

/77/ Cf. Evans' translation, Tertullian: Adversus Marcionem, 505.

2. [Assuming Marcion's acceptance of vss. 12-25 of the Emmaus-narrative]:   Disciples of Jesus, having already heard news of the resurrection (v. 21), fail to recognize the risen Lord as he walks beside them; in addition, they betray the magnitude of their false expectations ('Hēmeis de elpizomen hoti autos estin ho mellōn lytrousthai ton Israēl') and invite Jesus' rebuke (v. 25, omitting any reference to the prophets).

3. Apostles of Jesus gathered in Jerusalem are 'terrified and affrighted' at the appearance of the risen Lord, 'supposing they had seen a spirit' (v. 37). Jesus again reveals himself as the Son of the True God, and invites the apostles to witness the marks of his passion.   Thereafter, the apostles persist in their disbelief (v. 41a, omitting *apo tēs charas kai thaumazontōn'*).   At this point, Jesus vanishes from their sight (v. 31b, *'kai autos aphantos egeneto ap autōn'*) and only reveals himself beyond this to the True Apostle on the road to Damascus.

The silence of the fathers restricts what we can say beyond this about Marcion's use of this chapter.  It is likely that he rejected no verse which could be adduced in favor of his doctrine of false apostleship; and it is probable that these verses stood in bold relief in his source.  Tertullian does not take up any of the verses dealing with the post-resurrection enlightenment of the apostles.  But he does imply that Marcion 'deleted' these from Luke:  'Even after his resurrection . . .[Jesus] did not show them that he was any different from him they said they thought him to be' (AM 4.43.4). But in rejecting the uniformity of Jesus' teaching before and after the resurrection and asserting the faithlessness of the apostles, Marcion 'shows Jesus an author of error and a renegade from the truth' since 'he would not have tolerated this assumption about himself'.  Thus by implication Marcion is accused of rejecting the post-resurrection enlightenment of the Twelve.

As to the Emmaus-section of the narrative, it seems likely that Marcion accepted vss. 13-25, and almost certain that he accepted the climax of verse 25, as well as the false identification made by the disciples in v. 21 ('Nos autem putabamus . . . ipsum esse redemptorem Israelis'). The dramatic irony of the scene -- the glorified saviour walking unknown among the mourners -- can scarcely have failed to commend itself to Marcion, though the reason for its inclusion may well have been to supply a 'middle term' in the triple denial constituted by vss. 11, 25 and 41.  Here the revealer of the unknown God, himself unknown, is mistaken for a prophet 'mighty in deed and word'; his death is assumed to be a verdict on his mission (v. 21), as the 'one to redeem Israel'.  Jesus' castigation of these errors (v. 25) was a fitting judgment on the faithlessness of his own followers, and Marcion doubtless turned the scene to catechetical advantage in his effort to show that the unknown God remained unknown among the 'children of wrath',/78/ and that Christ had come to redeem all nations.

Marcion's use and interpretation of the resurrection-narrative was therefore consistent with his theological motives. We have no reason to suppose that Marcion knew of any tradition that proclaimed a belated 'correction' of the apolostic witness. The passages recorded by Tertullian relate chiefly to the errors of the apostles and the attempts of the risen Lord to convince them of the 'verity of the flesh'. Beyond this, we have Tertullian's statement to the effect that Marcion is 'sparing to statements which he proceeds to overturn by false interpretation as well as by deletion'./79/ But coming just after the suggestion that 'Marcion abstained from crossing out of his gospel certain matters opposed to him', in reference to 24.39f., the remark would seem to mean that Marcion rejected most of what did not comport with his doctrine of false apostleship in conjunction with his denial of the physical resurrection, with the exception of v. 39. This verse can be taken as the penultimate one in Marcion's resurrection-account. The final verse, on this reckoning, would have been a conflation of vss. 41 and 31, thus: 'Adhuc autem illis non credentibus [et] ipse evanuit ex oculis eorum'. In short, in arguing that Marcion has left v. 39 intact, or virtually so, Tertullian is not commenting on a general feature of marcionite exegesis. Rather, he is expressing surprise that Marcion has left untouched a passage potentially damaging to his docetic beliefs./80/

Marcion's doctrine of false apostleship would have prevented him from accepting any verse in Luke's gospel beyond 24.26, with the single exception of vss. 38-41a (revised) at the conclusion. Such an interpretation is consistent with the evidence supplied by Tertullian.

(B) Polemical Features in the Acts of the Apostles:

In the first chapter of Acts, Luke strives to heighten the confidence in

---

/78/ Harnack suggests as much: Marcion, 220*f., n. 25.

/79/ AM 4.43.7.

/80/ Moreover, it is all but certain that Marcion's text lacked the antidocetic vv., 24.30, 35, 40, 42-3. Cf. AM 4.43.6: 'De corporis autem veritate quid potest clarius?'

the apostolic witness still further. As a sequel to the eyewitness report begun with Lk 1.1, the work is designed to foster 'certainty' by means of 'many infallible proofs', not only in the Lord's resurrection, but, more directly, in the apostolic preaching. The period of post-resurrection instruction ('recapitulation') is specified as forty days, after which time (cf. Lk 4.2) the teaching continues under the aegis of the Holy Spirit in the absence of the risen Lord. The apostles are shown to compensate for the deficiency in their ranks by the election of Matthias (v. 26), thereby restoring the ideal number of Twelve. Finally, after having reached a magisterial accord (2.1), they are endowed with the power (dynamis) promised them by Jesus (2.4; 1.8; Lk 24.49b), and begin to teach a common doctrine (2.42; 'didache tōn apostolōn').

As Haenchen has commented, Acts is Luke's way of making the apostles' authority plain to the reader: Jesus chose them through the Spirit, and commissioned them before his departure./81/ For Luke, only the Twelve are apostles, and they alone represent the original ecclesia, centered on Jerusalem (cf. 1.4; Lk 24.47b, 49b), the site of the original apostolic witness to the resurrection, as well as the place where the consensus fidei had been arrived at, under the tutelage of Jesus himself./82/

Although one cannot establish conclusively that the unequivocal intention of Luke's work -- to invite confidence in the apostolic preaching -- is a specifically anti-marcionite intention, that appraisal cannot be ruled out in principle. The dangers of circular reasoning are evident here as elsewhere in the study of Maricon: On the one hand, we are obliged to begin with the fully-fledged Lucan narrative from which, according to his opponents, Marcion subtracted his gospel. On the other, the predilections of writers like Irenaeus and Tertullian led them to conclude without investigation that their fuller gospel had undergone heretical alteration. That their Catholic text was an expansion of a source known both to Luke and to Marcion was not an idea they could have seriously entertained. Given only these two certainties, together with the fact that Marcion was reckoned to have 'excluded' Acts from his canon,/83/ it is not impossible to postulate the existence of a 'proto-Luke' (Streeter) to which

---

/81/ Haenchen, Acts, 139.

/82/ Haenchen, Acts, 124f.; 139, n. 3.

/83/ AM 5.2.7.

Marcion had access and of which the expanded 'Catholic' Luke, together with its sequel Acts, was in part an apologetic response to Marcionism. Such is Knox's appraisal: 'The author of Luke-Acts', he argues, 'sought to reclaim both a gospel and Paul from the Marcionites'./84/ It was not Marcion who abridged, but the Church which expanded the gospel and, in the writing of Acts, redefined the position of Paul vis à vis the Twelve.

This emphasis on the apologetic aim of Luke-Acts, if not without difficulties, points the way to understanding the highly complex relationship between Marcionism and Catholicism in the second century of the Church's existence. For example, the 'apologetic' aspects of the resurrection-narrative in Luke's gospel are more easily explained if it is assumed that Luke knew of Marcion's attack on the apostolic preaching and the physical resurrection. So too, the curious picture of Paul that emerges from Luke's 'history' becomes explicable if we suppose that Luke knew of Marcion's attempt to limit the apostolate to Paul, and to denigrate the Twelve.

With regard to the Book of Acts in particular, however, Knox's theory presents difficulties. For while it is the case that the picture of Paul in Acts does not comport with that given in the epistles, one can scarcely say that Paul plays an insignificant part in Luke's work. Were Luke aware of Marcion's particular brand of paulinism, is this the strategy he would have employed to overcome it? Would not a different and more 'subordinationist' argument have been appropriate? Here we must ask whether the attempt to set Paul's mission alongside that of the Twelve in a way that Paul himself may have found objectionable, but which otherwise does no injury to his prestige, betrays an apologetic intention on Luke's part which can be construed as a response to Marcion's radical paulinism.

Haenchen denies emphatically that it was Luke's intention to subordinate Paul to the Twelve: 'On the contrary, Luke hopes to accredit him by having Paul show himself in Jerusalem . . . . He incorporates Paul into the recognized hierarchy of the Church, though not indeed among the Twelve, whose number is complete and admits of no thirteenth. Yet arm in arm with them Paul publicly appears, and this is tantamount to an official endorsement of his mission before it has properly begun'./85/ Yet the line

---

/84/ Marcion and the NT, 139; Blackman, Influence, 39.

/85/ Haenchen, Acts, 336; so too Kümmel, Introd., 182; Hengel, Early Christianity, 66f. (!); C. Burchard, Der dreizehnte Zeuge. Traditions-und kompositionsegeschichtliche Untersuchungen zu Lukas Darstellung der

between 'accreditation' and 'subordination' as drawn here is too fine to be visible. A thoroughgoing denigration of Paul's apostolate would have flown in the face of the evidence of the epistles/86/ and his reputation in the Asian churches: as a 'strategy', denigration was precluded. Moreover if Luke did envision Marcion's teaching in the making of Acts, he could have achieved nothing by laying claim to a hypothetical apostle who had announced his own inferiority to the Twelve! Thus, for the orthodox, everything hinged on putting Paul's claim in context, on the premise that Marcion's error was not in thinking of Paul as an apostle (albeit Luke withholds the title) but in thinking of him as the only apostle.

The character of Marcion's threat required the orthodox to wage a defense on two fronts: on the one, it was necessary to define the limits of Paul's apostolate; and on the other, to demonstrate the unity and integrity of the original apostolic witness as a basis for the (ongoing) rule of faith and the authority of bishops. Stripping Paul of apostolic rank would scarcely have been the appropriate response to the marcionite challenge, nor is such an enterprise Luke's primary aim in Acts.

The nature of the Lucan apologetic in Acts must be evaluated in the light of these two foci: the denigration of the original apostolate, and the elevation of Paul. Moreover, if it is assumed that Luke's apologetic intention consisted in both the wish to vindicate the original apostolic witness, as well as to 'reclaim Paul from the Marcionites' (Knox), it then seems reasonable to conclude that Luke's 'paulinism', which is ordinarily explained in terms of his unfamiliarity with the pauline correspondence, is rather to be explained by this intention. That is to say, whatever his acquaintance with the Paul of the epistles, he knew this to be Paulus Marcionis; and any response to Marcionism, as being an exaggeration of the pauline apostolate, would necessarily have resulted in a modification of Paul's claims as well. The theory that Luke had little or no knowledge of

---

Frühzeit des Paulus (1970), 174. (Not to quibble with Haenchen's use of the phrase 'recognized hierarchy').

/86/ G. Klein, ZKG (1960), 371, suggests that Luke knows the pauline epistles but owing to Paul's reputation in orthodox circles, cannot use them. Regarding the solitary attribution of the title 'apostle' to Paul at Acts 14.4, Klein writes (Die Zwölf Apostel [1961], 212): '[This use can only be explained] as a part of that mimicry under cover of which he accomplished the portentous modification of the traditional conception of the Apostle . . . . Luke accepts with the greatest composure (or should one say, the greatest cunning?) serious flaws in the objectivity of his presentation, so long as his primary intention remain undisturbed'.

Paul's epistles explains the discrepancy between the 'Lucan Paul' and the Paul of the church-letters only if it is presupposed that Luke's chief purpose in Acts was to offer an independent witness to the mission of a teacher, the main evidence for whose significance he had somehow managed to ignore. To put the matter another way, outside the evidence of the pauline correspondence, where Paul's claim to be an apostle is advanced, there is no warrant for assigning Paul even so significant a role as does Luke in Acts, which must lead us to wonder why, if Luke is unaware of Paul's arguments in the epistles, he is prompted to single him out from among the scores of christian missionaries -- some of whose stature may have exceeded Paul's -- for special treatment./87/ By Luke's day the contours of Paul's theology were well known. But for reasons best explained in terms of Luke's apologetic intention in Acts, the rough edges of Paul's theology had to be smoothed over, and his stature diminished in relation to that of the Twelve. As Haenchen acknowledges, 'In Acts we are listening to the voice of a man of the subapostolic age . . . someone of a later generation trying in his own way to give an account of things that can no longer be viewed in their true perspective'./88/

The question then is whether Luke 'is a stranger to the theology of Paul' (Bleiben)/89/ by apologetic design or by accident, and if the former, whether his apologetic intention has not led him (a) to subordinate Paul to the Twelve in some fashion/90/ by retouching the picture of the apostle that emerges from his letters,/91/ and (b) apropos the nature of the marcionite threat, to indemnify the Twelve against any imputation of error by insisting both on the priority of their gospel and the confirmation of their office by the dictum of the risen Lord: in short, by a revelation equalling and exceeding Paul's.

---

/87/ Cf. Holmberg, Paul and Power: The Structure of Authority in the Primitive Church (1978), 69: 'Paul was not the only christian missionary to Jews and gentiles, and not the first'; cf. p. 58. And see further, Bauer, Orthodoxy and Heresy, 233ff.

/88/ Haenchen, Acts, 116.

/89/ Cf. Kümmel, Introd., 161ff.

/90/ Thus, Klein, Die Zwölf Apostel, 115ff. v. C. Burchard, Der dreizehnte Zeuge, 135f.: 173ff.

/91/ M.S. Enslin, 'Once Again, Luke and Paul', ZNTW (1970), 253-71.

Clearly Marcion would have rejected any accreditation of Paul that depended on the priority of the original apostles, even if the effect of this accreditation were 'to place Paul's witness, though nonapostolic, on the same level as that of the Twelve Apostles'./92/ In Acts, however, Paul is referred to as 'apostle' only once (14.4), and then only in conjunction with Barnabas. At no point is he designated Apostolos Christou Iesou, the title by which he knows himself and his mission, as distinct from that of his opponents./93/ In contrast to Gal 1, Paul is said to have been in Jerusalem before the 'Apostolic Council', which he attends virtually by divine invitation. On this earlier excursion, Barnabas presents him to the Twelve as a Christian, and he becomes a neophyte in their ranks (Acts 9.28)./94/ But this is permitted only after the apostles overturn the verdict of the Jewish disciples 'who believe[d] not he was a disciple' (Acts 9.26f.).

Peter, not Paul, is acknowledged to be the first missionary to the gentiles (Acts 15.7 v. Gal 2.9b), and after the Apostolic Council, Paul takes the so-called 'apostolic decree' to Antioch, acting thereby as the apostles' emissary (Acts 15.25)./95/ As Marxsen has noted, Paul is here 'made dependent on the original apostles'./96/ Similarly, Luke causes Paul to appeal with pride to his Pharisaic past/97/ and to emphasize that his preaching, properly understood, is no different from Jewish preaching./98/ The circumcision of Timothy for the sake of the Jews (16.3), the taking of a Jewish vow (18.18; 21.24-6) are anomalies if viewed in the light of Paul's aims as expressed in the epistles. Marcion would have regarded this capitulation of the apostle to the works of the law with horror.

---

/92/ Thus, Burchard, Der dreizehnte Zeuge, 174.

/93/ 1 Cor 1.1; 2 Cor 1.1; cf. Rom 1.1; 1 Cor 9.1; Gal 1.1.

/94/ 'Epeirazen kollasthai tois mathētais . . . kai ēn met autōn eisporeuomenos kai ekporeuomenos eis Ierousalēm' (9.26, 28).

/95/ Cf. Dunn, Unity and Diversity in the NT, 254f.

/96/ W. Marxsen, Einleitung in das NT (1974): ET, 169.

/97/ Acts 26.5 v. Phil 3.7f.

/98/ Thus Marxsen, p. 169 re: Acts 26.27f.

Although Marcion's earliest opponents leaned heavily on the account in Acts in order to correct his radical paulinism/99/ there is no evidence to suggest that the Paul of Acts was known to Marcion,/100/ anymore than was the recapitulation of teaching that forms the climax of Luke's resurrection narrative. That the earliest references to Acts as an authoritative book/101/ are those that occur in anti-marcionite polemic increases the possibility that the book itself arose in response to the marcionite view of Paul's apostolate, and as an attempt to reclaim Paul from the Marcionites./102/

Theologically this view is reinforced by Vielhauer's reckoning that the Book of Acts 'contains not one specifically pauline idea',/103/ although there are a few traces of the realization that Paul was 'against' the law./104/ There is no question but that the marcionite Paul is more nearly 'pauline' than the Lucan Paul: but this is so because Marcion knew only the Paul of the epistles and did not credit the dilute paulinism of the ecclesiastical establishment. The Lucan Paul bears a message for a Church in which the gentile mission without the law needs no justification; it is a fact of christian history. Haenchen very succinctly says that 'Luke is unaware of Paul's solution'/105/ to the question of the law. Marcion on the other hand knows that solution, and concludes that the tension between the law and gospel cannot be historically rationalized and set aside. It was the ongoing fact of christian life that the law leads not to God, but into sin./106/ The

---

/99/ AM 5.1.6; Iren. Haer. 3.14.1f.

/100/ See J.C. O'Neill, The Theology of Acts (1961), 26f.

/101/ M. Dibelius, Aufsätze zur Apostelgesch. (1951), 127f.; so also, Haenchen, Acts, 9f. One notes also the testimony of the anti-marcionite prologue to Luke, where it is stressed that Luke wrote his gospel 'after the others were already written'. Cf. Heard, 'The Old Gospel Prologues', JTS 6 (1955), 1-16. Marcionism seems in this prologue to be characterized a 'Jewish fable': 'ne Iudaicis fabulis adtenti in solo legis desiderio tenerentur'.

/102/ Knox, Marcion and the NT, 139.

/103/ P. Vielhauer, 'Zum Paulinismus der Apostelgesch.', EvTh 10 (1950/51), 15 (= Aufsätze zum NT [1965], 9ff.

/104/ Marxsen, Einleitung in das NT, ET 169, re: Acts 21.21, 28.

/105/ Haenchen, Acts, 112.

/106/ Gal 3.19.

message of the alien God is the end of the law; Paul had preached nothing else (Rom 10.4). This perception remained valid even though the false apostles who thwarted Paul's mission had been succeeded by bishops who preached in Paul's name.

The Lucan view of the apostles and of Paul must be taken together at this point: Had Marcion known Luke's gospel and Acts, he would have had to reckon with texts that were plainly irreconcilable with the pauline letters that he himself had taken pains to assemble. According to these texts, he was given to understand that the Twelve had been perfected and transformed by a revelation rivalling and strangely similar to Paul's, but about which Paul (assuming the interpolative character of 1 Cor. 15.5-8) was completely silent. He was likewise given to understand that Paul himself, far from being an apostle in his own right, had solicited the approval of the Twelve, and was thereby implicated in their teaching. Had he known of such a tradition, Marcion would have had no hesitation in pronouncing it false.

Neither Luke's correction of the primitive tradition which Marcion found in his source concerning the faithlessness of the apostles, nor the view of Paul advanced in Acts, is explicable in the absence of a prior threat to the consensus fidei. To put the matter flatly, without the imputation that the apostles had corrupted the gospel, no defense of their apostolate would be necessary, and the apologetic offered in Luke-Acts would become, in historical-critical terms, extraneous. Likewise, in the absence of a radical variety of paulinism, such as that espoused by Marcion, namely a form which called into question the very basis of magisterial authority as Luke would have known it, the need to 'downgrade' Paul would scarcely have arisen. This is especially so in view of the fact that outside heretical circles there is no evidence that Paul's memory would have enjoyed a renaissance after the second generation. In short, the marcionite view of Paul's apostolate may explain the apologetic thrust of the Lucan corpus, the testimony of the Fathers concerning Marcion's corruption of the gospel (e.g., AM 4.2.4) notwithstanding. Considering the nature of the evidence no decisive proof is possible. However the principle 'lesser because later' (cf. AM 4.5.7) to which the Fathers appeal cannot be treated as a reliable form of argument. For Tertullian, the argument from tradition has become so established as to be merely a 'prescription' to be employed as argument requires: thus, 'Luke was not an apostle, but an apostolic man, not a master but a disciple, and in any case, less than his master and indeed even more of lesser account [tanto posterior quanto posterioris ] as being the follower of a later apostle, Paul . . . [such that ] even if Marcion had introduced his gospel under the name of Paul personally, that one single document would not be adequate for our faith if destitute of the support of his predecessors'./107/ Tertullian here infers nothing more than what the Lucan intention entitles him to infer, that because Paul is a later apostle, his authority is less than that of those who preceded him, since they had been perfected in the faith by Jesus himself./108/

Knox concluded that the Book of Acts serves the double purpose of 'exalting and idealizing Paul, and at the same time definitely subordinating him to the apostles in Jerusalem'./109/ It is clear that this view cannot be rejected on chronological grounds. There is virtually no evidence for the existence of the Lucan corpus prior to Justin Martyr's first Apology./110/ Even as late as 150 (+), Acts was not considered an authoritative book,/111/

---

/107/ AM 4.2.4.

/108/ So also the author of the anti-marcionite Prologue to Luke. Text: Aland, Synopsis quattuor Evangeliorum, 532f.; Regul, p. 16.

/109/ Haenchen would argue against the 'subordinationist' theory on the grounds that Paul is the real protagonist of Acts; after signifying their approval of Paul, the apostles actually vanish. The versus showing Paul and the 12 together in Jerusalem (9.19b-31) are the last in which the 12 alone constitute the whole of the Christian high command (Acts, 336). Against this, it should be stressed that Luke does not think in terms of 'subordination' as such, but in terms of priority; the very fact that the apostles act as an accrediting authority (9.26: 15.23) for Paul's gospel strongly suggests that Luke's apologetic intention can be satisfied merely by establishing their historical precedence. They have been designated infallible witnesses 'to the things pertaining to the Kingdom of God' (Acts 10.39). See further W. Eltester, 'Lukas und Paulus', Eranion (1961), 1-17; C.K. Barrett, Luke the Historian in Recent Study, 8-26; E. Hirsch, 'Petrus und Paulus', ZNTW 29 (1930), 63ff.; R. Eisler, 'The Meeting of Paul and the Pillars', Bull. of the Bezan Club (1937), 58-64; J.N. Sanders, 'Peter and Paul in Acts', NTS 2 (1956), 133-43; O. Bauernfiend, 'Die Begegnung zwischen Paulus und Kephas', ZNTW 47 (1956), 268-76.

/110/ 1 Apol. 39.3 v. Acts 4.13; 1 Apol. 49.5 v. Acts 13.48; and * 1 Apol. 50.12 v. Luke 23.49a, 24.25, 44f.; Acts 1.8. cf. O'Neill, Acts, 11f.

/111/ Wendt, Die Apostelgesch. (1913), 48.

and did not become such until a generation later, when Irenaeus feels entitled to cite it in the struggle against Marcion and the gnostics. 'So far as we know', Harnack observed, 'the Book of Acts was hidden in obscurity up to the time of Irenaeus'./112/ And significantly, the majority of Irenaeus' references to Acts occur specifically in the course of the anti-marcionite polemic of Book III of the Haer./113/ Here its use was dictated by the fact that 'from it one could demonstrate the untiy of the apostolic message'./114/

In view of what we have said about the dating of Marcion's teaching (pp. 37ff.), the relative lateness of the Lucan corpus makes it probable that Marcion's evangelion/115/ was an Urlukas, and without question an

---

/112/ Harnack, TLZ 53 (1928), 126.

/113/ Iren. Haer. 3.1.1; 3.12.1-15; 3.14.1f.

/114/ Haenchen, Acts, 9.

/115/ Hawkins at the turn of the century commented on Luke's 'disuse of the Marcan source', with special reference to 9.51-18.14, 6.45-8.26, and the passion-narrative ('Three Limitations to St. Luke's Use of St. Mark's Gospel', in Oxford Studies in the Synoptic Problem [1911], 29-94; and in the same volume, Bartlett identified Luke's special source as correlating with . . . the hellenistic side of the Judaen Church, just as Matt.'s Q seems connected with the Hebraic ('The Sources of St. Luke's Gospel', in ibid., 316f.). Oxford biblical scholarship in the next decade saw the appearance of B.H. Streeter's remarkable essay, 'Proto-Luke' (Hibbert Jnl. [1921]; rpt. The Four Gospels [1927], 214ff.), in which he identified proto-Luke as 'a kind of half-way house between collections of sayings like Q, and the biographical type of gospel [such as] Mark'. He assigned to proto-Luke the following passages: Lk 3.1-4.30; 5.1-11; 6.14-16; 6.20-8.3; 9.51-18.14; 19.1-27; 19.37-44; 21.18, 34-36; 22.14, etc. Unfortunately, Streeter remained confident that 'the author of proto-Luke -- the person who combined together in one document Q and the bulk of material peculiar to the Third Gospel -- was none other than Luke, the companion of Paul' (p. 218). Streeter also assumed that Luke added the passion- and infancy-narratives, together with the resurrection-narrative, at a later date, and inserted sections from Mark in seven parts: Lk 4.31-44; 5.12-6.19; 8.4-9; 18.15-43; 19.28-36; 19.15-21.33; 21.37-22.13. Some twenty years on, by Streeter's reckoning, Luke transcribed the travel-documents which he had composed while a companion of Paul; these became the Acts of the Apostles. At no point did Streeter take Marcion into his equation, judging his gospel 'to have been an expurgation of Luke' (p. 5f.). See further, H. Cadbury, The Making of Luke-Acts (1927), and V. Taylor, 'The Proto-Luke Hypothesis', ExT 67 (1955), 12ff.: T.E. Bleiben, 'The Gospel of Luke and the Gospel of Paul', JTS 45 (1944), 134ff.; H.C. Snape, 'The Composition of the Lucan Writings: A Reassessment', HTR 53 (1960), 27ff. Streeter's thesis (Proto-Luke = Q + 'Special Source') was called into question by J.M.

abbreviated version of the Third Gospel./116/ While Knox's theory is not demonstrable merely on chronological grounds, it shifts the burden of proof to the side of those who wish to deny the apologetic intention of Luke-Acts on the premise that the works were composed by Luke 'the companion of Paul' and reflect a first-century rather than a post-marcionite Sitz im Leben. It seems reasonable to conclude at the very least that Luke's intention in his two-part work corresponds to the foci of Marcion's theological challenge, viz., the denigration of the apostolic witness, and the radicalization of Paul's claim to apostleship./117/

---

Creed, who argued that the Marcan narrative is 'basic' to Luke, and is found not only in the Q and L sections (e.g., 4.16-30; 5.1-11), but is fundamental to the passion and resurrection narratives as well (Commentary on Luke, 1930). Nevertheless, whatever the weaknesses of Streeter's thesis as originally framed, it is worth noting that the advocates of the proto-Lucan hypothesis were agreed that the gospel 'QL' had begun at Lk 3.1 ('a capital beginning for a gospel', Streeter called it); and we know this to have been the first verse of Marcion's evangelion, a fact never brought out by the proponents of the thesis:
    AM 4.7.1: 'Anno quintodecimo principatus Tiberiani proponit (eum) descendisse in civitatem Galilaeae Capharnaum' =
    Lk 3.1: 'En etei de pentekaidekatō tēs hēgemonias Tiberiou Kaisaros' + Lk 4.31a: 'kai katēlthen eis Kapharnaoum polin tēs Galilaias'.

/116/ According to Harnack (Marcion, 183*ff.) Marcion's gospel lacked the following: chs. 1-3 [nativity, baptism by John, the temptation, Adamite genealogy]; 8.19 [ref. to the presence of Jesus' mother and brothers]; in ch. 9, all ref. to Jairus; 10.21; 11.29-32 [ref. to Jonah]; 11.49-51; 12.6-7 ['ouchi pente strouthia/allakai hai triches tēs kephalēs hymōn]; 12.28 [retaining 'oligopistoi']; 13.1-5 [ref. to the Galileans murdered by Pilate; ref. to those killed in Siloam]; 13.29-35; 15.11-32 [the prodigal son]; 17.10; 18.31-3; 19.1-17, 21-2; 22.16, 35-8, 39-51 [Gethsemane, etc.]; 23.43; 24.26-7, 36-6, 44-6, 48-53. It should be stressed that Harnack's estimate of Marcion's deletions is extremely conservative, owing to his methodological assumption that Marcion found canonical Lk in existence. Following Zahn, Harnack also assumed canonical status for the Book of Acts (cf. Marcion, 40f.; 78f.; 83, 149*). These assumptions were called into question soon after the appearance of the 1921 edition of Marcion by (inter alia) H. von Soden, ZKG 40 (1922), 191ff.; and see further the reviews by Lietzmann, ZNTW (1921), 94f.; W. Bauer, Göttingische Gelehrter Anzeigen (1923), 1ff.; M.J. Lagrange, Rev. B. (1921), 602ff.; H. Strohl, RHPhR (1923), 156ff.; A. d'Ales, RSR (1922), 137ff. The debate about Harnack's methodology has been reopened by B. Aland in 'Marcion: Versuch einer neuen Interpretation', ZTK 70 (1973), 420-47.

/117/ Cf. AM 5.3.5f: Tert. makes the right hand of fellowship the decisive mark of Paul's apostleship: Paul is 'nothing without the support of his predecessors' (AM 4.2.5). He did not make the gospel but 'found it already in existence'.

## 4.5 False Apostleship in Marcion's Gospel

Marcion's chief texts for the theory of false apostleship were Gal 1.6-9; 2.4 and 2 Cor 11.13-14. In these passages, he saw references to a large number of unauthorized and nameless teachers who, if not the Twelve, acted as outriders of the Jerusalem Church in spreading false doctrines among the congregations established by Paul./118/ According to Harnack, 'Sie werden zwar von den Uraposteln bestimmt unterschieden; aber M. hat sich überzeugt, dass diese eine ganz klägliche Rolle gespielt haben'./119/ But Harnack here overstates the distinction which Marcion himself seems to have made between the 'original' apostles and the false teachers.

Marcion followed Lk 6.13f. in allowing that Jesus himself had chosen the Twelve./120/ Tertullian asks, 'Quis tale de numeri defensione competit Christo Marcionis', that is to say, Can Marcion justify his retention of the Twelve, after having accused them of corrupting the gospel. From his own version of Luke, however, Marcion was aware that Jesus had expressed impatience during his lifetime with the 'perversity' and 'dullness' of his disciples, which persists even beyond the resurrection itself (24.11, 16, 25). Marcion interpreted these references in line with Paul's allusions to those who were endeavouring to undermine his mission, so that to this extent Jesus and Paul are understood to be up against the same problem. Having failed to perceive the hidden things of God as they were revealed during Jesus' lifetime, the apostles then embark on a campaign to impede the spread of the true gospel. If Paul himself had doubts about the provenance of his enemies, Marcion had none: He found in his version of Luke what was missing in the epistles, namely the 'source' of the apostolic error: The apostles had not realized that Jesus was the son of the alien God.

(A) The Faithlessness of Peter and the Super-Apostles

Peter's confession (Lk 9.20) was singled out by Marcion to epitomize this misunderstanding. Jesus' command, that Peter 'tell no one such a thing' ('ho de epitimēsas autois parēngeilen mēdeni legein touto': 9.21) was taken by Marcion to mean that Peter had mistaken Jesus for the son of a Creator and

---

/118/ Cf. Harnack, Marcion, 34ff. Cf. AM 4.3.4f.

/119/ Harnack, Marcion, 34; cf. 230ff.

/120/ Tert. AM 4.13.3f.; esp. 4.13.5.

was accordingly enjoined to silence: 'Immo, inquis, quia non recte senserat, noluit mendacium disseminari'./121/ The 'great secret'/122/ has nothing to do with an untimely identification of Jesus' true nature, but is rather a case of mistaken identity: the chief of apostles thereby shows his inability to come to terms with the meaning of revelation. In pauline terms, he still thinks 'after the flesh'.

Peter errs again, this time in concert with the rest of the apostles, in the (transposed) resurrection scene of the transfiguration (9.33ff.; cf. Mk 9.2-13)./123/ In this instance too, as in the case of the resurrection-discourse (Lk 24.38f.), Tertullian holds that Marcion has permitted damaging verses to stand: 'Nam et hoc vel maxime erubescere debuisti, quod illum cum Moyse et Helia in secessu montis conspici pateris, quorum destructor advenerat'./124/ For Tertullian the transfiguration is

---

/121/ Tert. AM 4.21.7.

/122/ Cf. Mk 8.30; 9.9; 1.34; 3.12. On the history of research, see H.J. Ebeling, Das Messiasgeheimnis und die Botschaft des Marcus-Evangelisten, ZNTW 1939 (suppl.); E. Percy, Die Botschaft Jesu, Lunds (1953), 271ff.; D.E. Aune, 'The Problem of the Messianic Secret', Nov. Test., 11 (1969), 1ff. Bultmann attempted to show (History of the Synoptic Tradition, 347) that the secret can be explained through the 'union of the hellenistic kerygma about Christ, whose essential content consists of the Christ-myth . . . with the tradition of the story of Jesus'. For Maricon, this corresponds to the hiddenness of the good God.

/123/ Lk 9.28-36 = Mk 9.2-8; Matt 17.1-8. Montefiore argues (Synoptic Gospels, I, 204ff.) that the story is intended to 'give a miraculous confirmation of the messiahship from heaven . . . .' In the story partly depends on Exodus 24.12-18 ('six days', the Cloud). (The Transfiguration in Mk 9.3 appears to be interpolated.) Harnack argued for the independence of the account as an authentic reminiscence of Peter (Sitzungberichte der preussischen Akademie der Wissenschaften [1922], 62-80): 'Wer hat die präzize Zeitangabe gegeben wenn nicht Petrus selbst'; and cf. E. Lohmeyer, ZNTW (1922), 185-214. Moffat (Introd. to the Lit of the NT [1918], 224) commented that 'the two-fold apologetic motive of the transfiguration story is fairly obvious: viz., to explain how the crucified Jesus could be the Christ of God'. Montefiore (ibid., 207) regards Mk 9.5.6 ('kalon estin hēmas hōde einai . . .') (= Lk 9.33) a later addition: '[It is] an awkward attempt to give the apostles something to say'. But Luke omits Mark's form of address ('Rabbi', v. 5) and substitutes 'Epistata' (v. 33). The Marcan identification of Jesus, even if put onto Peter's erring lips, would have been unacceptable to Marcion. Cf. Matt 23.8.

/124/ Tert. AM 4.22.1.

irrefragable proof that Jesus had not come to abolish the law and the prophets; Marcion, by admitting the incident, argues against himself. But here as before Marcion's interpretation of the transfiguration precludes Tertullian's gloating assessment.

Marcion apparently saw the transfiguration as the apotheosis of the Unknown God,/125/ the moment of revelation, as well as the moment when the law was finally abrogated (cf. Am 4.22.1).

Marcion made use of v. 33b as documentation for the apostolic error: Peter had misunderstood the revelation, thinking it a glorification of the law and the prophets (cf. Mk 9.6), *'Mē eidōs ho legei'*; the cloud which overshadows them betrays their ignorance (9.34 v. Mk 9.7a)./126/ In short, the apostles 'heavy with sleep' at the very moment of revelation and lost in a cloud (= law) when the moment is past and 'Jesus stands again alone' (v. 36; cf. Mk 9.8), fail in their vocation at the crucial time (cf. 22.45). They are non-witnesses to the revelation of the true God 'who until that moment had not been revealed'./127/ They interpret their vision as an elevation of Jesus to the stature of prophet (cf. 24.19b) rather than as a denigration of the old covenant.

While Luke's (apologetic) intention in his redaction of the Marcan transfiguration was to offer a defense both of the apostles' witness and of the retention of the OT by the Church, Marcion interpreted the same material (in whatever form he may have found it) to support his theory of false apostleship. For Luke, the climax of the transfiguration, as he has

---

/125/ Marcion rejected the doublet of 9.35b at 3.22, as well as the story of the baptism by John. But the longer v. may well have occurred in the apotheosis-section of Marcion's evangelion, thus supporting the idea of the abrogation of the law and the revelation of Jesus as the Son of the unknown God. Vss. 35-36a become clearer if they are taken to follow 32a.

/126/ The rare word diagrēgorēsantes (v. 32) reinforces the metaphor of sleep to signify the 'unknowing' of the disciples. The narrative is confused: 'They the disciples feared as they entered into the cloud'. Cf. Montefiore, Synoptic Gospels, II, 450; E. Norden, Die Geburt des Kindes (1924), 97 n. 1. *'En tō genesthai tēn phōnēn'*: When the voice speaks, Jesus is alone. Luke presses this point, whereas Mark's ref. is oblique (v. 8). It is undoubtedly meant to suggest that Moses and Elijah are far beneath Jesus in dignity; and it would not have been difficult for Marcion to interpret the scene as representing an abrogation of the law and the prophets.

/127/ Tert. AM 4.22.6f.

arranged it, is the appearance of Moses and Elijah beside Jesus (v. 30, cf. Mk 9.4), while for Marcion (to conjecture), it is the moment when the OT figures fade into the cloud/128/ and Jesus 'stands alone before them', his face changed, and his garments glistening (9.29, cf. Mk 9.3). The voice of the alien God calls them to bear witness; but while it speaks, the cloud (the symbol of the God of Israel) overshadows them (Mk 9.7 v. 9.34), and 'they enter into the cloud' (34b). There is no parallel in Mark for Luke's elaboration of the cloud-motif.

However Marcion may have known the incident, the primary blame for the 'unknowing' was attributed to Peter, who thought that Jesus was the Christ of Moses and Elijah,/129/ as previously he had mistaken Jesus for the Christ of God,/130/ and later/131/ 'makes a rash utterance and turns in the direction of denial'./132/

---

/128/ The symbol is commonly used in the OT to represent the presence of God: vid., Lev 9.22-4; Exod 33.9-10; 40.34-8; 1 Kings 8.10-11; and in Exod 24.16-$\overline{17}$; Numbers 9.15f. In Exod 40.35, the cloud is associated with the glory of YHWH, while in Dan 7.13-14, it refers to the Son of Man and divine judgment. In either case, Marcion would have understood the cloud as an essentially 'negative' symbol: that the apostles are 'overshadowed' by the cloud means that they are ignorant of Jesus' identity and still cleave to the belief that he is the son of the Creator. Marcion could also point to Lk 9.54b-55 to support his interpretation of the transfiguration: when asked by James whether he will enact miracles comparable to those performed by Elijah, Jesus rebukes them with the words, 'You know not what manner of spirit you are of' (on the MSS variations, cf. Harnack, 'Ich bin gekommen', in Erforschtes und Erlebtes [1923], 98ff.). Harnack attempts to show that the longer reading is the original; it is almost certainly the marcionite reading (cf. AM 4.23.9ff.; Marcion, 185*f. n. 50-56). The passage comes in Luke's so-called 'great insertion' -- the wedge which Lk (or his source) drives into the Marcan narrative, which is not resumed until 18.15. For Streeter ('Proto-Luke', 203) this section belongs to the hypothetical gospel underlying Luke's (final) redaction. 'The section Lk 9.51-18.14 is the centre and core of the Third Gospel. It occupies 25 out of the 180 pp. of Lk in the Greek NT before me, and it contains most of the parables and narratives peculiar to Lk as well as about half of the material in Lk which can plausibly be assigned to Q'. The 'long-reading' of vss. 55b-56a contains also the central marcionite theme of the contrast between the just and the good God.

/129/ AM 4.22.4: 'Quomodo nesciens? Utrumne simplici errore . . .' Tert. refers to Marcion's explanation.

/130/ Lk 9.20; cf. AM 4.21.7.

/131/ Lk. 22.31f.

/132/ AM 4.41.2.

Harnack was mistaken, therefore,/133/ in making so clear-cut a distinction between the false apostles and the Twelve: such a distinction was unknown to Marcion, even if it was assumed by Paul. The thrust of Tertullian's argument is precisely that while Paul himself specified the character of the falsifiers (viz., advocates of the circumcision)/134/ Marcion wrongly equated the two. 'We must differentiate the two cases', insists Tertullian, 'for if Marcion's complaint is that the Apostles are held suspect of dissimulation or pretense, even to the debasing of the Gospel, he is now accusing Christ by thus accusing those whom Christ has chosen ['Christum iam accusat, accusando quos Christus elegit']'. Marcion begins from the premise that the reputed pillars of the Church, Peter, James, and John, stand behind the corruption of the evangelium Christi, and represent the immediate threat to Paul's gospel. Had not Peter been rebuked to his face for dissimulation and pretense?/135/

(B) The Name of the True Gospel

We cannot accept at face value Tertullian's suggestion that Marcion's motive for pronouncing censure on the apostles was 'to overthrow the credit of the gospels, which are the apostles' own and published under their names'./136/ For one thing, it is far from clear that Marcion knew of any gospel by 'Luke, the companion of Paul'./137/ The Marcionites of Tertullian's day maintained that canonical Luke was 'falsified in respect of its title'

---

/133/ Harnack, Marcion, 32ff.; 81f.; cf. von Campenhausen, Formation, 154.

/134/ Tert. AM 4.3.4.

/135/ Gal 2.11.

/136/ Tert. AM 4.3.2.

/137/ Harnack professed to find echoes of other gospels in the Antitheses (Marcion, 160ff.), particularly of the johannine literature; but the notion was soundly put down by Loisy (Christian Religion, 320f). In a curious passage (3.8.1), Tert. suggests that the johannine epistles were conceived in order to refute 'the premature and abortive Marcionites, whom the apostle John pronounced antichrists' (cf. 1 Jn 2.18, 22; 4.3); but Tert. is here thinking of the Ephesus-tradition associated with John and Polycarp (Iren. Haer. 3.3.4). The fact that the reputation of Paul is under serious threat at Ephesus can be seen from such passages, as well as from the polemic of the Pastoral Epistles. Cf. Bauer, Orthodoxy and Heresy, 233.

and that their own gospel 'was not to be attributed to Luke'./138/ This opinion may well be rooted in a tradition going back to Marcion himself, although to the orthodox bishops of Tertullian's day it seemed possible to treat the suggestion with contempt./139/

The probable explanation for Marcion's refusal to identify his gospel by an apostle's name is the doctrine of false apostleship itself: the true gospel could be attributed to no one but Jesus Christ. Moreover, the Marcionites believed the orthodox gospel to be an adulteration of their own (AM 4.3.5) and provided they understood theirs to be given to them by Paul, there would have been little reason for them to adopt the tradition (cf. Haer. 3.14.1) that the gospel had been written by a companion of Paul. Nor is there evidence that Marcion knew the words ascribed to Paul by the author of 2 Timothy (4.11): "Loukas estin monos met emou', which represent the strongest textual support for the case which both Irenaeus and Tertullian bring against Marcion's 'rejection' of Lucan authorship. It is true that in texts which Marcion did know -- Col 4.14 and Philemon 24 -- Paul mentions Luke and explicitly excludes him from the 'workers in the circumcision'. But the companion-tradition, strengthened on the basis of 2 Timothy 4.11 and long since established for Irenaeus and Tertullian, is unknown to Marcion. There thus exists no rationale for a deliberate decision to exclude Luke's name from the gospel, since if the companion-tradition had been accepted by Marcion as legitimate, he could have retained the title without loss of credit to his expurgated text. But as the apostles had originally discredited the gospel of Christ in their preaching, denial of apostolic authorship was no further discredit, and indeed any such ascription rendered its content false. While there is no evidence that Marcion himself polemicized against the orthodox canon or the ascription of gospel-texts to apostles, his refusal

---

/138/ Tert. AM 4.3.5.

/139/ The tactic adopted by the orthodox in Marcion's case was not to repudiate the authorities he cited but to absorb the authorities into a more 'complete' alternative canon: thus, Clement of Alexandria (Strom. 7.16) can say that a heretical canon is partial and hence inadequate. Knox would argue that the Church's stance in absorbing the authorities of the heretics explains the content of the Catholic Canon (Marcion and the NT, 38). Cf. Loisy, Christian Religion, 19; Harnack, Hist. Dogma, II, 39, and n. 3. Harnack considered that the ecclesiastical canon was not established in the interest of immediate spiritual edification (thus, Marcion!) but of attesting and certifying the Christian kerygma (ibid., 41-2). See further, T. Zahn, Gesch. des NT kanons (1888), I, 603ff.

to put a name to the evangelion was a part of his larger endeavor to verify and repristinate the 'truth of Christ'.

(C) The Oneness of the Gospel

Marcion understood the pauline references to the gospel, like much else in Paul, in a highly literal fashion, as referring to a unique and unrepeatable kerygma: unique in the sense that it had been definitively proclaimed by Paul alone; unrepeatable because the gospel made known once and for all what could never again be hidden. The unknown God had been revealed as a God of love and mercy. Paul himself had implicitly rejected the existence of more than one gospel./140/ Marcion's task, therefore, was to get behind the corrosive process that threatened to obscure Paul's vision of the gospel as belonging to Christ and being Christ's alone to give. He had offered it to the apostles, but they had been unworthy of the gift. He had given it to Paul 'by revelation', and Paul had proclaimed it to the churches. But at no point did it become the property of the Church, as Marcion's opponents were wont to argue: 'It ought to be clearly seen to whom belongs the possession of the scriptures that none may be admitted to the use thereof who has no title at all to the privilege'./141/

Marcion interpreted the phrase 'kata to evangelion mou' (Rom 16.25)/142/ in accordance with Paul's belief that the gospel of Jesus Christ (evangelion tou Christou: Gal 1.7) was essentially the same as Paul's gospel, 'given through Jesus Christ' ('kata to evangelion mou dia Christou Iesou')/143/ according to the 'mystery of revelation, kept secret from the beginning of the world'./144/ In stressing the nature of this communication, and in regarding Paul as the only communicator of the truth, the gospel was thereby distinguished from the 'other gospels' of the false teachers. Which, if any, of these gospels Marcion may have known it is not possible to

---

/140/ Gal 1.6-7.

/141/ Tert. Praes. 15.

/142/ On this see Harnack, Marcion, 42: 'Es lag ihm daran, die Identität des Evangeliums mit dem Evangelium des Paulus im Eingang des Briefs zu markieren und damit sowohl das 'judaistische' Evangelium als auch Mehrzahl von evangelischen Schriften auszuschliessen'.

/143/ Rom 16.25a.

/144/ Rom 16.25b.

surmise./145/ We can be reasonably certain that the plurality of the gospel-witness finally canonized by his opponents would have verified Marcion's suspicion that the Chruch had enshrined contradictions, and in gathering its sacred books had paid scant attention to the warnings of Paul./146/

Marcion's theological reform was designed to achieve the consistency and simplicity of teaching which he thought had been the hallmark of Paul's gospel and which was reflected in the faithfulness of those pauline congregations which had remained true to the faith of the apostle./147/ Consistency was secured by the uniqueness of the gospel: one need not look beyond Paul for 'right teaching'. As a secondary development of the struggle against the heretics, the orthodox sought to attain a like consistency by other means, namely, by claiming that christian teaching had remained invariable from the time of the apostles, who had 'been ignorant of nothing' and who had 'delivered the whole truth' to the Church. Marcion's was an appeal to revelation; the orthodox' an appeal to history. But the historical appeal was made more problematical by the introduction of an 'expanded' canon purported to undergird the unity of Catholic teaching from the beginning. In advancing their claim to the plurality of the apostolic witness as the warrant of consistent teaching (e pluribus unum), the theory of a single gospel was foreclosed to the orthodox opponents of Marcion; and while the idea of a four-fold gospel was destined to mitigate the difficulties represented by the plurality of the canon,/148/ consistency of teaching, as connoted in the traditio ab apostolis, was bound to remain a dogmatic

---

/145/ Cf. n. 137, supra. and von Campenhausen, Formation, 159 (re: Harnack, Marcion, 81f., 249*): 'Marcion had no need to accept the other gospels, and he did not do so; as a general rule, at any rate, he simply ignored them. If this were not so it would not be possible to explain why neither Irenaeus, nor Tertullian, nor Origen ever mentions an explicit and reasoned "critique" of the canonical gospels on these lines, nor why such a critique was not rejected'.

/146/ Marcion, 303*ff., 162*f.

/147/ The existence of a doctrinal criterion for remaining faithful to Paul's gospel is presupposed in the Marcionite Prologues to his letters. See de Bruyne, 'Prologues bibliques d'origine Marcionite', Rev. bénéd. (1907), 1-16; and cf. W. Mundle, 'Der Herkunft der marcionitischen Prologe zu den paulinischen Briefen', ZNTW 24 (1925), 56f.; Harnack, 'Der marcionitische Ursprung der ältesten Vulgata Prologe zu den Paulusbriefen', ZNTW 24 (1925), 204ff.; M.J. Lagrange, 'Les prologues pretendus marcionites', Rev. B. 35 (1926), 161ff.

/148/ Haer. 3.11.8f.

construction in the Church. A relative consistency of teaching, as a correlate of the uniqueness of the gospel, was available to the Marcionites on the basis of their rigid delimitation of the written canon to include only the 'gospel' and teaching of Paul.

Not surprisingly, therefore, marcionite counter-polemic/149/ seems to center on the absurdity of the orthodox claim that the four-fold gospel provides the basis for a coherent (unified) christian teaching:

> [The Marcionites] laugh at us as if they alone knew the truth, though they have no proof of what they say./150/
>
> [When the heretics] are confuted from the scriptures, they turn around and accuse these same scriptures as if they were not correct nor of authority, and assert that they are ambiguous./151/
>
> Marcion strives hard to overthrow the credit of those gospels which are the apostles' own and are published under their names . . . with the intention no doubt of conferring on his own gospel the repute which he takes away from those others./152/

The marcionite ridicule of the 'pluralism' of the orthodox position prompts Tertullian to judge as 'false [all doctrine] which savours of contrariety to the truth of the churches, and the apostles of Christ and God';/153/ it is not sufficient for the Marcionites to condemn the canon by claiming 'that the apostles did not know all things'/154/ or that the truth was delivered only to

---

/149/ AM 4.4.1f. A tendency toward expansion may have been known to Marcion himself; consequently, the possibility cannot be ruled out that while the orthodox response to Marcion was to set limits on 'approved books', or what Knox prefers to call the 'closure of the canon' (Marcion and the NT, 21), the tendency towards pluralism in orthodox circles is the reason for Marcion's prior delimitation of sacred scripture. This would remain true even though Marcion had no intimate knowledge of 'other' gospels. Harnack alludes (Hist. Dogma, II, 44) to the fact that the canon 'emerges' in the same ecclesiastical district where we first find the existence of the apostolic regula fidei. 'We hear nothing of any apostolic authority belonging to the compilers, because we learn nothing at all of such persons'. Cf. Harnack, 'Die ältesten Evangelienprologe und die Bildung des Neuen Testaments', Sitzungsberichte Berlin. Akademie (1928), 339, n. 3.

/150/ Justin, 1 Apol. 58.

/151/ Iren. Haer. 3.2.1.

/152/ Tert. AM 4.2.3.

/153/ Tert. Praes. 21.

/154/ Tert. Praes. 22; Iren. Haer. 3.12.5, 6, 11, 13.

Paul,/155/ since it can be demonstrated from the very books that Marcion rejects, especially from the Acts of the Apostles, not only 'that the apostles were not ignorant', but that they -- together with Paul -- delivered scripture into the keeping of the Church./156/

(D) The Author of the Gospel

Later marcionites considered Paul himself or even Jesus the author of the evangelion,/157/ conjecture which Marcion may have fostered by refusing to assign a name to the text: 'Marcion evangelio, scilicet suo, nullum adscribit auctorem, quasi non licuerit illi titulum quoque affingere, cui nefas non fuit ipsum corpus evertere'./158/ Harnack contended/159/ that Marcion 'took it for granted that Jesus had need of an authentic gospel to be written down', as a witness to the revelation of the alien God,/160/ since the Creator had received his due in the OT. However that may be, the distinctive thing about Marcion's appeal to the 'gospel of Christ' is that it is an appeal to a written source, as compared to the oral tradition of the Church or the communication of secret wisdom among the gnostic sects. It is the complaint of the Marcionites, according to Adamantius,/161/ that the first apostles preached sine scriptura, and that as a natural consequence of this procedure, their words became increasingly distorted. The epistles of Paul had the primary advantage of being literae: the actual interpretatio evangelica had been given as letters which at least forestalled the process of ongoing corruption.

---

/155/ Iren. Haer. 3.13.1; cf. Tert. Praes. 23.

/156/ Tert. Praes. 25.

/157/ Thus Adam. Dial. 1.8; 2.13f.; Carmen Adv. Marcionem, 2.29; discussed in Harnack, Marcion, 266*ff.

/158/ Tert. AM 4.2.3.

/159/ Harnack, Marcion, 36.

/160/ Cf. Harnack, Marcion, 36; 246*f. Von Campenhausen notes that the idea of a gospel bestowed directly by Christ is not found elsewhere in the tradition, 'though it is in gnostic circles' (Formation, 156). But Marcion's motives for postulating a gospel 'not written by man' ('ekeryksan agrapha') had nothing to do with a tradition of secret wisdom as such.

/161/ Adam. Dial. 2.12; cf. Harnack, Marcion, 259*. But cf. Iren. Haer. 3.2.1: '[The heretics] allege that the truth was not delivered by means of written documents but viva voce'.

The Urevangelium, the gospel of Christ, remains largely an ideal in Marcion's theology. Correct the letters of Paul as one might ('Denique [Marcion] emendavit quod corruptum existimavit')/162/ one could never arrive by human endeavor at the evangelion tou Christou. At any event, such an endeavor was unnecessary, since according to the mystery which Paul had revealed, the letters of Christ were written on the tables of the heart./163/ Marcion's effort to locate the true gospel thus differed in conception from that of his opponents. He was not interested in developing an authoritative norm to be used as proof of doctrine, but only in restoring the gospel of truth. The appellate use of scripture, as defined in 2 Tim 3.16, was foreign to Marcion's theological outlook. The work of restoration was not dictated by the need to refute wrong opinions, but in order to 'let the glorious Gospel of Christ the image of God shine unto men'./164/

---

/162/ Tert. AM 4.5.6. H. Windisch, 'Das Evangelium des Basilides', ZNTW (1906), 245 argued that Basilides' editorial principles were not very different from those of Marcion. According to Harnack (Marcion, 72ff.) Tatian also was obliged to make excisions in compiling his harmony. Cf. further, F. Scheidweiler, 'Arnobius und der Marcionitismus', ZNTW 45 (1954), 45-8; F.G. Sirna, VC 18 (1964), 39-41. There is a slim chance that later Marcionites canonized further pauline letters and other gospels as well; Harnack (Marcion, 210) in evaluating the evidence of Adamantius (Dial. 2.16-20), Epiphanius (Panar. 42.3), Ephraem (Lied. 24.1), and Eznik (De sect. 4), concludes even that the Pastoral Eps. were finally accepted into the expanded marcionite 'canon': but he reasons this chiefly on the basis of Tert.'s remark (4.5.7): 'Cotidie reformant evangelium, prout a nobis cotidie revincuntur'. Additional evidence in Marcion, 172f.; cf. 134*, 132*, n. 2. But the revision of the gospel 'day by day' mentioned by Tert. is probably a reference to the editorial procedures of Marcion and his followers in the quest for the 'true gospel'; it therefore points in the direction of contraction rather than expansion, and the evidence cited by Harnack is too vague to be persuasive. Harnack cites Origen, contra Celsum, 2.27 (cf. Origen, hom. Luc., 25) as evidence of marcionite revisions, but the passage does not suggest that the Marcionites added to their canon; merely that even an outsider like Celsus could be offended at Marcion's use of the gospel. Cf. H. Chadwick, Origen: Contra Celsum (1965), 90 n. 2.; and W. Völker, Das Bild vom nichtgnostischen Christentum bei Celsus (1928), 90.

/163/ 2 Cor 3.3.

/164/ 2 Cor 4.4. Harnack, Marcion, 36: 'Ein authentisches schriftliches Evangelium muss es geben'.

### 4.6 Summary: The Inferiority of Paul and the Anti-Marcionite Defense of the Apostolic Tradition

Marcion believed that the Twelve had fathered a tradition of false teaching in the Church, the only remedy for which was the careful restitution of Paul's gospel. This theme was prevalent in marcionite counter-polemic against the orthodox, as is plain from the shape of the arguments used by Marcion's opponents. The 'genealogy of error' offered by Irenaeus is only the most ambitious attempt to rehabilitate the pedigree of christian truth by historical means:

> When we refer [the heretics] to that tradition which originates with the Apostles [and] which is preserved by means of the succession of bishops in the churches, they object to tradition, saying that they themselves are wiser, not merely than the bishops, but even than the Apostles, because they have discovered the unadulterated truth. [For they maintain] that the Apostles intermingled the things of the law with the words of the Saviour . . . . It comes to this: these men do not consent either to scripture or to tradition./165/

Tertullian follows a similar line of reasoning in the de Praescriptione:

> [The Marcionites] . . . branding the apostles as ignorant, put forth the case of Peter and those with him having been rebutted by Paul. . . . [alleging] that Paul added yet another form of the gospel than that which Peter and the rest had previously set forth./166/

Tertullian responds to this criticism of apostolic tradition by insisting that Paul became an apostle only because he shared with the Twelve 'a common belief and preaching', and interprets Galatians 2.9 as the token of his 'authorization'. Indeed, he cannot resist saying that the reason for Paul's going up to Jerusalem (Gal 1.18) had to do with Peter's position. And he stresses that there was no diversity in the gospel preached by Peter and Paul, merely 'a distribution of office',/167/ itself agreed by the apostolic college. With this consensus clearly in view, Tertullian is able to indict Marcion's theory of false apostleship: 'The original sources of the faith must

---

/165/ Iren. Haer. 3.2.2.

/166/ Tert. Praes. 23: That the Marcionites are the focus of this passage is not only clear from the run of the argument, but also from the reference to 'those who reject the Acts of the Apostles'.

/167/ Tert. Praes. loc. cit.

be reckoned for truth as undoubtedly containing that which the churches received from the apostles, the apostles from Christ, and Christ from God . . . We hold communion with the apostolic churches because our doctrine is in no respect different from theirs'./168/

The argument for the priority of truth (cf. pp. 72ff.) was foreclosed to Marcion because of his belief that the gospel had suffered corruption at the hands of the apostles themselves in their preaching./169/ The argument was open to Marcion's opponents, on the other hand, only at the expense of downgrading the importance of Paul's apostolate/170/ in the very process of claiming his teaching for the Church./171/ At the same time, as has been shown with respect to the Lucan corpus, there was a corresponding insistence on the apostolicity of the evangelical witness and the integrity of the apostles in communicating the Lord's words. Justin is moved to refer to 'the memoirs composed by the apostles, which are called gospels',/172/ and Irenaeus asserts,

> It is unlawful to assert that[the apostles ]preached before they possessed perfect knowledge, as some [heretics] venture to say, boasting themselves as improvers of the Apostles. For after our Lord rose from the dead, the Apostles were invested with power from on high, when the Spirit came upon them, were filled from all [his gifts ], and had perfect knowledge./173/

The apostles were thus prevented from teaching falsehood by the intervention of the Spirit of Wisdom./174/ Irenaeus equates them with the teleioi mentioned by Paul (1 Cor 2.6), such that Paul's defense of his own

---

/168/ Tert. Praes. 21.

/169/ Tert. AM 4.3.2ff.; 1.20.1f.; cf. Haer. 3.2.2; 3.5.1; Adam. Dial. 2.12.

/170/ AM 1.20.2; cf. AM 5.1.2f.; Tert. Praes. 23; Iren. Haer. 3.13.1f. Bauer, Orthodoxy and Heresy, 226f.; 234; Loisy, Birth of the Christian Religion, 322.

/171/ Blackman makes the valuable observation (Influence, 37) that in moving away from Paul, canonicity soon became identified with the idea of apostolicity. Cf. Tert. De bapt. 17; Harnack, Hist. Dogma II, 44 n. 2.

/172/ 1 Apol. 66; 1 Apol. 67.

/173/ Iren. Haer. 3.1.1.

/174/ Cf. Iren. Haer. 3.12.5f.

teaching (1 Cor 2.4; 2.10) is retrojected into the post-resurrection experience of the apostles./175/ 'These are the voices of the disciples of the Lord, the truly perfect who after the assumption of the Lord were perfected by the Spirit . . . [at a time and place] where there was no Valentinus, and no Marcion'./176/ The argument for the priority of the truth becomes possible through the assertion that the deficiency of the apostles is eradicated in the Easter-experience and its sequel, Pentecost. And this is taken by Marcion's opponents to mean a revelation equalling and exceeding that of Paul. Its 'equivalence' is suggested by Luke's description of the moment of revelation: 'Autōn de diēnoichthēsan hoi ophthalomoi kai epegnōsan auton' (Lk 24.31), and its congruence with the description of the Damascus-experience of Paul: 'Aneōgmenōn de tōn ophthalmōn autou ouden eblepen' (Acts 9.8). The central theme in either case is enlightenment, with reference both to scripture and understanding (Lk 24.32; 24.45) as well as to the 'enlightenment' (i.e., return of sight) that follows Paul's reception of the Holy Spirit (Acts 9.17b-18; cf. Acts 22.13b; 26.18)./177/

As has been suggested, a recapitulation of the Lord's teaching occurs only in the Lucan Corpus; in the gospels of Matthew and Mark, it is subsumed in the evangelical commission (Mk 16.15f.; Matt 28.19f.). In Mark particularly -- which in some of its aspects may be closer to Marcion's evangelion than Luke -- the motif of the apostles' disbelief remains central: 'Kai ōneidisen tēn apistian autōn kai sklērokardian hoti tois theasamenois auton egēgermenon ouk episteusan' (16.14). Luke mitigates the motif found in his Marcan source (24.11, 25, etc.), and turns the negative tradition of Jesus' upbraiding of the disciples into the positive concept of enlightenment, whereby 'their eyes are opened and they know him' (Lk 24.31 v. Acts 9.8). Mark's attribution of 'hardness of heart' to the apostles becomes in Luke an 'opening of the understanding'; but the echo of the older gospel can still be heard: 'Ouchi hē kardia hemōn kaiomenē ēn [en hēmin] hōs elalei hēmin en tē hodō, hōs diēnoigen hēmin tas graphas' (Lk 24.32). In respect of this

---

/175/ Acts 2.4; Lk 24.45.

/176/ Iren. Haer. 3.12.5; cf. Iren. Haer. 3.12.7, 13.

/177/ Cf. Paul's assertions that he has 'seen' Jesus the Lord: 1 Cor 9.1; 15.8; Gal 1.12.

revelation, which is linked closely to the impartation of the Spirit,/178/ the testimony of the original apostles is elevated to a position of greater historical credibility, as it is based on direct knowledge of the Lord's sayings. It is thus, in the strict sense, not 'revelation' but recapitulation.

Irenaeus goes a step further. Against Marcion's suggestion that Paul alone had known the truth, he argues that Paul had acknowledged his own inferiority to the Twelve:

> Paul acceded to [the request of] those who summoned him to the apostles . . . . And again he says, 'For an hour we did give place to subjection: [Ad horam cessimus subiectione" Gal 2.5], that the truth of the gospel might continue with you' . . . . Thus the statement of Paul harmonizes with, and is, as it were, identical with, the testimony of Luke regarding the apostles./179/

Following Irenaeus' argument, Tertullian advances a similarity subordinationist view of Paul's role:

> Paul writes that after fourteen years he went up to Jerusalem to seek the support of Peter and the rest of the Apostles, to confer with them concerning the content of his gospel, for fear lest for all those years he had run, or was still running, in vain -- meaning if he was preaching the gospel in any form inconsistent with theirs. So great as this was his desire to be approved of and confirmed by those very people who, if you please, you suggest should be understood to be of too close kindred with Judaism./180/

We may characterize the orthodox response to Marcion's doctrine of false apostleship as an attempt to reclaim Paul, and the whole of his gospel, for the Church. This task required a sharp differentiation of the false apostles who opposed Paul's gospel and the Twelve who preceded him 'according to the flesh'. And such a differentiation meant that in spite of Paul's fervent denials of the notion, he was in some sense inferior to the super-apostles: not in virtue of his gospel, which was construed as being essentially the same as that preached by the Twelve (AM 5.3.1) but in virtue of historical priority. As Tertullian would argue, that which is delivered from the beginning has the greater claim to truth (AM 1.1.6). The original apostles,

---

/178/ Lk 24.49a v. Acts 2.1f., and cf. Jn 20.22.

/179/ Iren. Haer. 3.13.3. Vulg. = 'Quibus neque ad horam cessimus subiectione, ut veritatis evangelii permaneat apud vos'. On the omission of hois oude in mss. cf. Aland, et al., Grk NT (1975), 651, n. 2.

/180/ Tert. AM 5.3.1; cf. Praes. 23; AM 1.20.2f.

according to the witness of the gospel which Marcion had curtailed, had enjoyed a prior and direct revelation of truth; they too had received the Spirit; but with a significant difference: the Spirit of Truth had been promised to them, as it had not to Paul. The very suddenness and immediacy of Paul's revelation made it questionable (Acts 9.26b). The disciples, speaking with the voice of the Church of Luke's day, 'believe not that Paul is a witness'. This shows the mind-set of a developed Catholicism which regards revelation less as an event than as a fulfillment of prophecy (cf. 2 Tim 3.15f.). Luke considers the confirmation of the apostolic witness by the Spirit the completion of scripture (Lk 24.49b). Paul's revelation is only 'verifiable' in comparison with their own -- a fact which may explain the striking similarities between Lk 24.16/31-32 and Acts 9.8a/18, in describing the respective events.

Despite Paul's protests, the original experience of the Twelve was closed to him by the Church. Insofar as his teaching comports with that of the Twelve, he is an apostle; but he stands virtually in the apostolic succession. This consideration and not the desire to highlight Paul's mission explains the disappearance of the Jerusalem Apostles after Acts 11.19./181/ It has been put in perspective solely on the basis of having been made posterior to the Pentecost-experience of the Twelve.

The reclamation of the gospel by the orthodox required less articulate means than the rehabilitation of Paul, since it could be shown that Marcion and his followers had mutilated the scriptures, 'not acknowledging some books at all; and, curtailing the gospel according to Luke and the epistles of Paul, they assert that these are alone authentic, that they have themselves thus shortened'./182/ And Marcion had rejected the Acts of the Apostles which provided the bridge between the apostolic witness and the (complementary) work of Paul: he counted the earliest church history, in short, a falsification of the birth and spread of the gospel./183/ Irenaeus challenged the Marcionites to accept the entirety of the gospel of Luke or to admit that they have no gospel at all./184/

---

/181/ Cf. E. Käsemann, 'Die Legitimät des Apostels', ZNTW (1942), 69-71.

/182/ Iren. Haer. 3.12.12.

/183/ Tert. Praes. 23.

/184/ Iren. Haer. 3.14.3-4. Irenaeus bases his argument on the so-called

Marcion's followers responded to the charge that he had corrupted the gospel with the specific counter-claim that he had been a renovator of a much older tradition: 'Aiunt enim Marcionem non tam innovase regulam separatione legis et evangelii quam retro adulteratam recurasse'./185/ This suggests the extent to which Marcion identified his mission with that of Paul./186/ His reading of the epistles not only confirmed his fears concerning the dangers confronting the gospel in the great Church,/187/ but they revealed something about how the 'great apostasy of the church had been allowed to develop'./188/ Moreover they demonstrated to Marcion's satisfaction that Paul had had a sacred duty to take a stand against error and to assert himself (Gal 2.11) against the other apostles.

This perception of Paul's struggle on behalf of the true gospel defines Marcion's understanding of the magisterial office. The mission of Paul was the prototype of his own attempt to preserve the message of Jesus concerning the unknown God from corruption by latter-day 'judaizers': bishops who had not yet been weaned from the law and continued to appeal to the OT as if it still counted for something;/189/ who spoke 'with authority' of 'a new law in Jesus Christ';/190/ gave thanks 'for the knowledge of the past';/191/ and declared that 'even Moses had spoken through the Spirit'./192/

For the orthodox it was clear that Marcion had bowdlerized the gospel for his own ends, forsaken the faith of the apostles,/193/ and in rejecting

---

/185/ Tert. AM 1.20.1: cf. AM 4.5.6f.

/186/ Harnack, Marcion, 37-40; 183f.; 231ff.; 38*; cf. Knox, Marcion and the NT, 14 ; Lindemann, Paulus, 383ff.

/187/ AM 4.3.2; cf. 1.20.1f.; Praes. 22f.; further, Harnack, Marcion, 296*.

/188/ Thus von Campenhausen, Formation, 154.

/189/ E.g., 2 Clement, 8.4; Ign. Smyrn. 1.1f.

/190/ Ep. Barnabas, 2.6.

/191/ Ep. Barnabas, 5.3; 5.7.

/192/ Ep. Barnabas, 10.2.

/193/ AM 1.1.5.

Acts, demeaned the consensus fidei./194/ His critics accused him variously of inconsistency, theological näivete, and intrigue; of attempting to overthrow the creed he had once embraced, and of being an absolute stranger to christian doctrine. Most of these accusations can be dismissed as polemical conventions,/195/ but the charge of theological näivete and inconsistency deserves comment.

Marcion, as we have seen, believed that the true gospel was revealed rather than received, and that one need not look beyond the epistles of Paul to locate the definitive teaching concerning this revelation. This was itself an act of faith, since Marcion seems to have exercised little critical judgment in appropriating Paul's gospel as the standard of christian teaching. Moreover, the structure which he imposed on Paul's teaching deprived it of its evocative character and reduced it to an oversimplified 'system' of contradictions:/196/ the antithesis between law and gospel became, in effect, a synecdoche for the whole of Paul's thought, while its most dynamic features -- including not least the ambivalence of the apostle himself toward the law -- were suppressed in the interest of consistency. In this respect, his designs were no less artificial than those of his opponents. His campaign against the orthodox issued in a demand that the true gospel and apostle should be specified in the teaching of the Church, and in this, his opponents followed his lead. In resisting the narrowness and simplicity of his vision, they accepted the premise from which he began./197/

There was very little in the way of a thoroughgoing and methodical critique of primitive Christianity about Marcion's enterprise. He knew essentially only one tradition concerning the first apostles -- that related by Paul -- and he accepted it without question on Paul's authority. His failure to resolve the tension in Paul's religious thought led him to declare against

---

/194/ AM 5.1.6f.; cf. Praes. 23.

/195/ Harnack, Marcion, 42; 250*.

/196/ On the possibility that Marcion's literalist approach to scripture derives from the rabbinical schools of his native Pontus, See Harnack, Marcion, 20 n. 3. Harnack suggests that Marcion developed his Antitheses in response to Jewish propaganda, and that 'his methods are not contrary at every point to those of his opponent and countryman, Aquila' (p. 21 n. 2). Cf. ch. 1, 'The Hellenistic Matrix'.

/197/ Cf. Knox, Marcion and the NT, 36; Harnack, 'Das Alte Test. in den paulinischen Briefen und in den paulinischen Gemeinden', Sitz. preussischen Akad. der Wissenschaften (1928), 124ff.

the unity of God, almost as an exegetical necessity rather than as a theological conclusion./198/

It is difficult to measure the significance of Marcion's theory of false apostleship. To be sure, by challenging the integrity of the first apostles he called into question the historical basis for christian teaching, and there could have been no more serious a threat to the backward-looking church of the second century: a church which had by and large rationalized its eschatological hopes and accepted its historical destiny. Moreover, his limited view of Paul's defense of the gospel was largely unsuited to a church that still required the law as a tutor, and the prophets to reassure it of its identity.

---

/198/ Harnack, Neue Studien, 20 n. 2.

# CHAPTER FIVE

# THE GNOSTIC TRAJECTORY OF MARCION'S THEOLOGY

## 5.1    Introduction:  Evidence of Marcion's Gnosticism

Marcion's theology is practical and biblical rather than speculative. There is no evidence that he based his doctrine of the two gods on a dualistic theory of the cosmos, as did his gnostic contemporary Valentinus or on a well-developed theodicy, such as that promoted by the Epicurean philosophers.    Indeed the attribution of the term 'gnostic' to Marcion was less common among the heresiologists than later scholarship has assumed to be the case. Irenaeus, as we have noted, includes Marcion among the 'gnostic' progeny of Simon Magus chiefly because his method obliges him to do so. But Tertullian makes explicit the distinction between Valentinus and Marcion,/1/ and nowhere in the <u>adversus Marcionem</u> does he use the term 'gnostic' in a descriptive way to refer to Marcion's religious theory./2/  In this respect at least the fathers were more judicious than later scholars who were inclined to cast Marcion among the gnostics on the basis of his ditheism, docetism, and 'anti-cosmic dualism' alone.  According to Jonas, 'the idea of the unknown God opposed to that of the cosmos, the very conception of an inferior and oppressive creator and the consequent views of salvation as liberation from an alien principle, are so outstandingly gnostic that anyone who professed them in their historical environment must be counted as one of the gnostics'./3/  Yet even those who are wont to characterize Marcion's religious thought as gnostic or quasi-gnostic have (sometimes inadvertently) emphasized the difficulty in putting a name to his theology. Streeter concluded that 'Marcion was  the  most formidable pre-

---

/1/ Cf. <u>Praes</u>. 38.  See the discussion in Harrison, <u>Polycarp's Two Eps</u>., 177f.

/2/ The connection is strongly suggested in Clement's discussion of the 'unreal continence' of the heretics, <u>Strom</u>. 3.4.25f.

/3/ Jonas, <u>Gnostic Religion</u>, 137.

cisely because he was the most Christian of the gnostics',/4/ and in his standard survey of early Christianity, A.C. McGiffert proposed that Marcion, like the gnostics generally, found his inspiration in the dualism of Paul:

> And so the antimony between Judaism and Christianity, and between the creating and redeeming God upon which most of them laid so much stress; the asceticism upon which many of them insisted, and the libertinism inculcated by others; their assertion of the impossibility of salvation for any man not endowed from above with a spiritual nature; their docetic views of Christ, and their identification of him with one of the pre-existing beings or aeons, which were supposed to bridge the chasm between God and matter; their denial of fleshly resurrection, and their insistence upon the purely spiritual character of eternal life -- all have their points of contact in the system of Paul, and may be recognized as more or less perverted and distorted reproductions of his views concerning the relation of law and gospel, the origin and nature of the Christian life, and the person and work of Christ./5/

More recently still, there have been a number of attempts to overcome Harnack's vigorous defense of Marcion's 'originality' and comparative independence of gnostic speculation. Bianchi,/6/ echoing Jonas' evaluation, has reasserted the gnostic 'themes' in Marcion's theology, including the emphasis on spirit-matter dualism, as reflected in the distinction between the sphere of the unknown God and the material world of the Creator. Bianchi has also stressed the exceptional significance attached by the Marcionites to the salvation of the soul and their disdain for the body. So too, Aland, in challenging Harnack's thesis, underlined three characteristics said to exhibit Marcion's relation to gnosticism: (a) the sharp differentiation between the Creator and the 'alien' God; (b) the idea of salvation from the world; and (c) the use and evaluation of the OT./7/ It should be stressed that none of these themes or characteristics was unrecognized by Harnack or his defenders, and their rediscovery by contemporary scholarship has shed

---

/4/ Streeter, The Four Gospels, 6.

/5/ McGiffert, History of Christianity in the Apostolic Age, 503.

/6/ U. Bianchi, 'Marcion, theologien biblique ou Docteur gnostique?', VC 21 (1976), 141-49.

/7/ B. Aland, 'Marcion: Versuch einer neuen Interpretation', ZTK 70 (1973), 420-47.

little light on the old question concerning the provenance of Marcion's religious ideas.

The general tendency of Marcion-studies in the last century, despite the intermission occasioned by the appearance of Harnack's monograph in 1921, has been to keep Marcion among the gnostics, even if with the proviso that Harnack did well to emphasize the distinctive features of the marcionite system. Blackman's reaction is typical of the trend: 'The gnostic systems were making a wide appeal. They offered the attraction of novelty and universalism, and many Christians, convinced that Christianity was a new way of redemption and for all men, were inclined to think that the christian creed and organization should conform to this model. From this direction came . . . Marcion. [His] attitude to Judaism was rooted in a repudiation of history which classes him with the gnostics, and it was a true insight which prompted the Church to designate him a heretic'./8/ This view of Marcion's influence comports with Jonas' verdict that for all his originality Marcion is to be accounted a gnostic 'not merely by way of classification, but in the sense that the gnostic ideas were abroad and actually shaped his thinking'./9/

The attempts to rank Marcion as the most 'christian' of the gnostics are generally characterized by a readiness to read into his elusive theology themes derived from those systems assumed to be contemporary with or parallel to his. Hence the motifs of spirit-matter dualism, docetism, and ditheism, as these emerge from the polemic against Marcion, are in circular fashion reckoned to show that Marcion's world-view is best described as gnostic because he participated in that hellenistic thought-world from which the gnostic systems also derived their themes. Such a reckoning presupposes that Marcion's 'entirely new twist' (Jonas), was geared to translate a pre-existing body of christian teaching into the familiar categories of hellenistic thought,/10/ and ignores the fact that Marcion's point of view was shaped by an archaic paulinism in which these motifs are already clearly programmatic.

The patristic tradition about Marcion prior to Origen warrants a 'gnostic' view of Marcion's theology only if we accept Irenaeus' story con-

---

/8/ Blackman, Influence, 125; cf. Burkitt, Church and Gnosis, 22f.; 126ff.

/9/ Jonas, Gnostic Religion, 137-38.

/10/ Cf. Clement, Strom. 3.3.13; Hippol. Ref. omn. haer. 7.18.

cerning Marcion's indebtedness to the teaching of Cerdo. According to this, Marcion becomes the continuator of the gnostic views of his master: *'Diadexamenos de auton Markiōn ho Pontikos euxēsen to didaskaleion, apērythriasmenōs blasphēmōn'*./11/ But this master-pupil relationship between Cerdo and Marcion is efficiently set aside by Tertullian, who reduces the connection to 'acquaintance' (Habuit et Cerdonem quendam)./12/ Here and elsewhere, it is fairly clear that Tertullian intends a distinction between the marcionite and gnostic systems. Among the 'sundry bypaths' to heresy challenged in the adversus Valentinianos (including the opinions of Heracleon, Secundus, Marcus Magus, and Ptolemaeus) Marcion does not figure./13/ And perhaps most significant of all is Tertullian's comment in the de Praescriptione, where he associates the heresy of Marcion with the teaching of the Stoics, while that of Valentinus he refers to platonic speculation. In the adversus Marcionem references to Valentinus are scant, but the most explicit of these indicates Tertullian's at least grudging acknowledgement of the distinction between Marcion's teaching and that of the gnostic schools: speaking of Marcion's recognition of two first principles, Tertullian asks 'why if two, there should not be more', since,

> if divinity were capable of number we should need to believe it the more richly endowed: more generous and more bountiful was Valentinus, who . . . [having conceived] of two, Depth and Silence, poured out a whole swarm of divinity, a litter of Aeons to the number of thirty, like Aeneas' sow./14/

The kinds of similarities between Marcionism and the gnostic systems to which F.M. Braun pointed/15/ do not belie Legge's observation that 'Marcion's views, unlike those of the gnostics, were original, and [were]

---

/11/ Eus. HE 4.11.2; cf. Haer. 1.27.2; Ps.-Tert., Omn. haer. 6.

/12/ AM 1.2.3.; by and large, as Mühlenberg has noted, our knowledge about Cerdo is so scant as to be useless, and 'there is little direct support for Marcion's connection with gnosticism'. 'Marcion's Jealous God' in Disciplina Nostra: Studies in Memory of Robert F. Evans, ed. D. Winslow (1979), 110.

/13/ Adv. Valent. 4; 33; the same distinction is implicit in the schemata employed by Ps.-Tert. in the Omn. haer. (cf. 4 v. 6).

/14/ AM 1.5.1; cf. Iren. Haer. 1.5-14.

/15/ Braun, 'Marcion et la gnose simonienne', Byzantion 25-7 (1955-7), 632-48.

formed . . . by a kind of centrifugal process [which] rejected in turn all pagan and Jewish elements as well as most of the traditions which had already grown up in the catholic church'./16/ Only a strained interpretation of the evidence permits us to conclude that Marcion's system was immediately derived from, or contributed to, the gnostic systems of the early second century, even though such a development cannot be ruled out definitively.

## 5.2 The Differentiation of Marcionism and Gnosticism

Marcion's teaching is free of the mythological fantasy and complexity that characterizes gnostic thought. Unlike his opponents, he does not speculate about first principles, nor develop a theory of the divine being. If his teaching is philosophically vulnerable to Tertullian's postulate that 'divinity implies unity' it is not vulnerable on the same terms as apply to the gnostic doctrine of diremption, since even according to the gnostics the divine being is ideally coherent (pleroma). No philosophical theory supports his belief in the creator. In the OT he found no rational arguments for the existence of God, but rather a history of his acts and laws. Moreover Marcion shared with the biblical writers the conviction that knowledge of God comes not by reason but by revelation. So interpreted, the OT became a book of supernatural history but, what is most significant, a closed book. He made no attempt to expurgate it or to allegorize its contents as the gnostics on the one side/17/ and orthodox on the other attempted to do.

The inconsistency and ingenuousness of marcionite doctrine, perhaps reflecting a lack of theological sophistication going back to the biblically-centered Antitheses themselves, can be discerned in the encounter between Rhodo and Apelles, recounted by Eusebius:

> The old man Apelles . . . used to say that it is not necessary to investigate the argument fully, but that each should remain in his own belief, for he asserted that those who placed their hope in the crucified would be saved, if

---

/16/ Legge, 'Marcion' in Forerunners of Christianity (1915) II, 203ff.

/17/ Origen, de princ. 2.5.2; cf. Letter of Ptolemy to Flora; cf. Tert. de res. 20: in the context of defending the term resurrectione carnis, Tert. complains that the heretics misuse allegory to confute orthodox teaching. Cf. Praes. 38.

> they persisted in good works. But . . . the most obscure
> part of all the doctrines he put forward was about God.
> For he kept on saying that there is only one principle, just
> as our doctrine states . . . and when I said to him, 'Where
> is this proof of yours or how can you say, that there is one
> first principle, tell us!', he said that the prophecies refute
> themselves by not having spoken the truth at all, for they
> are inconsistent and false and contradict themselves, but
> as to how there is one principle, he said that he did not
> know it, but merely inclined to that view. When I adjured
> him to speak the truth, he swore that he was speaking the
> truth when he said that he did not know how the unbe-
> gotten God is one, but that he believed it. But I laughed
> at him and condemned him because though he called
> himself a teacher, he did not know how to establish what
> he taught./18/

This remarkable exchange between the sophisticated catholic teacher/19/
and the elderly Apelles may serve as a summary of the marcionite doctrine
of c. 150: a disdain for philosophical speculation and argumentation; the
centrality of faith in the crucified as the mode of salvation; suspicion of the
allegorical interpretation of the OT, combined with a minimalist view of
prophecy; the doctrine that God is not the object of knowledge but the
subject of christian belief.

It is generally agreed that Apelles was a renegade from Marcion's
doctrines and a 'corrector' of his ditheism./20/ According to Eusebius'
recapitulation of Rhodo's testimony, Apelles, acting under the influence of
'a possessed maiden named Philoumene',/21/ was one of a number of
marcionite schismatics. Presumably he was a serious loss to the cause,
since even Rhodo acknowledges that 'he was reverenced for his life and old
age', and the well- attested story of his lapse into carnality may have
originated in marcionite rather than in orthodox circles./22/ It is equally
clear, however, that Rhodo was anxious to document the inconsistency and
diffuseness of the Marcionites in contrast to the unity of catholic teaching,

---

/18/ Eus. HE 5.13.5f.

/19/ Disciple of Tatian at Rome c. 180; Eus. HE 5.13.8. Cf. Ps.-Tert.
Omn. haer. 7.

/20/ AM 3.11.2 'desertor Marcionis'; AM 4.17.11: 'Apelles, Marcionis de
discipulo emendator'; cf. de anima, 23; de carne, 6-9; Praes. 30.

/21/ Cf. Praes. 30: 'vis et efficacia daemorum, quibus agebatur'; cf.
Praes. 6; Ps.-Tert., Omn. haer. 6 and Eus. HE 5.13.2.

/22/ Cf. Praes. 30.

so his testimony is not irrefragable proof that Marcion's teaching differed radically from that of his pupil. This recognition is the more important, as suggested by Harnack,/23/ since Rhodo is the first (independent) witness to the teaching of Marcion between Irenaeus and Tertullian, and unlike the others, the only one with direct experience of first-generation Marcionism. Setting aside his polemical design, Rhodo's testimony concerning Apelles yields the following outline.

(a) That there is one first principle, or more precisely, that the unbegotten God is a unity. He does not identify this god as creator of the world.

(b) That the prophecies are of an opposing Spirit (*'tas de prophēteias ex antikeimenou legei pneumatos'*)./24/

(c) He rejects the law of Moses (*Ho ge toi Apellēs houtos myria kata tou Mōyseōs ēsebēsen nomou, etc.*)./25/

(d) He acknowledges the primacy of faith and commends the doing of good works.

(e) He acknowledges the reality of the crucifixion, but denies the human birth of Jesus./26/

(f) He teaches the salvation of souls alone and denies the resurrection of the flesh.

---

/23/ Cf. <u>Sieben neue Bruchstücke der Syllogismen des Apelles</u>, (TU 6/37: 1890), 111-120. Idem., <u>Unbeachte und neue Quellen zur Kenntnis des Häretikers Apelles</u>, (TU 20: 1900), 93-100.

/24/ HE 5.13.2. Harnack has suggested that Apelles went much further than Marcion in his rejection of the OT. This is borne out by fragments of the <u>Syllogisms</u>, which originally comprised 38 books, preserved by Jerome in de <u>Paradiso</u>. Ps.-Tert. characterized the purpose of the work as being 'to show what Moses has written about God was not true but false' (<u>Omn. haer.</u> 6). The <u>Syllogisms</u> may be roughly characterized as a radical recasting of the <u>Antitheses</u> in which the dialectical structure of the earlier work was replaced by a simple polemic against the law.

/25/ HE 5.13.9; Origen, <u>contra Cels.</u> 5.54, declares that 'Apelles does not believe the books of the Jews which relate miracles'.

/26/ <u>Omn. haer.</u> 6; Tert. <u>de carne</u>, 6. According to Tert. and Hippol. Apelles went to some lengths to correct what he seems to have considered a weakness in the marcionite doctrine of the incarnation, softening Marcion's distinction between the reality and corporeality of Jesus by asserting a quasi-human body composed of aereal substances 'borrowed from the stars'. Cf. Hippol. <u>Ref. omn. hear.</u> 7.26.

(g)   He denies the creation of the world by the supreme God./27/

(h)   He accepts only the authority of Paul and the Gospel./28/

(i)   He stresses the 'shameful condition of the flesh'./29/

In essentials, Apelles seems to have agreed with Marcion that Christianity was based on the doctrine of the ultimate goodness of God and the salvation of the souls of men by faith in 'the crucified God'./30/ He was able to patch up the holes he discerned in Marcion's theology -- prëeminently the unresolved ditheism of his master's teaching -- at the expense of eliminating the OT altogether; "He has tried to prove . . . that whatever Moses has written about God is not true but false'./31/ The meaning of christian revelation was indeed radically new, but new because everything passing under the name of religion in the past had been a lie: Moses and the prophets had not anticipated the revelation of the true God, but instead had attempted to pass off the works of the Creator as the supreme manifestation of the divine purpose. The coming of Jesus had not (thus) shown the relativity of righteousness and love, as it had in Marcion's theology, but rather revealed all that had been spoken about God in scripture to be false: there was not one God in two dispensations, nor two gods, one known and one unknown; but one archon/32/ whose goodness had been obscured by the adherence of the Jews to the law 'of a certain angel of great renown' who had created the world and afterward repented of the act.

It can hardly be said, in view of the active opposition between God and the world which Apelles envisaged, that he 'rejected his teacher's dualism'./33/ And although his christology was designed to bridge the gap between the worlds of flesh and spirit and perhaps (but only perhaps) to supply a rationale for the redemption of the soul, it is certain that Apelles'

---

/27/ De carne, 8. According to Apelles, the creator repented of having made the world. Cf. J.-P. Mahé, 'Apelles' in Sources chrét. 216 (1975), 94-112.

/28/ Omn. haer. 6.

/29/ De carne, 8.

/30/ De carne, 5; cf. Eus. HE 5.13.5.

/31/ Cf. Omn. haer. 6; Eus. HE 5.13.9.

/32/ De carne, 8; Praes. 6.

/33/ So Quasten, Patrology I, 273.

religious ideas were of a more gnostic cast than those of his teacher. This suggestion seems curious in light of the fact that Apelles' purpose seems to have been to correct precisely those features of Marcion's theology which were most prone to philosophical attack from the orthodox, and those which have always been cited as the 'gnostic' elements of Marcion's religious thought: namely, the doctrine of two gods and the 'reality' of the flesh of Christ. Beginning with the testimony that Apelles acknowledged only one first principle/34/ and 'admitted that Christ really had a body' (Tertullian/ Rhodo), might not one conclude that Apelles had only retreated from the 'gnostic' themes of Marcion's thought, while preserving in substance the soteriological and biblical (pauline) emphases which had been a part of his training in the marcionite church?

Unfortunately, this conclusion is not warranted. Even Tertullian recognizes that Apelles' attempts to correct and supplement the doctrines of his teacher are a step farther away from the catholic faith than Marcion's heresy: Thus he complains that Apelles thought himself wiser than his teacher and that having fallen from the principles of Marcion, leapt out of the frying pan into the fire. The reasons for Tertullian's disapproval of Apelles, or rather his comparative preference for the 'old school' of Marcionites/35/ from which Apelles apostatized, cannot have only to do with his departure from the rigorist moral principles of 'his most abstemious master'. The suggestion that Apelles 'conceded to Christ real flesh without effect on [his] denial of the nativity',/36/ for example, can scarcely be seen as warranting Tertullian's belief that Apelles' heresy was a 'fall' from Marcionism. But if Apelles' system does not entirely comport with Marcion's, in what direction does it point: to Rome, or to Alexandria?

## 5.3 Marcionism and Nag Hammadi Gnosticism

In the transition from Marcionism to the teaching of his closest known disciple, we have an opportunity to discover, as we cannot for example in a

---

/34/ Rhodo in Eus. HE 5.13.5; cf. AM 3.11.2: 'Nam et Philumene illa magis persuasit Apelli ceterisque desertoribus Marcionis ex fide quidem Christum circumtulisse carnem, etc.'

/35/ Praes. 30; cf. AM 4.17.11; de carne 6.

/36/ De carne, 6.

comparison of Marcion's teaching with that of Valentinus or in searching the thought of Marcion for gnostic motifs and themes,/37/ the essentially original character of his radical paulinism. We may also discover why the attempt to correct Marcion's paulinism led almost inevitably to the philosophy of the gnostic schools, and to the semi-gnosticism of Pontitus, Basilicus, and to the eventual assimilation of Marcionism to Manichaeism. For in Apelles' system, the OT, which for Marcion still has the value of a distinct, historical revelation,/38/ dissolves into myth. The link between revelation and history is definitively broken in the claim that 'what Moses has written about God is not true but false'.

The parallels between Apelles' system and that of the gnostics is especially close at this point. In the Apocryphon of John, for example, the conventional motif of Adam's deception by the first Archon (Ialdabaoth) is directly linked to Moses' falsifying of the story: the refrain 'not as Moses said' becomes an exegetical device intended to extract the truth from the Genesis account, thus,

> And I said to the savior, 'What is the forgetfulness? And he said, 'It is not the way Moses wrote and you heard. For he said in his first book "He put him to sleep" [Gen 2.21], but it was in his perception./39/

A similar theme is broached in the Clementine Recognitions, where the heresy of Simon is made to turn on his scriptural proofs of the Creator's malefaction./40/ Here we have to do not with the declaration that the God whom Moses and the prophets preached was not the Father of Jesus Christ

---

/37/ Cf. Mühlenberg, 'Marcion's Jealous God', Disciplina Nostra, 110.

/38/ Harnack has pointed out that Marcion retained Lk 16.16-17: ('Ho nomos kai hoi prophētai mechri Iōannou') which is a recognition of the provisional (historical) validity of the law prior to the revelation of the alien God. That is to say, the God of Moses is only 'rejected' in virtue of the superior revelation of the 'stranger' (Ephraem). His law, which is absolute in historical terms, is relativised by the message of salvation. Harnack has stressed that Marcion 'thought appreciatively of the Mosaic Law', a conclusion based on his reconstruction of Marcion's gospel where he finds that Marcion failed to expurgate passages such as Lk 10.27 and 16.29, which allude favorably to the law (Lev 18.5-19.18) and to Moses and the prophets. Marcion may have retained Rom 13.8-10; 2.13, 20. Harnack, Marcion, 109f.; cf. Blackman, Influence, 114.

/39/ Apoc. John, II.1/22.21-25.

/40/ Recog. H-III, 38.1f. (NTA II, 550-551).

(ascribed to Cerdo, and according to Irenaeus, developed by Marcion),/41/ nor with the mediating (Valentinian?) speculation of Ptolemy's Letter to Flora which is close to the Apocryphon in terms of its approach to the Mosaic law. Rather, we confront the assertion that Moses was the dupe and scribe of the demiurge, who had blinded him to the truth;/42/ the counterfeit spirit had conspired to deceive Adam and his descendants (i.e., to hide from them the message of salvation). According to the Apocryphon of John, the archons delight in deception./43/ In marcionite speculation Moses shares in the general ignorance of the Jews regarding the existence of the alien God, and incurs no guilt by recording the righteous acts of the God of history./44/ Apelles, like the author of the Apocryphon, regards the OT first and foremost in terms of a masterful deceit perpetrated by the sons of the Creator, the choikoi, who cannot inherit the kingdom of God. Thus the revelation of Jesus Christ is fundamentally for Apelles the exposure of their deceit. As depicted by the visionary in the Apocryphon, the savior is the corrector of the false revelation handed down among the choikoi for the sake of perpetuating 'forgetfulness' of the imperium of the Creator-Archon's dominion over the soul of man:

> And he smiled and said, 'Do not think it is, as Moses said, "above the waters". No, but when she had seen the wickedness which had happened, and the theft which her son had committed, she repented. . . .
>
> He repented for everything which had come into being through him . . . . He planned to bring a flood over the work of man. But the greatness of the light of the fore-knowledge [pronoia] informed Noah, and he proclaimed [it] to all the offspring which are the sons of men. But those who were strangers to him did not listen to him. It is not as Moses said, "They hid themselves in an ark" [Gen

---

/41/ Iren. Haer. 1.27.1-2.

/42/ 2 Seth, VII.2/63.26f.

/43/ Apoc. John, II.1/21.21.

/44/ Tertullian does imply (5.11.10) that the Marcionites accused the Creator of 'threatening', in order to 'hide away the gospel of the unknown God', but elsewhere (1.9.2f.; 4.16.15; 1.19.1f., etc.) says that the Marcionites boasted of their God remaining hidden and that the Creator was ignorant of another God above him (1.11.9) and lacked foreknowledge (2.23.1, 3; 2.24.2; 2.25.1; 2.28.1). The contrast with the gnostic view of Moses is especially impressive in the marcionite imterpretation of Exod 32.32: 'Unde meliorem soletis affirmare Moysen deo suo, deprecatorem, immo et prohibitorem irae' (2.26.3).

> 7.7], but they hid themselves in a place, not only Noah
> but also many other people from the immovable race'./45/

In the revelation-dialogue from Nag Hammadi known as 'The Second Treatise
of the Great Seth' and given as a message of Jesus Christ to 'the perfect and
incorruptible ones', we find still other parallels to Apelles' teaching. In this
treatise, the God of this world (here identified with the God of the OT) is
both evil and ignorant:

> Moses . . . was a laughing stock, . . . [perversely bear-
> ing] witness concerning him [the OT God] who never
> knew me. Neither he nor those before him, from Adam
> to Moses and John the Baptist, none of them knew
> me . . . for there is a great deception upon their soul
> making it impossible . . . [since] I am he whom the world
> did not know, and because of this [the world] rose up
> against me . . . . [The Creator] was a laughing stock
> because he said, 'I am God and there is none greater than
> I. I alone am the Father, the Lord, and there is no other
> beside me./46/

The evidence will not permit us to say that Apelles derived his later teach-
ings from the schools of Valentinus of Basilides. But a reference in
Tertullian's de Praescriptione to the effect that Apelles 'withdrew from
Marcion to Alexandria',/47/ if it is taken as historical, may mean that his
'correction' was accomplished under the influence of the Valentinian gnosticism then flourishing in Egypt and represented in the generation after
Valentinus' death (c. 165) by Julius Cassianus (c. CE 190). The Testimony of
Truth,/48/ usually ascribed to him and included among the papyri discovered
in upper Egypt, suggests that the teachers of Alexandrian gnosticism toward
the end of the second century emphasized many of the same themes which
Apelles' correction of Marcion entailed. In going beyond the (marcionite)
claim that OT revelation had been provisional and inferior, and adopting the
view that it was no revelation at all, but rather a malicious design by the
Creator to obscure the nature of the supreme God, Apelles seems to have
joined hands with the Alexandrian teachers.

---

/45/ Apoc. John, II.1/13.18-23; II.1/28.32-29.10.

/46/ 2 Seth, VII.2/63.26-64.22.

/47/ Praes. 30.

/48/ Test. Truth, NHL, 406-416. Birger Pearson has correctly said that
Valentinian gnostic influence is evident throughout the Testimony 'even
though the Valentinians and Basilideans are there attacked as heretics'
(NHL, 406).

Nonetheless, many of these motifs or themes are sufficiently close to those developed by Marcion in the Antitheses, that Apelles on encountering them might well have been satisfied that they represented a necessary addendum to Marcion's christian ditheism. We find in the Testimony, concerning the expulsion from the Garden, this appraisal of the Creator's malice and ignorance:

> Of what sort is this God? First [he] envied Adam that he should eat from the tree of Knowledge. And secondly he said, 'Adam, where are you?' And God does not have foreknowledge . . . since he did not know this from the beginning. [And] afterwards he said, 'Let us cast him [out] of this place, lest he eat of the tree of life and live forever'. Surely he has shown himself to be a malicious envier [cf. AM 2.25.1: 'Inclamat deus, Adam ubi es? scilicet ignorans ubi esset']. . . .
>
> And he said, 'I am the jealous God; I will bring the sins of the fathers upon the children' . . . . And he said, 'I will make their heart thick and . . . their mind to become blind, that they might not know nor comprehend the things that are said'. . . . [This] is the [way] Moses [writes] in every book./49/

The aemulatio of the Creator was a sticking point for Marcion as well (cf. AM 1.25.6; 1.26.5; 2.29.3). The legalist Tertullian saw jealousy as the indispensable prerogative of a proprietary God and Judge. Marcion shared with the Alexandrian gnostics the view that the story of the expulsion from the Garden (Gen 3.9f.) testified to the ignorance and petulance of the Creator ('ad ceteras pusillitates et infirmitates et incongruentias'):/50/ and it is a short step from so viewing the matter to the position of Apelles and the Alexandrian gnostics: 'Surely he has shown himself a malicious envier'. But in distinguishing Marcion's theology from that of the Alexandrians, we must understand the significance of this step.

The gnostic Archon or world-creator is conventionally imagined as the disastrous product/51/ of an acosmic crisis in the pleroma. According to the Valentinian speculation, the godhead (in its unexplicated and perfect form) dwells in 'invisible and nameless heights'. He is pre-existent and

---

/49/ Test. Truth, IX.3/47.14-30; 48.4-13; 50.3-5.

/50/ AM 2.25.1.

/51/ General survey, G. Quispel, 'Gnosis' in Die orientalischen Religionen im Römerreich (1981), 413-434.

unbegotten. Nothing can comprehend him./52/ But he is not, so to speak, a homogeneous assembly./53/ The 'endless genealogies', mentioned by the author of the letter to Titus (3.9), refer to the systematic diremption of his divine characteristics 'through immeasurable eternities'. While he is not in any direct sense the 'Creator' (the gnostic cosmogony being a spatial hyperbole of the gulf between the pneuma and the pleroma), he is in some sense the conditio sine qua non of creation./54/

The Apocryphon of John, representing the Syrian or 'Sophia-gnosis', is perhaps the closest parallel in the Nag Hammadi literature to the Valentinian speculation detailed by Irenaeus./55/ The Apocryphon begins with the 'hypostatizing' activity of the first principle to form Barbelo, the aeons, seven archons, and (in parody of the higher creative activity by which Sophia and Ialdabaoth came into being, and out of which the lesser order originates) the archontic creation of 'psychical' man (= Adam). In an attempt to recover the power which she had passed on to her sons, the first archon, Sophia, contrives to assist the archons in their struggle to animate psychical man. When she does so, pneumatic man is born and begins to move. The natural inclination of the pleroma is hence downward toward formlessness. The crisis in the pleroma is fortified and sustained in the error of creation and the imprisonment of the pneuma. It becomes in effect the function of the world-creator, through his minions, to prevent the refunding of perfections to the pleroma and the salvation of (pneumatic) man. This is what is meant in the Testimony of Truth when the author says 'no one who is under the Law will be able to look up to the truth . . . but undefilement belongs to the light; . . . and they [turn] away from the light who are unable [to pass by] the Archon of [darkness] until they pay the last [penny]'./56/ The distinction between 'the light' and the law is also figured as the difference between 'imperishability', from which the son of man comes forth, and 'carnality', which is the realm of the demiurge, and those

---

/52/ E.g., GT I.3/22.27f.; Apoc. John, II.1/3.14f.; Iren. Haer. 1.1.1f.; Epiph. Panar. 31.5.1f.

/53/ Thus Jonas, Gnostic Religion, 181f.

/54/ Iren. Haer. 1.1.1; R.A. Markus, 'Pleroma and Fulfillment', VC 8 (1954), 193ff.

/55/ Jonas, Gnostic Religion, 177; Quispel, 'Gnosis', 420.

/56/ Test. Truth, IX.3/29.22-25; 30.1, 13-17.

who keep his law. The paulinist trajectory is evident in this dichotomy. We know enough of Apelles' system to be able to say that his christology presupposes these themes, and incorporates a typically gnostic view of the malice of the Creator (demiourgos) as part of an archontic plan to interfere with the redemption of the pneuma.

Marcion presupposes no such scheme. It is true that, like Apelles, Marcion denied the nativity of Jesus./57/ But this denial in itself is no trademark of gnosticism. Several of the Nag Hammadi authors attest belief in the 'human' birth of Jesus, even if the physiology implied in their accounts is ambiguous. Thus in the Tripartite Tractate,

> Not only did he take upon himself the death of those whom he thought to save, but also he accepted their smallness to which they had descended . . . because he had let himself be conceived and born as an infant, in body and soul./58/

And in the Testimony of Truth,

> What is the meaning of this mystery? John was begotten by means of a womb worn with age, but Christ passed through a virgin's womb. When she had conceived she gave birth to the Savior. Furthermore she was found to be a virgin again./59/

The rejection of the nativity-legend, or of the virgin-birth, cannot be accounted a proof of gnosticism, and its appropriation no proof of orthodoxy. This leaves open for the moment the possibility that Marcion's

---

/57/ In the de carne Christi Tert. complains that Marcion removed from his gospel the 'original records of the history of Christ', including the virgin's conception, pregnancy, and child bearing' and thus was unable to grasp the full idea of his flesh (de carne, 2). But that Marcion actually denied the nativity is unlikely. In all probability, Lk 1-3 did not appear in his source; and Paul, in line with his general indifference to 'knowing Jesus after the flesh', scarcely makes mention of the legend of Jesus' birth. Tert.'s diatribe in the second ch. of de carne ('Away with that eternal tax of Caesar, the squalid inn and swaddling clothes, the hard stable') does not reproduce any evidence from Marcion's works. Further on, Tertullian tells us that Marcion 'does not reject the assumption of a body as impossible or as hazardous to the character of God' (de carne, 4); nor did Marcion follow the habits of the gnostics in identifying the body of Christ with the personification of Wisdom (de carne, 5: AM 3.11.6) but asserted that Jesus' body was of a different substance than human flesh. Although Tert. is only sparing in his treatment of Lk 23, it is clear that Marcion conceived of the passion and death of Jesus in highly realistic terms. Thus Tert.'s insistence (AM 3.11.8) that nativity was not more disgraceful than the cross.

/58/ Tri. Tract. I.5/115.4-10.

/59/ Test. Truth, IX.3/45.11-19.

rejection of the nativity was due to his ignorance of or skepticism about the Lucan account, and to the profundity of Paul's silence on the subject. If this is so, then the christological implications which Tertullian adduces from Marcion's omission of Lk 1-3 are probably determined more by his own views on the subject of corporeality than by views expressed by Marcion./60/ What is significant is that Marcion's Christ suffers and dies. And this is precisely what the gnostic redeemer does not do, since the real 'passion' is the acosmic crisis in the pleroma itself./61/

It has often been pointed out that the views of Apelles concerning the reality of the flesh of Christ were less docetic than those of his teacher. According to Tertullian, Apelles believed 'that Christ borrowed his flesh from the stars and from the substances of the higher world'./62/ Tertullian also tells us that Apelles' followers 'lay great stress on the shameful condition of the flesh', which they hold to be furnished with souls by the author of evil,/63/ viz., the repentant angel who created the world. Such flesh, Apelles claimed, was unfit for Christ, who composed his body of celestial elements during his descent. Hippolytus offers a fuller version of the infor-

---

/60/ AM 5.10.7f.; de carne: de res. Tert. holds that 'the soul is corporeal, possessing a peculiar kind of solidity in its nature such as enables it both to perceive and suffer' (de res. 17); although the soul 'requires the conjunction of the flesh to endure suffering in order that by its aid it may be as able to suffer as, without its assistance, it was not fully able to act'. Because the soul and the flesh act together they are destined to be raised and judged together 'for that which is a suitable object to be judged is also a competent one to be raised' (de res. 14). In defending the resurrection of the flesh, Tert. glosses over the pauline dichotomy of body and spirit (cf. 2 Cor 5.6-7), or more precisely the distinction between 'the dead' and 'the bodies of the dead' which is central to Paul's thought. 'Corpus est quod amittit animam, et amittendo fit mortuum; ita mortui vocabulum corpori competit. Porro si resurrectio mortui est, mortuum autem non aliud est quam corpus, corporis erit resurrectio'; AM 5.9.3f.; cf. 5.10.6f.; cf. de res. 40-41.

/61/ A possible exception is the Valentinian Gospel of Truth, I.3/20.10f. And cf. Gos. Philip, II.3/56.15f.: 'Those who say that the Lord died first and then rose up are in error'. Though as Jonas has remarked (Gnostic Religion, 196 n. 28): 'It remains true that in the total theology of the Valentinians the suffering of the Sophia and not that of Christ, is the central fact, doctrinally and emotionally'. Cf. Apoc. James, I.2/6.1-5; 2 Seth, VII.2/55.15-30; Haer. 1.24.4.

/62/ De carne, 6-7, Apelles taking as his prooftext Lk 3.20, 21, which Marcion also took to contradict the nativity narratives being propagated by the judaizers'; AM 4.19.10f; cf. AM 3.11.3; 4.36.8f.; 4.26.13.

/63/ De carne, 8.

mation supplied by Tertullian.

> [Apelles] introduces one God in the infinite upper regions,
> and states that He made many powers and angels; beside
> him was another Virtue, which he affirms to be called
> 'Lord', but represents as an angel. By him he will have it
> appear that the world was originated in imitation of a
> superior world. With this lower world he mingled
> throughout a principle of repentance, because he had not
> made it so perfectly as that superior world had been
> originated . . . . [Christ] descended from the upper
> regions, [and] in the course of his descent he wove
> together for himself a starry and airy flesh; and in his
> resurrection restored, in the course of his ascent, to the
> several individual elements whatever had been borrowed in
> his descent: and thus -- the several parts of his body
> dispersed -- He reinstated in heaven his spirit only. /64/

A number of gnostic motifs, apparently of Valentinian provenance, are
present in this description of Apelles' system. The world is a product of
'deficiency' occasioned by the crisis in the pleroma: a mere imitation of the
'pure light which no eye can behold'. /65/ This corresponds to the 'Narcissus-
motif'/66/ that runs through much of the Nag Hammadi literature. According to the Tripartite Tractate, the Creator (Logos) 'begot in shadows,
models, and likenesses. For he was not able to bear the sight of the light,
but he looked into the depth and he doubted'. /67/

In the strictest sense (as Tertullian observes of Apelles' doctrine)
creation is an 'error', corrupt from its inception in the mind of the Creator;
it is an act of hybris to which the supreme God (Aeon) is not materially
connected. Because it is the product of hybris, it is the imperfect image of
the godhead. Thus, 'The Lord of the Universe is not called "Father" but
"First Father", the source of those that were to be revealed. [Now] he is
the beginningless First Father who beholds himself within himself as with a

---

/64/ Ps.-Tert., Omn. haer. 6.

/65/ Cf. Apoc. John, II.1/2.31f.

/66/ Or taken over from the hellenistic legend of the 'mirror of Dionysius',
Quispel, 'Gnosis', 420f.

/67/ Tri Tract. I.5/77.16-20.

mirror'./68/ Salvation consists in healing the deficiency, '[so] that the whole pleroma may again become holy and faultless',/69/ a transaction that calls in the first place for an end to the 'duplication' of 'those who belong to Adam' (i.e., to the flesh, and hence to the Creator). In the Apocryphon of John, which we have already mentioned in connection with Apelles' attitude toward the OT, it is said specifically that the Creator 'repented for everything which had come into being'./70/ And in the same document, the divine revealer (Pronoia) undertakes a descensus from the upper regions, and ascends again to the perfect aeon [II.1/30, 17-32]. In the Sophia of Jesus Christ, the revealer 'drops [down] from the light' to the lower regions 'so that he might reveal [to them] their molded forms' as a judgment on the Creator,/71/ in order to reveal the God who is above the Creator. So too in the Second Treatise of the Great Seth the Savior makes his way through the heavens by stealth: 'as I came downward no one saw me. For I was altering my shapes, changing from form to form. And therefore, when I was at their gates I assumed their likeness . . .'/72/ This journey parallels the cosmogonic process of the 'sinking of the soul', or the downward movement of the divine principle, often depicted as the light becoming enamoured of and sinking into the darkness, as in the Hermetic literature. In the Poimandres (c. 100: Dodd), where the antithesis of the Creator and the supreme God is absent, it is suggested that the divine emanation 'acquires' substance in its downward trajectory, becoming encased in the matter of darkness, which tries to retain it. So too in the Poimandres, the 'divesting' of these elements occurs during the ascent through the spheres, until such point as the light is disengaged from its earthly encumbrances. The motif is

---

/68/ Soph. Jes. Chr. III.4/98.22-99.3. In the Letter of Peter to Philip, the deficient aeons, themselves the offspring of the 'disobedience' of the mother, 'do not know the preexistent ones', but arrogance (authades: the personified emotion of the mother) continues to produce increasingly imperfect images: 'Untrue copies from the semblance which had emerged' (VIII.2/136.14f.; cf. Treat. on the Res. I.3/44.34-38).

/69/ Apoc. John, II.1/25/14f.

/70/ Apoc. John, II.1/28.33; cf. Gen 6.3, 6; cf. Clem. Recog. H-III, 39.4 (NTA II, 551).

/71/ Soph. Jes. Chr. III.4/119.6, 10f.

/72/ 2 Seth, VII.2/56.21-27f; cf. Letter of Peter to Philip, VIII.2/136.17-20; cf. Test. Truth, IX.3/32.22ff.

also suggested in the ceremonial 'passing through the gates' (climax heptaphlos) in the Mithra Liturgy known to Celsus./73/ Elsewhere the ascent is imaged in terms of a divesting of garments, or a loosing of knots. Irenaeus knows the process as 'the divestiture of the animal soul'./74/ One notes also the significance of fire among the elements in the Poimandres, and Apelles' claim that the souls are governed by a fiery spirit of evil (ab igneo illo praeside mali)./75/

All of this may serve to indicate a decided 'gnosticizing' of Marcion's teaching by his disciple./76/ That Apelles appropriated certain gnostic 'themes' from the Alexandrians in order to patch up the holes in Marcion's theology is clearly supported by evidence from gnostic literature, even if in comparison with Valentinus and Basilides, Apelles' 'gnosticism' is of a marginal type. Significantly, we are told that he holds to Paul as the only authority, and that, like Marcion, he teaches the salvation of souls alone. No mention is made of a tradition of 'knowledge' among Apelles and his followers. His doctrine of the flesh of Christ is sketchy and seems to have lacked the complex mythological detail typical of the Alexandrian gnosis. Indeed, Rhodo calls Apelles to task not because his system is overwrought, but because it is too simple. His 'stress on the shameful condition of the flesh', reported by Tertullian in the de carne Christi, may cause us to doubt Tertullian's other comments concerning Apelles' 'carnality';/77/ but whether the followers of Apelles based their asceticism on marcionite practice or on some belief derived from Alexandrian dualism cannot be determined. What is significant here, to repeat the assertion with which we began, is that

---

/73/ Origen, contra Cels. 6.22. Valuable information on this motif is supplied by Chadwick, Origen Contra Celsum, 334, n. 2; cf. further F. Cumont, The Mysteries of Mithra (1903), 144ff.

/74/ Haer. 1.7.1; cf. 1.21.5.

/75/ De carne, 8; cf. Hippol. Ref. omn. haer. 10.16.

/76/ There is no evidence that Apelles produced a fully-fledged cosmogony. By the same token Marcion is not known to have developed a coherent cosmogony; and his belief in the 'descent' of Christ is indicted by Tert. for precisely this fault: 'Nunc autem et reliquum ordinem descensionis expostulo, tenens descendisse illum'. Marcion seems to have said only that Christ 'appeared' ('Viderit enim sicubi apparuisse positum est' AM 4.7.2); though Tert. infers that the Christ of the alien God must have come through the Creator's territory (loc. cit.).

/77/ Praes. 30; Ps.-Tert., Omn. haer. 6; cf. Praes. 33.

Tertullian understands Apelles' system as a departure from Marcion's more conservative principles. Here we can suggest that Tertullian recognized this schismatic form of Marcion's teaching as a drift leftward toward the teaching of Valentinus. This would explain not only Tertullian's curious allusion to Apelles' insubordination ('Sed non est discipulus super magistrum'),/78/ but also the fact that according to the arrangement of de Praes. 30 Apelles is, in doctrinal terms, a transitional figure between the heresy of Marcion and that of Valentinus. This arrangement is more fully explicated in Tertullian's discussion of the various docetic heresies in de carne Christi: 'Apelles was first a disciple of his and afterwards an apostate'./79/

### 5.4 The Anti-Gnostic Trajectory of Marcion's Theology

As we can observe from this examination of the gnostic trend of Apelles' Marcionism, Paul's theology exercised a controlling influence on Marcion's thought which only begins to break down in the generation after his death. For if we accept that Apelles was a member of a 'schismatic' faction of the marcionite church, then we must also accept the existence of a 'mainstream' Marcionism which adhered more or less rigidly, if selectively, to the paulinism of the founder. It is Paul's controlling influence that distinguishes this 'orthodox' Marcionism from the speculative gnosticism of the Alexandrians, even if (ironically) precisely those motifs which Marcion singled out for emphasis in Paul's thought -- the meaning of revelation, salvation by faith, the use of the law -- are those that most readily admitted of a gnostic reconstruction. Although Marcion's radicalization of Paul's theology entailed the elaboration of such themes as were also near to the center of Alexandrian gnosticism, it is nonetheless clear that Marcion's treatment of these themes involved a control lacking in the gnostic speculation. And this must lead us to conclude, in the face of the evidence supplied by his opponents, that Marcion's salvation-centered theology involved an anti-gnostic strain no less self-consciously developed than the anti-judaizing stance represented in the doctrine of false apostleship. In this connection, Harnack's emphasis on Marcion's 'originality' leads us astray, for it encourages the belief that Marcion was free to follow the implications of

---

/78/ AM 4.17.11.

/79/ De carne, 1; cf. AM 3.11.2.

Paul's gospel in any direction he chose: that he did not formulate his dualistic theology in gnostic terms is thus explained as a consequence of his independence of Cerdo, rather than as a result of his dependence on Paul. But this is to put the accent where it does not belong. The internal dissension within the marcionite church toward the end of the second century centered on the belief that Marcion had not gone far enough. His fidelity to the ambiguous and unresolved dialectic embodied in the pauline epistles, unacceptable to orthodox and gnostic alike, can only be explained as a deliberate rejection of the gnosticizing of the apostle, in favor of a simplified and liberal, if philosophically näive, soteriology. If the conservatism of his approach to Paul caused dissatisfaction among his younger disciples, his solution to the 'meaning' of the epistles (about which there was no agreement even among his opponents: 2 Ptr 3.16) was looked upon as radical. One can assume that the second-century crisis in the marcionite church arose from the conviction that Paul's teaching could not easily be defended against orthodox revisions without revising it along different, that is to say gnostic, lines. The philosophical context for this revision was Alexandrian gnosticism. But for Marcion, this option was foreclosed: his appeal was not to rhetoricians and philosophers, but to those who pinned their hopes of salvation on faith in the crucified. His gospel-centered belief and refusal to allegorize or eliminate the OT as an independent and authentic source of revelation illustrates the antignostic and literalist strain in his theology. It suffers, not as Tertullian, Clement, and Hippolytus imagined./80/ from too much indulgence in Greek philosophy, but almost certainly from too little. In terms of his dependence on Paul's theology, he is not the most original, but perhaps the least inventive of early christian theologians.

## 5.5 Summary: Marcionism and Gnosticism

We can summarize the relation between Marcion's theology and that of the gnostic schools as follows:

(A) Marcion's teaching is free from the mythological speculation about first principles, acosmic crisis, and cosmic descent (diremption) which characterizes the theogonies of the gnostics. He does not postulate a plurality of divine and semi-divine beings extending from the supreme God to the world-

---

/80/ Tert. AM 1.25.3; 2.16.2; 4.15.2; 5.19.7; Clement, Strom. 3.3.13; Hippol. Ref. omn. haer. 7.17; 10.15.

creator and thence to the lower orders of creation. The actual bond between the creatures of the world and the Creator is not weakened by the idea that they are somehow alien to the world. That is to say, no necessary or causal links exist between the Creator and the supreme God, much less between the supreme God and man. Only once and only through one activity does the supreme God 'intervene' or reveal himself in history, namely, in the sending down of his son to redeem man from the justice of the Creator. But in no sense is this providential -- i.e., it does signify the beginning of God's stewardship of the world. It is, in the purest sense, a 'revelation' of a being and divine nature previously unknown./81/

(B) According to Marcion's gnostic contemporaries soteriology is an adjunct of necessity. The acosmic crisis in the pleroma, resulting in the spillage and descent of perfections into the created order, requires correction. This correction, in turn, entails the 'ingathering' of the dispersed (pneumatic) elements belonging properly to a higher order of being. As Marcion appears to have acknowledged no relationship between the unknown God and the Creator, soteriology has to do exclusively with the nature of God (goodness) and the plight of man (law); man does not participate in the nature of God; his soul is not an incarcerate fragment of divine being. But in some unspecified way, his soul is free from the constraints of the Creator's justice and hence worthy of salvation.

(C) Compared to the supreme God, the Creator is not absolutely evil,/82/ but in exercising his dominion over his property, he displays a kind of justice and jealousy which, in comparison with the perfect goodness of the alien God, can only be viewed as malice. The plight of man under the law is to be ignorant of anything beyond this justice which counts for goodness.

(D) Although Marcion did not think highly of the created order,/83/ he does not seem to have taught a 'gnostic' doctrine of creation: i.e., creation as an act of hybris directed at the Perfect Aeon and intended as an imitation of

---

/81/ AM 1.19.1.

/82/ Cf. Harnack, Marcion, 31-34.

/83/ The inference drawn by his more philosophical opponents was that Marcion's emphasis on continence entailed the belief 'that nature is evil because it was created out of evil matter' (Clement, Strom. 3.3.12; cf. Tert. AM 1.14.3f.; 1.29.5f.). Clement also provides that the Marcionites abstain from marriage because they 'do not wish to fill the world made by the Creator God' (loc. cit.); further Harnack, Marcion, 273*--77*.

his pleroma; it is an act performed in ignorance of the existence of the supreme God and of the nature of absolute goodness, and to that extent (implicitly) justifiable./84/ It should be stressed that Marcion's belief in the 'ignorance' of the Creator is almost certainly not a deduction based on cosmological speculation concerning divisions in the pleroma;/85/ the theme is present in Paul's thought (cf. 1 Cor 2.8).

(E) Marcion makes faith rather than knowledge the mode of redemption, and the only appropriate response to revelation. In this he follows Paul closely: *'Logizometha gar dikaiousthai pistei . . .'* (Rom 3.28). Faith as response to divine revelation means freedom from the law of death (Rom 3.28; 8.2) and life in the Spirit of Christ: the 'law of faith' (Rom 3.27). Marcion envisaged no 'cosmic ascent' of the soul as a correlate of faith; he accepted Paul's view of the resurrection as the revival of 'spiritual' man (1 Cor 15.48f.; cf. AM 5.9.2; 5.10.3), Christ's death and resurrection being the paradigm of the process (1 Cor 15.21-2; cf. AM 5.8.6f.; 3.11.7f.; 4.43.6ff.). Certainly Paul's reference to the 'destruction of death' (1 Cor 15.26), to the effect that God's enemies will be destroyed that 'God may be all in all' (*'Hina ē ho theos panta en pasin'*: 15.28) admits of gnostic development; but we have no evidence that Marcion thus interpreted the passage. It is important to keep in view that Marcion understood redemption not as the reintegration of the dispersed elements of the godhead, but as freedom

---

/84/ Apelles required the creator (Angel) to repent of creation, whereas Marcion understands creation in terms similar to those advanced later by Plotinus, viz., as the telos of the creator (2 Ennead 9.8). The ignorance and hybris of the creator is also a theme in Valentinian speculation (cf. Hear. 1.5.4). As Jonas observes (p. 45), 'Ignorance is the essence of mundane existence, just as it was the principle of the world's coming into existence'. In particular the transcendent God is unknown in the world: therefore revelation is needed. Cf. 2 Seth, VII.2/64.7-25; Test. Truth, IX.3/48.1.13; On the Origin of the World, II.5/99/3-9; and cf. especially Marcion's view given in AM I.II.9.

/85/ Marcion did not regard the significance of revelation as self-evident, as it is represented in much gnostic literature (cf. 2 Seth, VII.2/52.2-10), nor merely to consist in explicating the cosmic distance between the spiritual and material worlds which the metaphor of ignorance (otherwise 'numbness' or 'intoxication') connotes. Cf. GT I.3/17.1, 10, 29f.; 18.12ff. Revelation is not a 'call' to secret gnosis, but a declaration of the mysterion of divine love. But the idea that the creator's ignorance implicates him in the crucifixion is clearly an exaggeration of Paul's view and marks a conjunction between Marcion's thought and that of the (Alexandrian) gnostic Christians. Cf. e.g., Haer. 1.24.4: '[Basilides holds] that Jesus was crucified through ignorance and error'.

from the Creator's law. In saving mankind, the supreme God does not save his own but another's, a recognition which provoked the legalist Tertullian to remark that Marcion's God was no respecter of property: 'Totus ergo in alieno habitat deus Marcionis si non creatoris sumus templum'./86/

(F) The christology of Marcion bears only little resemblance to the eclectic revealer-myths of the gnostics. In the latter, Christ (or Christ and the female principle, Holy Spirit) are messengers sent to reveal to the perfect 'the hidden mystery',/87/ and thereby compensate for the error (creation) initiated by the hybris of Sophia. Marcion does not dwell on the negative content, the hiddenness of the mysterion revealed through the announcement of man's alienation from God, since this alienation is of an altogether different order than that envisaged in the gnostic myth of redemption. Rather, he stresses the positive content, in terms that preserve the dichotomy between the unknown God and the object of his revelation: Here too Marcion seems to refrain from carrying the pauline emphasis in a 'gnostic' direction, as for example that represented in the Gospel of Truth. To be sure, Paul provided for a sharp distinction between psyche and pneuma (protos and deuteros anthropos) and envisioned Christ as the heavenly man, but he postulated no cosmic descent or genealogy 'relating' Christ to man: salvation depends entirely on a unilateral action undertaken by God acting in Christ to change man from the first to second condition. Prior to this change, man is not in any respect 'spiritual' (ou prōton to pneumatikon alla to psychikon, epeita to pneumatikon); as a result of it, he bears the image of the heavenly (1 Cor 15.46, 49)./88/ The mystery for Paul consists in the metamorphosis itself (1 Cor 15.51): the process by which that which is 'corruptible' becomes 'incorruptible'. God's action in Christ, foretold in the resurrection (and in the appearance of the risen Jesus to Paul), is the guarantee that this change occurs (1 Cor 15.52b). But there is nothing in the nature of man that establishes or warrants his redemption; it takes place according to the 'hidden purposes of God'. It is precisely this emphasis on God's direct, saving action that gnosticism, with its emphasis on genealogy (the 'necessity' of salvation as a

---

/86/ AM 5.6.11.

/87/ GT I.3/18.15; cf. 1 Cor 2.6-7f.: 'Sophian de laloumen en tois teleiois . . . sophian en mystēriō'.

/88/ Cf. the Nag Hammadi Treat. on the Res. NHL, 50-53.

consequence of the primal diremption of the godhead) erodes. Thus, in stressing the grace of God as the motive of salvation and the only means of overcoming the division betwen the spiritual and created order, Marcion distinguishes himself from the metaphysical determinism of the gnostic schools.

(G) In the gnostic christologies, the message of the savior ordinarily involves the impartation of secret wisdom, marking the way of the soul's ascent through the cosmos./89/ Marcion does not seem to have developed this strain of Paul's theology (1 Cor 2.6): the 'mystery of faith' relates exclusively to the goodness of God and not to any 'perfection' inherent in man. According to Marcion, Jesus conforms to the terms of the Creator's law in order to 'purchase' mankind from sin and death./90/ He becomes the victim of 'the Creator's curse'./91/ But Marcion's interpretation of Paul's teaching does not lead, as in both gnostic and christian orthodox circles, to a theory of 'reconciliation'. Those whom Christ saves from the curse of the law are strangers to God./92/ Thus we must conclude that Marcion's understanding of atonement as a cancellation of the Creator's legitimate claim to his own property has little in common with gnosticism. With Paul, he acknowledges that 'the law is not against the promises of God'; but the promise of God intervenes to secure man's release from bondage to the law and hence to the justice of the Creator. The nuances of Paul's dialectic of law and grace, as we have noted, are commonly eroded in the gnostic systems, as a result of their disparagement of the created order.

---

/89/ Cf. GT I.3/17.1f; Test. Truth, IX.3/31.5-12.

/90/ AM 5.3.10 (Gal 3.13); cf. 1.11.8.

/91/ AM 1.11.8; cf. Gal 2.19-20: *'egō gar dia nomou nomō apethanon'* and Gal 3.13: *'Christos hēmas exēgorasen ek tēs kataras tou nomou genomenos hyper hēmōn katara . . .'*

/92/ An echo of this occurs in the Gos. Philip:' [Christ] ransomed those who were strangers and made them his own' (Gos. Philip, II.3/53.3f.). But the passage is anomalous in the context of the Gospel's teaching, which otherwise understands redemption in terms of a matrimonial image: 'Christ came to repair the separation which was from the beginning and again unite the two' (Gos. Philip, II.3/70.13f.).

## 5.6 Marcionite and Gnostic Anthropologies

Marcion's anthropology -- the doctrine that man belongs totally to the Creator -- differs from Syrian and Alexandrian dualism. Irenaeus tells us/93/ for example that Saturninus of Antioch preferred the teaching that 'man was the workmanship of angels, a shining image bursting forth below from the presence of the supreme power'. He possesses a 'divine spark' which comes to him from the pity of the power above him, a spirit which, by the intervention of Christ (who comes to destroy the God of the Jews) returns after death 'to those things which are of the same nature with itself', while the rest of the body 'decomposes into its original elements'.

In the metaphysical elaboration of this speculation among the Valentinians, a closer identification is made of those who possess the 'divine spark'. According to the Tripartite Tractate, 'mankind came to be in three essential types: the spiritual, the psychic, and the material, conforming to the triple arrangement of the Logos', from which the types emanate. This typology is not known except by revelation, however./94/ The Savior, who 'is concerned with the redemption of the totality' reveals each type for what it is: the spiritual 'is like light from light', in that it accepts revelation without hesitating; the psychic 'like light from a fire', since it hesitates to accept knowledge and assent to the revelation in faith. The earthy, however, are 'alien in every way'; they are satisfied with the darkness; they 'shun the dawning of the light, since its appearance destroys them'. The spiritual will receive complete salvation; the material 'destruction in every way'; while the psychic being of 'a double determination' will be saved by the grace of God, 'the salvific thought'. A similar anthropology is presupposed in the Apocryphon of James, the Sophia of Jesus Christ, and in the Authoritative Teaching,/95/ while in the Apocryphon of John, with its doctrine of reincarnation, the racial triadology is mitigated by the author's belief in apocatastasis. In The Concept of our Great Power the soul of man is depicted as the chart of salvation history, with the elect being subject both to the 'aeon of the flesh' and the 'coordinate psychic aeon' until the (spiritual) aeon which is to come, comes from the 'Logos of the power of

---

/93/ Haer. 1.24.1.

/94/ Tri. Tract. I.5/118.14-20.

/95/ Cf. Jonas, Gnostic Religion, 44.

life' (VI.4/42.7). The general anthropological view represented in the Nag Hammadi documents tends to confirm Irenaeus' appraisal of the Valentinians that,

> they conceive of three kinds of men, spiritual, material, and animal, represented by Cain, Abel, and Seth. These three natures are no longer found in one person, but constitute various kinds of men. The material goes, as a matter of course into corruption. The animal, if it make choice of the better part, finds repose in the intermediate place . . . [and] the spiritual . . ., attaining to perfection, shall be given as brides to the angels of the Savior [cf. Tripartite Tractate, I.5/122. 12-24] while their animal souls of necessity rest forever with the demiurge./96/

Common to the gnostic anthropology is the platonizing of Paul's dualism: 'Sarx kai haima basileian Theou klēronomēsai ou dynatai oude hē phthora tēn aphtharsian klēronomei'./97/ In its unqualified form, this dualism presupposes a principle of 'identity', whereby the flesh belongs to the flesh and the spirit to the spirit. God possesses no identity with the former; and man, except by the grace of God, no identity with the latter (1 Cor 2.11). Paul's division of the things of the flesh and the things of the spirit is accepted by Marcion as a literal description of God's plan for the world: it becomes, in effect, the prooftext for his ditheism as well as for his anthropology: 'Oida gar hoti ouk oikei en emoi, tout estin en tē sarki mou, agathon' (Rom 7.18a). According to Marcion's exegesis, that 'the natural man cannot obtain the things of the spirit and of God' did not establish (as in the gnostic exegesis) a separate race of psychics, but only reinforced the distinction between the wisdom of men and the power of God (1 Cor 2.5). It is evident that Paul's allusions/98/ to 'the perfect', the 'natural', and the 'spiritual' man supply the raw material for gnostic

---

/96/ Haer. 1.7.5.

/97/ 1 Cor 15.50; cf. e.g., 1 Cor 5.4; Gal 3.28 and Tri. Tract. I.5/132.2-133.7.

/98/ 1 Cor 2.14-15; 15.48f.; Rom 8.8f.; cf. Haer. 1.8.3.

development of an anthropological hierarchy./99/ But Marcion does not carry his exegesis of Paul in this direction. He knows nothing of man's extra-mundane origins, or of the incarceration of the pneuma by the 'seven soul vestments'; of man's intoxication by the poison of the world, his ignorance of the divine spark within, or his alienation from the source of his being. In short, man is at home in the world precisely because in its unredeemed state (Rom 8.23) flesh and blood have nothing to do with√ spiritual things. 'Man is both the property and the work and the image and likeness of the Creator, and is flesh by virtue of the Creator's earth, and / soul by virtue of his breathing'./100/ In Marcion's conservative reading of Paul, there is a rejection of any metaphysical (gnostic) interpretation of salvation that would reduce the meaning of revelation to an act of divine necessity./101/

The distinction between marcionite and the more speculative forms of paulinist anthropology is best indicated by reference to the exegesis of Lk 6.43 (*Ou gar estin dendron kalon poioun karpon sapron, etc*), which Tertullian asserts was the 'source-passage' for Marcion's ditheism./102/ Specifically, Tertullian tells us that the passage was meant 'to apply to men, not to gods', and in gnostic anthropologies, it was so applied, that is as a corollary of Paul's doctrine of identity: 'For evil cannot produce good fruit. For the place from which each of them is produces that which is like itself; for not every soul is of the truth, nor of immortality. For every soul of these ages has death assigned to it. . . . But the immortal souls are not

---

/99/ On the tripartite division of the soul, vid. Plato, Timaeus, 70f.; 35f. On the Valentinian model, the compound soul described by Plato dissolves into genera, as 'types', of men (Iren. Haer. 1.7.5; 1.8.3). While Plato establishes a genealogy of the gods (Tim. 40; 41ff.) and makes the creation of the supreme God (Tim. 69), the creative function of the latter is contrasted with the dissolvent tendency of 'an evil being' (Tim. 41). As that which is 'harmonious and happy', creation stands under God's guarantee: 'you shall not die, nor be liable to the law of death' (Tim. 41; cf. 1 Cor 15.51f.).

/100/ AM 5.6.11: Tert.'s sentence takes the conditional ('Si homo . . .') but the sentiment expressed seems to be Marcion's.

/101/ Cf. Treat. on the Res. I.3/49.2-5; 44.30f.; cf. Tri. Tract. I.5/133.7.

/102/ AM 1.2.1f.

like these . . .'/103/ Marcion's anthropology entails a violation of this principle of identity, i.e., the redemption of man by a God alien to his being (Rom 8.11). There is no singling out of a 'spiritual' class who belong by nature to immortality./104/

## 5.7 Conclusion

Thus far we have examined the way in which Marcion's understanding of revelation differed from that of his gnostic contemporaries, using the theology of Paul as a frame of reference. Here we may provisionally conclude that Marcion's use of Paul was essentially conservative, in the strict sense of that term: he did not carry the thought of the apostle to the metaphysical extremes of the Alexandrians, and in some cases, he seems to have refused gnostic interpretations of Paul's thought, even at the cost of conserving its ambiguity. Yet in stressing (with Harnack) the originality of Marcion's approach to Paul one cannot assume that he was not familiar with, or influenced by, the gnostic exegesis of Paul and the gospels. And in view of the motifs which occupy the center of Marcion's thought -- the doctrine of an unknown God, the conception of salvation as liberation from an oppressive and jealous Creator,/105/ and the belief in Christ as an immortal redeemer -- such familiarity is hardly to be denied. At the same time, this familiarity can only be compared to Paul's (similar) acquaintance with the motifs of gnostic and hellenistic dualism: that is to say, it does not result in a systematic appropriation of gnostic themes, or in a coherent attempt to interpret the gospel in such terms. Marcion's struggle with Paul's theology

---

/103/ Apoc. Peter, VII.3/75.7-16, 26f. On the use of the Gospel of Luke as a source document in defining the genera, cf. further, Iren. Haer. 1.8.3. Here Jesus' words: 'Let the dead bury their dead, but go [thou] and preach the Kingdom of God' (Lk 9.60) is taken to distinguish the spiritual class from the animal; cf. Lk 9.61, 62; 13.20f. (Three classes corresponding to the three measures of meal).

/104/ Further on the gnostic use of Paul's epistles as prooftexts of the spiritual hierarchy: Exegesis of the Soul, II.6/130.20-131.13; Apoc. Paul, V.2/20.1-20; Teaching of Silvanus, VII.4/107.20-108.30. Marcion's theology lacked what Jonas (Gnostic Religion, 124) has termed 'the very center of gnostic religion', namely, 'the [emphasis on] the discovery of a transcendent inner principle in man and the supreme concern about its destiny'. See AM 4.16.11: 'Quis enim poterit diligere extraneos?'

/105/ On jealousy as a theme in gnostic exegesis, cf. On the Origin of the World, II.5/99.3-11; 2 Seth, VII.2/64.18-25; Test. Truth, IX.3/47.15-30.

entailed struggling with the gnostic interpretation of Paul as well as with the emergent 'deutero'-paulinism of the orthodox. But his resolution of the struggle was as little gnostic as 'orthodox'. This fact explains the general sense of Justin, Irenaeus, and Tertullian, that Marcion, dangerous as his teaching was, was of a different breed than the other heretics, that he had not quite 'fallen into the abyss of madness and blasphemy against Christ',/106/ that in some sense Marcion spoke to 'believers' and not to a spiritual élite like the Valentinians,/107/ and even that he died in grace, reconciled to the teaching of the church./108/

Thus while we must conclude that Harnack's argument for Marcion's 'originality' is not borne out by the most recent evidence available in gnostic-studies, his desire to make Paul's gospel the norm and center of christian teaching has no analogue in the writings of the gnostics themselves (Haer. 1.27.4).

---

/106/ Cf. Haer., 1. praef. 2.

/107/ Tert. adv. Valent. 2.

/108/ AM 1.1.6; Praes. 30. In AM 4.4.4, Tert. contradicts his assertion (cf. de carne, 2) that the Marcionites acknowledged the genuineness of the letter ascribed to Marcion by the orthodox: 'Quid si nec epistulam agnoverint'. The amount of space Tert. gives to discussing the document would suggest that the Marcionites actively sought to scotch the story that Marcion had once been a 'believer of the doctrine of the Catholic church in the Church of Rome under the blessed Eleutherus' ('Quid nunc, si negaverint Marcionitae primam apud nos fidem eius, adversus epistulam quoque ipsius?' AM 4.4.3). Tert. evidently believes in the authenticity of the letter, which included the declaration that Marcion had 'agreed to the conditions imposed upon him' by the Bishop of Rome. But the fact that the Marcionites themselves held it to be an orthodox forgery suggests as probable (a) that the Marcionites knew of no connection between Marcion and the Church of Rome and (b) that they rejected the notion that Marcion had survived until Eleutherus' reign.

CHAPTER SIX

# THE MORPHOLOGY OF MARCION'S DUALISM

## 6.1 Introduction

Marcion's dualism is the best-attested feature of his theology, but also the most problematical. He advances it, as Blackman has pointed out, 'not as a theory of the universe nor as a contribution to the philosophy of religion . . . [but as the] expression of what were to him the fundamental facts of human life'./1/ Attempts to locate the source of Marcion's dualism in Iranian speculation, Jewish cosmology, gnostic thought, and in the philosophies of Plato, Empedocles, and Epicurus belong not only to modern scholarship, but to a tradition originating with the heresiologists themselves. The very mention of Marcion's heresy -- 'there is another god beside the Creator'/2/ -- provokes Justin to claim as belonging to christian revelation not only the testimony of Moses, but also that of Plato in the Timaeus, 'So that from Plato [as well as from] Moses we can learn that the world was made by the word of God'. Irenaeus tells us that Marcion 'received' and elaborated the 'doctrine of one who took his system from the followers of Simon [of Samaria] . . .' (Haer. 1.27.1), that 'the God proclaimed by the law and the prophets was not the father of the Lord Jesus Christ'. Rhodo states that Marcion introduced two principles (duo archas eisēgountai),/3/ as a simple solution 'to the division of things', and that those who came after him 'passed into [a] worse error'./4/ Tertullian tries,

_____

/1/ Influence, 71; but Blackman's implication that Marcion may have derived his dualism from Plutarch's extrapolation of a passage in the Timaeus (De Anim. Procreatione in Timaeo Platonis, 1015e) is surely inadmissible; Influence, 70, n. 2.

/2/ I Apol. 58; cf. Eus. HE 4.18.9.

/3/ Eus. HE 5.13.3f.

/4/ HE, loc. cit. Potitus and Basilicus are named by Rhodo as being faithful to Marcion's doctrine of two principles; he names Syneros as the founder of a new error. Interestingly, Eusebius connects (4.29.1f.) Tatian's heresy with that of Marcion ('condemning him who made male and female') (cf. Iren. Haer. 1.28.1); then goes on to credit Rhodo as Tatian's pupil at Rome (HE 5.13.1).

185

without any apparent thought for the coherence of assertions, to connect Marcion's dualism variously to Cerdo,/5/ to the Stoics,/6/ to Greek and Persian Philosophy, and to Mithraism,/7/ with a certain bias for the influence of Epicurus./8/ Hippolytus couples Marcion's teaching with that of Empedocles;/9/ while Clement of Alexandria considers Marcionism a misreading of the philosophy of Plato, Pythagoras, and Christ./10/ Epiphanius, who reckoned the Greek philosophical schools among the heresies, takes it for granted that Marcion's apostasy is grounded in hellenistic learning. By the fifth century, at least in Syria, Marcion was widely thought to have preached not two, but three first principles corresponding to the 'three heavens' mentioned by Paul./11/

---

/5/ AM 1.2.3.

/6/ Praes. 7.

/7/ AM 1.13.3: 'de quorum ingeniis omnis haeresis animatur'.

/8/ AM 1.25.3f.; 2.16.2; 4.15.2; 5.19.7; cf. Lucretius 5.146: 'The fine nature of the gods far withdrawn from our senses is hardly seen by the thought of the mind . . . and therefore they are [substantially] unlike us'. Tertullian was obviously thinking of the first of the 'Forty Articles' of the Epicurean creed, according to which 'a blessed and eternal being has no trouble himself and brings no trouble upon any other being; [he is] exempt from movements of anger and partiality', Diog. Laert. 10.139; cf. also Cicero, de nat. deor. 1.19.50f.

/9/ Ref. omn. haer. 7.17-18f.

/10/ Strom. 3.3.12f.

/11/ Eznik de Kolb, de sectis 4; Eznik was doubtless reporting (with what degree of accuracy we cannot be certain) the substance of the marcionite system in the churches around Bagrevard c. 445. The theogony is close to that of the gnostic communities: 'In the first heaven dwells the Stranger; in the second, the God of the Law, and in the third his armies (= archons)'. According to Eznik, the God of the Law is jealous of his creation, and sends 29 generations to hell before the alien God takes pity on man. The Son of the good God descends and empties Hades, whereupon the redeemed souls ascend (like Paul) to the third heaven: 'The Lord of the world seeing the god-head of Jesus knew that there is another God beside himself . . . and Jesus said to the Creator: I have a suit with thee, and let none judge between us but thine own law which thou didst write . . . . And when [they] produced the Law, Jesus said to him, didst thou not write that whoso killeth shall die, and whoso sheddeth the blood of a righteous man, they shall have his blood . . .' The debate between the redeemer and Creator continues, Jesus itemizing the benefits he has wrought for creation, and thus establishing his righteousness and the warrant for his suit. Redemption is accomplished in virtue of a legal technicality: the souls of the faithful are 'owed' to the Creator as required by his own law: 'Leaving the Creator, Jesus laid hold of

While the search for the sources and analogues of Marcion's dualism by the fathers set a scholarly precedent which has continued from their day to this,/12/ it is well to keep apologetic designs in mind when appraising the historical value of the information they provide. To show that Marcion's thought is not the gospel, but a new philosophy 'craftily decked out in an attractive dress',/13/ is a convention of anti-marcionite polemic from Justin to Epiphanius. It is epitomized in Tertullian's claim in the Praes. that pagan philosophy is the source of all heresy:

> Heresies are themselves instigated by philosophy. From
> . . . [philosophy] came Marcion's better God with all his
> tranquility; he came from the Stoics. Then, again, the
> opinion that the soul dies is held by the Epicureans; while
> the denial of the restoration of the body is taken from the
> aggregate school of all the philosophers; also when matter
> is made equal to God you have Zeno's teaching; and when
> any doctrine is alleged touching a God of fire then
> Heraclitus comes in. The same subject matter is
> discussed over and over again by the heretics and the
> philosophers; the same arguments are involved. Whence
> comes evil? -- Why is it permitted? -- What is the origin
> of Man? . . . . But what has Athens to do with Jerusa-
> lem? What concord can there be between the academy
> and the church, what between heretics and Christians?
> . . . . Away with all attempts to produce a mottled
> Christianity of Stoic, Platonic, and dialectic
> composition./14/

Locating the philosophical analogue for Marcion's dualism was entailed in the task of proving him a renegade from the gospel./15/ No matter that Marcion never mentioned Plato or Epicurus; it was sufficient for the purpose that an analogue could be found. That the pagan sources were not cited only showed the deceitfulness of the heretics. Hence Hippolytus understands Marcion's 'dependence' on Empedocles as an attempt to 'pass off' the

---

Paul and revealed to him the purchase and sent him to preach that we are bought with a price, and everyone who believes in Jesus has been sold by the just to the good'. From this we may gather that in the marcionite church in Syria Paul's idea of atonement (Rom 5.11) acquired a mythological mise en scène. Nonetheless, the central themes of Marcion's thought are still clearly to be discerned.

/12/ See for example August Bill's 1911 monograph, Zur Erklärung und Textkritik des 1. Buches Tertullians 'Adversus Marcionem'.

/13/ Iren. Haer. 1. praef. 2. Irenaeus specifies (1. praef. 1) those who 'falsify the oracles of God', but has in mind the gnostics generally.

/14/ Praes. 7; cf. AM 5.19.7.

/15/ E.g., AM 5.19.1, 7f.; cf. 1.25.3; 1.21.4f.

philosophical principles of discord and affinity (= the just and good gods) as christian doctrine,/16/ while Tertullian argues that the christian faith is the very opposite of 'subtle speech and philosophy'./17/ Such evidence as we possess will support no conclusion other than that which the fathers would have resisted the most strenuously: namely, that the source of Marcion's dualism is the religious thought of Paul (Rom 3.28; 6.14; 11.6; etc.). From the apostle he derived the primary antithesis between law and grace as well as the doctrine of two gods.

Marcion's ditheism probably did not arise, as Tertullian suggests, as a response to the problem of evil./18/ The concern with theodicy is one which Tertullian generally attributes to the heretics, and belongs to the polemical rather than to the substantive part of his argument./19/ There is no indication elsewhere in the adversus Marcionem that Marcion's primary or 'obsessive concern' was the origin of evil, or that his ditheism was advanced in the interest of providing an easy answer to the question.

There is less reason to question Tertullian's statement that the scriptural basis of Marcion's belief was Lk 6.43:/20/ 'A good tree brings forth no corrupt fruit, and a bad tree no good fruit'. The chiasmic structure of Jesus' pronouncements comported with Marcion's primary (pauline) antithesis of law and grace; thus, elsewhere he applied Jesus' words concerning the old and new wineskins to the distinction between the gospel and the law;/21/ and the parable, 'Can the blind lead the blind', to the Creator,/22/ who was ignorant of the higher divinity, and 'had no means of recognizing that the one of whom he had no knowledge was Jesus and the

---

/16/ Ref. omn. haer. 7.17. Cf. Epiph. Panar. 42.

/17/ AM 5.19.8.

/18/ AM 1.2.2; thus pace Blackman, Influence, 86; cf. Epiph. Panar. 24.6, mentions Basilides as having begun from the same principle.

/19/ Cf. Praes. 7.

/20/ AM 1.2.1-2. Cf. Epiph. Panar. 42.2; Philas. Lib. haer. 17.

/21/ AM 4.11.9-11.

/22/ AM 4.17.11.

Holy One of God'./23/ Like Valentinus/24/ Marcion found in Lk 10.21f.
support for the doctrine of the unknown God (Christus ignotum deum
praedicavit):/25/ 'You have hidden these things from the wise and
prudent. . .: No man knows who the Son is but the Father, and who the
Father is but the Son, and he to whom the Son will reveal him'. The
existence of such a pronouncement in the gospel seemed to comport with
Paul's words about revelation as the unfolding of a mystery, previously
unknown, even to the Creator (1 Cor 2.7; cf. Eph 3.9). Here almost
certainly we have an instance of the use of Paul's words as the touchstone
for determining the meaning of the true gospel; it is not the evangelion or
apostolikon alone that leads Marcion to conclude the existence of an
unknown father, but the coincidence of the two. Marcion saw in the Lucan
antitheses a reference to a God above the Creator; and this must be the
same God whom Paul knew as the father of Jesus Christ. Scripture thus
speaks clearly of two distinct gods, old and new; known and unknown; jealous
and good; judge and savior. The basis for this ontological distinction, as we
have already noted, is not a metaphysical theory, such as Tertullian
advances in favor of the unity of God,/26/ but the evidence of historical
revelation, as interpreted both according to Paul's gospel and the words of
the savior distilled from the 'corrupt' gospel: *'Hekaston gar dendron ek tou
idiou karpou ginōsketai'* (Lk 6.44). What the Creator is in himself is
explicated in his action toward man in the light of the revelation of the
unknown God. It is no longer possible to know the Creator (and the
Creator's justice) as an absolute value; it is only possible to know him in
relation to a new standard established by the revelation of the alien God,
who is in himself absolutely good (AM 2.29.3). In the sense which Marcion
adduced from the gospel, the primary distinction has to do not with a theory
of God but with how God has acted (AM 2.28-9). One can even say that the
use of the terms 'known' and 'unknown' to mark this distinction puts the
emphasis in the wrong place, since for Marcion the distinction is between
the revealed and (heretofore) unrevealed Gods. The appearance of the alien

---

/23/ AM 4.7.11.

/24/ Cf. Iren. Haer. 4.6.3-4.

/25/ AM 4.25.10.

/26/ 'Ergo unicum sit necesse est quod fuerit summum magnum' AM 1.3.5.

God relativizes what man had previously regarded as the good: namely, the Creator's law, and this relativity corresponds to the perspective of man 'under the law' and 'after faith'. If Marcion was consistent in applying the paulinist schema to the gospel, he might naturally have interpreted the 'blindness' of the false apostles,/27/ epitomized by Peter's identification of Jesus as the 'Christ of God' (*Christos tou Theou*),/28/ in line with Paul's words about spiritual discernment (1 Cor 2.14f.), Jesus' promise concerning the transformation of the perfect (Lk 6.40) paralleling 1Cor 2.16 ('*Hēmeis de noun Christou echomen*'). In any event, it seems probable that it was on the basis of his reading of Paul that Marcion read back into the gospel the 'doctrine' of the known and unknown God, and not the other way around.

## 6.2 Access to Marcion's Theology

What Marcion thought of the Creator has been the subject of considerable controversy./29/ The confusion arises over apparently contradictory reports in the writings of the fathers, and even within the works of individual fathers.

This inconsistency, in turn, raises as many questions about the extent of the patristic knowledge of Marcion's teaching as about the teaching itself. Irenaeus, the first to offer extensive information about Marcion's doctrine, does not claim to base his description on the texts considered sacred by the Marcionites themselves. Indeed Irenaeus shows no sign of knowing the name of Marcion's theological treatise, and though he purposes 'specially to refute him . . . out of his own writings . . . [and] the discourses of the Lord and Apostles which are of authority with him',/30/ he does not claim to have had access to these writings while composing his

---

/27/ AM 4.36.9-11.

/28/ Lk 9.20; cf. 9.45; 10.24a; 12.56b; 23.34; 24.16.

/29/ Cf. A. Bill, Erklärung und Textkritik (1911), 104ff. ('Die Zwei-götterlehre Marcions'); pp. 17-33.

/30/ Haer. 1.27.4.

general work against the heretics./31/

Similarly, it cannot be assumed that Tertullian, for all his extravagance in refuting Marcion's errors, possessed more than second-hand knowledge of his doctrines. His 'statements' are frequently suppositional: 'Secundum vero Marcionem nescio . . .' (AM 5.16.4); or inferential: 'Hic erit argumentatio haeretici . . .' (AM 5.14.7); 'Haec si Marcion de industria erasit' (5.14.9); (cf. 5.12.6: 'Si et pseudapostolos dicit, etc.'); conditional: 'Si quid tale Marcionis deus edidit vel edixit' (5.11.2); or merely interrogative: 'Aut si nihil de creatoris traditum est ei a patre, ecquomodo hominem creatoris sibi vindicat?' (4.25.8). Only at peril does one transform Tertullian's interlocution into a marcionite 'system'; and the number of antitheses and editorial emendations to the gospel that can be assigned with any confidence to Marcion is much smaller than Harnack imagined. Nor is Tertullian especially secretive about his method. In the midst of the crucial discussion of Marcion's ditheism in relation to 2 Cor 1-4, he cuts short his explanation of Paul's use of the phrase 'Ho Theos tou aiōnos', 'in order to prevent it from being of advantage to my opponent -- satisfied to have won my case: I am even in a position entirely to bypass this argument'./32/

But the extent of Tertullian's direct knowledge of Marcion's writings is not only called into question by rhetorical evidence -- the discursive, inquisitorial, and often conjectural nature of the polemic; the tendency to sidestep questions, and to reduce the opponent's argument to rubble on spurious textual grounds. It is also doubtful on the basis of Tertullian's own comment at the beginning of Book I. There he claims to have produced a 'first edition' of the text too hurriedly, and that a revised edition was 'stolen' from him by an apostate (AM 1.1.1). The literary sources for the third edition, therefore, are the first and second. Tertullian does not mention

---

/31/ Apparently, Irenaeus never fulfilled this ambition; cf. Eus. HE 5.8.9. One can only suppose that what he knows about Marcion comes from the no longer extant Logoi Kata Markionos from which he quotes (Haer. 4.6.2; cf. Eus. HE 4.18.9); cf. Photius, 125. But it cannot be determined whether he had other reports at his disposal; cf. Loofs, Theophilus von Antioch und die anderen theologischen Quellen bei Irenäus, TU 46/2 (1930). Eusebius mentions a noble treatise against Marcion by Theophilus of Antioch (HE 4.24.1) as well as treatises against Marcion by Dionysius of Corinth (Ep. to the Nicomedians, HE 4.23.4) dating from c. 170; Philip of Gortyna and Modestus (He 4.25.1). The fact that Modestus' work survived until Jerome's day (de vir. illus. 32) may mean that both Irenaeus and Tert. were dependent on it; but this is only conjecture.

/32/ AM 5.11.10.

having had access to Marcion's writings at any stage in the revision, and the quantity of authentically marcionite doctrine that can be distilled from his books is not significantly greater than that contained in Irenaeus' scattered references. In most respects, the adversus Marcionem suggests an enlargement and elaboration of Irenaeus' material. Tertullian derives from Irenaeus, for example, the idea that the goodness of the alien God is defective if it is neither revealed in judgment nor effective in saving all ('rursus bonus, si hoc tantum sit bonus non et probator in quos immittat bonitatem, extra justitiam erit et bonitatem, et infirma bonitas eius videbitur non omnes salvans, si non cum iudicio fiat')./33/ This literary dependence on Irenaeus extends to other matters of substance as well: thus Haer. 3.25.2: 'Rursus, ut increpatiuum auferrent a Patre et iudiciale, indignum id Deo putantes et sine iracundia et bonum arbitrantes se adinvenisse deum'; cf. AM 1.25.1: 'Quod attinet ad bonitatis quaestionem, his lineis deduximus eam minime deo adaequari, ut neque ingenitam neque rationalem neque perfectam, sed et improbam et iniustam et ipso iam bonitatis nomine indignam'./34/

Tertullian however made more extensive use of a second source, now lost to us, which reproduced in some detail the substance of Marcion's evangelion and apostolikon. As he uses Justin's Dialogue in Book III,/35/ there is reason to suppose that Justin's longer work on Marcion was one of his sources in Books I and II. That Tertullian had access to the Antitheses, or to any other of the 'writings' mentioned by Irenaeus, is only a dim possibility.

---

/33/ For Irenaeus (Haer. 3.25.2), the judicial function defines deity and validates the goodness of and wisdom of God. But a 'just' God who is not good lacks the other requisite of God: hence, 'Marcion igitur ipse dividens deum in duo, alterum quidem bonum et alterum iudicialem dicens, ex utrisque interimit Deum' (Haer. 3.25.3). Tert. expands on but does not really modify Irenaeus' argument (AM 2.13.5; cf. 1.22.5ff.; 1.23.1): 'Exigo rationem bonitatis'. On not saving all: AM 1.24.2; 1.24.4, 7; 1.26 passim; 2.28.2f.; 2.3.5. Cf. Eznik, de sectis, 4.

/34/ Cf. also AM 1.25.3; 1.26.1; 1.27.2; cf. Origen, de princ. 2.5.3f., where it is argued that the bonitas of God is identical with his justitia; and contra Cels. 6.53.

/35/ According to Quispel, the third ed. comprised Books 4 and 5; Book 3 uses the Dial. with Trypho and the Haer. 'Ad Tertulliani adversus Marcionem librum observatio' VC I (1947), 42; idem: De bronnen von Tertullianus AM (1943): A. Bill, Erklärung und Textkritik (1911), 6.16.

In approaching Marcion's theology, therefore, one must acknowledge (a) that the most detailed sources available for reconstructing his thought are based not on a first-hand knowledge of his writings, but on a variety of reports, all of them polemical and all, including the earliest, retrospective; (b) that the sources do not supply the wherewithal for retrieving the entirety of Marcion's theology, but rather supply hints as to its general structure and the themes that inform it; (c) that the later polemic against Marcion deserves little of the historical credit that has commonly been given it, reflecting in the main a later stratum of marcionite belief or an elaboration of earlier anti-marcionite polemic.

## 6.3 Marcion's Ditheism

Justin understands Marcion's ditheism in terms of the difference between a greater and lesser god; specifically, between a god who creates and a god 'who does greater works' (i.e., saves)./36/ Justin supplies no information concerning the scriptural or philosophical basis for Marcion's ditheism. For that we must look to Irenaeus, who provides the first clue as to the sources of Marcion's opinions, namely, the teaching of the philosopher Cerdo./37/

According to Irenaeus, Marcion postulated the existence of two gods 'separated from each other by an infinite distance'./38/ The use of a spatial metaphor to signify the separation of the demiurge from the pleroma as perfect aeon is also common in gnostic theogonies./39/ But Marcion does not appear to have personified the cosmic space, or emphasized its demonic

---

/36/ I Apol. 26; 58.

/37/ But cf. Haer. 2.31.1: Here Irenaeus refers to the 'school' of Marcion, Simon, and Menander, without mentioning Cerdo. Ps.-Tert. Omn. haer. 6, attempting to show that Marcion's assertions are 'identical with the heretic who preceded him', attributes Marcion's teaching wholesale to Cerdo, but he seems to have had no source other than Irenaeus and Tert., from whom he learned of Marcion's use of Luke.

/38/ Haer. 4.33.2.

/39/ Cf. Pistis Sophia (NTA I, 256f.); Naasene Psalm (NTA II, 807f.); Ginza, 454f. (cf. Jonas, Gnostic Religion, 67). Among Syrian Marcionites the common designation for God was simply 'the Stranger' (Ho agnotrios); cf. A.W. Mitchell, St. Ephraim's Prose Refut. of Mani, Marcion and Bardaisan (1921) II, lvii, lviii, lxiii.

implications. The infinite distance points to and reinforces the qualitative otherness of the supreme God, who is completely good, from the cosmocrator, 'who is proclaimed as God by the law and the prophets, declaring himself to be the author of evils,/40/ to take delight in war, to be infirm of purpose and even contrary to himself'./41/ Just as the cosmocrator's malice is manifest in the teaching of the law and the prophets, the alien God's benevolence is demonstrated by his saving activity. This action is manifested in Jesus Christ,

> who is derived from that father who is above the God that made the world and coming into Judaea in the times of Pontius Pilate the governor, who was the procurator of Tiberius Caesar, was manifested in the form of a man to those who were in Judaea, abolishing the prophets and the law and all the works of that God who made the world./42/

Thus the revelation of the alien God is not an acosmic theophany or an apparition of the divine revealer: it is an event grounded in history, and attested by the gospel: 'Marcion lays it down that there is one Christ who in the time of Tiberius was revealed by a god formerly unknown, for the salvation of all the nations' (AM 4.6.3). The historicity of Marcion's thought about this revelation is also signalled by the fact that he postulated no elaborate diremption or genealogy,/43/ but understood the coming of Jesus, broadly speaking, in line with Eph 4.9f.

Marcion seems to have derived this liberation-motif from the gospel, though it is also present in the letter known to the Marcionites as Laodiceans. In the Gospel of Luke, Jesus preaches liberation on the basis of a passage from Isaias: 'He has sent me to proclaim release to the captives . . . to set at liberty those who are oppressed' (Lk 4.18b). In Ephesians Marcion found a way of explicating the message: Jesus' proclamation to the children of the covenant was a declaration of freedom for the oppressed children of the lesser God. He had annulled the law with its rules and regulations, so as to create a new humanity out of himself (Eph 2.15; cf. Haer. 4.13.1). He had come to strangers (Eph 2.19; cf. Haer. 3.11.2) to

---

/40/ According to Tert. (AM 1.2.2) Marcion got this idea from Isa 45.7 and Luke 6.43f.

/41/ Haer. 1.27.2.

/42/ Haer. 1.27.2.

/43/ AM 4.7.2; cf. 1.19.2.

obliterate the alienation -- the infinite distance between man and God./44/ Christ was man's release from the judgment of a Creator (Eph 1.7), to whom man in his natural condition (tekna physei) belonged./45/ The fundamental antithesis underlying Marcion's dualism is clear from his reading of Ephesians (Laodiceans) 2.2f.:

> By nature we are [all ] under the dreadful judgment of the Creator [i.e., orgēs ] . . . according to the course of the world [and the ] cosmocrator, whose spirit works among the sons of disobedience; but [the supreme ] God, rich in mercy and love [saves ] us by his grace, and in union with Christ Jesus raises us up and enthrones us with him in the heavenly realms . . . . How great his kindness to us in Christ Jesus! By his grace and not by striving you are saved./46/

Marcion's understanding of the effect of salvation is summarized in his rendering of Eph 2.14: 'Gentiles and Jews he has made one, having broken down the wall of the hostility of the flesh'./47/ The soteriological myth of the descensus is grounded in Eph 2.15ff. The savior surprises the Lord of the world/48/ who is ignorant of the existence of the merciful God above him (Haer. 3.11.4; cf. 4.34.3; cf. AM 1.11.9; 1.22.4; 2.2.1; 5.18.1f.); he

/44/ Such passages as Lk 5.1; 24.36, etc. are echoed by Marcion: the Jesus who 'appears in their midst'; the literalist Tert. argues that the nativity narrative must be accepted and Marcion's account of revelation rejected ('Quis viderit descendentem, quis retulerit' AM 4.7.2). Almost certainly, Ephesians (Laodiceans) 4.9f. is the source for the descensus ad inferos attributed by Irenaeus to Marcion (Haer. 1.27.3) which apart from being the only mythological topos explicitly assigned to Marcion (cf. Eznik) is also the earliest expansion of the belief alluded to in 1 Ptr 3.19 (cf. Lk 23.43), expanded in the Evangelium Nicodemii, and included among the articles of the Apostles', Athanasian, and Constantinopolitan creeds. See J. Monnier, La Descente aux Enfers (1904); J.A. MacCulloch, The Harrowing of Hell (1930); J. Kroll, 'Gott und Hölle, der Mythos vom Descensuskampf', Studien der Bib. 20 (1932).

/45/ AM 1.23.3: Perfect goodness consists in its being expended upon strangers without obligation of kinship. Cf. Am 4.23.4f.

/46/ Eph 2.2-5; reconstruction, based on AM 5.17.10f.

/47/ Reconstruction based on AM 5.17.14.

/48/ Eph 3.10: Marcion reads: 'Occulti ab aevis deo qui omnia condidit' i.e., 'from [the ] God who created all things'; AM 5.18.1f.

reveals himself to those in hell,/49/ and appropriates the souls of those 'who walked in all sorts of abomination' by annulling the law (cf. Haef. 3.12.12; 4.13.1). Those 'who were pleasing to God' (i.e., the OT faithful) are not reckoned to partake in salvation, as they do not believe Jesus' announcement and choose to remain under the Creator's regime./50/ Thus, the souls of those who believe are eligible for salvation from the Creator's threatenings and the curse of the law.

On the basis of the themes broached in Ephesians and other letters written in Paul's name, Marcion makes a number of doctrinal points: (a) Salvation is given only to the soul which has received the teaching of the Spirit (cf. Haer. 1.27.3; 1 Cor 2.11, 13); the body, being from the earth is incapable of salvation (Haer. 5.19.2; 1.27.3; cf. 1 Cor 15.50); (b) God's salvation is universal and his mercy unqualified; he saved 'Cain, and those like him, and the Sodomites, and the Egyptians, and others like them';/51/ (c) There are some whom the alien God does not save; not because they fall outside the scope of his mercy, or because redemption is otherwise foreclosed to them (i.e., as a different 'genus'), rather because

> Their wits are beclouded; they are strangers to the life
> that is in God, because ignorance prevails among them
> and their minds have grown hard as stone (Eph 4.18)

These are the children of the lesser God, who remain under his law and judgment. Marcion saw Abel, Enoch, Noah, Abraham, and all the prophets as belonging to this category, a fact which caused Tertullian to declare/52/ that the goodness of Marcion's God is defective because it did not embrace the whole of humanity. But Irenaeus, giving more attention to the course of Marcion's thinking, suggests that the 'exclusion' of some of the children of the lesser God from salvation has nothing to do with the judicial sentiments

---

/49/ Haer. 1.27.3. On the originality of Marcion's view of the descensus, cf. Burkitt, Gospel History, 299f.

/50/ Haer. 4.8.1; cf. AM 1.22.2f., 6f.; 1.23.8; esp. 1.24.2f.; 2.28.3.

/51/ Haer. 1.27.3; cf. AM 1.23.2. The marcionite descensus takes on a distinctly anti-Jewish tone in Epiphanius' rendering, or misrepresentation: 'Cain, Korah, Dathan, Abiram, Esau and all the nations who had not obeyed the God of the Jews [he delivered] such as the Sodomites and Egyptians', Panar. 42.3; but this is contradicted by Tert.'s testimony, AM 4.6.3 ('in salutem omnium gentium').

/52/ AM 1.24.2.

of the supreme God. Rather, it is brought about in virtue of their past experience of the law of the Creator: 'Since these men, Marcion says, knew that their God was constantly tempting them, now [i.e., upon the revelation of the supreme God in Jesus ] they suspected he was tempting them and did not run to Jesus or heed his announcement'./53/

Marcion's radicalization of Paul's soteriology/54/ is really a means of expressing the fundamental opposition of law and grace and the 'infinite distance' between their executors (Haer. 4.33.2). For this he received hints from 2 Cor 4.4. It is this passage which the descensus mentioned by Irenaeus (Haer. 1.27.3) presupposes. Marcion deduced from it that there were those who had not received the gospel, less through their own fault than through the malice of the Creator (Rom 11.7-8). The determining principle in his soteriology was not the difference between saints and sinners, but the difference between the children of light and the children of darkness (1 Thess 5.5). Insofar as 'judgment' is entailed by this doctrine,/55/ it follows for Marcion on Paul's principle that revelation 'reproves' the law eo ipso: 'Ta de panta elegchomena hypo tou phōtos phaneroutai. Pan gar to phaneroumenon phōs estin' (Eph 5.13f.). The 'hidden purpose' of God and his essential goodness remained intact (Col 1.13); put simply, Marcion develops no theory of 'original' sin and hence regards man as a free agent when it comes to accepting the meaning of God's revelation. Man's experience of (the supreme) God's goodness is defective; but his acceptance of the gift of divine mercy is unaffected by this deficiency. This reckoning follows on Marcion's adherence to Paul's idea of christian liberty: The alien God's purpose is the freedom and liberation of man from the 'pettiness' and 'malignity' of the Creator's purpose (AM 2.28.1). Man's salvation is suspended, as it were, in this dichotomy of divine self-interest and depends on his acceptance of freedom from the law. That Marcion attributes the forfeiture of salvation by the OT faithful not to their adherence to the Creator's law, but rather to their suspicion of

---

/53/ Haer. 1.27.3; Tert. holds to the Stoic notion that it was the duty of a God perfectly good to come to the rescue of all men 'to conform to this primary rule of divine goodness' AM 1.22.2-3.

/54/ Blackman has called this 'Marcion's grossest exaggeration of Pauline teaching', Influence, 102; cf. Harnack, Marcion, 126ff.

/55/ AM 2.28.3: 'Tuus quoque deus quos salvos non facit utique in exitium disponit'.

him on the basis of his past actions, underscores rather boldly man's existential dilemma: either to doubt what is known, and be saved by faith; or to put one's faith in what one knows and be lost. Marcion expresses in his version of the <u>descensus</u> the pauline division of law and grace (cf. Rom 6.14) in its most radical form.

The paulinist foundation of Marcion's dualism can be traced even further in the <u>Haer</u>. Taking up his argument against the Marcionites anew in Book III, Irenaeus attempts to refute the heretics on the basis of 'that scripture which they have thus shortened' (i.e., Luke and the epistles of Paul)./56/ Here we learn as much about Marcion's teaching from the proto-credal affirmations of Irenaeus as from his positive assertions concerning Marcion's theory of God./57/ Thus in the course of discussing Marcion's 'heretical inventions' (3.4.2), Irenaeus is moved to give a summary of the orthodox positon, over and against that espoused by the Marcionites. This summary is not linked to a pre-existing baptismal formula, but rather, 'to the ancient tradition of the apostles'.

Indeed, Irenaeus makes the point that the <u>traditio apostolica</u> is credible because it admits of a theological construction which the apostles would have understood, whereas the inventions of the heretics would have

---

/56/ <u>Haer</u>. 3.12.12.

/57/ On the idea that Marcion's heresy lay behind the framing of the old Roman symbol, see McGiffert, <u>The Apostle's Creed</u> (1902), 171-3, 13; and G. Krüger, ZNTW (1905), 72-79. The only explicitly anti-marcionite symbol is one dating from the fourth century Laodicean church: *'Pisteuomen eis hena theon toutestineis mian-archēn, ton theon tou nomou kai evangeliou, dikaion kai agathon'* (Harnack, Marcion, 343*). Cf. Caspari, <u>Alte und neue Quellen zur Geschichte des Taufsymbols</u> (1879), 20. In view of the fact that Marcionism was strong in Laodicea, this statement is of special significance; the author of Rev 3.15 knows the church there as being 'neither cold not hot'(*'Oute psychros ei oute zestos . . . chliaros ei'*), a reference to its dubious 'orthodoxy' (cf. <u>Sib. or</u>. 7.20). It seems far from impossible that this is a reference to the Marcionism of the laodicean church, which from the marcionite point of view (Marc. <u>Prol. Laod</u>.) 'having accepted the word of truth [from the Apostle] persevered in the faith'. The effectiveness of the orthodox in overcoming Marcionism in the Laodicean church is also evidenced by the creed.

been unintelligible to them./58/ In making this claim (Haer. 3.5.1) Irenaeus effectively acknowledges the counter-claims of the Marcionites regarding the authority and credibility of the apostolic tradition. According to Irenaeus, the tradition of the apostles communicated through the church maintains, (a) Belief in one God (who is also) creator of heaven and earth. (b) That Jesus Christ was his son, born of a virgin; that he suffered under Pontius Pilate; united man through himself to God; rose from the dead; ascended to heaven; and will return in glory as judge. Irenaeus incorporates in the clause on judgment that 'those who transform the truth' (i.e., edit the written documents) and 'despise his Father and his advent' will be sent to eternal fire. There is no incipient article on the Holy Spirit,/59/ but this is not surprising since Marcion developed no triadological idea of the god-head. Irenaeus sticks closely to the several issues raised by Marcion's paulinism: the uniqueness of God; the identity of God the judge and creator with the father of Jesus Christ; the essential humanity of Jesus Christ and his relation to the father; the reality of judgment and resurrection./60/

---

/58/ Haer. 3.4.2; cf. 3.5.1; 3.9.1. Prestige, Fathers and Heretics (1940), 3, would argue that the 'creeds of the church grew out of the teaching of the church' and rather underrates the degree to which the creeds are arguments against heresy. Seeberg, 'Die Entstehung des Apostolikon', ZKG (1940), 30 remarks on a general tendency c. 200 toward strengthening the church's armaments. We may also refer to Kattenbusch's judgment that the creed is not 'negatively' (i.e., against heretics) but positively conceived (Das Apostolische Symbol, II, 327; cf. McGiffert, Apostle's Creed [1902 ]). Harnack considered, further, that the development of the regula fidei in Irenaeus and Tert. is 'anti-heretical without being specifically anti-Marcionite' (Marcion, 316*); but this opinion is contravened by the fact that Irenaeus and Tert. envisaged Marcion, if not exclusively Marcion, in their positive theological formulations, making it unlikely that their proto-credal assertions arise spontaneously. The same is true in the development of the regula in the Pastoral Eps.

/59/ Cf. Haer.3.17.1-4.

/60/ Cf. Haer. 3.6.4; 3.10.3; 3.9.1; 3.12.2, 11. It is significant that Matt 1.23 (cf. Lk 1.34f.) is introduced not in order to bolster an article of faith but in an attempt to overcome Marcion's teaching (that the reality of Christ's 'flesh' and suffering had nothing to do with his nativity) on the basis of scripture 'rejected' by him. To this theme Tert. returns again and again: 'Plane nativitatis mendacium recusasti: ipsam enim carnem veram edidisti': AM 3.11.6; cf. e.g., 3.9.2; de carne, 1-2.

The extent to which Paul's name had come to be associated with the marcionite 'error' is also suggested by Irenaeus' polemic/61/ From the argument of the <u>Haer</u>. we can discern the main sources of Marcion's dualism and ditheism in the epistles: It will serve here to summarize these (<u>Haer</u>. 3.3ff.):

(a) Gal 4.8, 9: 'For though you have served them which are not gods, you now know God, or rather are known of God' (cf. AM 5.4.5). Tertullian's reference to the same text elaborates upon Irenaeus' simple denial that it was not Paul's intent to make a separation between those 'who were not God and him who is God': Thus, Paul was 'castigating the error of physical and natural superstition, which puts the elements in the place of God'.

(b) 2 Thess 2.4: 'Who opposes and exalts himself above all that is called god or is worshipped . . .' Irenaeus claims that Paul refers to the anti-Christ; Tertullian does not deal with the passage.

(c) 1 Cor 8.4-6: 'If there be so-called gods, whether in heaven or on earth -- as indeed there are many gods and many lords -- yet for us there is one God'. It is impossible to know on the basis of Tertullian's reference to this passage (AM 3.15.2) what use Marcion may have made of it; both Tertullian and Irenaeus take the reference to 'those who are called gods' (8.5a) to refer to idols but Irenaeus suggests that in heretical exegesis the passage referred to the archons. Still, this would not describe Marcion's belief that there was but one Creator beside the supreme God (and 1 Cor 8.4b [*'hoti oudeis Theos ei mē heis'*] cannot have stood in Marcion's text of the epistle).

(d) 2 Cor 4.4: 'In whom the god of this world hath blinded the minds of them that believe not'./62/ Tertullian adopts Irenaeus' argument wholesale: 'Marcion captavit sic legendo: In quibus deus aevi huius, ut

---

/61/ The procedure of refuting Marcion 'out of his own Apostle' (<u>Haer</u>. 4.34.2; 3.13.1ff.) can be traced back at least to Polycarp (<u>Phil</u>. 3.1), and climaxes in the Pastoral Epistles. Irenaeus is able to bring the weight of these letters of 'Paul' to bear against Marcion's heresy. Hence, it is conceivable that Justin and perhaps Theophilus of Antioch, followed the same design in their own refutations of Marcion's error, although it is unlikely that Justin knew the Pastorals. At any rate, by Tert.'s day, the reclamation of Paul had been accomplished by a steady stream of anti-marcionite polemic; cf. Clement's statement, <u>Strom</u>. 2.11.52, to the effect that the heretics are 'convicted' by the Epistles to Timothy. Tert.'s assertion ('Nam mihi Paulum etiam Genesis olim repromisit' Am 5.1.5) is based on a long literary tradition. Cf. <u>Praes</u>. 25.

/62/ Cf. AM 5.17.7-9; 5.7.1.

creatorem ostendens deum huius aevi alium suggerat deum alterius aevi. Nos contra sic distinguendum dicimus: In quibus deus, dehinc: aevi huius excaecavit mentes infidelium: In quibus, Iudaeis infidelibus, in quibus opertum est aliquibus evangelium adhunc sub velamine Moysi' (AM 5.11.9). Tertullian claims the exegesis as his own.

(e) Gal 3.19: '[The law] was added to make wrongdoing a legal offence. It was a temporary measure, pending the arrival of the offspring [sperma] to whom the promise was made. It was promulgated by angels, through the hand of the mediator'. Tertullian omits discussion of this passage, on which account Harnack decided that Marcion had deleted Gal 3.15-25. But Irenaeus' citation makes it highly probable that Marcion retained at least 3.19 and 3.22-25; while Marcion would have rejected the connection between Jesus Christ and the 'promise to Abraham', he certainly would have embraced the declaration that 'faith having come, we are no longer under the tutelage [of law]'. Moreover, 3.20 appears, in this context, to be an interpolation, since it destroys the sense of 3.19 (*diatageis di angelōn en cheiri mesitou'). It probably did not stand in Marcion's text. Significantly, neither Irenaeus nor Tertullian cites Gal 3.20 against Marcion, which is curious since in the textus receptus it is perhaps Paul's most explicit tribute to Jewish monotheism. Marcion would not have disagreed with the pauline idea of law as paidagogos to Christ,/63/ but he would have placed a different sense on the word than praeparatio.

(f) 2 Thess 2.8f.: 'And then the one without law [ho anomos] will be revealed [the one] whom the Lord will consume with the spirit of his mouth and destroy in the brightness of his coming'. Irenaeus rearranges the order of this passage to ensure that anomos is modified by 'hou estin hē parousia kat energeian tou satana' (2 Thess 2.9a); thus, the 'lawless' one is made an agent of Satan. We can infer that Marcion took the anomos to refer to the Creator, or the 'Christ of the Creator', whose law is revealed as lawlessness by the 'revelation of Jesus'. So Tertullian: 'Secundum vero Marcionem nescio ne sit Christus creatoris' (AM 5.16.4). Tertullian's text of 2 Thess

/63/ Marcion would have found the language of Gal 3.19 congenial if construed along the lines suggested by Bultmann, ThNT I, 265-67 and Conzelmann, ThNT, 227.

seems to differ considerably from the textus receptus (cf. 5.16.2)./64/

(g) Lk 11.22 (= Matt 12.29ff); cf. 1 Cor 2.8: 'When one stronger [than the one strong ] assails and overcomes him, he takes away [his goods ]'. Haer. 3.8.2; cf. ÁM 5.6.7: 'Etiam parabola fortis illius armati, quem alius validior oppressit et vasa eius occupavit, si in creatoris accipitur apud Marcionem . . .' Irenaeus implies that Marcion's exegesis ran, 'He was not strong as opposed to him who bound him and spoiled his house'.

(h) Lk 16.13: 'No servant can serve two masters . . . . You cannot serve God and Mammon'. Haer. 3.8.1; cf. AM 4.33.4: 'in nummo scilicet injusto, non in creatore, quem et Marcion iustum facit'.

According to Marcion's radicalization of Paul's (oblique) distinction between the God of this world and the father of Jesus Christ, the good God is seen as alien to creation; he is separated from mankind and from the Creator by a gulf which can only be crossed through the unilateral saving action that also reveals God as the God above creation. Burkitt has suggested that Marcion's alien God really exists in a 'fourth' dimension,/65/ that the Creator, being closely identified with the world (Gal 6.14; Eph 2.2) is not a coequal deity but a lesser God who is destined to perish with his works. In the marcionite exegesis of 1 Cor 15.24ff., 'The Lord of this world destroys himself and his world eternally',/66/ that is to say, the continuation of the law and the works of the law after the revelation of Jesus Christ is self-destructive. The Creator progressively loses his grip on his handiwork. Harnack concluded,/67/ from Hippolytus' testimony,/68/ that the Marcionites recognized only one first principle and thus that Marcion was 'ultimately' monotheistic in his outlook. This may be saying too much on the basis of too little evidence, although there is ample material in the epistles of Paul that might have led Marcion to view the dispensation of the Creator as temporary.

---

/64/ Cf. D. Rivet, Tertullien et l'écriture (1938); R.P.C. Hanson, 'Notes on Tertullian's Interpretation of Scripture', JTS 12 (1961), 273; 79; G. Zimmermann, Die hermeneutischen Prinzipien Tertullians (1937).

/65/ JTS (1929), 279f.

/66/ Eznik, de sectis, 4; cf. Tert. AM 2.28.3; cf. 5.9.13; cf. 3.4.5.

/67/ Marcion, 141, n. 1.

/68/ Contra Noetum, 11.

The crossing of the gulf between the unknown and known represents an end, or the progressive elimination, of the law of death and its gradual replacement with the 'law of faith', '*hotan katargēsē pasan archēn kai pasan exousian kai dynamin*' (1 Cor 15.24b). In gnostic theogonies, and in the Gospel of John, this transition is commonly figured by the image of light shining in the darkness: ignorance is a condition of temporality ('*hē skotia auto ou katelaben*': Jn 1.5), while the light itself is eternal (cf. Rom 1.20a). Marcion thought in a similar vein, though he refused to acknowledge the one principle that might have brought his teaching into alignment with the orthodox system: Expressed classically in the Gospel of John it is that although the world owed its being to him, it did not recognize him (cf. Jn 1.10f.).

Here Marcion's error seems really to consist in supplying a rationale for the failure of the lesser God -- for mankind in general and the Jews specifically -- to recognize the redeemer: that he was wholly unknown prior to being revealed 'in the fifteenth year of Tiberius Caesar'. The Creator is fickle and cruel in his dealings with mankind; but he is not explicitly culpable, being ignorant of the higher revelation (AM 2.6.8). For the gnostics, the ignorance of mankind is inconsistently kept in check by a protective demiurge (cf. Jn 1.18), who lacks 'gnosis' of the pleroma. To the orthodox, as represented in the language of the Fourth Gospel, the failure to grasp the meaning of revelation hinges less on man's enforced ignorance of God's being or goodness than on an eternal intention (logos) hidden in the mind of the Creator. In either case, however, God 'comes to his own',/69/ either to a spiritual élite, who bear the imprint of God on their souls and are deemed worthy of gnosis, or in the widest sense, to mankind for the purpose of redeeming his own creation. But for Marcion, as for Paul, God comes to strangers (Eph 2.12), 'to the intent that now unto the principalities and powers in heavenly places might be known the manifold sophia of God' (Eph 3.10). It is human experience -- embodied in the law 'written in stone' and the Creator's mighty deeds/70/ -- that hides 'the breadth, length, depth, and height . . . and love of Christ' that excels gnosis (Eph 3.18). God is revealed, in other words, not as 'first principle' as in the gnostic systems,

---

/69/ Haer. 5.18.2: Irenaeus quotes John in this connection.

/70/ Cf. Tert. AM 2.21.1; 2.23.1f.; 2.24.1f.; etc.

nor as the father who creates, judges, and redeems as in the orthodox,/71/ but exclusively as a 'God rich in mercy, who with a great love has loved us' (Eph 2.4; Haer. 3.25.2; AM 1.27.2).

The fundamental distinction between the 'two gods, separated from each other by an infinite distance',/72/ is therefore not merely epistemological, as the distinction between 'known' and 'unknown' connotes. It is a distinction, rather, grounded in the evidence of human experience as recorded in the OT. The visible world, with its deception and delusion (cf. 2 Thess 2.10) teaches only sin, death, and despair. This is Marcion's interpretation of Gal 3.19, that the law leads only to destruction. It teaches nothing of a God of mercy. Creation does not show God to be a God of love (Rom 1.18f.) but only a God capable of mighty acts. Redemption was not a part of this God's plan. In their zeal to defend the catholic truth, critics like Irenaeus and Tertullian were bound to miss the point which Marcion labored to make in his interpretation of Paul's letters. How could this alien God be good if he 'draws away men that do not belong to him from him who made them and calls them into his own kingdom'./73/ Is not goodness what it is precisely in virtue of being exercised toward one's dependents -- in effect, an adjunct of duty or judgment? Irenaeus refuses to acknowledge the goodness of Marcion's God on the grounds that 'he does not give from what belongs to himself':/74/ as he has not been offended by sin, it is neither his responsibility nor his place to show mercy -- indeed, his mercy is an absurdity, since he can exercise no judicial power toward what does not belong to him./75/ In an argument that commends itself readily to Tertullian, Irenaeus points out that Marcion's God cannot be distinct from the Creator, because he exhibits the Creator's covetousness (aemulatio)

---

/71/ It should be remarked that nowhere does Marcion refer to the alien God as 'Father'; a fact which distinguishes him equally from his gnostic and orthodox contemporaries.

/72/ Haer. 4.33.2.

/73/ Haer. 4.33.2.

/74/ Haer. 5.17.1.

/75/ Haer. 5.27.1.

toward creation./76/ His goodness is defective precisely because he delayed revealing it 'until twenty-nine generations were in Hell',/77/ and because it lacks the essential element that would make it a credible revelation: that is to say, it is not 'a recapitulation of that disobedience which had occurred in connection with a tree'./78/ The Son of the alien God does not come to summarize human history,/79/ but to annul the law and to create in Jew and gentile 'a single new humanity in himself'./80/ This is a view of salvation which depends on an essentially pessimistic idea of human history and of the human condition before grace (Rom 7.5; 7.18a; 7.24; cf. Eph 2.12b). It stands therefore in sharp contrast to the view which arises from Irenaeus' monotheism, where the repetition of events according to the new dispensation does away with the effects of the old. From Irenaeus' standpoint, the interloping God who steals another's property, whatever theory may be advanced about his incarnation, cannot have summed up human nature because he came to vindicate another order of things./81/ He belongs, in other words, across an infinite divide which separates not man and his creator, but both man and his creator from a God the belatedness of whose revelation makes his goodness suspect.

In fact Marcion seems preëmptively to have acknowledged this objection in his interpretation of the descensus in Eph 4.9f.: the OT faithful, having grown suspicious of the Creator's fickleness toward them, refuse the gift of salvation and choose to remain under his law. We can read no anti-Jewish sentiments into Marcion's theology at this point. As we have seen, he emphasizes the paulinist idea that faith in Jesus has broken down the partition between Jew and gentile. In no sense is Marcion's teaching an indictment of the Jews, nor even of the OT; he neither 'allegorizes' the Pentateuch nor proscribes it as a malicious piece of Jewish propaganda designed to put a flattering face on the evil doings of the demiurge. It was not Marcion's prosaic mind that caused him to treat the OT as a book of

---

/76/ Haer. 5.18.1.

/77/ Eznik, de sectis, 4; J.M. Schmid's trans., 184.

/78/ Haer. 5.19.1.

/79/ Haer. 5.23.2.

/80/ Eph 2.14ff.; AM 5.17.14.

/81/ Haer. 5.14.2.

historical revelation, but his belief that the gospel relativized its 'absolute' value, and showed the God who had acted throughout the course of history to be other than the God who would bring history to a close. Marcion was wrestling not only with pauline dualism in trying to sharpen the distinction between law and grace, redemption and judgment, but indirectly with the problem which confronted Paul out of his own pharisaic past: the difference between Elohim (Gen 1.1) who 'created' heaven and earth, and YHWH Elohim (Gen 2.4), that is to say, the distinction betwen God the strict judge, and (YHWH) God who is merciful./82/

Clearly, Marcion's alien God shares with the God of Jewish thought the characteristic of being remote without being 'hidden in silence', like the 'inexpressible first Father' of gnostic speculation. He is ignotum, but he is this only in contrast to the Creator ('sicut enim ignotum eum fecit deus notus creator');/83/ he is not a deus absconditus, since he is known by revelation and certain things can be said about him on the basis of his redeeming activity. Thus, he is 'placidus et tantummodo bonus atque optimus'./84/ Tertullian settles on the designation 'formerly unknown' ('utrumque, opinor, et nunc incerto et retro ignoto'),/85/ which distinguishes him from the one 'unknowable in his nature'/86/ or the 'invisible one within the all' of the Valentinans./87/

### 6.4  Summary

We can profitably summarize at this point what we learn of Marcion's theological dualism from Irenaeus:

(1) The God proclaimed by the law and the prophets is not the father of Jesus Christ. The former is known, the other unknown; they are separated

---

/82/ See E.P. Sanders, Paul and Palestinian Judaism (1977), 123ff., who argues that in the rabbinical literature 'God's mercy predominates over his justice': i.e., middat rahamin vs. middat ha-din and middat pur 'anut.

/83/ Haer. 4.20.6; cf. AM 1.9.2.

/84/ AM 1.6.2; cf. 1.25.7.

/85/ AM 1.9.2.

/86/ Tri. Tract. I.5/55.28.

/87/ Tri. Prot. XIII.1/35.24.

by an infinite gulf and the Creator is 'ignorant' of the existence of the alien God./88/

(2) Jesus is derived from the God above the world: he was historically revealed in the time of Pontius Pilate. He came to save the souls of believers./89/ (We learn nothing from Irenaeus about the 'Creator's Christ', known by Tertullian and implicitly by Justin [1 Apol. 58 ]).

(3) The distinction between the Creator and the alien God is ontological: the 'lesser' god is not derived from the greater; nor has the greater any stake in creation as such. Mankind is thus the 'property' of the Creator./90/

(4) Marcion maintained that the prophets were 'from the Creator', such that their testimony relates only to the (historical) dispensation of God as revealed in scripture. In no sense does prophecy adumbrate the revelation of the alien God./91/

(5) The appropriate description of the Creator is 'just';/92/ he is acknowledged to be 'the God that made the world'./93/ But in contrast to the alien God, he is not good; indeed he is the 'author of evils'./94/ He has 'blinded the minds of those who do not believe'./95/ His justice is revealed as infirmity of purpose; he is contrary even to himself./96/

(6) In contrast to the Creator, the alien God exercises no providence or judicial power./97/ He calls men to salvation and confers eternal light;/98/ he saves those who receive him/99/ Thus, the appropriate description for

---

/88/ Haer. 4.33.2; 4.34.2-3; 3.11.4.

/89/ Haer. 1.27.3.

/90/ Haer. 4.33.2; cf. 4.32.1; 5.18.1; 4.36.6; 3.11.2.

/91/ Haer. 4.34.1, 5.

/92/ Haer. 3.25.3.

/93/ Haer. 1.27.2; cf. 3.7.1-2.

/94/ Haer. 3.12.12; 1.27.2.

/95/ Haer. 4.29.1.

/96/ Haer. 1.27.2; 4.28.3; 4.29.1.

/97/ Haer. 5.27.1; 3.25.2f.; 4.33.2.

/98/ Haer. 4.36.6; cf. 1.27.3.

/99/ Haer. 4.28.1; 1.27.3.

the alien God is 'good'./100/

(7) The will of the alien God is man's release from the law of sin and death; he is moved to have mercy and bestow grace purely in virtue of his nature, which is goodness;/101/ and to this end he overturns the precepts of the past (i.e., he expropriates the Creator's property).

(8) The alien God 'suffers' in the person of Jesus Christ, according to the terms of the Creator's law, in order to win salvation for man./102/

---

/100/ Haer. 3.25.2; 4.33.2; 3.12.12.

/101/ Haer. 3.15.2; cf. AM 1.26.1.

/102/ Haer. 4.33.2. That Marcion recognized the passion is suggested by Irenaeus' argument against Marcion's docetism. His objection, like Tertullian's, is that denial of the nativity amounts to denial of the humanity and hence of the suffering of Jesus. Cf. 5.14.2. See further, Harnack, Marcion, 124ff.; Chronol. II, 125.

# CHAPTER SEVEN

## THE CONSTRUCTIVE THEMES OF MARCION'S PAULINISM

### 7.1 Cosmology

According to Marcion the world made by the Creator reveals nothing of the goodness of the unknown God. But unlike the cosmic hyperbole employed in the gnostic systems to indicate the demonic nature of the gulf between the supreme God and the demiurge, the 'infinite space' between the God of this world and the unknown God is neutral: it expresses a difference of function in the separation between creating and judging, on the one side, and loving and saving on the other./1/ The world itself stands as the supreme achievement of the Creator; it shows forth his power and declares him to be God in his own right ('non negantis creatorem deum')./2/ But while Marcion did not deny that the Creator is a god, he regarded him (thus his works) as unequal and inferior to the God who is 'solely kind and supremely good'./3/

While the work of the Creator with man as the crowning achievement/4/ warrants his being considered God, the revelation of the God formerly unknown/5/ diminishes the values which men previously assigned to the natural world. Marcion seems to have expressed this new order (in a simile apparently misconstrued by Tertullian) in terms of the distance between God and man./6/ The alien God is as far above man as man is above the insects; yet in caring for such 'distant' things the true goodness of the alien God is established and the old order in which the justice and providence of the Creator was the supreme good is abolished.

---

/1/ AM 1.6.1; 2.12.1; 2.29.4.

/2/ AM 1.6.2; 1.11.9; 1.13.2; 2.16.5.

/3/ AM 1.6.2f.; cf. 1.11.9. Tert. argues that as by definition 'God' is that which is supremely great, Marcion has 'set in opposition two supreme greatnesses' (1.5.1f.; 1.6.4).

/4/ AM 1.14.2: 'placebit tibi vel hoc opus dei nostri'.

/5/ AM 1.9.2; 1.11.9.

/6/ AM 1.14.1; 1.17.1.

Here Marcion seems to have in mind Paul's discourse on weakness in 2 Cor 12.9f. (*'hē gar dynamis en astheneia teleitai'*): the superior God enters into the 'prison house of the creator',/7/ coming down from the third heaven, and suffering crucifixion for man's benefit. If the allusion to 2 Cor 12.2 ('de tertio caelo descendere'; cf. AM 1.15.1) belongs to the marcionite creed from which Tertullian is apparently quoting, then it is clear that Marcion was heavily dependent on Paul's cosmology; it would seem that he developed no supplementary theory of the cosmos (cf. AM 4.7). Hence also Marcion's acceptance and elaboration of the idea that the Creator is the God of this aeon/8/ and his view of redemption as a cosmic drama/9/ consisting of liberation from the powers of the world./10/ He may have posited a separate (physical) sphere over which the alien God had control;/11/ but it is likelier that this is Tertullian's attempt to show Marcion's philosophical ineptitude:/12/ to what world does the alien God bring the souls of those he saves? Where is the visible evidence of it? If the alien God is truly God, why could he not have made a world of his own to save instead of tampering with the possessions of another? These arguments may respond to Marcion's suggestion, itself derived from Paul (Gal 6.15; 1 Cor 15.21f.; 15.44ff.), that the alien God in revealing his love brings about a new creation. But they may only represent Tertullian's spatio-materialist interpretation of the doctrine ascribed to Marcion by Irenaeus: 'Jesus is derived from that Father who is <u>above the God</u> that made the world'/13/ which he is then able to call his own.

---

/7/ AM 1.14.3. The phrase is often adduced as a marcionite synecdoche for the cosmos. But the prison-metaphor may have occurred to Marcion on the basis of 2 Cor 12.10, the incarnation being God's entering the 'prison of the flesh'. Cf. 'in haec paupertina', AM 1.14.2.

/8/ 2 Cor 4.3f.; cf. AM 4.38.7f.; 5.11.9f.; 5.17.1-9; cf. Iren. <u>Haer</u>. 3.7.1; 4.29.1.

/9/ AM 5.18.12f.; 3.23.5.

/10/ 1 Cor 2.6 = AM 5.6.7; cf. Lk 11.21.

/11/ AM 1.15.2: 'Ecce enim si et ille habet mundum suum infra se'; 1.15.5.

/12/ AM 1.15.1f.

/13/ <u>Haer</u>. 1.27.2.

## 7.2 God in Himself: Consistency as Supremacy

The revelation of a God who acts toward the world without the jealousy (aemulatio) of the Creator casts a new light on the historical relationship between the Creator and the world. In pauline terms, the dying aeon is shown for the first time to be corruptible. Marcion would not dispute Tertullian's claim that judgment and power are the proof of God ('Digna enim deo probabunt deum');/14/ but given the revelation (AM 1.26.1f.) of a God whose action is not to judge, but to save, the proof of the Creator's power only reveals his malice/15/ and jealousy. In a passage that can almost certainly be traced back to Marcion himself,/16/ the unity of purpose displayed by the unknown God in his saving action reveals (probare) the known God to be auctor alteri -- the author of opposites,/17/ who 'commands what he has forbidden and forbids what he has commanded, smiting and healing'. In a phrase that may mark Marcion's attitude toward the monism of his opponents, the OT God is 'contrary even to himself'; as author of the world's evils, as judge, and provoker of war,/18/ he is ontologically distinct from that self-consistent deity who acts towards the world only once and in only one way./19/ Thus while Tertullian argues from

---

/14/ AM 1.18.2.

/15/ AM 1.17.4; 1.22.3; etc.

/16/ Cf. Iren. Haer. 1.27.2.

/17/ AM 1.16.4; cf. AM 2.23.1f.; 2.21.1; 2.25.1.

/18/ Iren. Haer. 1.27.2. Cf. AM 2.21.1f.

/19/ As McGiffert has observed (God of the Early Christians (1924), 153), Marcion interpreted the Christian God 'in exclusively moral terms', a solution unacceptable to his contemporaries who understood salvation in 'physical as well as spiritual terms [which] included the resurrection of the flesh'. If God did not exercise physical control over the world, including in this control the right to judge men for the inherent and actual sins of the flesh, then God must be of necessity weak and imperfect. Marcion's opponents argued that neither the OT nor the preaching of the apostles supplied evidence of a God whose 'morality' was not exercised in judgment as well as in salvation. But for Marcion, the meaning of revelation was strictly bound up with the salvation of men's souls: one may even say that his ontology is derived from his soteriology, since there is in the nature of the alien God nothing that can contradict his absolute goodness and love, as evidenced in his design to free men from the God of justice and judgment. This alien God is wholly other, not in a metaphysical sense; rather, he is radically other than man's experience of God.

the premise that 'that which is supremely great is necessarily singular'/20/ and deduces from this the singularity of God as creator, judge, and saviour; Marcion seems to have indicated that <u>that which is supremely great is that which does not differ from itself</u>,/21/ and deduces (not philosophically, but on the basis of the Creator's revelation in the OT) that there is another God besides the Creator whose unity of purpose makes him supreme.

Marcion seems to have pushed the distinction between the God of this world and the alien God as far as possible, on the basis of 2 Cor 4.4 and other dualistic themes in Paul's teaching./22/ Hence, the unity of purpose which the alien God directs toward the world is not manifest in works: it is hidden;/23/ it is not revealed <u>ab origine</u>, like the created order of the lesser God, but once and once only in Jesus Christ ('Deus noster, etsi non ab initio, etsi non per conditionem, sed per semetipsum revelatus est in Christo Jesu')./24/ This summary of the faith, according to Marcion, corresponds to the original gospel of Paul: it is this message that the apostles had debased in continuing to preach Christ as the Son of the Creator./25/

## 7.3 The Nature and Plight of Man

In his interpretation of Paul's Epistle to the Romans, Marcion undoubtedly saw the judicial action (Rom 5.18f.) which brings men to condemnation as appropriate to the Creator's malice and jealousy. By contrast, the 'free gift' of love which justifies men's faith corresponds to the nature of the alien God (Rom 5.16ff.). Marcion emphasized Rom 5.13 as the explanation of 5.12, 19: It is the <u>aemulatio</u> of the Creator, as expressed in the law, that brings about the disobedience of man and the 'death that reigned from Adam to Moses'. But in Marcion's thought, 'sin' in

---

/20/ 'unicum sit necesse est quod fuerit summum magnum', AM 1.3.5f.

/21/ Cf. AM 1.26.1 (the laudation of goodness as God's only attribute); cf. 1.17.1; 2.27.8; 1.24.7; 1.25.3; 1.27.1f.

/22/ Gal 4.8-9; 2 Thess 2.4; 1 Cor 8.4; Gal 3.19 etc.; cf. Tert. AM 1.19.4; 1.21.6; 1.2.1; Iren. <u>Haer.</u> 1.27.2.

/23/ Tert. (AM 1.18; 1.23-24) argues <u>with</u> Irenaeus that a completely good God was bound by duty to act on his <u>goodness</u>.

/24/ AM 1.19.1.

/25/ AM 1.20.1, 4; cf. <u>Haer.</u> 3.5.1.

the sense of a guilt-accruing or punishable transgression is unknown. It is true that sin is patent to the nature and condition of man under the law; but it is finally the law itself to which guilt must attach, since 'sin is not imputed when the law does not exist' (*hamartia de ouk ellogeitai mē ontos nomou . . .*', Rom 5.13; cf. 4.14). Marcion might have accepted the Augustinian interpretation of Paul which envisaged man before grace as incapable of not sinning./26/ But the idea that sin must be imputed to the law itself, and thus to the malitia of the Creator (AM 2.9.1), distinguished him sharply from his orthodox contemporaries and from later 'orthodox' paulinists like Augustine. "The blame', writes Tertullian, 'should be imputed to [man] himself and not to God' (AM 2.6.1). Indeed, Tertullian even acknowledges Marcion's probable response to the orthodox doctrine: 'If the freedom and control of man's will was found to have ruinous effect, man ought to have been differently constituted'./27/

Marcion's ditheism is both his solution to the problem of evil and the key to his anthropology. By postulating the Creator as the author of the law which leads unavoidably to the vicious cycle of sin and retribution, Marcion removed the stumbling block over which many an orthodox theologian tripped: namely, the difficulty of reconciling the omnipotence and goodness of God with the existence of a defiant creation which operates contrary to his will (AM 2.5.2). The solution to the problem for the orthodox was to be discovered in the relationship between the constitution of human nature and the expedient of judgment adopted by an ingenerately good God in consequence of man's misuse of reason ('Ita prior bonitas dei secundum naturam, severitas posterior secundum causam', Tert. AM 2.11.2). But for Marcion the solution was to be sought in a differentiation of Gods, neither of whom is omnipotent: the good God can do nothing contrary to goodness, and so cannot create or judge; but the God of this world is equally powerless;

---

/26/ Cf. e.g., de pecc. mer. 3.8.15; Serm. 294.15; 151.4: Marcion possessed something of Augustine's sense that man's imperfection was the result of a 'profound and permanent dislocation'.

/27/ Tert. argues that man received absolute freedom with the breath of God, having been constituted in his image and likeness, the intention being to enable man to exhibit the goodness that by nature belongs to God alone: freedom of choice is thus reckoned to be a conveyance of the good: ('de institutione adscripta est illi quasi libripens emancipati a deo boni libertas et potestas arbitrii, quae efficeret bonum, . . .') AM 2.6.5.

constricted by the exercise of his power, he cannot save what he has created. Rather, he substitutes for the good that which he considers just, according to the completely arbitrary designs he has established for the governance of the world.

In the strictest sense of the word, then, man is a creature of the cosmocrator;/28/ he is not only under the law, but he mistakes the law for the highest good. He is therefore as much a stranger to the alien God as he is a creature under the 'law of sin and death' administered by the Creator. Being so constituted, he is 'guilty' only under the second condition; under the first, he is merely renegade from an unknown good: in pauline terms, he is man before and after faith: *'Ara oun hōs di henos paraptōmatos eis pantas anthrōpous eis katakrima, houtōs kai di henos dikaiōmatos eis pantas anthrōpous eis dikaiōsin zōes'* (Rom 5.18). Marcion does not speak in terms of man's 'freedom of choice'; the understanding is radically clouded (cf. Eph 1.18; 2.2f.; 1 Cor 13.12). According to nature, men belong to the lesser God (AM 1.17.1; cf. Eph 2.3b) and are strangers to the God above him (cf. AM 2.23.1; Eph 2.12);/29/ it is not primarily by man's free choice (AM 2.6.5) but by the love and mercy of the alien God that they come to freedom.

This 'breaking through' and taking possession of man was early on seen as a violation not only of man's freedom of choice/30/ but also of the Creator's natural right to his possession./31/ Irenaeus and Tertullian both invoke the law of property against Marcion's God, claiming that his goodness is diminished by an act of theft./32/ And Origen quotes Celsus as saying,

> Why does he secretly send to destroy the creations of this God? Why does he force his way in by stealth . . . and lead astray? Why does he lead off those whom, as you say, the Creator has condemned and cursed? . . . . Why does he teach them to escape from their master? Why should they flee from their Father? . . . . Why does he

---

/28/ Iren. Haer. 4.33.2; Tert. AM 1.23.8f; 1.17.1.

/29/ 'Hominis alieni: in extraneos': These are Marcion's words, almost technical terms of the Marcionite theology' (Evans ed., AM [OECT], 61, n. 1). Cf. Iren. Haer. 4.33.2; further, Harnack, Marcion, 265*.

/30/ AM 2.6.4f.; 2.7.2f.; etc.

/31/ Cf. AM 2.28.2.

/32/ Haer. 4.33.2; 5.18.1; AM 1.23.7f.: 'ceterum qualis bonitas quae per iniuriam constat, et quidem pro extraneo?'

> lay claim to be the Father of the strangers? . . . . An
> impressive God, indeed, who desires to be the father of
> sinners condemned by another and of poor wretches who,
> as they say themselves, are but dung . . ./33/

The significant term, then, for understanding Marcion's anthropology is that of 'stranger'; 'Diligere iuberis inimicum et extraneos'./34/ Man is alienated from God not by reason of sin as in Tertullian's anthropology,/35/ nor is he a stranger 'to the plenitude to which his soul belongs', as in the Valentinian systems; rather, he is by nature a stranger to God and God to him. He is a sinner not in virtue of being a descendant of Adam, but because he is a child of the lesser God (AM 1.17.1)/36/ 'whose very essense [substantia] is capable of sin'./37/

Paul's libertarianism is clearly programmatic for Marcion's anthropology: The blame attaching to the exercise of free choice must be referred to the Creator, and not to the creature ('nec potest non ad originalem summam referri corruptio portionis')./38/ Man is guilty under the law; but as a stranger to the good he is free: 'Those who were strangers to the promise, having no hope, and without God in the world: [the same] who were aliens have been drawn close by the blood of Christ' (Eph 2.12-13). Man stands between two opposing principles; in his natural state, he has no case to plead before God:/39/ 'Horremus terribiles minas creatoris':/40/ We stand in fear of the Creator's terrible threatenings.

---

/33/ Contra Cels. (Chadwick trans.) 6.53; on Origen's handling of Celsus' question about good and evil in relation to Marcion's God, 6.54ff.

/34/ AM 1.23.4f.: 'a primordio extraneum'. Cf. Evans, Prose Refutations, 61, n. 23.

/35/ Cf. de paen. 3; cf. de anima, 40-41.

/36/ 'O deum maiorem, cuius tam magnum opus non potuit inveniri quam in homine dei minoris!'

/37/ AM 2.9.1f. According to Tert. the breath (afflatus) but not the spiritus of God was potentially capable of disobedience as the conveyancer of free choice, though this disobedience could never be 'referred back' to God himself. The blame attaching to freedom of choice accrues only to man, who makes it function.

/38/ AM 2.9.1.

/39/ Cf. AM 1.23.5; 1.27.3f.; 2.12.1f.

/40/ AM 2.13.3; cf. however Blackman, 'Marcion had nothing convincing to say about the anomalies and errors of human existence', Influence, 79.

In the light of revelation, man's existential plight, previously known only to the alien God, becomes clear to man himself: that he is confronted with a choice, in pauline terms, between the law of death/41/ and the law of Christ (freedom)./42/ Marcion expressed this plight by pointing to the record of the Creator's dealings with mankind: the God who forbids labor on the Sabbath (Exod 20.9f.) commands the ark to be carried around Jericho on the Sabbath;/43/ the God who forbids the making of idols/44/ commands Moses to shape the image of a brazen serpent./45/ He variously requires sacrifices and rejects them;/46/ ennobles those he has chosen/47/ only to repent of his selection later./48/ Worse than his capriciousness and lack of foresight (improvidentia) is the Creator's admission that he creates evils (Isa 45.7), sends them against man and then repents of having done so./49/ The facts of revelation imported that man under the law was the image of the Creator. Of Marcion's interpretation of Gen 3.22 ('Ecce Adam factus est tanquam unus ex nobis') there remains only a faint trace in Tertullian's polemic; but it is likely that the myth was construed by Marcion to refer to man's acquiring the traits demonstrated by the Creator himself: ignorance, caprice, and malice. Tertullian aptly remarks that Marcion 'has put human

---

/41/ Rom 8.2; 1 Cor 15.56.

/42/ Gal 6.2; cf. Gal 2.4; 5.18; 5.23; Rom 6.14; 7.1f.; 3 Cor 2.7-18, etc.

/43/ AM 2.21.1.

/44/ AM 2.22.1.

/45/ Num 21.8f.

/46/ Isa 1.11, 13f.

/47/ AM 2.24-25.

/48/ Thus Marcion's interpretation of Jonah 4.2; 1 Sam 15.11.

/49/ Jer 18.11; AM 2.22.2; 2.24.7ff. Marcion may have used 1 Sam 15.28f. ('quia non sicut homo est ad paenitendum') to suggest that God was capable of repenting wrong-doing. On this point, Tert. argues that paenitentia does not signify a confession of wrong-doing, but means simply that God could change his mind: the philological point scarcely goes to the heart of Marcion's argument that God lacked foresight (cf. AM 2.25.1ff.). Marcion makes a similar point referring to Gen 3.9, 11, 'Ubi es Adam?'. Tert. argues that God feigned ignorance to give Adam an opportunity to repent. 2.25.5; also Theophilus, ad Autol. 2.26.

characteristics in God rather than divine characteristics in man';/50/ and this is almost certainly the way in which Marcion would have understood the significance of God's words to Adam. That man is made in God's image (Gen 1.26) does not attest to man's capacity for the 'gentleness, patience, mercy and goodness',/51/ which characterize the alien God, but rather to his capacity for anger, jealousy, small-mindedness, and pride. What man is under the law tells him what the law-maker is in himself: 'Quomodo ergo in deo humanum aliquid existimas, et non divinum omne?'./52/ Marcion may have derived his understanding not from a straightforward exegesis of the OT passage, but from Paul's declaration in 1 Cor 15.49: *Ephorēsamen tēn eikona tou choikou* -- that is, the image of the God of this world (AM 5.10.10).

Marcion both accepts and expands upon Paul's distinction between psyche and pneuma by averring that soul and spirit originate with different authors. Either Marcion changed Paul's ending of 1 Cor 15.45, or knew a reading which differed considerably from Tertullian's text: The first man, Adam, was made a living soul; the last Lord a life-giving spirit./53/ Tertullian objects with some justice to the rhetorical imbalance of Marcion's rendering; Marcion, for his part, seems only to have objected to Paul's use of Adam as a prototype of Jesus and probably regarded the usage as an orthodox interpolation: in view of 15.46, how could the natural (Adam) adumbrate the spiritual change which was to come about in Christ? 'It is not the spiritual which was first but the physical: later came that which is spiritual'. For Marcion the transformation (1 Cor 15.47f.) from choikos (natural man or man as created by the just God), to epouranios (man according to faith) was an absolute metamorphosis effected by the alien God and attested by the saving action of Jesus (1 Cor 15.57)./54/ Marcion's idea of resurrection is simply a corollary of the idea that the natural body cannot be saved because it belongs to the Creator (AM 5.6.11), whereas the

---

/50/ AM 2.16.5f.

/51/ AM 2.16.6.

/52/ AM 2.16.5; cf. Eph 2.2b-3.

/53/ Based on AM 5.10.7f.

/54/ Cf. AM 5.11.15ff. Tert. is carried away by argument, using the passage to defend his view of bodily resurrection. Cf. de carne 3; Marcion of course denied the doctrine (Haer. 1.27.3; AM 5.10.3).

spiritual body, animated by the transforming action of the alien God, is equipped for salvation. But just as Marcion's idea of the alien God is non-physical, so his view of the resurrection (AM 5.10.3): what is saved is a transformed and reconstituted spirit. Almost all that can be said on this point is that Tertullian's understanding of bodily resurrection is far removed from the marcionite doctrine of spiritual transformation./55/ According to Marcion's theory, the transformation is required by the principle that nothing in the constitution of man corresponds to anything in the nature of the alien God;/56/ while for Tertullian the same God acts in Adam and in Christ ('Quare secundus, si non homo, quod et primus?')./57/ Tertullian can complain that the alien God's appropriation of the souls of men is illegitimate precisely because man is the image and likeness of his Creator./58/ Marcion's anti-materialism let his critics to taunt that the wholly good God fails to save the whole man since the flesh does not rise again; and as man's salvation is incomplete God's goodness must come into question:/59/ 'Quid erat perfectae bonitatis quam totum hominem redigere in salutem, totum damnatum a creatore, totum a deo optimo allectum?' (cf. de paen. 3)./60/

---

/55/ Tert. de carne, 4-5; AM 3.11.6; de res. 42-54.

/56/ De carne, 3; AM 3.8.1-2; cf. 1 Cor 15.50b; Rom 8.5.

/57/ AM 5.10.9.

/58/ AM 5.6.11f.; 2.16.5f.

/59/ AM 1.24.3f. Tert. seems to have had no other sources for his contention than Irenaeus (1.27.3; and cf. AM 1.24.2 and Haer. 4.33.2), along with some knowledge of marcionite ritual ascesis, which he attacks in 1.14 and 1.28-29. But the passage in Irenaeus only implies a denial of the resurrection of the flesh as 'being taken from the earth'. Tert. takes this up in the context of 1 Cor 15.37: 'Marcion enim in totum carnis resurrectionem non admittens et soli animae salutem repromittens' (AM 5.10.3); this is gleaned from Irenaeus, but with the addition that Marcion makes resurrection 'not a question of attributes but of substance'. Irenaeus does not indicate that Marcion raised the question of substantia or materia, but suggests that Marcion(?) declared the body suffers corruption (Haer. 5.4.1). That Marcion thought in terms any more sophisticated than Paul is to be doubted.

/60/ AM 1.24.4. By the 'whole man', Tert. refers to his physiological theory of the soul and body as divisible corporeal entities. The former 'sprung from the breath of God, immortal, possessing body, having form, simple in substance, intelligent in its own nature, developing its power in various ways, free in its determinations, subject to changes of accident, in

Marcion defined man primarily in terms of his relation to the Creator. His transformation (2 Cor 3.8; Phil 3.21; Rom 8.29) -- his expropriation from the law of sin -- has nothing to do with any possibility available to him as a man under judgment./61/ Tertullian failed to detect that this anthropology was less dualistic than his own: Marcion denied that man was a 'composite being'. According to Paul, what man is in relation to the Creator defines his true and essential nature. What he is ('how' he is transformed) by the grace of God has nothing to do with his nature: nothing he can do 'according to the flesh' or in order to attain 'wisdom' aids him in achieving the transformation from the carnal to the spiritual state. By nature he is a slave to spiritual powers; by grace he is a new creation. It is unlikely that Marcion was familiar with any philosophical or pseudo-philosophical theory of the soul other than that enunciated by Paul. And Tertullian's idea of spirit as an operation of the soul, 'planted' in it from birth/62/ would scarcely have commended itself to Marcion, who evidently equated the operation of the 'will' with the contrary purposes of the known and unknown Gods./63/ While he may have acknowledged the existence of some rarefied materia which constitutes the soul in man/64/ there is confusion over whether Marcion understood this soul in the active sense as willing or only in the passive sense of being. In any event, the soul does not 'participate' in its own salvation. It seems doubtful that Marcion would have recognized the will as an independent authority (to autexousion), capable of transacting its salvation, since ignorance belongs absolutely to the condition of man under the Creator's law.

Thus while we cannot assume that Marcion made a functional

---

its faculties mutable, rational, supreme' (de anima, 22). Significantly, while Tert. mentions Apelles among the heretics who wrongly speculate about the origin of the soul, Marcion is not mentioned. Cf. ibid., 23; further, de res. 40.

/61/ Cf. AM 5.17.10; 2.27.8: 'Iudicem eum designatis'; 2.21.1.

/62/ De anima. 11.

/63/ Tert. incorrectly argues that Marcion left no room for free will, in imputing all initiative to the Creator (AM 2.6.1f.; cf. de anima. 21) and to the alien God.

/64/ The exact nature of Marcion's theory cannot be deduced from Tert.'s discussion in the de anima (21). But at 5.10.3, Tert. tells us that Marcion's denial of the resurrection turns on the question of substantia; so too AM 3.8.3: 'an credam ei de interiore substantia qui sit de exteriore frustratus?'

distinction between mind and will (cf. Tertullian, de anima, 12), he may have wanted to suggest that it is the mind (nous) of man which the Creator's law had clouded, his will remaining to some unspecified degree 'free', if also impaired by virtue of its dependence on the superior function of nous (cf. AM 2.5-7). This would be a deterministic view of human nature which nevertheless allowed some room for the outreach of the soul confronted by the mysterion of divine grace. The idea of choice is implied in Irenaeus' report that 'Salvation will be the attainment only of those souls who learn his doctrine', and in the acceptance/rejection motif provided in the descensus. Moreover the emphasis on revelation as a clearing away of the clouds of ignorance and the breaking of the law of death seems to hinge on there being minds capable of receiving this revelation. But the initiative according to which the transformation occurs remains God's, and has nothing ultimately to do with man's 'will' to be saved.

Marcion may well have disputed Tertullian's reading of 1 Cor 15.29-58 concerning the resurrection of the body. For Marcion, apparently, the salvation of the whole man consists precisely in being freed from the body of death; 'flesh' is that which is no part of the new creation: 'et in hoc totum salutis sacramentum carnem mergit exsortem salutis' (cf Rom 8.8; 1 Cor 15.50, etc.)./65/ Man does not possess this animus in the sense of an 'inextinguishable divine spark' but solely by virtue of being man; he is ignorant of the good; he is not incapable of responding to revelation. Put differently: because Marcion did not postulate sin as an offense against a God who is perfectly good, he was not compelled to argue the depravity of man's reason as a consequence of transgression. To say that man is 'ignorant' by nature (AM 2.6.1) is only to say something about his historical situation in the world, and not about his capacity to grasp the meaning of revelation.

### 7.4 The Christ of the Alien God

The distinctive feature of Marcion's christology is its dependence on the 'docetic' elements of Paul's religious thought (Rom 8.3: en homoiōmati sarkos hamartias; cf. Phil 2.6-8; Col 1.15). The ancient witnesses proscribe

---

/65/ On Marcion's view of the unworthiness of the flesh: AM 1.28.3f.; 3.11.7; de carne, 4; and cf. Iren. Haer. 5.4.1.

Marcion for his rejection of the virgin birth;/66/ and it is this feature of Marcion's thought that causes Irenaeus to enunciate his own view of the 'natures' of Christ as against those who 'transform the truth, and despise his Father and his advent'./67/

As we have noted in considering the historical question, the identification of Marcion with the 'docetist' mentioned by Polycarp in his Letter to the Philippians is already assumed by Irenaeus./68/ Thus, according to the earliest strand of the tradition still discernible Marcion's heresy was known as having a christological dimension: He denied that Jesus had come in the flesh ('en sarki elēluthenai'), and more ambiguously, 'he [did] not confess the testimony of the cross'. Significantly, Polycarp does not say that Marcion denied that Jesus suffered and died on the cross, but rather that he falsely interpreted the evidence (martyrion) before him. We know from later writers that Marcion took seriously the reality of Jesus' suffering. Tertullian remarks that he has doubts about the sincerity of Marcion's belief 'that God was crucified',/69/ since Christ did not take on true flesh (3.10.1; 3.8.2). Tertullian elsewhere suggests that the logic of Marcion's position requires him to attribute real flesh to Christ (3.11.6; cf. 3.8.3: 'An credam ei de interiore substantia qui sit de exteriore frustratus?'; 2.27.2; 1.24.5). This apparent contradiction can be explained by Tertullian's doctrine of corporeality and the physiology of human conception:/70/ no flesh that has entered the world other than through natural childbirth can undergo death. Emphasis on this aspect of Marcion's heresy is occasioned therefore not because a docetic theory of Christ's nature is presupposed in his theology, but for just the opposite reason:

---

/66/ E.g. Tert. de carne, 2-4; AM 1.19; Haer. 4.33.2; Adam. Dial. 2.9; and cf. Chrysostom (Hom. 123.6), cited by Harnack, p. 368*

/67/ Iren. Haer. 3.4.2. According to Irenaeus, Jesus 'condescended to be born of a virgin, and united himself to God and man through himself' ('ipse per se hominem adunans Deo'); cf. Haer. 3.11.3; 4.33.2; 4.6.2. It is possible that Irenaeus bases his knowledge of Marcion's docetism on Justin's testimony, Logoi kata Markiōnos, also mentioned by Photius, 125.

/68/ Haer. 3.3.4; Polyc. Phil. 7.1; cf. 2 Jn 7.

/69/ AM 2.27.7.

/70/ Cf. de res. 17; de anima. 25; 27-37.

because Marcion, unlike the gnostics, stressed the reality/71/ and historicity (Haer. 1.27.2) of Jesus' humanity and suffering (de carne, 5) while at the same time -- illogically to Tertullian -- denying that he had been born./72/ Tertullian argues that Marcion's error lay in overturning the fact that nativity and flesh bear mutual testimony to each other's reality since without nativity, there can be no flesh (cf. de carne, 1)./73/ But it is doubtful whether Tertullian knows more about Marcion's christology than what is indicated or implied by his opponent's alleged rejection of the nativity-narrative of the gospel./74/

In Paul's christology, Jesus is a divine being, the 'Lord' himself (1 Cor 1.31; 2 Cor 3.16; 2 Thess 1.9). He is the image of the invisible God (Col 1.15f.; 2.9; cf. Phil 2.6). In a passage which Marcion is said to have

---

/71/ Cf. Harnack, Marcion, 188*; 310*; in AM 5.13.12 it is suggested that Marcion distinguished between sōma and sarx in the interpretation of Rom 7.4. But Tert. does not seem to be confuting Marcion at this point; merely conceding a hypothetical objection to his argument which he proceeds to withdraw. See J.P. Mahé's discussion, Sources chrét., 216 (1975), 93.

/72/ The extent to which the concepts of realitas and substantia are linked in Tert.'s mind can be seen from his preliminary excursus against Marcion in the de carne. There he considers self-evident the proposition that 'Marcion, in order to deny the flesh of Christ, denied his nativity' (de carne. 1). Irenaeus argues in relation to Marcion's docetism: (a) that Jesus declared himself son of man; (b) that this title implies human birth; (c) that to forgive sins, he had to be an agent of the Creator, i.e., the offended party; (d) that there would have been no issue of blood at the crucifixion if Christ possessed no human flesh. Irenaeus anticipates Tert. in making the reality of the passion contingent on the nativity (cf. Haer. 4.33.2).

/73/ Cf. AM 4.8.3. Tert. quotes Lucretius, I.305, to the effect that a body must be tangible to be a body ('Tangere enim et tangi nisi corpus nulla potest res . . .'); but he makes the exegesis of Lk 4.30 to turn on the denial of the visibility of Christ's body, an extraneous point since Maricon had not said that Jesus deceived the men by becoming invisible; cf. Lk 24.36.

/74/ We cannot take seriously Tert.'s taunting suggestion that Marcion despised the generative process and was horrified at the sight of the newborn (de carne, 4; echoed by Clement, Strom. 3.3.12), and that this caused him to omit the birth narrative from the gospel; conversely, the fact that Tert. preoccupies himself with the generative process may suggest that it is only on this point that Marcion differed significantly from the mainstream christologies. This is strongly suggested by the challenge Tert. puts further on: 'Either take away nativity and then show us your man, or else withdraw the flesh and then present to our view the being whom God has redeemed' (de carne, 4); cf. Chrysostom, Hom. 123.6 (Harnack, Marcion, 368*): 'Markiōn hora ti phēsin ouk edunato ho theos sarka analabōn meinai katharos'.

rejected (Rom 9.5), Christ came 'according to the flesh'; but the same passage seems to imply that Christ and God are one *(ho ōn epi pantōn theos')*./75/ It is impossible to know whether Marcion would have accepted either affirmation, taken by itself; but the idea that Christ according to the flesh is to be equated with God would have been intolerable to him. About the most we can say is that in failing to embrace Tertullian's equation between the flesh that is born and the flesh that is capable of suffering and dying, Marcion need not have rejected the idea that Christ came and suffered according to the flesh, and suffered as the dispensation of God toward creation (e.g., AM 1.11.8).

The elimination of Rom 9.5 suggests that Marcion made at least a primitive distinction between Christ and God. The <u>reality</u> of Jesus as the mode of God's revelation 'according to the flesh' cannot entail that the flesh of Christ is 'created', i.e., composed of substances belonging to the Creator (thus Apelles) since this would mean that Jesus himself belongs to the Creator and hence that the Creator is within his rights in taking away the life he has given. Whether Marcion thought in the forensic terms of his opponents is uncertain; it is likely that he reached for his solution no further than Rom 7.4, if indeed he reached at all./76/

There is an element of theological sophistication in Marcion's christology, but it stops short, from what we can discover, of being a sustained attempt to explain the relation between the supreme God and his Christ. Perhaps properly understood, Marcion's christology is no more imprecise in this respect than that of Ignatius,/77/ 'John', or the author of the <u>Epistle to Barnabas</u>./78/ However that may be, the saying attributed by

---

/75/ Thus McGiffert, <u>God of the Early Christians</u>, 27.

/76/ See further, Blackman, <u>Influence</u>, 100.

/77/ Cf. Ign. <u>Eph</u>. 18.2: *'Ho gar theos hēmōn Iēsous ho Christos'*. Even in insisting on the nativity of Jesus, 'according to the family of David' (<u>Eph</u>. 20.2), Ignatius still prefers to speak of the incarnation as a phanerōsis of God (<u>Eph</u>. 19.3) in language tinctured by gnostic speculation. Elsewhere, he speaks of 'the passion of God' (<u>Rom</u>. 6.3) and expresses a <u>contemptus carnis</u> no less severe than Marcion's in declaring that 'nothing visible is good' (<u>Rom</u>. 3.3). The (pauline) docetic emphasis is also presented in his allusion to Jesus being 'clothed' in flesh (<u>Smyrn</u>. 5.2).

/78/ The author of the <u>Epistle to Barnabas</u> understands the flesh of Christ to have been concession to human perception (5.10).

Adamantius/79/ to the marcionite Megethius suggests the extent to which Marcion's theory of redemption was determined by Paul (cf. Rom 7.13a): 'The death of the Good became the salvation of men' (cf. AM 1.11.8). We may therefore see Marcion as struggling toward a doctrine which he does not manage to articulate. Even in this, his failure may have as much to do with his fidelity to Paul as with his own theological inconsistency: none of Marcion's contemporaries succeeded in making Paul's teaching coherent. Marcion, in all probability, stuck closely to the idea (Phil 2.7f.) that Christ was both *en morphē theou* and *en homoiōmati anthrōpōn:* 'God dwelt in human shape', and laid low the high estate of his glory, making it subject to death on the cross./80/

In holding the idea that the revelation of God in Christ is transitory rather than intrinsic to the godhead itself Marcion anticipates the modalist-Monarchians such as Praxeas and Sabellius. If Marcion could not have accepted that God suffered,/81/ the conclusion is nonetheless unavoidable that his christology led him in the direction of patripassianism; i.e., the alien God's temporal manifestation is as the suffering savior. In this mode, he truly undergoes death (Phil 2.8b = AM 2.27.2f.) in obedience to the Creator's law, his suffering being a paradigm for all humanity. In this respect Marcion's christology does not lack the element of 'summary' (anakephalaiōsis) around which Irenaeus organizes his own christology. But there is an important twist. While for Irenaeus and Justin the incarnation evidences that there is one divine purpose at work in creation and redemption,/82/ Marcion seems to have regarded the suffering of Jesus as the compendium of man's relation to the Creator./83/

---

/79/ Cited by Harnack, Marcion, 296*; cf. Apelles, sic. Rhodo, HE 5.13.5.

/80/ AM 2.27.2f. Whether Tert. has firsthand knowledge of a creed used by the marcionite priests is not clear, but there is no reason to think that the Marcionites would have less reason than the orthodox to provide a formal profession of belief at some point in the life of the community.

/81/ Adv. Prax. 28-30.

/82/ Cf. Haer. 3.9.1; 4.9.3; 3.18.1: 'Sed quando incarnatus et homo factus, longam hominum expositionem in seipso recapitulavit, in compendio nobis salutem praestans . . .').

/83/ 'Quantenus et ipsi deum in figura et in reliquo ordine humanae conditionis deversatum iam credidistis. . .' (AM 2.27.2). Here Tert. purports to refute the Marcionites out of their own faith.

According to the terms of Irenaeus' doctrine, the humanity of Christ must have been identical with that of Adam (Haer. 5.14.2) in order for the recapitulation to occur: In taking on flesh and blood, Jesus recapitulated in himself 'not some other, but the original handiwork of the Father seeking out that thing which had perished'. That this recapitulation is generic rather than paradigmatic Irenaeus attempts to show from a section of the gospel which Marcion is accused of eliminating: 'The pedigree which traces the generation of our Lord back to Adam contains seventy-two generations, connecting the end with the beginning, and implying that it is He who has summed up in Himself all nations dispersed from Adam downwards, and all languages and generations of men, together with Adam himself'./84/ The extent to which Irenaeus' doctrine of recapitulation is a response to Marcion's christology has not been documented. But it is certain that Marcion's 'rejection' of the Lucan genealogy/85/ and his insistence on the historical sense of prophecy/86/ required just such a response.

To Irenaeus, it was apparent that the voice speaking in such passages as Exod 3.7f. ('I have seen the affliction of my people and have come down to deliver them') was the voice of God in his disposition as the logos: The word of God was 'accustomed from the beginning to ascend and descend for the salvation of those who were in affliction'./87/ But Marcion regarded such evidence of the Creator's beneficence as proof of his inconsistency and 'infirmity of purpose': Christ does not 'summarize' or 'recapitulate' this God's dispensation. What he summarizes instead is the human condition in itself: man as stranger (to God), and man the sufferer in relation to the law of the Creator. In avoiding the deeper metaphysical problems entailed by such a christology, Marcion fell prey to the criticisms of definition-prone opponents such as Tertullian (AM 4.7; 4.8.2: '. . . iam de substantia eius

---

/84/ Haer. 3.22.3.

/85/ Tert. de carne, 2; AM 1.19; 4.7.1f.; Iren. Haer. 1.27.2; Adam. Dial. 1-3.

/86/ Iren. Haer. 1.27.2; AM 4.7.4; 4.15.1f.

/87/ Iren. Haer. 4.12.4; cf. Tert. AM 3.5.2f.; 2.27.3. Further, on the belief that the voice of God in the OT was the son acting as messenger of the father, Justin, Tryph., 56ff.; Tert. adv. Prax. 14-16; Eus. HE 1.2.2f.; Prudentius, Apotheosis.

corporali praefinire', cf. 3.8.3f.)./88/ But free from the constraint of proving the hidden meaning of OT prophecy, and of developing a christology based on the divine metanoia,/89/ Marcion was able to stress the theme of divine love and the consistency of God's purpose as revealed uniquely in Christ: 'Sufficit unicum hoc opus deo nostro'./90/ The central theme of Marcion's christology, however imperfectly developed, is close to that developed by Paul, and exponents of Paul's theology, where the salvation of man is linked to the power of God's love operating in Jesus (2 Cor 13.4).

## 7.5 The Christ of the Jews and Judaism: Marcion's Second Christology

Marcion's literalist reading of the OT persuaded him that the Creator's Christ was still to come./91/ Of this aspect of his teaching, there is evidence reaching back as far as Justin./92/ The Christ of the Creator promises the Jews regathering out of dispersion, the rëestablishment of the kingdom,/93/ and when life has run its course, 'refreshment with those beneath the earth in Abraham's bosom'./94/ This is evidence that the appropriate designation for Marcion's Creator is 'righteous', rather than evil/95/ and that the alien God is not opposed to every purpose of the Creator./96/ With obvious sarcasm, Tertullian writes, 'You make your good God exempt from every bitterness of feeling and [thus] from hostility to the

---

/88/ On Tert.'s use of OT prophecy, AM 3.6-7.

/89/ 'Mutavit sententias suas deus noster . . . Paenituit mali in aliquo deum nostrum, sed et vestrum. Eo enim, quod tandem animadvertit ad hominis salutem, paenitentiam dissimulationis pristinae fecit debitam malo facto . . .', AM 2.28.1-2.

/90/ AM 1.17.1: Tertullian here offering a hypothetical marcionite argument. Cf. 1.26.1; 2.27.8; 2.7.1; 1.24.7.

/91/ AM 3.23.6; 4.6.3f.; 3.4.4ff.

/92/ 1 Apol. 58.

/93/ AM 4.6.3.

/94/ AM 3.24.1.

/95/ AM 4.33.4; 2.12.1; cf. Haer. 3.25.2.

/96/ Cf. AM 1.25.3; 1.27.2.

Creator';/97/ and although the alien God disapproves of the Creator's order, toward the Creator himself the alien God is only lukewarm (tepidus),/98/ as he does not intend setting up a barrier against the Christ who is still to come.

That Marcion chose to emphasize the hope for Israel by means of this 'second' christology shows once again the extent of his dependence on Paul's religious thought and (with a view to his omission of the anti-Jewish polemic of Rom 9, and emphasis on the 'new man' anthropology of Eph 2.15) the pro-Jewish orientation of his theology. This does not mean that Marcion goes beyond Paul's ambivalent concern for the welfare of the Jews (Rom 3.1f.; 10.1; 11.1ff.). He regards Judaism only as the point d'appui of revelation in Christ. But there is an element of empathy in Marcion's theology: Israel has suffered most under the Creator's regime. Blinded by suspicion, the Jews refuse the Christ who offers salvation/99/ and choose to remain in Abraham's bosom,/100/ awaiting the Christ who offers the restoration of the political kingdom. Doubtless Marcion had found warrant for this interpretation in Paul's references to Israel's recalcitrance and 'ignorance'./101/ His use of the descensus Christi to illustrate the promise is also dictated by Paul (Rom 10.7: 'E, tis katabēsetai eis tēn abysson?', cf. Eph 4.9f.), who regards the enlightenment of the jews as a desideratum in its own right (Eph 1.17-23 = Rom 10.2), accomplished on equal terms with the salvation of the gentiles (Eph 4.17f.; Rom 10.19). Marcion may have accepted Paul's notion (Rom 11.7f.) that the conversion of the gentiles is a spur to the Jews; but he seems not to have emphasized the catalytic idea of the gentile mission as

---

/97/ AM 2.29.3f.; cf. 5.4.14.

/98/ AM 3.4.4; cf. AM 3.24.1: 'O deum etiam ad inferos usque misericordem!'

/99/ Iren. Haer. 1.27.3.

/100/ Cf. AM 3.24.1. Marcion seems to have used the term 'Abraham's bosom' to refer to the locus of 'those who have obeyed the law and the prophets' (4.34.11). Tert. defines it (AM 4.34.13), 'etsi non caelestem, sublimiorem tamen inferis, interim refrigerium praebituram animabus iustorum, donec consummatio rerum resurrectionem omnium plenitudine mercedis expungat . . .' One cannot be sure from Tert.'s assumption that Marcion himself understood the 'heaven' of the alien God as local (AM 4.7.2; 3.24.13), but it is not unreasonable to suppose that Marcion accepted Paul's cosmology as being correct.

/101/ Rom 10.19; 11.7; 11.23; 10.2f., etc.

such. The gentiles, being removed from the law, have a natural advantage over the Jews. Since 'the exceeding riches of God's grace' are not adumbrated in the experience of Jew or gentile (Rom 3.9, 23; Eph 2.7), it is possible for Marcion to stress the equality of men as (former) strangers to the mercy of God (Eph 2.3b-4; 2.11f.; 2.19; 3.6; Rom 10.12f.) and God's love for Israel (Rom 11.2; Gal 3.7f.).

Marcion's second christology is historical: the 'Judaic Christ'/102/ will gather the children of Israel out of dispersion, whereas the Christ of the alien God purposes to deliver the whole human race (AM 4.6.3). The Christ of the Jews will be known as Emmanuel (AM 3.12.1; Isa 7.14); he will be a warrior and deliverer (AM 3.13.1f.), 'born of a young woman' (AM 3.13.5f.); he will take up the strength of Damascus and the spoils of Samaria against the king of the Assyrians (Isa 8.4; AM 3.13.1). In nature, he is 'the son and the spirit and the substance of the Creator' ('filius et spiritus et substantia creatoris')./103/ But it is not prophesied in scripture that he will suffer and die on a cross./104/ It is this Christ whom the Jews expect and whom the Creator, in a moment of compassion, promised to the children of Israel; of any other savior, both the Creator and the Jews are ignorant./105/ Marcion, stressing this ignorance, evidently diverged from the popular view that the Jews actively despised 'the word and spirit, the Christ of the Creator' in times past./106/

Not only is this second christology an affirmation of Jewish messianic expectations; it is also an attempt to absolve the Jews of any responsibility for the death of Jesus. How could they have known, Marcion asks, that Christ had come to rescue them from the Creator? The blame for the death of Jesus must be charged to the God who has blinded the minds of men, and not to those who, ignorant of any higher good, seek to keep his commandments (AM 3.6.8; 2.28.3; 5.6.5; Haer. 4.29.1). Christ comes not to his

---

/102/ AM 3.21.1; 4.6.3.

/103/ AM 3.6.8.

/104/ AM 3.18.1f.; cf. ad Nat. 1.12; Justin, Tryph. 91, 94, 112.

/105/ AM 3.6.8; 1.11.9.

/106/ AM 3.6.8. Tert.'s view of the Jews as Christ-killers gets its fullest treatment here: 'The Jews both rejected Christ and put him to death not because they took Christ for a stranger, but because though their own, they did not accept him', AM 3.6.9; cf. 1 Cor 2.8.

own, but for the sake of all nations (AM 4.6.3); he comes to the Jews as a stranger (AM 3.6.2), because they have suffered the most under the 'Creator's terrible threatenings' (AM 2.13.3). Had they known that he came from a God of mercy and in order to free them from the law, they would have spared him (1 Cor 2.8). This ignorance applies equally, even prëeminently, to the apostles who mistakenly identify the gospel proclaimed by Jesus with the fulfillment of prophecies and, in preaching to the Jews, hesitate to proclaim to them 'another God besides him in whom [the Jews] believed'./107/ Thus in developing his christology Marcion supplies a rationale for false apostleship which is wanting in Paul, but which nevertheless does not assume an anti-Jewish character. On the contrary, the apostles are neither more nor less enlightened than other men, Paul (because of his special revelation) being the only exception./108/ The crucifixion shows forth the infirmity of the Creator's purpose./109/ But precisely because 'inconsistency' is patent to the Creator's nature, he promises (and apparently desires to effect) deliverance for his chosen people,/110/ at least from the political misfortunes that they have suffered on account of their faithfulness. In this he shows forth his justice.

## 7.6 The Pro-Jewish Trajectory: Marcionism as 'Jewish Error'

Conventional interpretations of Marcion's theology have paid but scant attention to the pro-Jewish element in his thought, emphasizing instead his presumed 'rejection' of the OT and his denigration of the Creator. Certainly Marcion's exaggerated paulinism turned on the premise that the law was at an end/111/ and that the prophets were from another God than the God announced in the gospel./112/ But as we have seen, where Marcion differs from Paul, it is in the direction of emphasizing the love and forgiveness of

---

/107/ Haer. 3.12.6; cf. 3.12.2.

/108/ Iren. Haer. 3.13.1.

/109/ AM 5.6.7; cf. 5.17.10; 5.6.6.

/110/ Tert. AM 4.6.3; 3.24.1f.

/111/ Haer. 4.13.1; 4.34.2-3; cf. 4.12.3; cf. Rom 3.20ff.; 6.14; 7.4; 3.28.

/112/ Haer. 4.34.1.

God for the 'children of wrath', rather than the recalcitrance and hard-heartedness of the Jews.

While our ability to piece together Marcion's text of Rom 10-11, where the problem of Israel's unresponsiveness is broached, is severely limited -- we have no way of knowing the extent of the intercisa scriptura noted by Tertullian/113/ in this epistle -- it can be no accident that he left unaltered Rom 11.33 (= Eph 3.18f.; cf. Col 3.16a), concerning the mystery of God's purpose. One notes also the close linguistic resemblance between the opening sentence of the Antitheses ('O wealth of riches . . .') and the ekstasis of Paul in Rom 11.33, and its echoes in Eph 2.7; 3.18f. (Col 2.3; 3.16). It is also significant that Marcion 'removed' prōton after Ioudaiō at Rom 1.16,/114/ with the resultant reading 'The power of God is given to salvation to all who believe: to the Jew as well as to the Greek'. In this editorial decision we see again Marcion's refusal to make a strategy of the gentile mission, while the elimination of the rest of the chapter in toto can only be explained in terms of Marcion's revulsion at the ideas he found there. The Paul of Rom 9.22 is unknown to Marcion./115/ Moreover, it would have been impossible for him to read Rom 1.20f. ('The invisible things of him from the creation of the world are closely seen . . .') as coming from the hand of the author of Rom 16.25b (!) (cf. 11.33f.; 3.11a; 1 Cor 2.8). Even if Marcion had known such a text,/116/ he would have considered it spurious: and whether he did or did not, the imputation of guilt to the Jews was theologically precluded by suggestion that the God of wrath manifest in them (Rom 9.22) was the God who poured forth his mercy on Jew and gentile

---

/113/ AM 5.14.6; cf. 5.13.4. But Rom 11.31-32 probably did not appear in Marcion's text. Harnack, Marcion, 354*f.; Burkitt, JTS (1929), 219f.

/114/ AM 5.13.2f.

/115/ AM 5.13.4f. It is worth underlining that Marcion did not consider Rom 1.24, 28b even an adequate characterization of the Creator -- or so the absence of 1.19ff. would suggest; in the same connection, we must question just how much of ch. 1 following 1.9 Marcion accepted or knew.

/116/ Kümmel: 'We do not know how the truncated text attested by Marcion originated. . . .It is just as possible that Marcion found it truncated as that he shortened it himself', Introd. to the NT, 317. So too, Klijn, Introd., 79; de Bruyne, 'Les deux derniers chapitres de la Lettre aux Romains', Rev. Bénéd. 25 (1908), 423ff.; and P. Corssen, 'Zur Überlieferungsgeschichte des Rom.' ZNTW 10 (1909), 79ff. suggested that Marcion's shortened text represents the point of origin for the textus receptus but also that Marcion shortened the epistle.

alike (cf. Rom 3.9)./117/

Marcion clung to the tenet best expressed in Eph 2, that God's very being is revealed in his mercy and not in judgment. It was not part of his interpretation of Paul that God shows his wrath to the 'vessels fitted for destruction'. This theme is driven further by the inclusion of the marcionite doxology (Rom 16.24ff.) at the end of Rom 14.23 (Marcion omitting chs. 15-16):/118/ 'According to the revelation of the mystery which was kept secret since the world began, [and is ] now made manifest, by the oracle of scripture by the eternal God's command, made known to all nations, to bring them to the summons of faith'./119/

The Jews too stand under the wrath of God (Rom 3.9; cf. Eph 2.3f.) and their hearts have been darkened. But they are eligible for reprieve from the law of death that reigned from Adam to Moses (Rom 5.14, 8.2). There is no compelling evidence to support the judgment that Marcion's theology is anti-Jewish in design, and the familiar view that his 'rejection' of the OT made him the arch-antisemite of the ancient church is uninformed./120/ To be sure, Paul himself envisages a 'judaizing' error, which consists in following after the law of righteousness, rather than attaining to the perfection of faith. This is the great stumbling block to salvation. But Marcion rejected the expressly anti-Jewish sentiments recorded by the author of Rom 9, by eliminating -- if indeed he knew -- the chapter from his

---

/117/ 'The heretic will raise a quibble', writes Tert. (AM 5.14.7), that it was the superior God that the Jews did not know, and that 'against him they set up their own righteousness'. According to Tert. Marcion's text of Rom 10.3a imported that it was God himself -- the true God -- whom the Jews do not know; whereas the 'righteousness' of God (the Creator) they know full well (10.4).

/118/ Origen, Comm. in ep. ad Rom. 10.43 (PG 14, c. 1290 A-B): 'Caput hoc [Rom 16.25ff.] Marcion, a quo scripturae evangelicae et apostolicae interpolatae sunt, de hac penitus abstulit; et non solum hoc, sed ab eo loco, ubi scriptum est "omne autem, quod non est ex fide, peccatum est" [viz., 14.23], usque ad finem cuncta dissecuit'. Cf. Harnack, Marcion, 165*f.

/119/ Cf. J. Dupont, 'Pour l'histoire de la Doxologie finale de l'Épitre aux Romains', Rev. Bénéd. 58 (1948), 3-22; R. Schumacher, 'Die Beiden letzten Kapitel des Römerbriefs' in Neutest. Abhandlung 14.4 (1929). Michel, Der Brief an die Römer (1957), 4.

/120/ Tert. attributes the destruction of Judaism to Marcion's God: 'Quid illi cum Judaico adhuc more, destructori Judaismi?', AM 5.5.1.

edition of the letter./121/ Even assuming that Marcion was acquainted with chapter 9, we must find his deletion of it revealing, not only from the standpoint of his editorial judgment but from a theological standpoint as well. Chapter 10, which appears in Marcion's apostolikon, restores the soteriological initiative interrupted at 9.1: the hope for Israel (cf. 11.26). Marcion could not have found himself in disagreement with its fundamental themes: that Christ is the end of the law 'for those who believe'; the formula of salvation in v. 9; and the germ of Ephesians 3.14 in vv. 12-13: 'There is no difference between the Jew and Greek, for the same Lord is rich unto them that call upon him; whoever calls upon the name of the Lord shall be saved'./122/ The conclusion is inescapable that if Marcion here exercised editorial judgment over the epistle in its received form, those sections that he chose to omit are those that refer to God's exclusion of Israel from the covenant. The crucial passages for Marcion were those that stood in opposition to the prophecies and testified to the goodness of the alien God: that 'Christ is the end of the law' does not mean that only gentiles are to be saved (Rom 11.1-2, 11); for it is God's will 'that all Israel be saved' (11.26, 28b), and that even unbelievers shall obtain mercy (11.31). In the sentence from Romans which he paraphrases at the beginning of the Antitheses (Rom 11.33), the mercy of God is the true gnosis confronting Jew and gentile: 'O profundum divitiarum et sapientiae dei, et investigabiles viae eius'.

It is important in the face of the evidence to distinguish between Marcion's attitude toward the Jews and toward the judaizers./123/ The former, like Paul (Rom 11.1), were the seed of Abraham, the covenant-people of the Creator. The message and mercy of the alien God is directed in the first instance to them, since they have been exceptionally dutiful children of the lesser God. They are beckoned to faith in the mystery of divine love 'hidden for ages from God the creator of the universe' (Eph 3.9)

---

/121/ AM 5.14.6.

/122/ Vs. Harnack who believed Marcion would have eliminated 10.5-11.32 'with its many OT quotations'!

/123/ This distinction bears important implications for the discussion of Marcion's arrangement of the apostolikon. Statements such as this by Souter are common: 'The arrangement was determined by Marcion's theology, as Galatians is the most anti-Jewish of all the Epistles', Text and Canon (1954), 152. Cf. chapter 3.

and to partake in the riches of salvation (Eph 3.9; Rom 11.33). But their historical relationship with the Creator has clouded their understanding, and caused them to be naturally suspicious of the revelation of unconditional grace. This does not mean the exclusion of the Jews from the promise, but quite the reverse: that God's mercy is magnified in the attempt to save the children of wrath (Eph 2.3f.; 11; cf. Rom 3.22b-23).

The judaizers, on the other hand, /124/ are those who reject the gospel and fall back on the security of the law (Haer. 3.12.6ff.). The 'judaizing' error, which Marcion derived from Gal 1.6ff., is not so much treason against the gospel of Christ, as a failure to communicate to those still under the law the radical newness of the revelation in Jesus Christ.

### 7.7 Conclusion

At no point does Marcion's opposition to the 'judaizing' of Paul's gospel become opposition to the Jews: the latter attitude is not, as has sometimes been assumed on the basis of a too superficial reading of the sources, the determining factor in Marcion's theology and exegesis./125/ Moreover, even Marcion's opponents recognized the Jewish trajectory in his religious thought. Because he rejected the allegorical interpretation of the OT and explained its predictions as referring to the messiah of the Jews, still to come, Marcions was accused by Tertullian of 'forming an alliance with the Jewish error'./126/ 'From the Jew the heretic has accepted guidance in this discussion [regarding the Messiah], the blind borrowing from the blind, and has fallen into the same ditch'./127/ Marcion's 'Jewish' error consisted chiefly in his depriving Christianity of its apologetic proof, namely the proof

---

/124/ One is obliged to note the inadequacy of this term, stemming from the liberal NT theology of another time and place: Marcion does not know the error as 'Jewish'; he knows only of false apostles who have corrupted the gospel.

/125/ E.g., Blackman, Influence, 44ff. Thus, too Enslin, Christian Beginnings, 463: Harnack, Hist. Dogma, (ET: 1900/1961) I, 282; cf. 283-85, bespeaks the psychologism of his era when he observes that Marcion 'was not able to translate himself into the consciousness of a Jew'.

/126/ AM 3.6.2f.; cf. 'Disce et hic cum partiariis erroris tui Iudaeis', 3.16.3; Marcion interpreted Isa 7.14 to mean 'a young woman', not 'a virgin'. Cf. also Tert. adv. Jud. 9.

/127/ AM 3.7.1; cf. 3.8.1; 3.16.3f.; 3.23.1f.

from antiquity. But it cannot be overlooked that his opponents detected in his theology and soteriology a more positive attitude toward the Jews than they themselves were inclined to exhibit./128/

/128/ AM 3.21.1; cf. 1 Thess 2.15f.; Acts 3.14: 'hymeis de ton hagion kai dikaion ērnēsathe . . . ton de archēgon tēs zōēs apekteinate . . .' Justin, I Apol. 38; Tryph. 44; 133; 136, passim.; Ep. Barnabas, 3.6.

# CHAPTER EIGHT

## THE RECLAMATION OF PAUL:
## THE ORTHODOX CRITIQUE OF MARCION'S PAULINISM

### 8.1 Introduction

Irenaeus argues in the adversus Haereses for the existence of four gospels, to match Marcion's 'mutilated one', and makes extensive use of the deuteropauline 'Pastoral' epistles in the attempt to show Marcion's corruption of the Apostle's works. Consequently, the idea that Marcion had reduced rather than established a canon of scripture was prevalent before the end of the second century, as also was the connection between Marcion and Paul. We cannot be certain when the association of Paul and Luke became fixed: Irenaeus is the first to take it for granted,/1/ but as he bases his opinion on the connection between Luke and Paul in the Pastoral Epistles (cf. 2 Tim 4.11; Haer. 3.14.1) themselves anti-marcionite and perhaps written around the same time as the anti-marcionite sections of canonical Luke (see above, pp. 107ff.), we may venture the guess that the tradition grew up specifically in response to marcionite claims on behalf of their gospel.

Irenaeus attempts to show that Marcion, in subtracting Luke from the four-fold gospel, had violated a natural principle: 'Neque autem plura numero quam haec sunt neque rursus pauciora capit esse Evangelia'./2/ In violating this principle, Marcion had 'cut himself off from the blessings of the gospel'/3/ and the consensus of apostolic teaching which, in virtue of their number, they establish, namely,

> Unum deum fabricatorem huius universitatis, eum qui et per prophetas sit adnuntiatus et qui per Moysen legis dispositionem fecerit, Patrem domini nostri Jesu Christi adnuntiantia, et praeter hunc alterum deum nescientia neque alterum Patrem./4/

---

/1/ Haer. 3.14.1.

/2/ Haer. 3.11.8.

/3/ Haer. 3.11.9.

/4/ Haer. 3.11.7.

Tertullian's reason for rejecting Marcion's gospel is more technical, hinging on the idea that the regula fidei was passed on to Paul at the hands of the apostles, after his having agreed to the essentials of the faith (capita fidei). Hence it is possible to say that the apostles, with John and Matthew, 'introduce' (insinuare) the regula, while Luke and Mark 'give it renewal' (instaurare). What authority Luke possesses, he possesses by virtue of the compact made between Paul, his master, and Paul's predecessors, the apostles. Having put the authority of Marcion's gospel in perspective vis à vis the authority of Paul,/5/ Tertullian repeats Irenaeus' contention that Paul and thus Luke had acceded to the regula established by the apostles: '. . . quantum ad unicum deum attinet creatorem et Christum eius, natum ex virgine, supplementum legis et prophetarum'./6/ Tertullian's introduction to the question of Marcion's use of scripture is sharper than Irenaeus'; Irenaeus emphasizes the positive aspect of Luke's attachment to Paul, and also 'the things [of the gospel] which we learn from Luke alone'./7/ Marcion's error is to 'reject [by omission] that gospel of which he claims to be a disciple'. Tertullian emphasizes the negative side of the relationship: Luke's gospel cannot stand alone because it comes from an apostle subordinate to the discipuli domini. It must be collated with the 'records of the apostles' delivered to the church (AM 4.2.2f.; cf. Haer. 3.11.7; 3.14.1; 3.12.13). Hence, Marcion's error is to believe 'that the Christian religion with its sacred content begins with Luke's discipleship [of Paul]'./8/ The polemic of both Irenaeus and Tertullian reveals not only a strategy designed to overcome Marcion's exaggerated claims for Paul's authority,/9/ but also the extent to which Marcionism was identified with the teaching of Paul: 'Qui dicunt solum Paulum veritatem cognovisse'./10/

Moreover, the goal of the polemic is not merely to refute Marcion's interpretation of the Apostle's teaching, but to reclaim that teaching for

---

/5/ AM 4.2.4: 'tanto posterior quanto posterioris apostoli sectator'; cf. Haer. 3.14.1.

/6/ AM 4.2.2.

/7/ Haer. 3.14.3.

/8/ AM 4.3.1.

/9/ Cf. Haer. 3.13.1f.; AM 4.3.1ff.; 5.2.7.

/10/ Iren. Haer. 3.13.1; cf. Tert. AM 5.1.1ff.

orthodoxy. It would be too much to say that Paul's reputation is built on the confrontation between Marcion and his opponents, since it is certain that the letters of the Apostle were read in christian communities that had come under paulinist influence <u>before</u> Marcion affected to make Paul's teaching the exclusive basis and norm for christian belief./11/ But that Paul's canonical status was secured by the need to defend his letters against marcionite and other heretical claimants seems more than likely./12/ Otherwise, we have no adequate way of explaining how his 'Christ-intimate theology'/13/ should have commended itself to a church struggling toward organizational and doctrinal identity,/14/ and which found many of Paul's ideas difficult to understand and to accept./15/ Against the 'domesticating' tendency which occurs in the attempt to bring Paul's theology into line with the teaching of the church stands Marcion's radical view that the church's teaching must conform to the gospel of Paul, to the exclusion of all other sources and norms.

---

/11/ See the discussion in D. Rensberger, <u>As the Apostle Teaches: the Development of the use of Paul's Letters in Second Century Christianity</u> (1980) and J. Clabeaux, <u>The Pauline Corpus which Marcion Used: the Text of the Letters of Paul in the Early Second Century</u>, Ph.D. (in progress) Harvard.

/12/ For a dissenting view, see Andreas Lindemann, <u>Paulus im Altesten Christentum: Das Bild des Apostels und die Rezeption der Paulinischen Theologie in der Frühchristlichen Literatur bis Marcion</u> (1979); Lindemann concludes that Paul was honored by the 'orthodox' but was viewed primarily as the apostle to the gentiles and foe of heresy, and that he was opposed and rejected by Jewish Christianity. The use of Paul by the gnostics and Marcion did not (so Lindemann) prompt the church to eschew the apostle; instead, the absence of pauline influence from much early christian literature is to be explained by factors of geography and <u>Gattungsgeschichte</u>. The weakness of Lindemann's argument is that it seriously underestimates the orthodox ambivalence toward Paul, and exaggerates the (conventional) significance of his 'rejection' by Jewish Christianity in terms of its effects on orthodox writers of a later period.

/13/ Deissmann, <u>Paul: A Study in Social and Religious History</u> (ET, 1926), 299.

/14/ Cf. H. v. Campenhausen, 'Polycarp von Smyrna und die Pastoral-briefe', in <u>Aus der Frühzeit des Christentums</u> (1963), 205; and <u>idem.</u>, <u>Kirchliches Amt und geistliche Vollmacht</u> (1953), 116f.

/15/ Lindemann (<u>ibid.</u>), acknowledges this difficulty perfunctorily, but draws no conclusions from it. The Tübingen professors long ago called attention to Paul as the 'target' of Rev 2.9 and 3.9 (cf. 2.2; 2.20; 2 Ptr 3.16); and cf. Bauer: 'It was precisely orthodoxy that rejected Paul' (<u>Orthodoxy and Heresy</u>, 233; cf. 214f.).

Although active opposition to Paul's teaching cannot be substantiated as the reason for the failure of the johannine literature to mention the Apostle, the existence of an exaggerated or 'heretical' paulinism in the churches of Asia Minor may underlie the polemic of Rev 2.14, 20, 24ff.; 3.14, and point to a waning of the Apostle's influence, mitigated only by the literary endeavors of a 'pauline school' conceivably in Ephesus itself./16/ The decline in Paul's reputation is indicated by the sentiment expressed in James 2.24 ('A man is justified by works and not by faith in itself') aimed, as it would seem, at Rom 3.28 (cf. Gal 2.16f.). A similarly unpauline view prevails in James 2.18ff. where faith becomes accession to certain 'proofs' and must be accompanied by works (*hē pistis chōris tōn ergōn argē estin*). The author has evidently abandoned Paul's teaching in favor of what Marxsen styles 'a reduced understanding of faith' as belief in doctrine: 'What he attacks is the idea that the pauline formula should be accepted as valid'./17/ The concept of christian liberty (1 Cor 6.12; 1 Cor 10.29; 2 Cor 3.17; Gal 5.13) is replaced by the 'law of freedom' (James 2.12). This tendency is carried even further in 1 Clement and Polycarp's letter to the Philippians where the message of the Apostle is transformed into a simple church piety. As Käsemann comments,/18/ even the early disciples of Paul moderated the severity of his theology in favor of edification, as in Lk and the Pastorals, or they subsumed it under a new theme, as in Eph. The reference to Paul's epistles in 2 Ptr 3.16 (*en hais estin dysnoēta tina*) suggests just how unintelligible his teachings had become by the mid-second century;/19/ while the reference to the 'twisting' of Paul's words by 'the unlearned and unsteady' (*hoi amatheis kai astēriktoi streblousin*) parallels

---

/16/ E. Käsemann, 'Paulus and Frühkatholizismus', ZTK 60 (1963), 75-89; G. Bornkamm, 'Ephesus' in Paul, ET (1971), 86. Assuming a period of some years between the writing of Ignatius' Letter to the Ephesians and the johannine literature, this silence may point to the success of the heretics mentioned in Eph. 9.1. But cf. O. Cullmann, The Johannine Circle (1971), 98f.; C. Maurer, Ignatius von Antiochien und das Johannesevangelium (1949), 110; and esp. H. Köster, 'Geschichte und Kultur im Johannesevangelium und bei Ign.', ZTK 54 (1957), 56ff.; J. Weiss, Early Christianity, II, 783, on the relation of this 'school' to the marcionite community in Asia Minor, and especially to Laodicea/Ephesus.

/17/ Marxsen, Introd. NT (1974), 230.

/18/ Käsemann, 'Paulus und Frühkatholizismus', 76.

/19/ E. Fascher, RGG$^3$ 5 (1961), 259f.

Irenaeus' judgment of Marcion: 'vani omnes et indocti et insuper audaces qui frustrantur speciem Evangelii . . .'/20/

It is clear in any case that within the NT itself we have evidence of the waning of Paul's influence (the johannine literature, esp. Rev 2.14f.; 3.4f.; James 2.14ff.; 2 Ptr 3.16), as well as material that can be construed as polemic against his teaching, and attempts to rehabilitate, revise, or to subsume his teaching under a new rubric (Acts 9.26ff.; Lk 24.27ff.; Ephesians; Colossians; the Epistles to Timothy and Titus, etc.).

It has not been sufficiently recognized that the marcionite 'error' in calling the church back to Paul belongs to the life-situation and perhaps at the very center of the struggle to come to terms with Paul's theology. In 2 Ptr 3.16 this struggle is presupposed. Paul remains Peter's 'beloved brother', to be sure, but his doctrine is implicitly subordinated to the clarification offered by the 'primary' Apostle. And in the literature of the johannine circle, an attempt is made to resolve the problem described in 2 Peter at Paul's expense. It is conceivable that Marcion's radical paulinism develops in response to the supplanting of Paul's theology in the churches of Asia Minor by a 'johannine' or Ephesian orthodoxy (Rev 2.2ff.), that is, to provide an explanation of Paul designed to overcome the Ephesian aversion to his theology. We shall return to consider this suggestion presently.

With the exception of the anti-marcionite polemic of the Pastoral Epistles and the considerably revised (marcionite) themes in the Epistle to the Ephesians, the NT testifies more to the struggle against Marcion's interpretation of Paul than to the nature of the teaching that provoked it. But it is worth emphasizing that the struggle itself belongs to a different life-situation than even Marcion's earliest critics assumed to be the case or were prepared to concede. This recognition is of vital importance if we are to avoid reading Marcion's heresy in the wrong light -- as Schlatter did when he concluded, without any mention of Marcion's role in the process, that 'the teaching of Paul was preserved as the title deeds of the church, [the epistles being] collected by the churches he founded and added to the Gospel'./21/ Such confidence evaporates with the rejection of Irenaeus' assertion that Marcion's activity was securely removed from the apostolic

---

/20/ Haer. 3.11.9.

/21/ Schlatter, The Church in the NT Period (1926/ET 1955), 315f.

age ('Non enim communicat mendacium veritati'),/22/ and the 'reckoning of
dates' proposed by Tertullian/23/ in order to prejudge as corrupt that which
comes later than the apostolic faith. Only an unwarranted confidence in the
praeiudicatio counts against the conclusion that 'the beginning of Marcionism
was so early that the church writers of the end of the second century, who
are our best authorities, do not seem themselves able to tell with certainty
the story of its commencement'./24/

A healthy skepticism toward the patristic evidence about Marcion's
heresy, such as that exhibited in the last century by Professor Westcott,/25/
but inconsistently carried through in Harnack's otherwise masterly mono-
graphs, is also necessary if we are to grasp the fact of Marcion's significance along with the consequences: 'That no christian teacher holds so
significant a place in the history of the ecclesiastical canon as Marcion'/26/
is an inexplicable assumption unless Marcion belongs to a period of doctrinal
ferment during which not only the status but also the substance of Paul's
teaching was hotly disputed. In the parts of the NT 'missing' from Marcion's
canon, the extent of this dispute is clearly visible. According to the Lucan
'settlement' even the earliest converts, Paul among them (9.26f.), 'hold fast
to the doctrine of the Apostles' (Acts 2.42). It is this form of didaskalia
that the 'Paul' of the Pastoral Epistles (2 Tim 4.3; Titus 1.9; 2 Tim 2.13; 1
Tim 1.3) invokes against 'all those in Asia who are turned away from me' (2
Tim 1.15). But it is anachronistic to conclude, with Marcion's opponents,
that Acts and the Pastorals were eliminated by Marcion from his canon
because they presented a picture of the apostolic age which contradicted his
own belief that the apostles had perverted the gospel of Paul (Haer.
3.12.12; 3.5.1). Beneath Marcion's doctrine of false apostleship is the
historical struggle over the right to Paul's authority, and the proper
interpretation of his letters. If this is the same situation reflected in 2 Tim
1.15, and more emphatically in Rev 2-3, from the orthodox perspective,
then we can say with some confidence that Marcion belongs to the very age

/22/ Haer. 3.5.1.

/23/ Am 4.4.1f.

/24/ G. Salmon, DCB, 818f.

/25/ Westcott, General Survey of the History of the NT (1896), 318-24.

/26/ Zahn, Gesch. Nt.lichen Kanons (1888) I, 603ff; II, 409ff.

from which his opponents labored to remove him and that his heresy was one side of an ecclesiastical triangle which had Paul's letters at its base and the domesticating efforts of the orthodox, such as the author/redactor of Luke-Acts, the Pastorals, and the 'church' (johannine?) editor of Ephesians/Laodiceans opposite.

With reference to the precanonical phase of the (anti-marcionite) deuteropauline literature (c. 150) we can depict the struggle in this schematic way:

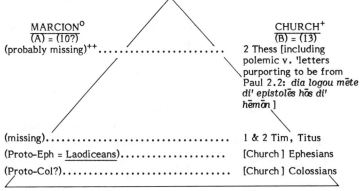

MARCION[o]
(A) = (10?)
(probably missing)[++] . . . . . . . . . . . . . . . . . . . . . . . . . . .

CHURCH[+]
(B) = (13)
2 Thess [including polemic v. 'letters purporting to be from Paul 2.2: *dia logou mēte di' epistolēs hōs di' hēmōn* ]

(missing) . . . . . . . . . . . . . . . . . . . . . . . . . . . . . .     1 & 2 Tim, Titus
(Proto-Eph = Laodiceans) . . . . . . . . . . . . . . . . . . .     [Church] Ephesians
(Proto-Col?) . . . . . . . . . . . . . . . . . . . . . . . . . . . . .     [Church] Colossians

(X) = (7?) Letters of Paul: [1 Thess; Gal; 1 & 2 Cor; Phil;
Philemon; Romans & Rom 16(?)]

[o]  Apud. Latin Marcionite Prologues (cf. de Bruyne, Rev. Bénéd. 24 [1907], 1-16; Corssen, Zeitschrift für NTliche Wiss., 10 [1909], 37-9).

[+]  Apud. Mur. Can.

[++]  Marcion did not differentiate the Thess correspondence, and it cannot be concluded on the basis of AM 5.16 that 2 Thess figured in the mariconite canon.

This diagram is not set forth as a 'solution' to the tangled history of the pauline canon. It is rather a model of the trajectories discernible in the early controversy between Marcion and the orthodox on the basis of their common claim to represent Paul's teaching accurately. At the base (X) a prëexisting corpus of (perhaps) seven pauline letters, of which Marcion was at least arguably the first collector and editor; on the one side (A) a radicalization of Paul's soteriological, dualistic, and Christ-mystical themes which, we may reasonably conclude, is simultaneous with the process of collecting;/27/ and (B) a counter-attempt to domesticate, explain, and supplement these themes and bring them into the service of the great church.

## 8.2  The Epistle to the Laodiceans

As the most important city in the Lycus valley,/28/ and the most prosperous trading center of the Cybyratic dioikēsis, Laodicea was well-positioned to attain to the rank of a christian see.  Its early status is attested by the fact that two 'apostles' in succession, one depicted as writing from captivity (Col 4.10), the other (Rev 1.9) in exile at Patmos, address the church in Laodicea on the reckoning that from this center their words will reach a wide audience.  In every respect, Laodicea was a more significant city than Colossae, lying some twelve miles to the east.  Writes Lightfoot, 'The political supremacy of Laodicea and the growing popularity of Hierapolis gradually drain the strength of Colossae'./29/  Strabo, Marcion's countryman, writing about two generations before Paul,/30/ describes it as a 'small town' (polisma) in the district where Laodicea is capital: 'While Laodicea and Hierapolis both hold important places in the early records of the church, Colossae disappears wholly from the pages of history.  Its comparative insignificance is still attested by its ruins, which are few and meagre . . . .  Without doubt Colossae was the least important

---

/27/ That Marcion knew 2 Thess is doubtful in the extreme.  Harnack assumed that Marcion omitted only 1.8 ('en pyri phlogos . . .) and altered 2.11.  In fact however, it is difficult to imagine how Marcion might have countenanced 2.9, in view of his soteriology or 2.15 (cf. 3.6b); 2.2 presupposes the existence of letters purporting to come from Paul.  Nor can we fail to relate this theme to the reference to the 'fantasies about the anti-Christ' (Kümmel, Intro. to the NT, 264) which are also foreign to the theology of the authentic pauline letters, and can scarcely have commended themselves to Marcion (cf. 2 Jn 7).  In any event, it will scarcely do to argue an early date for the epistle on the grounds that it is attested in the marcionite canon and cited by Polycarp (Phil. 11.4), since the spurious themes may as easily have their Sitz im Leben in the battle against Marcion.

/28/ The position of Laodicea among the churches of Asia Minor has been exhaustively documented by Lightfoot, Colossians and Philemon (1892), 1-70.  Cf. Strabo, 12.8.13, 15; Cicero, ad. Att. 5.21; Pliny, Letters, 5.29.0.

/29/ Lightfoot, Colossians and Philemon, 16.

/30/ Strabo, 12.8.13.

church to which any Epistle of St. Paul is addressed!'/31/ The injunction (Col 4.16) to the christian community at Colossae to share their letter with the church at Laodicea, as well as to read the one addressed to Laodicea, points to the prestige of the Laodicean church and the existence of a fuller expression of pauline teaching having been (previously?) delivered to that community. Following this hint further, we may expect the Colossian letter to have been a 'summary' of the one to the Laodiceans, assuming for it a life-situation corresponding closely to that of the latter epistle. We shall consider the question of authorship further on; presently we turn our attention to the life-situation of the epistles themselves.

## 8.3 The Jewish Population in Colossae/Laodicea

The Epistle to the Colossians presupposes the existence of a powerful Jewish colony in Laodicea and the surrounding townships. This reckoning is based not only on the epistle itself, but also on independent testimony. According to Josephus,/32/ Antiochus the Great and Antiochus II transplanted 2,000 Jewish families from Babylonia and Mesopotamia into Lydia and Phrygia, and it is likely that the majority of these families settled in the thriving cities founded by the Syrian kings. The mint-surname of the city's tutelary deity (Zeus) Laodicensus-Aesis points to the tie between the religious practice of the city and that of the east, particularly Syria,/33/ in the three generations before the time of Paul.

The evidence for a substantial Jewish presence in Laodicea is unambiguous: When Flaccus, propraetor of Asia (BCE 62), forbade Jews to contribute to the Temple and confiscated money due to be exported to Palestine, he seized twenty pounds weight in gold. Calculated at the rate of a half-shekel for each man (Shekel = 110 gms.: Rom. lb. @ 5050 gms.) this sum represents a population of more than 11,000 adult freemen/34/ in a single district of which Laodicea was capital. Somewhat later, we have a

---

/31/ Lightfoot, Colossians and Philemon, 16.

/32/ Josephus, Antiq. 12.3, 4f.

/33/ Evidence in Lightfoot, Colossians and Philemon, 8f.; 20, n. 1; Strabo, 12.8.13, 15.

/34/ Lightfoot, Colossians and Philemon, 20, n. 4; Cicero, pro Flacc. 28; Josephus, Antiq. 14.7.2.

document said by Josephus/35/ to be a decree of the Laodiceans in which they thank the Roman consul for a measure granting Jews the liberty of observing their sabbaths and practicing the rites of their religion. Added to this may be the passage in the Talmud/36/ in which Elijah, appearing to Ishmael ben R. Jose, says 'Thy father fled to [Sardis]; flee thee to Laodicea'; and an inscription, found in the Jewish cemetery of Porta Portuensis in Rome, which carries the legend, *'entha keitai Amonia Ioudaia apo Laodikeias'*. According to the Talmud, when King Sapor massacred 12,000 Jews who had taken part in an insurrection in Caesarea (Cappadocia), 'the wall of Laodicea was cloven with the sound of the harp-string'./37/ One can suppose that Laodicea was singled out for mention because of its significance among Jewish settlements of the diaspora./38/

While the influence of Judaism in Laodicea is well-attested, the origin of the christian church in that city is obscure: There is no evidence that Paul visited the region; nor, unless we take as pauline the references in Col 2.1 and 4.13f., that he knew of the existence of a christian community there. Luke mentions (Acts 16.6) that Paul 'passed through the Phrygian and Galatian country', but the term Phrygia cannot be explained in this context as referring to or including Laodicea. The Paul of Colossians, moreover, represents himself as 'having heard' of their faith in Christ and recalls the day when he first learned of their christian profession and zeal (Col 1.4, 9: *dia touto kai hēmeis, aph' hēs hēmeras ēkousamen, ou pauometha . . .'*); thus a pauline foundation for the churches of the Lycus is excluded whether one accepts the authenticity of Colossians and Ephesians or not: 'I would have you know', writes the author, 'how great a conflict [agōna]/39/ I have for you and them that are in Laodicea and as many as have not seen my face in the flesh' (2.1). It is said in Col 1.7 that the

---

/35/ Josephus, Antiq. 14.10.21.

/36/ Talm. Babl. Mœd. Katon 26a, in Neubauer, La geographie du Talmud, 319; cf. Talm. Babl. Baba Metziah 84a (Neubauer, 311).

/37/ Talmud, loc. cit.

/38/ Lightfoot calls attention to Laodicea's reputation in the manufacture of dyed wool, observing that this trade 'had a particular attraction for the Jews'; cf. Acts 16.14; Rev 3.17; also Talm. Babl. 'Sabbath', 147b; Neubauer, 317.

/39/ A reference to the controversy captioned in Col 2.4.

church had been established in the gospel by the labors of Epaphras./40/ But it should not be assumed that he was Paul's 'delegate': the expression 'fellowservant' serves only to separate him from the corrupters of the gospel against whom Paul himself rails in Galatians. The Colossian church seems to look back to Epaphras rather than to Paul as its founder, while the author of the epistle written in Paul's name makes Epaphras the Apostle's co-worker and a member of the congregation (Col 4.12).

Laodicea and Colossae come onto the scene in the NT not as churches which have remained true to the Apostle's teaching but as heretical churches in need of 'apostolic' correction. Two decades prior to Ignatius, the apocalyptic Seer finds the Laodicean community 'wretched, miserable, . . . and blind' (Rev 3.17b); and in the apocryphal Acts of John,/41/ Paul's reputation in Laodicea has been supplanted (c. 55-58; cf. Rev 1.11)/42/ by the memory of John's (later?) success there. Significantly, it is johannine rather than pauline 'orthodoxy' which is put forward as the doctrinal desideratum for the Laodiceans.

The 'Paul' of 2 Tim 1.15 complains that 'all Asia is turned away from me'. This lament, assigned to Paul by the author of the Pastorals, cannot be squared with the complaint of Demetrius, the silversmith of Acts 19.26: that Paul with his propaganda has 'perverted crowds of people, not only at Ephesus but also in almost the whole of Asia'. The explanation of this disparity must be sought in the definition, or rather the struggle over the definition, of 'orthodox' paulinism at the turn of the century./43/ Ignatius himself, who largely supplies that definition, addressed only the churches in Ephesus, Smyrna, and Philadelphia among those in Asia Minor, omitting those of Pergamon, Thyatira, Sardis (cf. Rev 2.13f.; 2.20f.; 3.4f.), and

---

/40/ Who is also credited with the care of the churches in nearby Laodicea and Hierapolis. Epaphras is thus the doctrinal 'link' between the churches of the Lycus Valley.

/41/ Fourth c. Cf. Eus. HE 3.25.6; Hennecke, NTA II, 190ff.; Epiph. Panar. 47.1.5.

/42/ Cf. Zahn, Forschungen zur Gesch. des Nt.lichen Kanons, 6 (1900), 197f.

/43/ Cf. Bauer, Orthodoxy and Heresy, 78ff.

(notably) Laodicea./44/ In contrast to the church at Ephesus,/45/ 'which has tried those who have claimed to be apostles and rejected them as liars' (Rev 2.2b), these heretical churches are denounced by the Seer directly (and by Ignatius implicitly) as 'synagogues of Satan' populated by those 'who say they are Jews and are not' (Rev 3.9, 2.13). The connection between these 'synagogues' and the marcionite communities is suggested circumstantially, (a) by the extant inscription discovered in the village of Lebaba near Damascus,/46/ identifying the ruins of a marcionite synagogue;

(b) by the parallels between the heretical churches as 'seats' of Satan (thronos tou Satana: Rev 2.13; 3.9), and the attested activity of Marcion in Asia Minor. Toward the end of the second century, the christian poet Bardesanes composed dialogues against Marcion in Syriac. It is evident from Eusebius' account (HE 4.30.1) that Bardesanes considered Marcionism the greatest heretical danger in Syria at the time. Further, the Chronicle of Edessa establishes the early flourishing of marcionite communities in the region (c. 138). Theophilus of Antioch and Justin, in their lost treatises against Marcion, also testify to the prominence of Marcion's teaching in Syria; both of these were composed toward the middle of the second

---

/44/ Concerning Laodicea, which the Marcionites regarded as having persevered in the faith of the Apostle (Marc. Prol. Laod.; cf. de Bruyne, Rev. Bénéd. 24 [1907], 1-16; Corssen, ZNTW 10 [1909], 37-9; Harnack, Theol. Literaturzeitung, 32 [1902], 138ff.; Burkitt, Gospel History [1907]) we have the dissident view of the author of the christian Sibylline (c. 200) (7.22): 'Woe to Laodicea thou that hast never seen! Audacious thou liest; but the wave of Lycus surges over thee' (Hennecke/Schneemelcher, NTA II, 721) and the rebuke of the Laodicean church in Rev 3.15: 'Because you are tepid . . . I will spit you out of my mouth'. Moreover, it is doubtful that Ignatius was acquainted with many of Paul's letters (cf. H. Rathke, Ignatius von Antioch. und die Paulusbriefe [TU 99: 1967], 27-40; and W.R. Schädel, in Jewish and Christian Self-Definition, 51, 224, n. 65), and his sympathy with the substance of Paul's teaching is at least questionable on the basis of Eph. 8.2: 'Ha de kai kata sarka prassete, tauta pneumatika estin'. That Ephesus, unlike Laodicea, was considered a bastion of episcopal orthodoxy after CE 70, cf. B. H. Streeter, The Primitive Church, 55 (Ign., Eph. 9.1).

/45/ Marcion is said by Philastrius to have visited Ephesus (Haer. 45; cf. Harnack, Marcion, 13*; Salmon, DCB, 818f.) and to have been rejected there by Papias and the elders; cf. Harnack, Marcion, 15*

/46/ Le Bass-Waddington, Inscriptions grecques et latines, III, 582-3; Inscription 2558. The inscription dates c. 318. 'It is noteworthy that the Marcionites anti-Jewish as they were, should have called this place of worship a synagogue' (!) (Salmon, DCB, 819b). Especially significant is the ascription to Paul; cf. Harnack, Marcion, 341*f.

century. Philastrius, writing in Brescia (c. 385) looks back to Marcion's activity in Ephesus, as does the author of the anti-marcionite Prologue to the Fourth Gospel, which may itself reflect a tradition dating back to the second century./47/ Tertullian's claim, 'Faciunt favos et vespae, faciunt ecclesias et Marcionitae', is borne out by the proliferation of anti-marcionite polemic in Asia Minor: The heresiological work of Adamantius, Epiphanius, Theodoret, and Eznik witness to the success of Marcion's teaching in the eastern Empire, and Celsus expounds on Marcion in his Alēthēs Logos./48/

(c) The geographical matrix of Marcionism is more comprehensible if we imagine a mission centering, in the first place, on Pontus-Bithynia in the north, reaching outward through Galatia (where Marcion may first have encountered Paul's theology in the missive that became the centerpiece of his collection of the Apostle's letters) and thence to Ephesus, where he may for a time have associated himself with the johannine circle. It is the memory of this association which seems to be enshrined in the anti-marcionite Prologue to John and at least implicitly in the Latin prologue preserved in the Codex Toletanus./49/ We cannot be certain where Marcion went after his cool reception in Ephesus but a reasonable conclusion would be Smyrna to the north (the meeting with Polycarp?) or to Philippi (a warning to the congregation in advance of his coming?). If a marcionite error is envisaged in Ignatius' epistles, then it is equally plausible that Marcion was active in the interior of the peninsula, in and around the Lycus Valley (Thyatira, Colossae, Laodicea, and Sardis). As Ignatius writes to

/47/ In A. Harnack, 'Die Ältesten Evang.-Prologe und die Bildung des NTs.', SAB Phil.-histor. 24 (1928), 322-41; cf. B. Bacon, 'The Anti-Marcionite Prol. to John', JBL 49 (1930), 43-54; and JTS 23 (1922), 134. Challenged by E. Gutwenger, 'The Anti-Marcionite Prologues', TS 7 (1946), 393-409; R. Grant, 'The Oldest Gospel Prologues', Angl. Th. Rev. 23 (1941), 231f.

/48/ Contra Cels. 5.62; 5.54; 6.52ff.

/49/ De Bruyne, 'Les plus anciens Prologues Latins de Evangiles', Rev. Bénéd. 40, 208; but de Bruyne could not accept that Marcion had been repudiated by John; the same Prologue speaks of Papias as 'one of John's cherished disciples'. De Bruyne believed that the prologue was known to Irenaeus, but was unable to draw any conclusion from this. Cf. Stroebel, ZNTW 49 (1958), 132, n. 5. It should be stressed that the evidence for the johannine authorship of the Fourth Gospel and the Apostle's residence at Ephesus is to a great extent identical with the question of Marcion's attendance on John.

none of these churches, the possibility that he had no friendly congregation to address in the region cannot be ruled out./50/ Based on evidence still to be discussed, we can provisionally conclude that the center of Marcion's influence, and the nexus of marcionite activity, was Laodicea. In all probability, he ended his days as a teacher in the christian community there.

## 8.4 The Sources

According to the anti-marcionite Prologue to the Fourth Gospel:/51/

> The gospel of John was made known and given to the churches by John while he yet remained in the body, as one Papias by name, of Hierapolis, a beloved disciple of John, has related in his Exoterics, that is in his last five Books; but he wrote down the gospel at the dictation of John correctly. But Marcion, the heretic, when he had been censured by him because he held heretical opinions was cast off by John. [Marcion] had brought writings or letters to him from the brethren in Pontus./52/

We have in this Prologue evidence of a tradition that links Marcion with the churches of Phrygia and the Lycus generally, and with the johannine circle in particular.

Much later Jerome records that John wrote his gospel 'when he was in Asia at the time of the seeds of heretics, Cerinthus, Ebion and others who deny that Christ came in the flesh, whom he himself also calls antichrists in his Epistle and at whom the apostle Paul frequently lashes out'./53/ Although Marcion is not mentioned by Jerome, the tradition linking the writing of the gospel to the spread of heresies survives. Jerome may have been persuaded, on the weight of Irenaeus' testimony, to place Marcion later. On the other hand, Clement of Alexandria, who also associates John with Ephesus, points to a heretical tradition according to which Marcion was a contemporary of the apostles./54/ Tertullian's testimony is not very

---

/50/ Thus Bauer, Orthodoxy and Heresy, 79-80.

/51/ Vatican, Cod. Reg. 14, 9th century.

/52/ D.J. Theron, Evidence of Tradition (1957), 32f.; Lightfoot, 'Papias of Hierapolis', in Essays on the Work Entitled 'Supernatural Religion' (1880), 210.

/53/ Jerome, com. Matt., in Theron, Evidence of Tradition, 52f.

helpful: in the fourth book of the AM he distinguishes the churches founded by Paul from those which are <u>alumnae</u> of John, and goes on to distinguish a third variety: those founded by Marcion: 'Habet plane et illud ecclesias, sed suas, tam posteras quam adulteras . . .' (AM 4.5.3f.).

This evidence in itself is rather more tantalizing than conclusive; but to it we must add the evidence <u>about</u> Papias himself. Eusebius disputes Irenaeus' statement that Papias was 'the hearer of John and a companion of Polycarp',/55/ citing the preface to his five books as proof that he had not received the articles of faith from the apostles but from those who had known them./56/ Eusebius also observes that it was from the Lord's disciple, the presbyter John, rather than the beloved disciple (to whom the gospel was ultimately credited) that Papias learned 'the articles of faith'; and Eusebius finds it probable that the Revelation was composed by this 'second' John -- i.e., the presbyter./57/ The tradition concerning Marcion depends on our associating him with the John whom both Polycarp and Papias knew personally at Ephesus. But it is possible, as Eusebius suggests, that Irenaeus confuses John the son of Zebedee and John the presbyter./58/

---

/55/ <u>Haer</u>. 5.33.4.

/56/ Eus. HE 3.39.2ff.

/57/ Cf. Raymond Brown, <u>Gospel of John</u> (1966), xci. In Rev 18.20 and 21.14 the author writing from Patmos (1.9) refers to the Twelve as if he were not one of their number. Ignatius does not seem to know of the Apostle John's tenure at Ephesus; cf. Justin, <u>Tryph</u>. 81; <u>Acts of John</u>, 18 (NTA II, 215f.); and Polycrates, according to Eus. HE 5.24.3f.

/58/ Irenaeus identifies John the presbyter with John the 'disciple' who 'leaned upon the breast of the Lord', and the author of the gospel (<u>Haer</u>. 3.1.1); thus he establishes a line of succession between John, Paul, and Polycarp, only the latest of whom knew Marcion (2.22.5; cf. 3.3.4; 3.11.1f.). Irenaeus hardly ever calls this John an Apostle. Irenaeus also ascribes the Revelation to John 'the disciple of the Lord' (4.20.11) and we find the same phrase introducing a passage from 2 John 11 (<u>Haer</u>. 1.16.3). The crucial reference to Marcion in 3.3.4 occurs as a non-sequitur attached to a story about John rebuking Cerinthus at Ephesus: Irenaeus, in other words, appears to know of another tradition, one which links Marcion to Ephesus and conceivably to the johannine circle there; but he has reduced the details of the account to the retort, itself gleaned from elsewhere, and eliminated the vital geographical information: 'Et ipse autem Polycarpus Marcioni aliquando occurrenti sibi . . .' (<u>Haer</u>. 3.3.4). Tert. may preserve a memory of this tradition when he refers on the basis of 1 John 2.18, 22 (cf. 4.2) to 'premature and abortive Marcionites whom the Apostle John pronounced antichrists', though in context Tert. regards these heretics as Marcion's predecessors. (3.8.1).

By the fourth century a far from secure ecclesiastical canon/59/ recognized the 'second' John as successor of the first:/60/ 'John, bishop of Ephesus appointed by John [the Apostle]'. Here it is sufficient to say that the tradition linking Papias and Marcion to John, the author of the Fourth Gospel, is slightly more secure than the identity of John himself. But it should be noted that the repudiation of Marcion by 'John' at Ephesus, supposedly because of the texture of his interpretation of Paul, is far from unlikely given the existence there of a 'circle' devoted to perpetuating, explaining, and 'domesticating' the theology of the Apostle. This may mean that the altercation between 'John' and Marcion or between Marcion and the other 'editors' of Paul's letters was over how best to preserve or propagate the Apostle's teaching. That Marcion settled on a revised version of an older gospel and a collection of epistles, while other members of the community/61/ chose to produce a totally new gospel, would on this theory point out his literary conservatism. On the theological side however, it is little wonder that his 'solution' was regarded as unacceptable/62/ and that his insistence on reading Paul as a ditheist resulted in his exclusion from the community, one can only assume with a collection of Paul's letters in his possession.

It is not improbable that Marcion continued to preach his version of Paul's gospel in the cities and towns in the interior of the peninsula. Our guide in this must be the marcionite Prologues to the Epistles of Paul, presupposing as they do some criteria for fidelity to the Apostle's teaching.

---

/59/ Apostol. Const. 7.46; Funk ed., 453-55; further: J.E. Bruns, 'The confusion between John and John Mark in Antiquity', Scripture 17 (1965), 23-26; K.A. Eckhardt, Der Tod des Johannes (1961); F.V. Filson, 'Who was the Beloved Disciple?'. JBL 68 (1949), 83-88.

/60/ See the discussion in Brown, The Gospel of John, Anchor Bible Commentary (1966), 29 LXXXIXff.

/61/ Cf. Brown, The Community of the Beloved Disciple, (1979), 103ff.; cf. JBL 97 (1978), 5-22; Culpepper, The Johannine School (1978). Writes Cullmann (The Johannine Circle, 54): 'The marked liturgical orientation of Revelation brings us quite close to the Gospel of John . . . . If the author belonged to the same circle -- and this cannot be ruled out -- we must at any rate assume that this circle held a variety of views, despite the features which it had in common'.

/62/ The 'millenarianism' which Papias seems to share with the author of Revelation and the johannine epistles (cf. Eus. HE 3.39.12) but entirely missing from Marcion's interpretation of Paul, may point to another reason for his expulsion. Cf. 2 Thess 2.8f.

According to these paragraphs, the christian communities of Galatia, Corinth, Rome, and Colossae 'were reached by false apostles' and tempted away from 'the faith of truth' (Prol. Gal.). Only the Laodiceans, Philippians (!), and Thessalonians are considered to be secure in the faith of the Apostle, though it is said that the Thessalonians were also reached ahead of time by judaizing apostles ('praeterea nec receperunt ea quae a falsis apostolis dicebantur . . .'). In short, the following picture emerges: The church considered 'lukewarm' and 'wretched' by the apocalyptic seer ('which has tried the ones calling themselves apostles and found them liars', Rev 2.2) is by Marcion's standard the only church that has escaped completely the assaults of false apostles. And by the same token, the church at Philippi, which Polycarp enjoins to return to the faith of Paul (Phil. 9.1) and to avoid the 'false brethren . . . who bear the name of the Lord in hypocrisy' (6.3), is considered by the Marcionites to have 'persevered in the faith [of Paul]'. In the seer's estimation, the Laodiceans are 'blind'; in the words of the Sibylline Oracle, they have 'failed to see God' and insolently deceive themselves (Sib. or. 7.22f.). But the author of Colossians testifies that the faithful Epaphras (who according to the marcionite Prologue in Philippians is the amanuensis for that letter) has labored in Laodicea, Hierapolis, and Colossae 'that they may stand perfect and complete in the will of God' (Col 4.12f.). How can congregations that stand so near to Paul by one reckoning merit the rebuke or indifference of the Ephesian (johannine) community in the west?

The answer would appear to be that the Marcionites considered Laodicea the center of paulinist orthodoxy whereas the Ephesians, regarding the Marcionites as 'those who bear the name of the Lord in hypocrisy' (Polyc. Phil. 6.3; cf. Justin, I Apol. 26), found Laodicea lost ('blind') to the faith of Paul.

The evidence for this rivalry is not only to be found in the scattered allusions to Laodicea in the Apocalypse, but also in the competition over the titulus of the epistle, which Marcion knew as being addressed to the Christians at Laodicea, but which comes down in the tradition as an epistle addressed to the more steadfast congregation at Ephesus.

We must also keep in mind the terms of this rivalry. Although it is no longer possible to accept so simple an opposition between the gospel of Paul and that of 'John' as the Tübingen School assumed, there was almost certainly opposition to the marcionite version of Paul's gospel by a circle interested in refining the thought of the Apostle. The tradition outlined here points to a dispute over Paul's teaching, represented by 'John' and the Ephesian litterateurs on the one side, and Marcion and his followers on the other, which in terms of the reaction of the former comes close to eclipsing the reputation of the Apostle in the process of reclaiming his teaching for orthodoxy./63/ Doubtless this is so because the Marcionites tied themselves to a radical interpretation of some of the most difficult and ambiguous themes in Paul's theology and thereby made it difficult for the literary community at Ephesus to reformulate the Apostle's teaching in less obscure terms (cf. 2 Ptr 3.16). This reckoning may help to explain why, for all the points of contact between pauline and johannine theology, the debt to the apostle is not acknowledged in the literature of the johannine circle. But the Marcionites for their part were equally disinclined to accept a reconstituted 'paulinism without Paul' (the Fourth Gospel), or the reactionary paulinism of the Pastoral Epistles, which originate in the same area, perhaps at Ephesus itself./64/ Unlike the author of 2 Ptr, Marcion did not find Paul impossible to read; but his interpretation was not one that commended itself to a church whose Apostle ordered the brethren to 'obey the word of the epistle' and 'the tradition which is received from us' (2 Thess 3.14a, 6). It is against this background -- the rivalry between two christian communities, devoted in different measure and advocating different approaches to Paul's teaching -- that the Epistle to Laodicea/Ephesus takes shape.

## 8.5 The Epistle to the Laodiceans: Thematic Structure

Although it cannot be shown that Laod. is a 'cover-letter' to accompany the pauline correspondence, or was designed as a master-summary of Paul's teaching, the epistle presupposes the existence of the corpus paulinum./65/ Theologically, Laod. is as much a correction and interpretation as it is a synopsis of Paul's letters. Writes Köster, 'The theological theme in this situation is identical with that of universality,

---

/63/ Lightfoot is typically judicious when he says (Colossians and Philemon, 50f.) that the Tübingen School failed to mark the coincidence between Paul's thought and that of John.

/64/ Thus E. Lohse, The Formation of the New Testament (ET: 1981), 104.

/65/ As Köster has pointed out: 'Die verkirchlichung der paulinischen Theologie', Einführung, 705.

which Paul develops in his mission to the Gentile Church, . . . as its author learned from Romans, with the question of Jew and Gentile'./66/ Here we must address the question whether this correction was modeled on the teaching of Paul as preserved intact at Laodicea (so the Marcionites), or whether on the doctrine of Ephesus, as the Pastor (1 Tim 1.3b) and Ignatius prescribe and the author of the johannine revelation implies (Rev 2.2f.). In canonical Ephesians we have a composite document (a) in part, originating in marcionite circles ('Laodiceans'), serving as a 'selective affirmation' of the Apostle's essential teaching, and incorporating corrections of the 'interpolations' which the Marcionites believed to exist in other epistles -- notably Romans and (arguably) Colossians. It is possible that Marcion was acting on the hint (Col 4.16?) that such an epistle did exist and made Colossians, or an early version of it, the point d'appui for Laodiceans. Such a reckoning may also provide a clue, albeit an ambiguous one, about the nature of Ephesians' dependence on Colossians;/67/ (b) a revised letter, 'to the Ephesians', an Ephesian (johannine?) correction of the marcionite summary of Paul's gospel provided in Laodiceans.

If the community in Laodicea (given even the present look of Col) had known of a letter purporting to be from Paul addressed 'to the faithful [!] in Christ Jesus in Ephesus [tois hagiois tois ousin en Ephesō]', it is most unlikely that such a letter would have survived or been credited among the strict paulinists there. This presupposes, of course, the dependence of modern Ephesians on Colossians; but there is reason to suspect, with Holtzmann,/68/ another stratum, at which the theology of Colossians was generally closer to the errors that the modern epistle condemns. The cross reference to Laod. may date from this ('heretical') stage in the history of the text; or it may be a marcionite interpolation indicating (Marcion's) Laod. as the corrective to a now-corrupt Colossians. The question of interdependence seems impossible to resolve with any degree of certainty. Tertullian's discussion of Col is little more than a digression on the nature of Marcion's heresy. Against the suggestion that Laod. is a 'corrective' to Col

---

/66/ Einführung, 706-07.

/67/ But cf. Klijn, Introd., 102; Kümmel, Intro. to the NT, 346ff., 358f.; Köster, Einführung, 706ff.; Thompson, Cent. Bible Com., 89f. ('Col. the earlier letter'); E. Käsemann, Das Interpretations-problem des Epheserbriefes: Exegetische Versuche und Besinnungen, II (1964), 253-61.

/68/ Holtzmann, NT Theologie, II (1911), 262ff.

is the fact that Marcion is not known to have made any major alterations in the text of Col, while he stands accused of 'removing whole pages' in Eph./69/ Accordingly, we are obliged to conclude that even if the Baur-Holtzmann hypothesis is correct/70/ -- Col being an orthodox reworking of a much shorter 'epistle of gnostic [!] provenance' -- the Urbrief cannot be shown to have originated in marcionite circles./71/

The situation is quite different in the case of Laod. We begin from the premise that the shortened version of the Epistle, which Tertullian regards as a 'mutilated' (i.e., shortened) Eph, is in reality an epistle originating in marcionite circles in Laodicea and not yet worked over by the orthodox community at Ephesus.

(a) It is difficult to ascertain from what Tertullian tells us about Laod./Eph exactly what Marcion's text of the Epistle included./72/ Only Gal and Rom are cited as having suffered comparable omissions and alterations, although this information only serves to indicate that Marcion's was a much shorter epistle than that known to Tertullian. A few hints are provided nonetheless. From the structure of Tertullian's argument we can gather that the greatest number of discrepancies between his text and Marcion's occur following chapter three and that the texts begin (markedly) to diverge at the crucial passage, Eph 3.9: where Tertullian's text read 'dispensatio sacramenti occulti ab aevis in deo qui omnia condidit' (= *oikonomia tou mystēriou tou apokekrymmenou apo tōn aiōnōn en tō theō tō ta panta ktisanti . . .').*/73/ Laodiceans showed 'occulti ab aevis deo qui omnia condidit': 'hidden from the ages from [the] God who created all things'. As for the rest of the letter (4-6), we have Tertullian's statement that Marcion 'not ony abstracts odd syllables . . . [but] filches away whole pages'. At

---

/70/ J. Knox, Jesus, Lord and Christ (1958), 158, n. 20; against pauline authorship of Col: Conzelmann, Lohse, Marxsen, Bornkamm, Käsemann, Schneke, Saunders, Fuchs; survey in E. Schweizer, 'Zur Frage der Echtheit des Kol. und Eph.', ZNTW 47 (1956), 287.

/71/ One must however stress that there is nothing inherently improbable about such a provenance; Tert.'s testimony is of little help.

/72/ Here the assumption is that, in the absence of any clear theological motive, it is not in itself likelier that Marcion excised a given passage than that the passage did not occur in his source.

/73/ AM 5.18.1-2.

5.18.5, he breaks off discussion of the theology of the epistle and launches into a discussion of the OT allusions (e.g., 4.8b referring to Ps 45.3), which Marcion had overlooked in the letter, and the precedents for the ethical discourse beginning at 4.25./74/ Tertullian bases his claim to Paul here as elsewhere on the prophetic dispensation of the OT, but the echoes of the passages he cites as forming the basis of Paul's discourse are faint. Outside Eph 4.8 (Ps 68.18; cf. Col 2.15) we encounter no formal citation of the OT./75/

(b) We have reason to suspect that a foreshortened version of the Eph ethical discourse occurred in Marcion's Laod. since we observe that he 'cut out' ('abstulit') the parenthesis at 6.2: 'Hoc est enim primum in promissione praeceptum'./76/ One might expect such an omission in view of Marcion's ideas on marriage and divorce. But the parenthesis can equally well be explained as a response to Marcion's attitude toward marriage and procreation, since there was nothing to prevent him blotting out 5.2ff. if he had considered the passage uncongenial (cf. Col 3.18ff.). What is significant is that the passage is a recasting of 1 Cor 14.34ff., which is perhaps a later interpolation into Paul's text, and which Marcion did not know, or certainly omitted, because of its emphasis on the law. The theme of 'mutual subjection' (cf. Phil 2.3) which characterizes the revised passage comports far better with Marcion's idea of church order than with the hierarchically-oriented structure described in 1 Tim 3.1-13, itself a variation on the same pauline theme, and which points to the organizational pattern of the orthodox communities. Moreover, it should be stressed that Marcion's attitude toward marriage remains ambiguous. While Tertullian accuses him repeatedly of contempt for the flesh, he expresses uncertainty over whether Marcion follows Moses' or Christ's practice regarding marriage (4.34.1f., 7f.). Marcion seems to have credited Luke 16.18f. and retained Lk 20.5./77/ An examination of the relevant passages indicates that while he prized celibacy, and forbade cohabitation/78/ even to married members

---

/74/ Ps 4.4; 18.26; Deut 21.21; Isa 52.11; 5.11, 7; Amos 2.12.

/75/ Holtzmann, NT Theologie II, 256.

/76/ AM 5.18.11.

/77/ AM 4.34.1f; 4.38.7f.

/78/ AM 5.7.6; 5.12.6f.; cf. 4.29.6.

of the church, he also forbade divorce for those already married./79/ This is in keeping with Paul's advice in 1 Cor 7.9ff., but qualified by an emphasis on 1 Cor 7.27ff./80/ Marcion's generally high regard for women/81/ is also indicated by Tertullian (5.8.12), 1 Cor 11.5 being used to the exclusion of 1 Cor 14.34 (cf. 1 Tim 2.11f.). The most plausible explanation is that Marcion's opponents exaggerated his teaching on marriage, while the ambiguities of the teaching itself must be sought ulitimately in Marcion's dependence on Paul.

(c) The ethical discourse in Laod. must also have included 5.18, 'Inebriari vino dedecori', which is to be contrasted with the sentiment expressed in 1 Tim 5.23. The inclusion of this maxim is hardly surprising, in view of Marcion's literalist interpretation of Lk 22.18 and Paul's injunction in Rom 14.21./82/ Marcionite presbyters apparently substituted water for wine in the celebration of the eucharist./83/

(d) We can assume from Tertullian's final rally that Marcion's Laod. included the bulk of Eph 6.10ff. Theologically, the situation of this battle between good and evil presupposes a number of antecedents:/84/ the Syro-Babylonian myth of the warfare between Marduk and the powers of Chaos for example, as well as OT analogues. Eph 6.14b corresponds closely to Isa 59.17: 'God put on righteousness as a breastplate, and a helmet of salvation upon his head; he put on garments of vengeance for clothing, and wrapped himself in fury as a mantle' (RSV). So too, in the Wisdom of Solomon: 'The Lord will take his zeal as his whole armour, and will arm all creation to repel his enemies. He will put on righteousness as a breastplate and wear

---

/79/ AM 4.34.1f., 5f.

/80/ AM 5.8.3.

/81/ Praes. 41. I have dealt with this aspect of Marcion's religious thought in my article, 'De Statu Feminarum: The Correlation of Gnostic Religious Theory and Social Practice', Église et Théologie (Oct. 1983). One cannot exclude the possibility that the polemic against the women teachers in the church in Thyatira, Rev 2.20, envisages marcionite church practice.

/82/ Bauer has suggested (Rev. B. [1921], 611) that Lk 22.19b-20 is a marcionite interpolation based on 1 Cor 11.24. See also Blackman, Influence, 7.

/83/ Epiph. Panar. 42.3.

/84/ Cf. G.H.P. Thompson, The Letters of Paul to the Eph., Col. and Phil. (1967), 93ff.

impartial justice as a helmet; he will take holiness as an invincible shield and sharpen stern wrath for a sword' (5.17f.). For the most part, however, the OT allusions have been denuded of any reference to the wrath and vengeance of God. The dualistic struggle between God and the world-rulers has been deliberately transformed: the 'garments of vengeance and fury' (Isa 59.17f.; cf. 2 Thess 21.8ff.) have become the 'girdle of truth' and the 'shield of faith' (Eph 6.16), to be used for protection against the 'fiery darts of the wicked'; the 'stern sword of wrath' becomes 'the sword of the spirit, the word of God'; and, perhaps most significantly, the 'mantle of fury' is replced by the 'shodding of the feet with the gospel of peace' (*hypodēsamenoi tous podas en hetoimasia tou evangeliou tēs eirēnēs*', 6.15; cf. Rom 10.15). Marcion equated the 'spiritual hosts of wickedness' (6.12; cf. 2 Thess 2.8; AM 5.18.12) with the 'power of the Creator'. Laod. knows the Creator as the *archon tēs exousias tou aeros*, 'the prince of heavenly powers', and makes explicit the contrast between his authority ('spiritual wickedness in high places'; cf. 2 Thess 2.7f.)/85/ and the mercy and love of God (Eph 2.4, 7; 1.19). This merciful God is 'high above every principality and power'/86/ that the world names God (Eph 1.21)./87/ His sole purpose is the redemption of mankind and the showing forth of his mercy towards mankind. The mysterion by which this transformation takes place, nascent in Paul's discourse in 1 Cor 15.51f., becomes in Laod./Eph an 'appropriation' of another's property, effected by the Christ whose grace has made man 'accepted in the beloved' (Eph 1.5f.). This purpose is not established in prophecy; notably absent is the typology of 1 Cor 15.45f., or any hint of a recapitulation based on the OT. It is God's will that man be saved (Eph 1.5; 1.9; 1.11b); put more succinctly (1.9), the appropriation of mankind takes place kata tēn eudokian, i.e., according to his pleasure. This for the

---

/85/ Cf. AM 1.15.5f. In this connection Schlatter's observation is noteworthy: 'It is hard to imagine any writer before John picturing Christ as a warrior going forth to battle. Such a notion comes perilously near to being irreconcilable with the christian conception of God', Church in the NT Period (ET 1965), 283. One should not overlook analogies in the Qumran War Scroll (the battles between the children of light and the children of darkness); but the thematic similarities between Qumran and Eph have often been asserted at the expense of underlining the essential differences in the way the motifs of conflict are developed.

/86/ Cf. AM 1.15.2-3.

/87/ Cf. Tertullian's discussion of the 'evidences' of God, AM 1.10,3f.: 'Iudacorum enim deum dicunt animae deum'.

author of Laod. is the explanation of the mysterion, its content being redemption and forgiveness through the riches of God's grace (1.9a; cf. 1 Cor 15.49). This God stands in opposition to the world: he is not its creator, but its savior. The dualistic themes of the epistles have here been expanded and radicalized (cf. 2 Cor 4.4; Gal 4.8, 9; 3.19; 2 Thess 2.4, 8; 1 Cor 8.4).

In essential details the God described by the author of Laod. corresponds to the alien God of Marcion's Antitheses. His mercy and grace are extended to strangers (2.3f.) who are by nature children of the God of wrath./88/ He is a God of infinite compassion (Eph 2.7);/89/ and a stranger to the cosmocrator (Eph 1.21 v. AM 2.28.1f.; 1.11.9; 5.18.3). He is a God of mercy who cannot be moved by works, his salvation being a free gift of grace, accessible by faith (Eph 2.8; cf. Rom 2.4). This access is entailed (cf. Rom 4.18; 3.20f.) by the fact that man in himself, man acording to nature, means nothing to the good God. As we have seen (pp.266f.) it is precisely this theme that underlies Marcion's anthropology and doctrine of redemption:/90/ God loves his enemies without expecting return./91/ Man's inability to influence God's decision has to do with the ontological rift which separates them. It is true that the epistle does not eliminate the need for good works, but they are linked post hoc to being 'new creatures' in Jesus Christ. Good works belong to the nature of adoption to sonship./92/

The nature of God's revelation as described in Eph also corresponds to Marcion's view of the 'divine disclosure' transacted by the alien God in Jesus. We have already noted Marcion's reading of Eph 3.9, which Tertullian took to be a revision of the original text. But as the theme is developed

---

/88/ Cf. AM 4.25.8; 4.26.7; 4.16.11f.; 1.23.1ff.; 1.17.1.

/89/ Cf. AM 4.6.3; 4.8.7; 1.26.1; 1.27.2f.

/90/ AM 4.17.4, 7; cf. Lk 6.36.

/91/ Am 5.5.4; 4.31.5; 5.4.14.

/92/ Cf. V.P. Furnish, 'Ephesians', ICB, 739a. It should be emphasized that the term poiēma (RSV: 'workmanship') refers specifically to the 'new creature' (Eph 2.15b). It does not constitute a reference to God as Creator. A better translation would be 'deed' or 'act' (cf. 1 Cor 1.30; Gal 6.15 [!]).

elsewhere in the epistle, in terms similar to those employed by Marcion, it is hardly likely that Tertullian's reading is the one which stood in the Epistle to the Laodiceans, and Marcion's text seems scarcely to have diverged from Tertullian's before 3.9. The author of Laod. stresses that God has chosen man 'since the foundation of the world' but in operation he is not linked to the God of Genesis who 'establishes' the foundation: that his purpose (1.9) arises only in conjunction with the act of the Creator may have been more strongly put in Laod. The Marcionites may have taught that the goodness of God is 'revealed' in response to the 'foundation of the world'. The heresiologists were quick to point out that a God perfectly good could not have waited 'until twenty-nine generations were in Hell' before revealing his goodness if his purpose was eternal (Eznik, de sectis, 4; cf. AM 1.22.3, 6ff.; 1.23.4f.). Nonetheless, the idea that man's salvation is God's pleasure -- unmotivated by any ontic or external necessity -- is cardinal to Marcion's theology (see above, pp. 214ff.). The prothesis of God is designed to unfold at the 'opportune moment', namely, when there can be an ingathering of Jew and gentile according to the 'gospel of salvation' (1.13: cf. Rom 11.26f.). The address to the Jews as 'those who first trusted in Christ' is entirely consonant with Marcion's theology (cf. Rom 11.28) as we have described it; and a pro-Jewish stance is also in keeping with the (assumed) provenance of the Epistle, specifically the paulinist congregation at Laodicea, which must have included a large number of Jews. More decisive however is the contrast between the pro-Jewish language in Eph, which we know Marcion accepted, and the 'anti-Jewish' sections of Romans, especially ch. 9, which he rejected or did not know.

At this juncture we may pause to consider the proposition that the theological formulations in Eph are to some extent 'corrections' of or responses to the theology of Romans.

### 8.6 Romans and Laodiceans

(a) Rom 1.16b agrees with Eph 1.12 that the Jews first trusted (Rom: 'believed') in Christ. In the passage following (Rom 1.18f.), rejected by Marcion, the author asserts that the 'wrath of God is manifest' (orgē) in the gentiles. Eph contrasts this 'wrath' (orgē) with the richness of God's mercy, and distinguishes the Jews from 'the children of disobedience' (Eph 2.3), i.e., those who still do the work of the law.

(b) The author of Rom 1.20 declares that 'the invisible things of [God] are clearly seen from the beginning of the world, being understood from the things that are created'. The gentiles, having ignored the signs of God's dispensation, 'are without excuse'. The author of Laod., on the other hand, records that 'the mystery of Christ [= God's purpose] . . . was not made known in other ages to the sons of men' (3.5a) but was 'hid from the beginning of the world from the God who created all things'. Their understanding has been darkened (cf. Rom 11.8f.) because 'they are alienated from the being of God' (Eph 4.18), not because they have rejected 'what God has shown to them' (Rom 1.19; cf. AM 1.11.9). The polemic of Rom 1.21ff. is replaced in Eph by the declaration that the gentiles should be fellowheirs, and 'of the same body and partakers of the promise in Christ Jesus through the gospel'. If the cue for this expansion comes from Rom 9.24, it lacks any reference to the exclusion of the Jews from the promise (but cf. Rom 9.25ff.). The bifurcation of Jew and gentile in relation to the law is replaced in Eph by the distinction between the 'old' and 'new' man in relation to the gospel (Eph 4.22-24).

(c) At the point where Marcion rejoins Romans (10.1), Paul enunciates his hope for Israel's salvation (cf. Rom 11.26); further on (Rom 10.12f.) he espouses the familiar conviction that 'there is no difference between Jew and Greek' (Gal 3.28; 1 Cor 1.24; 1 Cor 12.13). In Eph, this is expressed in terms of the 'equidistance' of gentiles and Jews from the mercy of God (Eph 2.4f.; 2.12f.; 2.16ff.), the two being constituted as 'one creature' by the Christ who 'breaks down the partition . . . that he might reconcile both unto God in one body by the cross, thereby bringing the hostility [according to the flesh] to an end' (2.15a).

(d) The question found in Rom 10.6b-7 ('who shall ascend into the height . . .') is actually answered in Eph 4.8ff.: *'anabas eis hypsos ēchmalōteusen aichmalōsian'*. The allusion to Ps 68.18 is clearly meant to refer to the captivity of men in contrast to the 'gift of grace given to everyone' (4.7) by a merciful God. The cosmology implied in this ascent/descent parallels that which characterizes Marcion's soteriology, /93/ and is especially close to the *descensus ad inferos* ascribed by Irenaeus to Marcion. /94/

---

/93/ AM 1.15.1f.; 1.19.2; 4.7.1f.

/94/ Haer. 1.27.3.

(e) The theme of Israel's salvation as a byproduct of their jealousy of the gentiles' acceptance of the gospel (Rom 11.11b-14; 10.19) is replaced in Eph by an inversion of priority, i.e., the gentiles come to the gospel by way of the Jews, with whom they are 'fellowheirs'. Nor is there any hint in Eph that only 'a few of the Jews' will be saved (Rom 11.14; Eph 2.12; 3.6). Likewise, the theme of jealousy -- God's over Israel and the Jews' over the salvation of the gentiles -- is replaced in Eph by the theme of 'God's kindness in Jesus Christ' (2.7; 2.17f.). The language used to express 'the unsearchable riches of Christ' is ultimately taken over from Romans (Rom 8.39; 11.33 = Eph 3.18ff.). In Romans, the power of Christ's love is literally stonger than the powers that rule the world (Rom 8.38; cf. 2 Thess 2.8; 1 Cor 15.24ff.). The motif of conquest 'in Christ' is transposed and elaborated in Eph 6.12ff. Missing from Eph, however, is any implication that God conspired to effect the ignorance and unbelief of mankind (Rom 11.32f.) in order to be able to show his mercy; instead, it is the agency of the principalities and powers that enforces the blindness of Jew and gentile. The revelation of mercy is an overcoming of the condition of 'hopelessness in the world' (Eph 2.12b) 'to the effect that the manifold wisdom of God might be made known to the principalities and powers in the heavenly places' (Eph 3.10). The 'astronomical' allusion of Eph 3.18b, in its transposition from Rom 8.39, is hence made to refer not to the inimical powers themselves, but rather to the extent of Christ's love: *'to platos kai mēkos kai hypsos kai bathos'*. Marcion uses comparable language in describing the meaning of the gospel./95/

## 8.7 Ephesians/Laodiceans and Romans in Relation to Marcion's Theology

The essential paulinism of Ephesians/Laodiceans cannot be denied; but we encounter here a modified form of the Apostle's teaching. This is clearest when we stop to consider the differing descriptions of man's existential plight:

/95/ Cf. Harnack's reconstruction, Marcion, 354*f.; cf. Eph 2.7; 3.19.

| Rom 1.21f. (cf. 11.8) | 'Eph' 4.17f. |
|---|---|
| Because they did not glorify | (Being alienated) from the |
| God as God . . . but became | life of God in the vanity |
| vain in their imaginations | of their mind, and having |
| . . . their foolish heart was | their understanding |
| darkened [by God] . . . | darkened through their |
| [Therefore] God gave them | natural ignorance, because of |
| up [paredōken] to | the blindness of their heart |
| uncleanness [akatharsian] | . . . who ceasing to hope having |
| through the lust of their own | given themselves over [paredōkan] |
| hearts to dishonour. . . | to licentiousness, greed and |
| themselves. (1.24) | unclean practices [akatharsias]. |

In the passage which Marcion rejected in Romans, it is God who blinds the hearts of men and God who gives them over the carnality and unclean practices. In 'Eph', however, it is man's alienation from God -- his situation as a stranger to mercy -- that darkens the heart, and hopelessness that causes men to 'engage in unclean works'. This alienation applies to Jews and gentiles equally, in relation to God who acts in Christ to break down the 'natural' barrier (i.e., the law) that stands between them (2.15). But the author of Laod. speaks as a Jewish Christian to a surrounding gentile population (3.1). His emphasis is thus on alienation as it applies to those who have only heard of Christ (4.21) and who are strangers to the promise of God as it was first delivered to the Jews (1.12). They are 'strangers', 'foreigners' (2.12; 2.17-19), and aliens from the life of God (4.18; 2.12b): 'apellotriōmenoi tēs zōēs tou theou' (4.18a); 'apellotriōmenoi tes politeias tou Israel . . .' (2.12a). The gentile like the Jew is brought into 'the habitation of God' (2.22) by embracing the promise which the Jews 'first trusted in Christ' (1.12f.).

The themes singled out for emphasis in Eph/Laod. parallel the central motifs of Marcion's theology. Man is by nature a stranger to the good, as God himself is an alien from the world;/96/ man belongs by nature to a God of 'wrath, severity, and judgment'/97/ who is ignorant of the existence of

---

/96/ AM 1.23.1ff.; 4.16.11. See further, note 39, p. 195.

/97/ AM 4.8.7.

the alien God;/98/ while the God of mercy exists in his own heaven, high above the spiritual powers who govern the Creator's world./99/ His sole purpose is the salvation of mankind and the revelation of his goodness./100/ This purpose however has been hidden from ages past, both from the Creator and from mankind: it is not revealed by any work of the alien God. We make our clearest approach to the authorship of Laod. by considering the following:

(a)  Rom 1.20:

The hidden [aorata] things of God are clearly seen from the creation of the world; being made known by the things of creation.

Laod./Eph 3.2bf.:

The dispensation of the grace of God . . . was not made known to men in other ages . . . [and] the mystery has been hidden from the beginning of the world from the God [Eph: in God] who created all things (3.2b, 5a, 9).

Marcion:

Our God, though not revealed from the beginning or by virtue of any creation, yet has by his own self been revealed in Christ Jesus./101/

(b) We make a further approach if we examine the crucial passage (Rom 11.7f.; cf. 1.20b) concerning the blindness imposed on the Jews by God in response to their recalcitrance, and the antithetical passage in Eph 4.17bf. 'Rejecting' the verse in Rom, Marcion claimed that 'the whole

/98/ AM 2.28.1f.; 5.18.3f.

/99/ AM 1.15.1f.; 4.7.1f.; cf. Gal 4.3b.

/100/ AM 1.25.1ff.; 1.26.1; 1.27.2; 1.17.1f.; cf. Eph 2.7.

/101/ AM 1.19.1; cf. 1 Jn 1.1-3.

imputation of Jewish ignorance since the first beginning refers not to Christ, but rather to God himself' (AM 3.6.8f.), that Christ was not despised and unrecognized by the Jews in the past,/102/ and that Christ had not been foretold beforehand./103/ Marcion stands accused of forgiving the Jews their mistake/104/ and of 'forming an alliance with Jewish error': as a result, the Jews committed no sin against Christ./105/

(c) Finally we must consider the transformation of the OT passages in Eph 6.11ff./106/ where we note the deliberate manipulation of the military symbols to exclude such terms as 'the garments of fury and vengeance', 'the helmet of Justice', and the substitution of such phrases as 'girdle of truth' and 'shield of faith'./107/ It is significant that Marcion is accused by Tertullian of precisely such manipulation, i.e., of subverting the sense of OT passages/108/ where Christ is (prototypically) depicted as a warrior. The bellicose imagery of Ps 45.3 ('Gird thee with a sword upon thy thigh') Marcion applied to the Christ of the Creator, who was to come at some future time as a warrior to restore the Jews to their former (political) estate (cf. Rom 11.26)./109/ The Christ of the alien God prohibits retaliation/110/ and so must be characterized in terms of the *evangelion tēs eirēnēs* (Eph 6.15), the gospel of peace, which is sufficient footing for the man

---

/102/ AM 3.6.8.

/103/ AM 3.6.2; 3.18.1.

/104/ AM 3.6.2.

/105/ AM 2.28.3; 3.6.2; cf. 3.16.3; 3.8.1f.

/106/ Isa 59.17; Wisd 5.17-20; Isa 11.5; 52.7; Hos 6.5.   Marcion is mistakenly accused by Tert. (4.29.13f.) of just such a procedure in relation to Lk 12.51 where the marcionite text read 'division' rather than 'sword' (cf. Matt 10.34).   So too Eznik (de sectis 4) who claims Marcion cast 1 Cor 15.25 in the passive so that Christ would not appear a warrior.

/107/ Cf. the apocatastatic emphasis of Rom 10.12-15, which is the point d'appui for the theology of Eph.

/108/ AM 3.14.2-3, 4.

/109/ AM 3.24.1f.; 3.21.3f.; 3.21.1f.   We can see from such passages the extent to which Marcion's thought was uninformed by any kind of eschatological thinking.   This serves also to explain his attention to the founding of churches in Asia Minor.

/110/ AM 2.28.2; 4.8.7.

shielded by faith. Tertullian himself prefers the stronger stuff of the Apocalypse (Rev 1.16)/111/ and complains that Marcion has refused to acknowledge John. But in his lecture to Marcion on the meaning of the allegorical armour of Christ,/112/ Tertullian loses track of his argument: it is Marcion himself who subscribes to the paulinist interpretation of the spiritual warfare described in Eph:

> Quodsi Ioannem agnitum non vis, habes communem magistrum Paulum, praecingentem lumbos nostros veritate et lorica justitiae, et calciantem nos praeparationem evangelii pacis, non belli, adsumere iubentem scutum fidei, in quo possimus omnia diaboli ignita tela extinguere, et galeam salutaris, et gladium spiritus, quod est, inquit, dei sermo. (AM 3.14.4 = Eph 6.14f.)

Moreover, we know from Irenaeus as well as from other statements made by Tertullian/113/ that Marcion interpreted the parable of the 'strong man armed' in his gospel (Lk 11.21f.) as a reference to the contest between the Lord of this world and 'the one stronger' (ischyroteros autou) who overcomes him and despoils him of his property (Eph 6.10f.). It seems entirely possible that we have in Eph/Laod. 6.14ff. Marcion's own elaboration of this contest, in pauline terms (cf. Rom 8.37ff.)./114/

(d) The theme of 'appropriation of another's property' (= adoption) (Eph 1.5: hyiothesia) is well-attested as a central motif of Marcion's paulinism, and is prominent in the genuine letters of Paul./115/ The emphasis on becoming God's by adoption comports with the theology of Marcion's revision of Gal 4.4.5: 'Cum autem evenit impleri tempus, misit deus filium suum',

---

/111/ AM 3.14.1, 3f.; 4.5.2 (Marcion's rejection of the Apocalypse).

/112/ AM 4.14.4f.

/113/ AM 5.6.7.; Haer. 4.33.2; cf. 5.17.1; 5.18.1.

/114/ Cf. the mythological descriptio in Rev 12.7f.

/115/ Rom 8.15, 23; 9.4; Gal 4.5. In Rom 8.15, Paul refers to the pneuma hyiothesias; in 8.23 he seems to equate redemption of the body (?) with adoption, while the author of 9.4 refers to the 'adoption' of the Israelites (anomalous in the context of Paul's argument). Laod. here seems to envisage the thrust of Paul's words in Gal 4.5 (4.4b being perhaps an orthodox interpolation): 'hina tous hypo nomon exagorase, hina tēn huiothesian apolabōmen'. Thus preeminently adoption has to do with redemption. The emphasis on 'expropriation of property' is not misplaced, since Paul seems to think in terms of the Roman practice of ensuring inheritance in the absence of a natural heir. Cf. A.H.M. Jones, The Decline of the Ancient World (1966), 13f.

omitting 'born of a woman, born under the law', but not v. 5: 'To redeem [those] that were under the law, that we might receive adoption as sons'. Harnack does not count this 'alteration', but it is to be assumed both from the sentence following the citation ('Erubescat spongia Marcionis')/116/ as well as from the fact that Gal 4.4b is missing from Tertullian's citation. Although the tone of the epistle is markedly pro-Jewish (Eph 4.17ff.), the 'problem' of the law, in Paul's sense of the word, is wanting; thus:

(e) It can be assumed that the law as a dividing line between Jews and Christians is a dead issue (2.15). The practical instruction offered beginning at 4.17 and comprising an appeal to renounce paganism (4.17-19; cf. Rom 1.21-25), and the duties of christian life (5.21-6.9) is analogous to the discourse in Col 3-4. But Eph 4-5 lacks the moderately libertarian trajectory of Col 2.16-23, or more specifically the contradiction between certain libertarian and ascetic emphases (Col 3.5-6 v. Eph 5.2-7; cf. Rom 1.18, Col 3.6). The most significant difference between Col and Eph in this connection is the statement in Col 3.10 that the new man is made *'kat' eikona tou ktisantos auton'* (cf. Gen 1.26f.) -- in the image of the Creator. The author of Eph (4.24) declares that the new man is created *'kata Theon . . . en dikaiosynē kai hosiotēti* -- and thus implicitly denies that the transformation from carnal to spiritual has anything to do with the Creator. This may point to a theological connection between (marcionite) Laod. and Col, Laod. finding correction in Col 3.10f. The germ of the motif is present in Paul's authentic letters (cf. Rom 13.14; Gal 3.27), but the speculation about how the new creature is to be constituted clearly suggests a post-pauline dispute over the meaning of his words.

(f) There are other points at which Col may preserve an original (marcionite) reading which has been altered in the Ephesus-redaction of the epistle. Thus: Col 2.7 ('rooted and grounded in Christ') v. Eph 2.20f. ('built on the foundation of the apostles and prophets . . .'; cf. 1 Cor 3.11). Eph 3.5 speaks of a revelation to 'the holy apostles and prophets', while Col 1.26 of a 'revelation to his saints'.

(g) Whether one assumes the priority of Col or not, it marks a different stratum in the development of the theme, 'that in Christ is neither Jew nor Greek', from that represented by Eph (Col 3.11; Eph 2.3-22; cf. Gal 3.28; Rom 3.9b) and an elaboration of the catalogue of vices given in

---

/116/ AM 5.4.2.

Rom 1.18-25./117/ Where Col diverges from Eph, it is generally in an 'anti-marcionite' direction. We cannot imagine such passages as Col 1.15b or 1.16b coming from Marcion; whereas 1.15a and 1.19, given Marcion's docetism, would have invited no serious objections; and Col 1.20 is echoed clearly in Eph 2.13, as is the 'stranger' motif in Col 1.21a (= Eph 2.13, 15, 19f.), not otherwise developed in Col, but theologically central to Eph. At the same time the anti-docetic Col 1.24 ('in his body of flesh') is excluded, if not contradicted, in Eph (2.14f.) where the 'building' is the christian community itself (cf. Col 1.23f.; 2.7)./118/

(h) The abbreviated ethical discourse (Col 3-4) does not differ markedly from the more expansive treatment given the subject in Eph 5-6, but this should not surprise us, since the high ethical standards of the marcionite communities are widely attested (cf. AM 1.27.5) and the church order (and practice) in Ephesus, Colossae, and Laodicea may not have differed greatly./119/ In any event one should expect to find the same virtues, if in differing order of priority, commended and honored in these christian communities even despite their theological disparity: compassion, lowliness, patience; the purity of love; harmony in the community; thanksgiving; christian service; prayerfulness; and fair treatment of slaves (documented in Philemon 15).

But there are signal differences even in the ethical discourses: In Eph 5.28, the author seems to emphasize the need for men to 'love their wives as their own bodies'. This idea is missing in Col. Tertullian, belaboring his point, cites the 'survival' of the verse as a lapse in Marcion's

---

/117/ Eph 5.6 is a doublet of 4.14, covering the same subject, and feasibly taken over from Col 2.4 (2.8a + 3.6). Some mss. add 'epi tous hyious tēs apeitheias', i.e., Eph 5.6b to Col 3.6.

/118/ Further: Col 1.10 (works) v. Eph 2.9 (cf. Rom 3.24; 9.32; 1 Cor 1.29, etc.); Col 1.27 (God's grace to the gentiles) v. Eph 3.6 (gentiles as fellowheirs with the Jews, Eph 3.8b); but Col 1.26 (the mystery hidden, made manifest to the saints: cf. Eph 3.4-5; 1.17f.; Col 2.2f.; cf. Eph 3.18f.; Col 2.2bf.; cf. Eph 4.14; Col 2.4f.; cf. Eph 6.10ff.); Col 3.6a v. Eph 2.4 and (!) 5.1f. But Col 2.14; cf. Eph 2.15.

/119/ The polemic in Rev 2.20 would seem to indicate a difference in church practice between Ephesus and the churches to the east: the marcionite churches encouraged women to prophesy: Epiph., Panar. 42.3-4; Eznik, de sectis, 4.16; Tert., Praes. 41; cf. Polyc., Phil. 4.2-3; Ign., Polyc. 5.2; and 1 Tim 2.12-15.

docetism./120/ Eph 5.6 (cf. Eph 4.14) is evidently interpolated from Col 3.6, and totally foreign to the theology of Laod. The initiative toward the Jews is not found in Col (Eph 4.17). And more suggestive, in view of marcionite ascesis, is the absence of any reference in the Col discourse to 'drunkenness and wine', proscribed in Eph 5.18f. (cf. Rom 14.21)./121/ and the tacit contradiction of the proscription in Col 2.16, 20ff. (cf. 1 Tim 5.23; 1 Tim 4.3), where ascesis is declared a false way of checking the indulgence of the flesh. It is also significant that Col 3.20 seems to represent a reading closer to Marcion's than Eph 6.1-2, which according to Tertullian lacked the parentheses, 'for this is the first commandment with promise' (Col: 'for this pleases the Lord'). As Eph/Laod. seems complete in its own right with the phrase, 'for this is right' ('touto gar estin dikaion'), it seems probable that Eph 6.2 is an interpolation designed to provide an OT basis for the aphorism in v. 1. Likewise the theme of divine retribution (Col 3.25) is missing from the advice to masters in Eph 6.9, while the theme of divine impartiality is present in both epistles.

Some provisional conclusions might be advanced on the basis of this analysis of Eph/Laod.:

The strongly pro-Jewish bias of the epistle known as Ephesians -- indicated by the confusion of audience (3.1 v.4.17f. but cf. Col 1.27) as much as by its unique development of the reconciliation-motif (Gal 3.28 but Col 3.11f.: alienation from the promise first delivered to Israel) -- suggests a place of origin where the christian congregation included a considerable number of Jews. This in itself does not preclude Ephesus, since it too had a large Jewish politeuma./122/ But the epistle presupposes a conversance between Jews and gentiles which, in the light of historical evidence, especially that supplied by 'Luke',/123/ does not seem to have

/120/ AM 5.18.9.

/121/ Cf. Epiph. Panar. 42.3.

/122/ Josephus, Antiq. 14.7.2; Sib . or. 3.271; Philo, vit. Mos. 2.27; cf. C. Guignebert, The Jewish World in the Time of Jesus (1939), 213ff.

/123/ Acts 19.1-7 indicates that Paul found Ephesian 'christians' defective in the spirit: curiously, they are said 'only to have received the baptism of John' -- presumably the Baptist -- but the text may reflect the memory of Paul's difficulty with a prëexisting 'johannine' (?) Christianity in Ephesus; cf. Haenchen, Acts, 554f.

existed in Ephesus. The historical evidence is supplied by Josephus, who
remarks that the Greeks of Ephesus petitioned Marcus Agrippa to exclude
Jews from the isopolity or 'potential citizenship'/124/ which they enjoyed in
other hellenistic cities, including Laodicea./125/ Political conditions in
Ephesus were thus hardly conducive to a 'breaking down of the barriers' such
as that indicated in Eph 2.14.

This information is corroborated in 1 Cor 15.32 and 16.9, where Paul
acknowledges the difficulties his gospel encountered in Ephesus, and
indirectly in 2 Cor 1.8-9 (cf. Acts 18.19-21, 24-26 [Apollos too knows only
John's baptism]; Acts 19.9, 13ff., 23ff.)./126/ Moreover, Eph (incredibly)
does not reflect the conflict with the Jews that informs the theology of the
Apostle's letters to Corinth, Galatia, and Philippi, written from
Ephesus./127/ This conflict is nonetheless visible in a recollection preserved
by 'Luke' in Acts, where we are told of Paul's expulsion from the synagogue
by the Jews at Ephesus 'who disbelieved the Way' (19.8)/128/ and his removal
to the home of a gentile Christian named Tyrannus (Acts 19.8-10). By the
same token, 'Luke' credits the story of Demetrius the silversmith, who is
able to incite the Greeks in the city to riot over the issue of Paul's gospel
(19.26ff.): 'When Paul wished to address the crowd, his disciples held him
back; and the Asiarchs . . . requested that he not venture into the theater'
(19.30f.). Even more remarkable, in view of Paul's difficulties at Ephesus,
is the idea (despite Luke's idealized denouement, Acts 19.17-20; cf. 19.26)
that that community should have 'persevered in the Apostle's teaching' to
produce the summary we find in canonical Eph. As Bauer correctly
observes,/129/ if Rom 16 (unknown to Marcion) represents a letter to the
Ephesians, then on the basis of vv. 17-20 we must conclude that during the

/124/ Tarn, Hellenistic Civilization, 176: the so-called 'Ephesian' process.

/125/ Cf. Josephus, Antiq. 12.8; Mac 2.30; cf. bell. Jud. 7.44.

/126/ Cf. Deissmann, Light from the Ancient East (1927), 112ff.; Bruce,
NT History (1969), 328.

/127/ According to the marcionite Prologues the letters to Galatians,
Corinth, and Colossae were written from Ephesus; Philippians from Rome;
cf. G. Bornkamm, Paul (ET: 1971), Appendix I, 241f.

/128/ G.S. Duncan, 'Paul's Ministry in Asia -- The Last Phase', NTS 3
(1957), 211-18.

/129/ Bauer, Orthodoxy and Heresy, 82.

Apostle's lifetime he encountered rival teachers there threatening division in the community. But we may go even further than Bauer: on the basis of the evidence of the Epistles and Acts, we have no reason to believe that Paul encountered any _initial_ success whatever in Ephesus,/130/ being rejected both by the synagogue and by the gentile population. The 'paulinism' of the Ephesus-community must have been marginal from the first, and the _prominence_ of the Apostle/131/ a byproduct of the struggle to reclaim his teaching form the heretics. Thus in Acts, Paul is reported as having warned the Ephesian Elders (_presbyteroi_) (Acts 20.30) in his farewell to them at Miletus that 'from their own midst' men would arise to draw Christians away from them, 'speaking perverse things' (cf. 2 Tim 3.1ff.; 4.3). This prediction actually describes the situation in and around Ephesus at the time of the composition of Acts; by most reckonings, at about the time Eph/_Laod_. must have been written (c. 110). One must wonder why this difficulty would not be reflected in an epistle directed to the Ephesian church.

To this consideration should be added three further points:

(a) That Ignatius thought that Paul was founder of the Ephesian community may be doubted (_Eph_. 12.2) since he envisages already in that community a prior apostolic foundation and body of doctrine to which the church there assents (11.2)/132/ 'in the power of Jesus Christ'.

(b) In the johannine Apocalyspe originating at Patmos, the memory of Paul's foundation of the Ephesian church seems to have been completely lost, or

---

/130/ Thus vs. Köster, 'Gnomai Diaphoroi' in _Trajectories_, 155f.: Köster has pointed out that 'several early christian groups . . . must have existed simultaneously [at the turn of the first century in Ephesus ]'; but he considers the church there 'originally pauline', and the author of Ephesians a 'Qumran-influenced paulinist'. Köster does well to point to the 'Jewish-christian "school" engaging in a daring interpretation of the OT' as the center for the production of Eph, but he considers Cerinthus the likeliest candidate for author, despite the fact we know next to nothing about Cerinthus beyond what Irenaeus records (_Haer_. 3.11.1). Further, even in Luke's romantic account of Paul's mission to Ephesus, it is plain that Paul is not regarded as 'founder' of the christian community there (19.1).

/131/ Tert. knows 'churches which are _alumnae_ of John' and churches 'nourished' by Paul (AM 4.5.2); Ephesus being one of the latter; but Irenaeus knows Paul as founder and John as continuator: 'Sed et quae est Ephesi Ecclesia a Paulo quidem fundata, Johanne autem permanente apud eos usque ad Traiani tempora, testis est verus apostolorum traditionis', _Haer_. 3.3.4.

/132/ Cf. Bauer, _Orthodoxy and Heresy_, 83.

perhaps deliberately suppressed (cf. Rev 2.4f.): only the names of the twelve apostles are found on the foundations of the New Jerusalem (21.14). The same process of erosion is evident in the Ephesus-section of the apocryphal Acts of John, which may have come into existence at around this time.

(c) By the time Irenaeus sets out to attack the heresies, Paul has been almost totally displaced in the consciousness of the church at Ephesus by John. In short, given Paul's avowed troubles in the city, his failure to find adherents there for his teaching, and the lack of success of his gospel thereafter, it is difficult to imagine this summary arising out of Jewish-Christian circles in Ephesus (cf. Eph 1.1; 1.15!).

The memory of Paul's troubles at Ephesus would have been especially vivid to Marcion if he experienced similar stubbornness and opposition there. An attempt to reintroduce (or rehabilitate?) Paul's teaching in a community where the memory of Paul's apostolate was already threatened may even point, however uncertainly, to a psychological explanation for the prominence of the doctrine of false apostleship in Marcion's theology.

Moreover, on direct evidence the prosperous Jewish polis of Laodicea is a likelier candidate as the provenance of the epistle than recalcitrant Ephesus: (a) because Paul does not mention writing a letter to Ephesus, or of having gained an audience there during his mission (cf. 1 Cor 15.32; 2. Cor 1.8-10), and (b) because Col, which may itself be an orthodox ('Ephesian'?) reworking of an originally marcionite document closely related to Laod., five times mentions/133/ the existence of a paulinist community in Laodicea for which the Apostle has great concern (Col 4.13), and which possesses a Church in which other letters of Paul are read (Col 4.16). This comports with the evidence of the marcionite Prologue to the Epistle to the Laodiceans, which finds that church secure in the 'word of truth' which they accepted from the Apostle, while the existence of such a church in Ephesus is at least e silentio denied. (c) Most significantly, the crucial sentence in Col 4.16b enjoins the Colossians to read the epistle 'from Laodicea',

----

/133/ Col 2.1; 4.13, 15, 16[2]. Holtzmann attempted to show that Eph was a revision of a not yet interpolated Colossians, and that Col itself originated in gnostic circles, Kritik der Epheser und Kolosserbriefe (1872); cf. E. Käsemann, RGG³ II (1958), 517ff.; E.P. Sanders, 'Literary Dependence in Col.', JBL 85 (1966), 28ff.; C. Anderson, 'Who Wrote the Epistle from Laodicea', JBL 85 (1966), 436ff.; H.J. Cadbury, 'The Dilemma of Eph.', NTS 5 (1958/59), 91ff.; R. Batey, 'The Distinction of Eph.', JBL 82 (1963), 101.

implicitly a pastoral letter left there by Paul/134/ rather than a letter of reproof. By their silence the Marcionites deny Paul's interest in the Ephesian church; or put the other way around tacitly confirm his failure there. The Paul who survives the Ephesian mob is familiar to the Laodicean church; the Paul who 'dismisses the assembly', an unknown figure (Acts 19.35, 41).

This suggests in turn that Laod., unlike those epistles devoted in whole or part to overcoming heresy, might be expected to lack, as it were, a distinctive problematic,/135/ or life-setting, comparable to the outbreak of enthusiasm at Corinth, the incursion of a 'false gospel' in Galatia, and the question of the parousia in 1 Thess. The brief sally against 'the cunning of men' (Eph 4.14) (parallel to Col 2.8, but lacking the doctrinal implications of the latter passage),/136/ does not really constitute such a problematic. In substance, therefore, and in its lack of a concrete life-setting, Ephesians is the kind of letter Laodiceans might be expected to be, viz., (a) a letter 'summarizing' the teaching of Paul, written by someone with access to the bulk of Paul's correspondence;/137/ not improbably, an itinerant teacher engaged in collecting Paul's letters to the churches in Asia; (b) a letter which reflects the social composition of that community -- in the case of Laodicea, a conglomerate of Jewish and gentile Christians, united by the teaching of Paul; and (c) a letter which affects to explain the Apostle's hope for Israel (Rom 11.26):/138/ thus the doctrine of the 'new creation' as the basic unit of church order after Christ himself (Col 1.24, 2.6; Eph 4.11ff.; 2.15ff.). In Eph, the pauline idea that Christ is the sacred point of convergence between Jew, Greek, male, female, slave, and free is

---

/134/ But cf. Tert. AM 5.17.1.

/135/ Thus, R.P. Martin, 'An Epistle in Search of a Life-setting', ExT 79 (1967), 296f.

/136/ Cf. Marxsen, Introd. NT, 187; and Kümmel, Intro. to the NT, 364.

/137/ With the possible exception of 2 Thess. This may count as further evidence that Marcion did not know 2 Thess, though later Marcionites may have assumed it to be Paul's work; Harrison, Paulines and Pastorals, 40f.; C.L. Mitton, The Epistle to the Eph. (1951), 98ff., 120, 333ff.

/138/ There is no hint in Eph of the attitude which inspired the writing of 1 Thess 2.14ff.

decisive;/139/ (d) a letter which reflects the religious syncretism of the christian church in the city of Laodicea. In Ephesians, this syncretism is more obvious than in any other deuteropauline letter, with affinities to Syro - Babylonian dualism,/140/ mainstream Judaism, and arguably to the conceptual world of the Qumran community./141/ At the same time, the household admonitions come from hellenistic-Jewish tradition, and the syzygy between the 'new man', 'Christ' and the 'church' (as the body of Christ) is best understood 'against the background of a christianized mythological gnosis'./142/ As the likeliest candidate for 'Laodiceans', the Epistle to the Ephesians satisfies each of these conditions: It is not a letter,/143/ but in the strict sense of an interpretation of Paul's theology. It presupposes a familiarity with the bulk of the pauline corpus; it addresses a situation in post-pauline christianity and assumes the existence of a fixed church order, faithful to the Apostle's teaching and in need of instruction rather than correction; it reflects a marked convergence between Jewish and gentile Christians and a syncretistic theology which is clearly more developed than Paul's. A final obtrusive piece of evidence should be put forward: namely, that Marcion knew this to be the Epistle to the Laodiceans, and he is our earliest witness to the titulus. The words 'at Ephesus' did not

---

/139/ Käsemann, 'Das Interpretationsproblem des Eph.', TLZ 86 (1961), 3.

/140/ Eph 6.12f.; 5.7ff.

/141/ Furnish, ICB, 835. So K.G. Kuhn, 'Der Eph. im Lichte der Qumrantexte', NTS 7 (1960), 334f.: The language of Eph 'recalls the conceptual world of the Qumran text' and 'manifests appearances of semitic syntax four times more frequently than all the other letters of the pauline corpus'; can we conclude from this that Marcion's ascesis may have derived from a practical knowledge of the Qumran tradition in Judaism, mediated through the Jewish population in Laodicea? So too Köster (Trajectories, 154), who notes that 'parallels to Qumran in early Christianity seem to be much more conspicuous after CE 70 [i.e., the dispersion after the Jewish war] than in the [historical] teaching of Jesus and the genuine letters of Paul'.

/142/ Thus, e.g., Käsemann, RGG[3] II (1958), 517ff.; P. Pokorny, 'Eph. und gnostische Mysterien', ZNTW 53 (1962), 160ff.; H. Schlier, LThK III (1959), 916f.; C. Colpe, 'Für Leib-Christi Vorstellung im Eph.', Judentum-Urchristentum-Kirche, Festschr. J. Jeremias, ZNTW 26 (1960), 172f.

/143/ F. Cornelius, 'Die geschichtliche Stellung des Eph.', ZRGes 7 (1955), 74ff.; H. Rentdorff, Das Neue Testament Deutsch, 8 (1933), 44.

stand in the original document./144/

Given that Eph marks a clear development beyond Paul, and at least in part a correction of the Apostle's teachings, we are bound to look to the circle from which the epistle originated and its theological structure in order to locate its author. On this reckoning, there seem to be no insurmountable objections to assuming that Marcion himself -- known even by his opponents as the corrector of Paul -- was the author of the Epistle to the Laodiceans, and that both Eph and perhaps Col represent orthodox versions of letters originating in the marcionite community of Laodicea./145/ As we have already observed, this community stands in tension with the johannine circle at Ephesus over the interpretation of Paul; and it is this tension that stands behind the confusion over the titulus: orthodox (johannine) Ephesus or heretical (marcionite) Laodicea? At least by the late second century the issue had been resolved in favor of Ephesus, since the Muratorian Canon records a letter of Paul to the Ephesians but rejects the 'marcionite' epistle to Laodicea./146/ We can only assume that the canonist regards the marcionite letter a corrupt version of church-Ephesians. The apocryphal Acts of John may reflect the gradual displacement of Marcionism by a johannine (or gnostic-johannine) theology in Laodicea (Acts Jn. 58-60),/147/

---

/144/ P$^{46}$ and taken over in the oldest codices; not given in B $\aleph$ (Codex 1793), which goes back to a very ancient prototype, or by the corrector of miniscule 424. P$^{46}$ reads 'tois hagiois kai pistois'. Origen did not find 'at Ephesus' at the beginning of his copy, but assumed that it was intended. The idea that Ephesians had no titulus because it was intended as a circular letter to the churches has little to commend it (viz., is this the summary of Paul's teaching that the Ephesian church would have published?). Kümmel notes that a letter without prescript and a gap for subsequent insertion of an address is without parallel in antiquity (Intro. to the NT, 355). On the general conclusion that Laodiceans is 'mistitled' Ephesians, see Souter, Text and Canon (1913), 152; idem., Expositor (1911); Harnack, Sitzungsber. der preussischen Akad. der Wiss. (1910), 693-709; and A.H. McNeile, Introd. to the Literature of the NT (1953), 176ff.; cf. Loisy, Christian Religion, 27: 'Eph probably appeared first as the Letter to the Laodiceans mentioned in Col 4.16'. Carl Franklin (Paul and the Early Christians, 1978) arrives at a similar conclusion.

/145/ I must here concur with Schille's thesis, that both Eph and Col derive from the same tradition, which is more clearly visible in Eph than in Col (cf. 'Der Autor des Epheserbriefes', TLZ [1957], 325ff).

/146/ Text, E.S. Buchanan, JTS 8 (1906), 537-45; Can. Mur. 64f.

/147/ On the dating of the Acts., see Schäferdiek, 'The Acts of John' in Hennecke, NTA II, 189f.

envisaging as it does the Disciple's success in that city. If there is a kernel of historicity in the report of the writer, it is possible that the Ephesian 'correction' of Laodiceans arose in conjunction with the success of the johannine mission to the 'heretical' see, and that the titulus was supplied at the same time.

With a view to the theological motifs appropriated from other of Paul's letters, but radicalized in Eph, the case for Marcion's authorship of Laod. is a persuasive one: In summary:

(a) Eph: the emphasis on faith as 'access' to salvation and the exclusion of works: 2.8f.; 3.12b; 3.17. Marcion: faith v. works: Adam. Dial. 2.6, 9, 'dia tēs pisteōs' (cf. Harnack, Marcion, 296*: 'tōn pisteuontōn patēr estin ho agathos' and Hist. Dogma, I, 268); Rhodo, in Eusebius, HE 5.13.7, 'mē epistasthai pōs heis estin agenētos Theos, touto de pisteuein'; Tert., AM 4.18.1ff. (exegesis of Lk 7.36-50); 5.13.2 ('ex fide legis in fidem evangelii').

(b) Eph: the opposition between the God of love and the power ruling the world: 1.21; 2.2; 2.4; 2.14f.; 3.9ff.; 6.10ff.; 2.16b; 3.5b. Marcion: the opposition between the God of love and world-maker: Tert., AM 2.28.2; 1.2.1f.; 1.5.1; 1.6.2; 1.11.9; 2.12.1; 2.29.3f.; 3.15.3; 4.1.11; 4.6.3; 4.14.8; 5.11.9; 5.18.3ff.; Iren., Haer. 1.27.2; 3.6.5; 3.12.12; 3.25.3; 4.33.2.

(c) Eph: revelation as enlightenment and a mystery recently disclosed: 1.9; 1.17; 3.3; 3.5; 3.9f.; 5.13f. Marcion: revelation as a mystery, recently disclosed: Tert., AM 1.11.9f; 1.17.4; 1.18.2; 1.19.1f.; 1.22.5ff.; 2.2.1; 3.4.1; 3.19.7; 4.5.3; 4.16.13f.; 4.19.5; 4.25.1; 4.25.10f.; 4.33.7; 5.11.10 [evangelium dei ignoti].

(d) Eph: the 'richness' of God's love and mercy: 1.6-7; 2.4; 3.7, 8b; 2.5b; 3.16f., 19; 4.2, 15. Marcion: God's love and mercy as a gift: Tert., AM 1.17.1f.; 1.19.1; 1.24.7; 1.25; 1.26.1f.; 2.17.1; 3.24.1; 4.8.7; 4.16.7; 5.4.14; 5.11.2-3; Iren., Haer. 3.25.2; 4.33.2.

(e) Eph: the ignorance of men and the Creator before revelation: 1.17; 2.3; 3.5; 3.9; 4.17-19; 5.8f. Marcion: Ignorance of men/alien God: Tert., AM 1.9.1-2f.; 1.10; 2.5.2; 2.24.2; 2.28.1; 2.6.8; 4.6.3f.; 4.20.4f. (cf. Eph 6.10f.); 5.6.5ff.; 5.18; Iren., Haer. 3.12.7; 4.34.3 [ignorance of the apostles].

(f) Eph: man's relation to the 'God of judgment': 2.2-4; 6.12f.; 4.14a; 4.22; 5.6b. Marcion: man's relation to the Creator (The righteousness and malitia of the Creator): Tert., AM 1.27.3; 2.6.1; 2.7.3;

2.9.1; 2.10.1f.; 2.13.3 (Horremus terribiles minas creatoris); 2.14.2; 2.21.1f.; 2.23-24; 2.27-28; 4.15.5f.; 4.33.4; 4.34.11; 5.7.11; 5.15.1; Iren., Haer. 4.29.1; 4.30.1.

(g) Eph: his condition as 'stranger' to the God of mercy and love;4 2.3; 2.11f., 13, 17, 19; 4.18 (cf. 'i'). Marcion: man as alien to God: Tert., AM 1.11.1; 1.23.5ff.; 4.16.11; Iren., Haer. 4.33.2; cf. 5.14.2, 3; 5.17.1; 5.26.2.

(h) Eph: man's condition after revelation: 5.8ff.; 4.23f.; 5.15; 4.14a (cf. 'i'). Marcion: man after revelation: Tert., AM 5.13.2; 1.17.1.

(i) Eph: salvation as 'appropriation': the christian as 'new creation' in Christ: 2.10; 2.15f.; 2.16f.; 3.16f.; 3.11; 3.20; 4.22f.; 1.5b; 4.24b. Marcion: the alien God's appropriation of the Creator's property: Tert., AM 2.28.2; 1.23.8; 3.4.3; 4.25.8; 4.39.17; 5.6.11; Iren., Haer. 4.30.3; 4.33.2; cf. 5.18.1; Origen, contra Cels. 6.53.

(j) Eph: Christ as God's disposition of mercy towards strangers: 1.4; 1.20; 3.16; 3.18-19; 2.13ff. Marcion: Christ as God's love: Tert., AM 1.19.1f.; 4.16.11 ('Quis enim poterit diligere extraneos?'); 1.23.1ff.

(k) Eph: the syzygy of Christ and the Church: 2.19ff.; 1.22f.; 2.16; 3.6; 4.15f.; 4.25b; 1.10; 5.29-30, 32. Marcion: Christ and the Church: Tert., AM 3.23.7; 4.5.3.

(l) Eph: moral ascesis and morality without the law; 2.15; 4.2; 4.25-30; 5.3-6; 5.15-20, 21, 24; 6.1-4, 5ff. Marcion: morality: Tert., AM 1.14 (Prohibition of food, etc. [Rom 14.21]); 1.28.4; 1.29; 4.11.8f.; 5.7.6; Hippol. Ref. omn. haer. 7.18; 10.15.

(m) Eph: the Gospel: 1.13; 3.4; 6.15; 3.9; 6.19b; 3.6. Marcion: Gospel: Tert., AM 1.19.4f.; 1.20.1; 1.21.5; 4.5; 4.6; 5.2.5 [evangelium dei novi]; 5.11.10.

(n) Eph: the faithfulness of the church: 1.1 (cf. Col 4.13, 16; 2.1); and Paul's care: 1.15; 4.16; 4.20f.; 2.19b. Marcion: faith of the church: Marcionite Prologue to Laodiceans.

(o) Eph: Paul, as the guardian of God's grace and his special insight into the 'mystery of Christ': 3.2f.; 3.4f.; 3.7ff. Marcion: Paul: Tert., AM 1.15.1; 3.14.4; 4.2-4; 5.1; Iren., Haer. 3.13.1 (cf. Eph 3.3); Origen, in Luc. hom. 25.

(p) Eph: baptism as the seal of purity: 5.26; 1.13b (as liturgical formula); 2.13b; 1.7. Marcion: baptism: Tert., AM 1.23.9; 1.29.1ff.

(q) Eph: cosmology: 1.20ff.; 2.2; 4.9f.; 6.12. Marcion: cosmology: Tert., AM 1.15; 1.16; 4.7; 4.26.12 ('vel sic potuisset videri

superasse validior ille deus Marcionis'); 4.29.16f. ('qui deum iudicem iustum
destruebat?'); 4.36.11 ('Ab illo deo descendisse Iesum ad deiectionem
creatoris . . .'); 5.16.2 ('nolente Marcione, crematoris dei Christus . . .');
5.18.11f./148/

---

/148/ The following passages, briefly annotated, suggest themselves as the
likeliest candidates as orthodox additions to Laod. But it should be stressed
that the criteria are not sufficient to establish them as part of a general
process of orthodox 'correction'. They remain in the context of Marcion's
expressed religious views anomalies only: 1.7a (forgiveness of trespasses);
2.1 (trespasses and sins) (cf. 2.5 [!]; 1.7; 2.13b, redemption by blood: cf.
Rev 1.5b); 2.10b (cf. 2.9b) (works); 2.20 ('foundation by apostles and
prophets'): tampered with according to Tert. AM 5.17.16; but it is curious
that Marcion would have acknowledged the 'apostles' while omitting only
'prophets'. As Tert.'s knowledge may be second-hand (i.e., as his source
may have cited only the omission), a more plausible solution is that the
original reading corresponded to 1 Cor 3.10-15, and Marcion could not be
expected to alter Paul's statement there: rather, the addition of apostles
points to the 'Ephesian' phase in the development of the epistle (cf. Ign. Eph
11.2; 2 Ptr 3.2) while the inclusion of 'prophets' is an anti-marcionite
interpolation. 3.14-15 (God as the author of fatherhood). 3.9b (God who
created all things; cf. AM 5.18.4f). Following Eph 4.1 the anomalies
become more extensive: 4.4-8 (v. 7f. seems to follow from an entirely
different premise); 'One Lord, one faith, one baptism, one God and father
of us all' (directed at Marcion's ditheism and double-christology; conceivably
also at his sacramental practice); 4.4ff. is not a 'recapitulation of the
argument of chs. 1-3' (Furnish, ICB, 841b). A trace of the original idea
may occur in Col 3.14-16 (= Eph 4.15, 'deceivers', which plausibly connects
to 4.1-3). 4.11-14 may be an interpolation; cf. 1 Jn 3.7; 4.14f. + 5.6f.,
certainly presupposes a heretical aporia, but may as easily have originated
within the marcionite community as outside it (cf. Col 2.8f.). 4.24: 'true
righteousness' -- a designation which Marcion is known to have applied to the
Creator (AM 4.33.4); 4.30 (offending the Spirit of God: Marcion's God could
not be offended: AM 5.5.4; 5.4.14) and the following vv. concerning
Christ's forgiveness (4.32). The formula 'ho Theos en Christō' is more
sophisticated than any christological formula in the epistle (cf. 2.17f), and
the form of address in 5.1 (tekna agapēta), together with the emphasis on
the 'love of Christ' and his death as sacrifice to God shows affinities with 1
Jn 2.1. But these affinities do not disqualify the passages if we assume that
Marcion had been a member of the School from which the concepts came,
and the 'love of Christ' is certainly a theme of Marcion's theology (cf. 1 Jn
2.1: teknia; 4.1 agapētoi; 1 Jn 2.28; 3.2, 7; 5.1, etc.; sacrifice, 1 Jn 2.2;
4.10; forgiveness, 1 Jn 2.12; 1.7b). So too Eph 5.6ff. (the children of light
and darkness, cf. 1 Jn 2.10-11), were the ethical implications are worked
out in terms of apocalyptic thought (1 Jn 2.18; 2 Tim 3.1ff.). One need not
look to Qumran for this motif (cf. 2 Thess 2.1ff.). Cf. further, Eph 5.13 /
1 Jn 2.8b (!); Eph 5.15 also bears the traces of being a johannine
interpolation (cf. 1 Jn 2.18f.), but the apocalyptic theme is not developed,
and the ethical résumé continues in v. 18 (Marcionite). Eph 6.2: a doublet
of 6.1, concerning filial duty; cf. Col 3.20. 6.10-19 seems in the main
Marcion's recasting of familiar OT themes. The idea that the vv. could not
have come from Marcion because such themes are employed is uninformed:
Marcion's use and understanding of the OT presupposes such a reevaluation,

We must also take note of the following 'negative factors' or 'missing motifs', bearing on the evaluation of this epistle: (a) Just as the epistle lacks the tone of 1 Thess 2.14ff., its pro-Jewish tenor does not involve a positive assessment of the law and prophets: 'the law of commandments' has been broken down, and is a dead issue for the 'new man', who is neither Jew nor gentile. Israel belongs to the (new) covenant of promise (cf. Rom 11.7) and stands first in the 'wisdom and knowledge of revelation' (Eph 1.17bf., 9; 3.4f. v. Rom 11.8) which is being extended outward to incorporate the gentiles in the habitation of God (2.22; 2.12, 18f.; 3.9). But God does not make this promise through the prophets. Rather, it is hidden from the God of this world (3.9; cf. 1 Cor 2.7), and the Epistle wants any appeal to the OT as a provocation to faith, such as we find in Rom 9-11. (b) The epistle lacks any authentic interest in the eschatological hope of the community (but cf. 5.14-15; 2 Tim 3.1f.). The ongoing life of the church is summarized in the attempt to create the 'new man in Christ' (4.12f., 24). This 'de-eschatologizing' of Paul's thought (cf. Col 3.4) comports with Marcion's failure to develop the theme of a second-coming/149/ For the author of Eph, the operation of God is in the past: its realization is accomplished in the spread of the gospel (cf. Eph 2.15; Col 2.14-15; Eph 3.10)./150/ (c) Eph/Laod. for all its apocalyptic terminology does not belong to the same thematic matrix as the johannine literature, and may even mark a self-conscious modification of it./151/ (d) Whereas Paul enjoins believers to, 'cast off the works of darkness and put on the armor of light'

---

and the structure of the Antitheses depended on it. Parallels with 1 Jn (2.13b, 14b) can be discerned (cf. Eph 6.16; and further: 1 Jn 3.8b; 4.4b; 5.4f.; 5.18f.). But the similarities are not decisive in the last case (6.10ff.), since we might expect Marcion and John to have shared a common conceptual and even linguistic universe (cf. 1 Ptr 2-3). Generally, with respect to chs. 5-6, the originally brief ethical discourse has been enlarged in line with the 'Ephesian' theology, represented graphically in 1 Jn (and cf. Eph 5.3; Rev 21.8). The brief allusion to the end-time (5.16, pars., 2 Thess 2.3f.; 2 Tim 4.3f) is otherwise foreign to the epistle, and may constitute no reference at all.

/149/ Cf. 1 Cor 11.26; 7.26; 7.29-31. Phil 3.20; 1 Thess 1.10; 3.13b; 4.15f.; 5.2; and Heb 9.27 (!); Jas 5.7-8; 2 Ptr 3.1-4; 3.5-14; 1 Ptr 1.7b; 4.7; 4.13.

/150/ Cf. AM 1.17.1; further, 5.16.1f. where Marcion stands accused of crossing out 2 Thess 8. The future action of (the good) God pertains to the Creator and the Creator's Christ (3.23.6; 3.24.1f.).

/151/ But cf. Köster, Trajectories, 154f.; Käsemann, 'Apocalypticism', JTC 6 (1969).

(Rom 13.12), the author of <u>Laod</u>. declares, 'you are in the light. . . act
like children of the light' (Eph 5.8b)./152/ The darkness that clouds the
mind (1 Cor 4.5) is declared a thing of the past in Eph (5.8a; cf. Eph 1.22;
Phil 3.20-21). (e) So, too, there is no reference to judgment by the agency
of Christ, or indeed to the judgment of God, in Eph (cf. 2 Cor 5.10; Rom
14.9): Jesus is the means by which God appropriates mankind to himself
(Eph 1.5b) and eliminates the natural ('fleshly') impediments to sonship (Eph
2.14; cf. Phil 3.21). Christ (1.6) is the manifestation of God's disposition
of mercy and love (2.4; 4.32b; 1.7f.; 2.7; 3.19; 5.2[?]); the means by which
the mystery of divine love is revealed to man (1.9; 1.17; 1.20; 3.4); the
model of salvation (2.5-6; 2.10; 4.15); and the original of the 'new man'
(4.24 v. 1 Cor 15.45f.). (f) The significance of the death on the cross is not
broached but it is envisaged as having had cosmic effects (Eph 1.20-22;
2.13-15); the author addresses himself (cf. Col 2.13ff.) specifically to what
God in Christ has done for mankind. We find no christological formula such
as exists in Phil 2.6-8 (though 2.9 is echoed in Eph 1.20; 2.6) or Col 2.9 (cf.
Eph 1.23). Nonetheless, the christology of the epistle is summarized at
3.11-12: Christ is God's purpose and man's access, *'dia tēs pisteōs autou'*.
The christology of the epistle thus conforms to that which Marcion derived
from Paul's letters.

---

/152/ The echo here to the Qumran 'War Scroll' is faint: 'Lay thy hand on the
neck of thy enemies, and thy foot on the heaps of the slain, smite the
nations, thy adversaries and let thy sword consume guilty flesh': cf. Eph
6.13 (!). Still, on the assumption that Marcion's theology derives from
Jewish circles, it is far from impossible that he was engaged in a conscious
reworking of themes that were also dominant in Essene Judaism. Besides
the emphasis on moral rigor, one can also point to more specifically
theological parallels: the contest between God and Belair, for example; the
theme of false teaching (<u>Damasc</u>. doc., I) and the raising up of the unique
teacher (<u>ibid</u>., VIII); the hiding of the knowledge of salvation (<u>Damasc</u>.
<u>doc</u>., II), etc. The Qumran community also postulated two messiahs, one
priestly, the other political. This, so far as I can discover, is the clearest
parallel in all of ancient literature to Marcion's doctrine of two Christs.
Scarcely to be ignored is the fact that the marcionite <u>synagoge</u> of Lebaba,
dating from the fourth century, lay only three miles outside Damascus. One
cannot exclude the possibility that Marcion derived his doctrine of true and
false apostleship from the Qumran diaspora. Barrett suggests (<u>Essays</u>, 102)
that while no basis for the 'accusations and counter-accusations that occur in
the Pauline literature' can be found in rabbinic literature, 'there are closer
parallels in the Qumran literature, especially perhaps in the Habakkuk
pesher, which sets over against the teacher of righteousness one who is
variously described as the preacher of falsehood and the man of falsehood'.
The 'antithetical' structure of Marcion's paulinism may have its roots in this
intellectual environment.

## 8.8 Conclusion

Based on a close consideration of this evidence, it seems possible (if only possible) to conclude that the disciple of Paul responsible for the writing of the Epistle to the Laodiceans, no longer extant but still visible beneath the surface of the church redaction carried out in the Ephesian circle, was Marcion. The Epistle, on this reckoning, represents his attempt to summarize and to define the central themes in the Apostle's thought, but reflects a situation quite different from that which obtains in Paul's lifetime. Moreover we can provisionally conclude that Marcion stood at the center of the paulinist circle at Laodicea, and that it may well have been here that his final canon of Paul's letters took shape.

CHAPTER NINE

THE MARCIONITE ERROR IN THE 'PASTORAL EPISTLES'

**9.1 Introduction**

The pauline authorship of the Pastoral letters has been disputed since Schleiermacher in his Sendschreiben an J.C. Gess (1807) challenged the traditional view of 1 Tim on linguistic and historical grounds. Several years later (1812), J.G. Eichhorn applied Schleiermacher's judgment to all three letters; and in 1835 F.C. Baur demonstrated the links between the polemic of the Pastorals and the gnosis of the second century. Since the nineteenth century, the view has become widespread that pauline authorship of the Pastoral letters is impossible/1/ and reflects a historical situation that cannot be located in the Apostle's lifetime. We cannot linger over the persuasive linguistic evidence against pauline authorship. It is sufficient to note in passing that the vocabulary of the three letters (901 words) includes 306 not found in any other pauline epistle (33%), and 335 not found elsewhere in the NT. This percentage is considerably higher than that for any other deuteropauline letter./2/

---

/1/ The objections to Paul's authorship were first collected by Holtzmann, Die Pastorals, kritisch und exegetisch bearbeitet (1880); cf. O. Küss, Paulus (1971), 30f., 77; W. Bauer, Orothodoxy and Heresy (1971), 88f., 222f.; A.T. Hanson, Stud. in the Past. Eps. (1968); N. Brox, 'Zu den persönlichen Notizen der Past.' BZ, NF 13 (1969), 76f.; idem., 'Historische und theologische Probleme der Past.', Kairos, NF 11 (1969), 81; Hegermann, 'Der geschichtliches Ort den Past.', Theolog. Versuche 2 (1970), 47ff.; Hans v. Campenhausen, 'Polykarp von Smyrna und die Pastoralbriefe', in Aus der Frühzeit des Christentums (1963), 197ff. A number of scholars of whom the most representative are Harrison (The Problem of the Past. Eps., 1921) and Kelly (The Pastoral Eps., 1963) argue for Paul's authorship or the existence of authentic pauline fragments in the letters.

/2/ R. Grant, Historical Introd. to the NT (1963), 211; cf. Harrison, Paulines and Pastorals (1921). Harrison showed (a) that of the hapax legomena of the Pastorals which are not encountered in the rest of the NT, a larger percentage are (also) not found in the LXX than is the case with Paul; (b) that a significant number of these hapax legomena are not attested before the end of the first century (pp. 16ff.). Metzger ('A Reconsideration of Certain Arguments against the Pauline Auth. of the Pastoral Eps.', ExT 70 [1958-9], 91ff.) has objected that the Pastorals are too brief to support

As we have already noted, the Pastorals are first attested as being letters of Paul by Irenaeus; that is to say, they first appear on the scene in the heresiological literature of the late second century. They are similarly reported by Tertullian and the Muratorian Canon, /3/ by which point their use as weapons against heresy is well established. They do not feature in the Gospel of Truth, or in the third-century Codex P.46 (Chester Beatty Papyrus)/4/ and there exist no marcionite prologues for the letters to Timothy and Titus. The idea that linguistic similarities between the Pastorals and the letters of Ignatius and Polycarp indicate their dependence on the Epistles has generally given way to the theory that they all stand in the same cultural tradition/5/ and suggestions, which must figure in our consideration, that Polycarp/6/ or 'Luke'/7/ wrote the letters: 'One places the Pastorals, with the Letter of Polycarp, and the Epistles of John and Ignatius, in a row', contends von Campenhausen, 'and sees in these roughly contemporaneous documents a parallel development towards catholic religious thought, a development indeed which addressed the same problem'. /8/

---

conclusions based on word-statistics. R. Morgenthaler, Statistik des NT. Wortschatzes (1958), 28ff., 38. It has also been shown that the relation between the logarithms of vocabulary and length-of-text in the Pastorals varies markedly from the same relation in the letters of Paul as a whole (Grayston-Herdan, 'The Authorship of the Pastorals in the Light of Statistical Linguistics', NTS 6 [1959], 1ff.). According to Kümmel, 'The language and style speak decisively against the pauline origin of the Pastorals' (Intro. to the NT, 373).

/3/ v. Campenhausen, 'Polykarp von Smyrna', in Aus der Frühzeit, 200: 'Eindeutig erst bei Irenäus im Rahmen seines antihäretischen Hauptwerks, dessen Titel nach 1 Tim 6.20 gebildet ist, und bei Clemens von Alexandrien'. Kelly concludes that 'Marcion did not include them in his pauline corpus . . . because of his dislike for their anti-heretical tone' (Pastoral Eps. 4). In the Muratorian Canon, 60, they are mentioned directly before the rejection of the marcionite 'Epistle to the Laodiceans'.

/4/ The idea that the missing leaves of $P^{46}$ may have provided space for the Pastorals is obviously not an argument in favor of their antiquity.

/5/ Kümmel, Intro. to the NT, 370.

/6/ v. Campenhausen, 'Polykarp von Smyrna'; also, Goguel, Introd. NT 4/2 (1926), 555; Bauer, Orthodoxy and Heresy, 226: 'The Pastorals originate in the same circles of orthodoxy as Polycarp himself'.

/7/ Wilson, Luke and the Pastoral Eps., 1979.

/8/ v. Campenhausen, 'Polykarp von Smyrna', in Aus der Frühzeit, 197; cf. D.W. Riddle, Early Christian Life (1935), 195-216; Enslin, Christian Beginnings (1938), 306, n. 20; Knox, Philemon among the Letters of Paul², 74; Bauer, Orthodoxy and Heresy, 226.

Enlarging on Conzelmann's idea of a 'Lucan circle' in Ephesus after the Apostle's lifetime/9/ and proposals put forth in slightly different form by C.F.D. Moule/10/ and A. Strobel,/11/ S.G. Wilson has attempted to show the linguistic and stylistic similarities between Luke-Acts and the Pastorals,/12/ 'which in view of [their ] brevity. . .are remarkable'. But Wilson's further contention, that these similarities involve not only language but 'often identical ideas' is not borne out in his discussion of the evidence; and the stylistic argument (as Brox pointed out) is far from conclusive: One can point to a number of other documents that have closer affinities with the Pastorals:/13/ 2 Peter, 2 Thess, and Polycarp's Letter to the Philippians being the most obvious examples. Quinn has recently suggested that 'Luke' 'edited' the Pastorals and that they were published as the third volume of Luke-Acts./14/ But Quinn's monograph, like Wilson's, does not explore the relationship between Polycarp and 'Luke', or envisage a common life-situation for the Pastorals and Polycarp's Letter to the Philippians. Nonetheless, if the relation between the 'Pastor', 'Luke', and Polycarp must remain fugitive in our analysis, this need not be true of the identity of the heretic or the heresy envisaged in the letters. Moreover, if we accept Knox's contention that Luke-Acts was designed 'To reclaim Paul for orthodoxy', then we should not be surprised to find many hands at work on these pseudonymous epistles of Paul and a decision as to whether the letters were the work of Polycarp, 'Luke' or yet another member of the Ephesian circle is less critical than the recognition that the claimants of Paul's

---

/9/ Conzelmann, 'Luke's Place in the Development of Early Christianity', in Studies in Luke-Acts, ed. Keck & Martin (1968), 298-316.

/10/ Moule, 'The Problem of the Pastoral Eps.: A Reappraisal', BJRL 47 (1965), 430-52. Moule however argues that Luke wrote the epistles during Paul's lifetime, and 'at Paul's behest'.

/11/ Strobel, 'Schreiben des Lukas?: Zum sprachlichen Problem der Pastoralbriefe', NTS 15 (1969), 191-210; refuted by Brox, 'Lukas als Verfasser der Pastoralbriefe', JAC 13 (1970), 62-77.

/12/ Wilson, Luke and the Pastoral Eps., 136.

/13/ E.M. Sidebottom, James, Jude, and 2 Ptr (1967), 97ff.

/14/ Quinn, 'P$^{46}$: The Pauline Canon?', CBQ 36 (1974), 379-85, 385 n. 36; cf. 'The Last Volume of Luke: The Relation of Luke-Acts to the Pastoral Eps.', in C.H. Talbert, Perspectives on Luke-Acts (1978).

authority were treading on common ground.

That this lucan 'school' developed in or near Ephesus, perhaps as an offshoot of the pauline school that was destined to recede (or be displaced?) in the wake of the johannine theology, seems probable. The postulation of 'schools' of various denominations takes us beyond the historical evidence, however. As von Campenhausen points out, we have a firm grip on only one historical personage, namely Polycarp himself./15/ What is more, we have persuasive evidence (a) that Polycarp was a contemporary of Marcion, and that he knew of Marcion's success in Asia Minor; (b) that he was associated 'with John and others of those who had seen the Lord'; and (c) that he presided over a christian community less than forty miles to the north of Ephesus and a hundred miles to the northwest of the 'heretical' churches of Laodicea and Colossae. Moreover, in writing to the church at Philippi, across the Aegean (c. 115) Polycarp evidences a knowledge of Marcion's error which clearly echoes the language of 1 John (4.2; cf. Phil 2.7f.) and 2 John 7, themselves concerned to refute a christological error. (d) Polycarp complains that the heretics are claiming Paul's 'wisdom' as their own (3.2) and (what is perhaps decisive) envisages Marcion's doctrine of false apostleship (9.2). If it is the case that the Pastorals form a 'third' section of Luke-Acts, itself conceivably an anti-marcionite offering from johannine circles in Ephesus, then we must contend with the idea that the 'problem' which unifies this literature -- namely the heresy of Marcion -- also points in the direction of Polycarp as the likeliest author. Nor does it seem improbable that the altercation between John and Marcion, known to the author of the anti-marcionite Prologue to the Fourth Gospel, is behind Polycarp's warning. That is to say, it was Marcion's error to revive an archaic form of paulinism along specifically ditheistic lines that led to his expulsion from a circle that included at least 'John', Aristion, Polycarp, and Papias besides./16/ It is also possible that Ignatius was a member of the

/15/ v. Campenhausen, 'Polykarp von Smyrna', in Aus des Frühzeit, 198f.

/16/ Iren. Haer. 5.32.4; Eus. HE 3.39.14. This leaves open for the moment the identity of 'Luke', but also opens the possibility that canonical Lk was a collective literary effort on the part of the Ephesian community designed to remedy the situation created by the publication of the marcionite Urevangelium, which they had originally shared. Irenaeus calls Papias a companion of Polycarp and according to Eus.: '[Papias] quotes other interpretations of the words of the Lord given by Aristion . . . and traditions of John the Presbyter' (HE 3.39.14).

circle at an advanced stage in its existence./17/

The extent to which the thought of Paul was programmatic for the theological work of this community is uncertain; but it is at least arguable that the introduction of paulinist ideas stands behind what Käsemann and Robinson have termed the 'gnostic-docetic' trajectory in the Fourth Gospel./18/ However this may be, the 'school' seems to have become fragmented early on over the extent to which the Apostle's thought could be brought into line with the changing spiritual and political requirements of the larger christian community (2 Ptr 3.16)./19/

Marcion's solution, clearly the most radical, if also the truest to the substance of Paul's thought, was unacceptable here. The hearing for his version of Paul's gospel came not at Ephesus, but at Laodicea (arguably at Colossae and Thyatira as well) where the epistolary summary of the Apostle's thought ('Laodiceans') was carried out, the Antitheses framed, and the gospel (which he may have learned at Ephesus from 'Luke') edited (pp. 260f.). The literary activity at Smyrna and Ephesus can thus be seen as a reaction to Marcionism. This is consistent with what we have said concerning the 'anti-marcionite' additions to the Urlukas, and to the publication of the 'Acts' of the Apostles where the memory of Paul's difficulties in Ephesus has been obscured, but not erased. Since it is probable that Polycarp and others in the Ephesian circle were well acquainted with marcionite polemic against the apostles (Phil. 9.2) and with their exclusive claim to Paul/20/ as the authority for their gospel, it appears likely that the heresy combatted from Ephesus, after Marcion's expulsion or departure from that city is his radical interpretation of the letters he had collected during his travels. We can only conjecture that the lost works of

---

/17/ Cf. Cullmann, The Johannine Circle, 119, n. 3; C. Maurer, Ignatius von Antiochien und das Johannesevangilium (1949), and H. Köster, 'Gesch. und Kultur im Johannesevangelium und bei Ign.', ZTK 54 (1957), 56ff. See further, Brown, Community, 103ff.

/18/ Cited in Cullmann, The Johannine Circle (1973), 58. Cullmann detects an anti-gnostic emphasis in the johannine literature; but he does not comment on a possible relationship between Paul and the circle. Cf. Robinson, 'The Johannine Trajectory', in Trajectories (1971), 266.

/19/ 2 Ptr: c. 130-140. So Käsemann, ZTK (1952), 272. If this late date is accepted, then the epistle may well acknowledge the difficulty in the 'domesticating' of Paul's theology. Cf. Brown, Community, 99ff.

/20/ Polyc. Phil. 3.2.

Justin and Theophilus of Antioch preserved the memory of Marcion's successes in the region.

Moreover, if we take Justin's Dialogue with Trypho (c. 140) and the Epistle of Barnabas (c. 130) to exemplify the apologetic of christian teachers 'against the false position of the Jews', then it can hardly be maintained that the conciliatory paulinism of the Epistle to the Laodiceans is typical of the churches recognized by Ephesus as 'orthodox'./21/ Neither 'John' nor Justin nor 'Barnabas' invokes Paul's memory, despite the ascription of an epistle to a companion of the Apostle. On the other hand, if we regard such paulinism as the 'Epistle from Laodicea' embodies as going against the grain of the anti-Jewish stance taken in the Ephesian community,/22/ resulting, as it were, in a conspiracy of silence against the Apostle, then we find it possible to explain the need for such 'pastoral' advice as the letters to Timothy and Titus contain. Together with 'Luke' they establish a 'companion tradition' through which the radical paulinism of Laodicea can be combatted: The heretical interpreters of Paul were given to consider a body of literature which not only contravened their version of the Apostle's teaching, but purported to come from his most trusted associates. Though the epistle ascribed to Barnabas stands (technically)

---

/21/ Cf. Clement, Strom. 2.6, 7; Origen, contra Cels. I.63; Com. in Rom. 1.24.

/22/ If we identify the Ephesian community with the johannine circle on Cullmann's terms, then we are required to see heretical ('Jewish') Christianity or 'heterodox' Judaism as one of the informing elements of the johannine literature. Cullman calls attention to the tradition preserved in the pseudo-Clementines as indicative of the structure of this non-conformist Judaism: 'The milieu of the gospel is to be seen as a Judaism influenced by syncretism in the area of Palestine and Syria. The homeground of the johannine circle is to be sought here' (The Johannine Circle, 38). On redaction-critical grounds, Cullmann discerns a development beginning in heterodox Judaism, including in the course of its progression, (a) the disciples of the Baptist; (b) a circle of disciples of John; (c) a special hellenist group in the early community in Jerusalem; and (d) a johannine community or circle responsible for the Fourth Gospel and the Epistles written under John's name (86ff.). The anti-semitisms of the literature are explained thus as the response of an originally marginal Judaism to 'official' Judaism. Cullmann's hypothesis suffers from its own ingenuity: his attention to internal, redaction-critical matters has caused him to overlook the compelling historical evidence that bear on the case. The dispute over the theology of Paul, for example, is not mentioned. See Köster, 'Gnomai Diaphoroi', in Trajectories, 114ff., and Robinson, in ibid., 232f. The neglect of Paul is an especially regrettable omission, since the existence of a johannine circle must be tied to the evidence for a pre-pauline Christianity in Ephesus (Acts 19) claiming the baptism of John.

outside this corpus, it belongs nonetheless to the orthodox tradition of enlisting the Apostle and the Apostle's companions in the fight against the heretics. As Bauer has commented:

> [The Pastoral Epistles are to be seen] as an attempt on the part of the church unambiguously to enlist Paul as part of its anti-heretical front and to eliminate the lack of confidence in him in ecclesiastical circles. As its answer to the heretical Apostle of the epistles to Laodicea and Alexandria 'forged in the name of Paul' ['Paulae nomine finctae': Mur. Can. 64f.] the church raised up the Paul of orthodoxy by using the same means./23/

## 9.2 The 'Jewish Error' in the Pastorals in the Light of Marcion's Theology

It is clear that Justin, 'Barnabas', and the authors of Luke-Acts and the Pastorals are of one voice in saying that any form of Christianity not based on the typological interpretation of the OT amounts to Jewish error,/24/ whatever else the 'Jewish' error may consist in. This point should be stressed, since it is often assumed, on the premise that Marcion's heresy was 'anti-Jewish', that references to nomodidaskaloi (1 Tim 1.7) and Ioudaikoi mythoi (Titus 1.14) rule out the possibility that the error proscribed in Paul's name belongs to Marcion. Kelly's opinion may be taken as typifying this view: 'The daring identification [of the heresy as Marcion's] has little, if anything to recommend it . . . . [He] was violently anti-Jewish, whereas the error of the heretics is a distinctly Jewish form of gnōsis. More generally, there is nothing to show that they professed any of Marcion's characteristic doctrines'./25/

As we have observed, however (p. 228), Marcion was known by his opponents to have 'formed an alliance with the Jewish error', in respect of refusing the allegorical interpretation of scripture, and his literal reading of the prophecies led him to embrace the view that the messiah-redeemer of Israel had not yet come (cf. Rom 11.26). This feature of his thought must

---

/23/ Bauer, Orthodoxy and Heresy, 226.

/24/ E.g.: Eps. Barnabas, 1.7; 4.7; 7.1; Justin, Tryph. 7, 11, 12, 44, etc.; 1 Tim 1.7; 2 Tim 3.8a, 16a; Titus 1.10b, 14; 3.9b. Goodspeed (Hist. Early Christian Lit. [1966], 102) remarks that 'Justin's contention that the Jewish prophecies are fulfilled in Christ is so contrary to the position taken by Marcion in the Antitheses, that the Dialogue may be taken as a counterblast against Marcion's book'.

/25/ Kelly, Pastoral Eps. 151f.

have been known in orthodox circles in Ephesus, since it is condemned already in Justin's first Apology. The 'Jewish myth' referred to in the Epistle to Titus may therefore be evidence in favor of seeing Marcion as the false teacher envisaged in the letter, and certainly cannot be taken as proof against the idea.

So too, the reference to 'legalists' or 'law-teachers' mentioned in 1 Tim (1.7a) may be no more than an allusion to the moral rigorism of the Marcionites, or so the ethical discourse in ch. 4 would lead us to believe. The dietary and purifactory laws of the Marcionites are well attested, and not easily distinguishable from the Jewish practices which the 'orthodox' Paul was known to have rejected (Rom 14.3: unattested by Marcion; cf. Eph 2.15; Col 2.14). Irenaeus makes Marcion the spiritual father of the Encratites (Haer. 1.28.1), and thus establishes by the association a Jewish provenance for the ascesis of the Marcionites./26/ A similar confusion characterizes the attitude toward the law in Col 2.16f. (v. Col 3.5f.). Col 2.8 ('kata tēn paradosin tōn anthrōpōn'; cf. Eph 5.6a) corresponds closely to the entolais anthrōpōn in Titus 1.14b, where the 'commandments' are assigned specifically to 'men who pervert the truth' (cf. Polyc. Phil. 7.1). The Pastor does not envisage the law precisely in the sense of Mosaic legislation. In 1 Tim 1.5 he speaks of the end of the 'command' (parangelia) and not of nomos; and even when he resorts to the use of the word nomos (1 Tim 1.8) in explicating the 'use' of the law (chreia), he adopts a most unpauline stance (cf. Rom 7.12ff.; 8.4f.; Gal 3.19, 21-25). For the Pastor, the law is designed not to 'lead into sin', but to prevent the disobedience and sinfulness of those who 'oppose sound doctrine' (1 Tim 1.10b; cf. 2 Thess 3.6, 14)./27/

---

/26/ Cf. Blond, RSR 31 (1944), 159-210.

/27/ Wilson notes: the Pastor understands the law 'pragmatically' rather than 'speculatively': 'the purpose of the law is seen to be prescriptive and concerned primarily with piety and ethics, which for the Pastor are virtually indistinguishable. The law's function is as a guide to morals' (Luke and the Pastoral Eps., 91f.). Wilson points out further that the notion that the law is good is 'thoroughly pauline' while the idea that its goodness lies in the restraint of evildoers is not. Clearly the Pastor's position toward the law is closely tied up to the restraint of heretics, the primary evildoers. Implicit in this connection is a differentiation of the law: those 'claiming to be law-teachers' are not necessarily teaching the Jewish law, but an interpretation of the law which differs from that envisaged in the epistle.

In short, the 'law-teachers' about whom the Pastor complains are teaching a different and conceivably more paulinist line concerning the law than he himself proposes when he counsels, 'The law is good if anyone use it lawfully [nomimōs], understanding that the law . . . [is laid down] for the lawless and disobedient [anomois de kai anupotaktois]' (1 Tim 1.8f.)./28/ Wilson suggests that the Pastor's knowledge of Paul may have come from phrases learned by oral tradition, but that 'he did not fully understand the way Paul would have used [them]'/29/ and Scott remarks that 'in his effort to repeat Paul's criticism of the law the writer has laid himself open to his own stricture on the false teachers', that 'they do not understand the things on which they insist'./30/ But it might also be the case that the Pastor's view of the law is put forward as a deliberate recasting of Paul's teaching, and conceivably as a response to a heretical teaching of the law -- such as Marcion's -- which preserves its speculative (antithetical) value, while at the same time rejecting its pragmatic use. We have no reason to believe that the Pastor's discussion in 1 Tim 1.6ff. is based on a näive misunderstanding of Paul's attitude, since in so doing we must also assume that the Pastor intended to represent, summarize, or repeat Paul's view, and this is clearly not the case.

Neither the allusion to those aspiring to be law-teachers nor the reference to 'Jewish myths', thus interpreted, is sufficient to exclude Marcionism as the heresy envisaged in these letters. On the contrary, the references may well point in Marcion's direction. We need only imagine a 'teaching of the law' corresponding to Gal 5.18ff. (cf. Rom 8.2f.; 1 Cor 6.12a; 2 Cor 3.6b), understood (on Paul's terms) by the heretic as that which

---

/28/ Cf. Moule, 'The Problem of the Pastoral Eps.', BJRL 47 (1965), 432: 'In what a different world of thought this stands from the noble Pauline conception of the law as . . . liable to abuse precisely when it is used lawfully'.

/29/ Wilson, Luke and the Pastoral Eps., 92.

/30/ E.F. Scott, The Pastoral Eps. (1936), 11. Wilson (p. 30) observes that the term nomodidaskaloi occurs elsewhere in the NT only in Lk 5.17 and Acts 5.34, there referring without pejorative intent to Jewish experts in expounding the law. But this meaning does not fit the context of 1 Tim 1.7, because of the participial phrase thelontes einai -- i.e., the persons in question 'aspiring' to be law-teachers. Cf. Kelly: 'The errorists are Judaisers who concentrate on the far-fetched minutiae of rabbinical exegesis to the detriment of the gospel'. This certainly takes us beyond the epistle. Kelly finds the Pastor's approach to the law fully in line with that expounded in Rom 7.7-25 and Gal 5.13-26 (p. 45).

leads into sin. Likewise, we need only assume that the 'fables' and 'Jewish myths' put about by the heretics are related to Marcion's 'alliance with the Jewish error'; that is, his adherence to the historical value of OT prophecy, including a belief in the restoration of the kingdom. What is more is the fact that among known heretics, Marcion alone seems to have preached such a 'Jewish fable',/31/ or as Tertullian puts it, to have 'shared half the error of the Jews'./32/ If therefore we are to imagine the heresy proscribed in the Pastorals as stemming from christian circles, an obvious choice is the marcionite-paulinist community in Laodicea.

## 9.3 Marcionite Motifs in the Pastoral Epistles

If Marcion cannot be excluded as the heretic described by the Pastor on the reckoning that 'he was violently anti-Jewish',/33/ do the Pastoral letters provide compelling evidence that the error is his? We must look for the answer to this question to the letters themselves.

We may begin with a general characterization of the heresy envisaged in the Epistles. 'Paul' addresses Timothy as his 'true child in the faith', using the intimate form teknon to underline the relationship of trust and confidence./34/ The writer mentions having left Timothy in Ephesus for the purpose of ensuring that certain persons there 'teach no other doctrine, nor give their minds over to myths and endless genealogies which promote speculation' (1 Tim 1.3f.; cf. Titus 3.9). Apparently the error is a stubborn one, since the author imagines Paul's intention to return to Ephesus shortly (1 Tim 3.14; 4.13). Meanwhile, he charges Timothy to keep to the 'sound teaching' that he has personally received from Paul at Ephesus (2 Tim 3.10; 1 Tim 1.10; Titus 2.1, 8; cf. 2 Tim 1.13; 4.3). It is said that Timothy has kept close to the Apostle's faith ('tēn parathēkēn phylaxon, ektrepomenos tas bebēlous kenophōnias kai antitheseis tēs pseudōnymou gnōseōs, hēn tines epangellomenoi peri tēn pistin ēstochēsan': 1 Tim 6.20).

---

/31/ Cf. AM 3.21.1; 3.23.1; 3.6.1f.; 3.7.1f.; 3.8.1f.

/32/ AM 3.16.3.

/33/ Kelly, Pastoral Eps. 151.

/34/ Kelly, Pastoral Eps. 40; cf. Acts 16.1ff.; 1 Thess 3.2; 1 Cor 4.17; Rom 16.21.

This caption does not really tell us very much about the substance of the heresy in question, and gives only a rough idea of its provenance. The scattered references to 'myths', 'genealogies', 'babblings', 'unlearned questions', and 'so-called knowledge' are polemical conventions and do not add up to a heresy of a certain genre./35/ Likewise, there is no more reason to think that the reference to 'opposing tenets' (= antitheses) in 1 Tim 6.20b is a veiled allusion to Marcion's work of that name than a more general indictment of the false doctrine; that is to say, tenets opposed to the sound teaching advocated by the writer of the epistle (cf. Titus 2.8)./36/ The conclusion that a 'Jewish-gnostic' heresy is imagined is uninformative:/37/ from what quarter does it come? How does it relate to the christian community in Ephesus, understood by the writer to be free from the law (1 Tim 1.7)? What 'Jewish' heresy can we point to in the primitive church which 'denied the power of God' (2 Tim 3.5), ordered the 'corruption of families' (Titus 1.11; 1 Tim 4.3ff.; 2 Tim 3.2; cf. 1 Tim 5.11ff.), or granted women prerogatives over men (1 Tim 2.11f.)? We have already noted that the case for a 'Jewish' heresy cannot be supported on the basis of Titus 1.14, since the myth can as easily be explained as affirmation of the Jewish belief that the Messiah of the Jews had not yet come -- that is, as an article of marcionite teaching. And if the reference following can be associated with the mention of those 'who desire to be teachers of the Law' (1 Tim 1.7), then it is fairly clear that the law in these instances is not the Jewish law but the 'commandments of men' who advocate certain practices which the Pastor derides as being 'Jewish' (cf. Rev 3.9). Moreover, is it possible to imagine a 'Jewish'-(gnostic) heresy making inroads among the gentile-christian population of Ephesus, in view of the hostility between Jews and gentiles in that city, and the memory of Paul's troubles there?/38/

On the basis of the situation which the writer's admonitions presuppose, we can gather (a) that the Ephesian church, as whose spokesman the

---

/35/ Cf. R.J. Karris, 'The Background and Significance of the Polemic of the Pastoral Epistles', JBL 92 (1973).

/36/ Bauer, Orthodoxy and Heresy, 226.

/37/ Wilson, Gnosis and the NT (1968), 43.

/38/ The memory of Paul's failure in Ephesus is also preserved by the author of a coptic fragment belonging to the genre of the Acts of Paul; cf. RHPhR (1960), 45ff. NTA II, 387.

author writes, knows of a heresy which is opposed to their interpretation of Paul's teaching. Ephesus has not yet been seriously affected by the false doctrine, since it still holds to a form of words which Paul has entrusted for safe keeping to Timothy (1 Tim 6.3; 6.20; 1.18, 11; Titus 3.10; cf. Rom 16.17; 2 Thess 3.6); (b) that the struggle to keep the faith is nonetheless intense: men of 'corrupt mind' threaten to steal the deposit. The danger looms geographically near to Ephesus/39/ since Paul's presence there is required (1 Tim 3.14). 'Paul' charges Timothy as his 'true son' (cf. Titus 1.4) to stand fast (1 Tim 1.8) and to 'fight the good fight of faith' (1 Tim 6.12) as a good soldier of Jesus Christ (2 Tim 2.3; cf. 4.5, 7). (c) While in the context of a pseudonymous epistle one should not expect to find the heresy captioned as a false paulinism,/40/ this can be inferred from the fact that Timothy and Titus are characterized as the legitimate heirs of Paul ('gnēsios', lit., the legitimate son; 1 Tim 1.2a; 2 Tim 1.2; Titus 1.4: 'kata koinēn pistin')./41/ It is therefore implicit that the contradictions mentioned by the author constitute an illegitimate form of Paul's gospel (cf. 2 Thess 2.2; 2.15), or point in the direction of a gospel being passed off by the heretics as coming from Paul himself. In short, the struggle is understood by the writer (who is perhaps acquainted with a pauline corpus)/42/ as a defense of the orthodox teaching of Paul, and not least of a church order which is thought to have its foundation in the Apostle's teaching. Put in its exaggerated form in the orthodox interpolation in the Epistle to the

---

/39/ Cf. Acts of John, 30. NTA II, 222.

/40/ Cf. Torm, Die Psychologie der Pseudonymität (1932); Aland, 'The Problem of Anonymity and Pseudonymity in Christian Literature of the First Two Centuries', JTS 12 (1961), 39ff.; and Wrede, ZNTW I (1900), 78, n. 1; Meyer, 'Religiöse Pseudepigraphie als ethischpsychologisches Problem', ZNTW 35 (1936), 262ff.; Schneemelcher, Apostolic Pseudepigrapha, NTA II, 88ff.

/41/ Kelly, Pastoral Eps. 40; but Kelly draws no conclusion from his observation.

/42/ So Campenhausen, 'Polykarp von Smyrna', Aus der Frühzeit, 210: 'Der Verfasser der Past. briefe fühlt sich als Pauliner'; but I cannot agree with Campenhausen that there is 'no other document that stands so near to Paul or brings the themes of his theology more perfectly to expression'. The themes here do not arise spontaneously, and in many ways the doctrines they attack stand substantially closer to Paul than the Pastorals themselves. On the Pastor's acquaintance with the pauline corpus, see A.E. Barnett, Paul Becomes a Literary Influence (1941), 25lf.; Spicq, Commentary (1966), 180f.; Harrison, Problem, 87ff.

Ephesians (2.20), this foundation is enlarged to include the apostles and prophets, but is not thought to include Paul! (d) The life-setting of the author is that of someone who is involved personally in the struggle with the heretics, and who feels himself able, on the basis of his acquaintance with Paul's teaching to address the church in Ephesus in the Apostle's name (cf. Polyc. Phil. 11.2; 3.2). This conclusion indirectly lends support to the idea that Polycarp was the author of the letters, despite, or even in view of his disclaimer in the letter to the church at Philippi: 'Oute gar egō oute allos homoios emoi dynatai katakolouthēsai tē sophia tou makariou kai endoxou Paulou' (Phil. 3.2). We cannot read Polycarp's warning as an oath that he would not attempt to counter the assaults of the false teachers by intro-ducing letters which he believed to reflect 'the word of truth, delivered accurately and steadfastly' to the churches.   The sentence testifies to Polycarp's intention; issuing letters in the name of the Apostle would only amount to a counter-claim corresponding to the 'false' claims advanced by the heretics./43/  Later claims were issued in an ultimately unacceptable form by the authors of the Acts of Paul/44/ and the apocryphal Epistle to Laodicea, which Harnack was mistakenly led to believe is 'the only complete writing which has been preserved to us from the Marcionite Church of earliest times'./45/  The author of 2 Thess (2.2b) knows of letters purporting to come from Paul, and has no qualms about condemning them by means of false letters of his own.

## 9.4 The Threat to Ephesus

Leaving aside the rhetorical aspersions which the writer directs at the counter-claimants -- including in this category the 'prophecy' in 2 Tim 4.3ff. (cf. 3.3ff.) that false teachers will arise to subvert the congregation -- we can turn to consider the substance of the threat to the Ephesian community.

---

/43/ Aland, JTS 12 (1961), 39ff.

/44/ The Acts date from the late second century, and may represent another stratum of anti-marcionite polemic in Asia Minor.   Cf. Schneemelcher, NTA II, 349. Cf. Loofs, Theophilus von Antiochien adv. Marcionem (TU 46/2: 1930), 148ff.; Kasser, RHPhR 40 (1960), 45ff.

/45/ Marcion, 149*; cf. Quispel, 'De Brief aan de Laodicensen: een Marcionitische vervalsing', Nederl. Theol. Tijdjd. 5 (1950), 43-46; Lightfoot, Colossians and Philemon, 274-300; Knox, Marcion and the NT; Pink, Biblica 6 (1925), 179ff.

(a) The doxology given in 1 Tim 1.17 has no direct parallel in the letters of Paul (but cf. 1 Cor 8.4ff.; Rom 16.27, not attested by Marcion). The emphasis is enlarged in the declaration that there is only one God (cf. Rom 3.30) who is also savior (1 Tim 2.3; cf. Titus 2.10, 11; 3.4), and one mediator, 'the man Jesus Christ' (cf. Phil 2.6ff.; Ign. Eph. 7.1-2). The docetic and ditheistic emphases of the heresy can be inferred from these affirmations./46/ Although we cannot on the basis of these references arrange the false teaching according to major and minor tenets, it is clear that the writer is concerned first of all to insist on the oneness of God, the uniqueness of the mediation of the man Jesus Christ (1 Tim 2.5ff.), and to set to rest certain false ideas about the power of God (2 Tim 3.5; cf. 1 Clement 11.2). Implicitly, a 'second' christology, plausibly to be related to the mythoi mentioned in Titus 1.14a, is rejected. We note also that the designation for God is sōtēr (1 Tim 2.3; Titus 1.3) but for Jesus mesitēs: the man Jesus is the mediator of God, but it is the one God who saves. It is at least possible that a repudiation of Marcion's strong soteriological emphasis in intended (cf. Titus 2.13b; Ig,. Polyc. 8.3; Rom. 3.3; Rom. praef.; Trall. 7.1; Eph. 17.2). It is also possible to call Jesus Christ saviour (Titus 3.6); but the saving power of God is exercised as mercy in spite of offenses against him (Titus 3.4f.), that is, in remission of debts. The Pastor combats a heresy which imagines the resurrection to be already past (2 Tim 2.18) and which also denies the physical resurrection of 'the man, Jesus' (2 Tim 2.8). He appears to link his admonition to Paul's counsel in 1 Cor 15, where certain people are said to deny the resurrection./46a/ But, as Bauer

---

/46/ We have to do with the identification of the Apostle's doctrine over and against the teaching of 'men of corrupt mind': on the basis of his intention, we must assume that most of what these letters contain, including the sections on church order and practice, arises in response to specific contradictions.

/46a/ Lock (The Pastoral Epistles [1924], 99) calls 2 Tim 2.18 'a natural perversion of the teaching of St. Paul (Rom 6.1-11) and of the Fourth Gospel (Jn 17.3)', which may encourage speculation that the heresy proscribed is Marcion's radical paulinism. The belief was held by certain gnostic teachers, as well, cf. Iren. Haer. 1.23.5 (Menander); 2.31.2 (Simon and Carpocrates). A more obscure comparison is that between the heresy envisaged in 2 Tim 2.18 and that represented in the Acts of Paul and Thecla (14), according to which men do not rise at all but only live on in posterity (see above, note 44). As represented by the paulinist author of the Pastorals, however, the heresy seems to comport with the marcionite view of resurrection (cf. AM 5.9.1f.; 3.8.7; 3.8.2f.; Haer. 4.33.2). The Pastor may mean to connect this 'perversion' of Paul's teaching with the problem broached by Paul himself in 1 Cor 15.12ff.

observes of 1 Cor 15, Paul's belief in bodily resurrection 'involves neither flesh nor blood'./47/ The one God has not (as the heretics seem to teach) been fickle in his dispensation toward mankind (2 Tim 1.7): his 'purpose was given in Jesus Christ before the world began', though it is only 'made manifest by the appearing of the saviour Jesus Christ' (2 Tim 1.9f.). The writer advocates the use of prophecy as proof that God has remained steadfast in his promise (1 Tim 1.18; 2 Tim 3.15-16).

(b) The attitude of the writer toward women does not comport with Paul's (1 Tim 2.11; 1 Cor 11.5)./48/ In the church-order he commends, women are 'forbidden to have authority over men' and required to keep silence in the churches. While the order corresponds generally to that mentioned in 1 Cor 14.34 the writer offers an additional warrant for his admonition, itself derived from 1 Cor 11.7f.: woman is the transgressor, an inferior (derivative) creature according to the scriptures (Gen 3.1ff.; cf. 1 Tim 2.13f.). The orthodox order is thus thought to reflect accurately God's plan for creation, which entails the subordination of women in the church as the result of their original insubordination. The writer knows of a different order, one in which women are permitted to exercise certain ministerial functions. The reference to keeping silence ('einai en hēsychia') suggests that the office in question is that of teacher or prophetess. Here again we can plausibly assume that the marcionite church practice (in Laodicea?) is the source of the writer's alarm: Tertullian, Hippolytus, Epiphanius, and Eznik assert that marcionite women served in precisely these offices./49/ The Pastor has no thought of celibate clergy: bishops (1 Tim 3.2), deacons (3.12), and young women and widows (5.11, 14) are encouraged to marry. The reference in 1 Tim 4.3 to a sect which forbids marriage supports the idea that the church order recommended by the Pastor

---

/47/ Orthodoxy and Heresy, 234. R.M. Grant notes that the heresy possesses 'certain features of the thought of the opponents of Paul at Corinth and at Colossae' (Historical Introd., 213); but the notion of 'incipient gnosticism' does not take us very far in the direction of identifying this 'Ephesian' heresy. Cf. Kümmel, Intro. to the NT, 379.

/48/ Cf. also the tradition preserved in the Acts of Paul and Thecla, 3.39 (Thecla as Teacher) NTA II, 363; the emphasis on continence (3.20), and the stress laid on Paul's preaching to women, Acts of Paul 7 (NTA II, 369). Cf. p. 311.

/49/ Tert. Praes. 41; AM 5.8.12; Epiph. Panar. 42.3-4; Eznik, de sectis, 4.16.

does not arise spontaneously, but in response to the moral rigorism of the proscribed doctrine; further,

(c) The writer warns of 'deceitful spirits' who go about 'teaching the doctrine of devils' (1 Tim 4.1ff.). Their emphasis on ascesis includes the separation of those already married,/50/ as well as a commitment to continence for those who are not (1 Tim 4.3); thus the Pastor's emphasis on those who are 'really widows' (*hē de ontōs chēra . . . memonōmenē*: 1 Tim 5.5; cf. 5.3; 5.16b), that is to say, those who have not been separated from their husbands as a consequence of 'the commandments of men'. The writer finds this teaching an affront to God the creator (1 Tim 4.3f.), who has declared 'that nothing is to be refused'. Sexual abstinence is displeasing to God, the author of life; thus 'women will be saved by childbearing' (1 Tim 2.15a; cf. Titus 2.4). Both Ignatius and Polycarp know of a heresy which involves the divorcing of husbands and wives, and Ignatius points to 'corrupters of families' already at work in Ephesus./51/ In his letter to Polycarp, he implores him to 'speak to the sisters, that they may love the Lord and be content with their husbands', though he refuses to name the false teachers./52/ Polycarp and Ignatius are determined that the identity of the heretics should remain secret, for fear of publicizing their mistake and giving them the proselytic advantage: 'It is right to refrain from such men, and not to speak of them in public or private' (Ign. Smyrn. 7.2; cf. Titus 3.10). The author knows that some women in the congregation have been carried away by 'silly myths' (1 Tim 4.7) and 'have turned aside after Satan' (5.15) (cf. Polyc. Phil. 7.1). Families have been disrupted (Titus 1.11; cf. Ign. Eph. 16.1: *'Hoi oikophthoroi basileian theou ou klēronomēsousin')*. The Pastor ties the 'seduction of weak women . . . who will listen to anybody' (2 Tim 3.6) to the signs of the last days (cf. Polyc. Phil. 6.3). In this oracle, we can detect the clear outlines of Marcion's teaching on marriage: 'Quis enim tam castrator carnis castor quam qui nuptias abstulit?'./53/ Tertullian likewise lampoons the 'saintly Marcionite females' for flaunting their rigorist moral principles and impugning the

---

/50/ Cf. Acts of Paul and Thecla, 3112 (NTA II, 356).

/51/ Polyc. Phil, 4.2-3; Ign. Eph. 16.1; Polyc. 5.2; cf. Titus 2.4f.

/52/ Ign. Polyc. 5.1; cf. Smyrn. 5.2-3.

/53/ Tert. AM 1.1.5; 1.29.1; 4.34.1ff.

purposes of the creator./54/

(d) There is a further indictment of moral rigorism in the letters: While the writer counsels the women to be discreet and sober (Titus 2.3 = Polyc. Phil. 4.3) and the men to keep themselves pure (1 Tim 5.22 = Polyc. Phil. 5.3), he repudiates the 'heretical' practice of using only water (in the eucharist?: 1 Tim 5.23) and abstaining from certain foods (cf. Rom 14.20a; 1 Tim 4.3). Although Jewish food prohibitions are not envisaged,/55/ a form of dietary observance is in evidence. The reference in 1 Tim 1.8 to the goodness of the law ('Oidamen de hoti kalos ho nomos') is designed to countervail the heretical proscriptions regarding food and marriage (cf. AM 1.14.1ff.; 1.29.1ff). The author has taken over the language of Rom 7.12 for this purpose. Significantly, Rom 7.4ff. formed the basis for Marcion's discussion of Paul's use of the law. Tertullian complains, 'Piget de lege adhuc congredi'./56/ We can imagine that the same text served as the prooftext for Marcion's prohibition of marriage, and Rom 14.21 as the basis for the dietary laws of the marcionite church. However, these stand in tension with Paul's admonition in Rom 14.14. The Pastor, by the same token, has reduced Paul's cautionary note to a simple request for discretion (Titus 2.3!), and declared the law as a restraining power good. As we have already noted, Marcion accepts the speculative value of the law as that which 'makes sin appear as sin' ('hina genētai kath'hyperbolēn harmartōlos':

---

/54/ Tert. AM 5.8.12; Praes. 41. Vööbus, Celibacy: A Requirement for Admission to Baptism in the Early Church (1951); Klijn, Acts of Thomas (1962); and Chadwick, 'Enkrateia', RAC 5 (1962), 343ff., discuss the promise of virginity required for baptism in the early Syrian Church. Wilson (Gnosis and the NT, 41) thinks that this may point to gnostic influence. We have already mentioned the possibility that certain supposedly Essene motifs are present in the marcionite proto-Ephesians ('Laodiceans'); it is here worth mentioning the practice of celibacy and lustration among the Essenes. Schürer notes, 'Since the act of marriage itself made an individual unclean and necessitated a levitical bath of purification, the effort to attain to the highest degree of purity might lead to the repudiation of marriage' (History of the Jewish People [1885] II, 211). Assuming that the (dispersed) members of such rigorist Jewish sects were influential in the marcionite synagogue in Laodicea, and even in the formation of the christian community of that city, we may be able to point to a Jewish stratum in marcionite ascesis, one which resulted in just such a repudiation. See further, F. Bolgiani, 'La tradizione eresiologica sull' "encratismo" ', Atti Acad. Torino (1962), 1-128.

/55/ Cf. Josephus, bell. Jud. 2.8.2; but cf. Kelly, Pastoral Eps., 95, re. Titus 1.10ff.

/56/ AM 5.13.1.

Rom 7.13b). The Pastor's preoccupation with marriage and diet has as its explanation a dualistic worldview which disparages the things of the creator and his power (2 Tim 3.5; cf. 1 Clement 11.2), though it is admitted that the heretical community possesses 'a form of piety' *('echontes morphōsin eusebeias')*. The argument presented by the Pastor is reminiscent of the one Tertullian advances against Marcion: Creation cannot be alien to the creator (AM 1.11.1); and in despising the things of the creator, the Marcionites despise God himself (AM 1.14.1f.; cf. Titus 1.15f.). 'Quanta obstinatio duritiae [Marcionis]' (AM 1.14.5).

(e) Finally, the Pastor emphasizes the importance of doing good works (Titus 2.14b; 1 Tim 5.25; 2 Tim 3.17; cf. Polyc. Phil. 10.2 v. 1.3 [!]; 5.1; Ign. Polyc. 6.2). Faith is a communicated body of doctrine (2 Tim 3.15ff., etc.) which serves as a spur to the doing of works (2 Tim 3.17; Titus 3.14). A similar emphasis characterizes the anti-pauline polemic in James 2.17ff., though the Pastor's advice obviously stands much nearer to Paul. What the writer means to combat is a teaching which countenances faith alone as the medium of salvation; against this, the writer argues that good works are the 'proof' of belief (Titus 3.8). The heretics 'profess they know God, but . . . they are reprobate [adokimoi] to the doing of works' (Titus 1.16). The presence of this theme in the letters does not necessarily suggest Marcionism as the error, but it supports a case which is already strong on other grounds./57/

There are four further clues to the identity of the unnamed heresy:

(a) The orderly transmission of teaching authority and church office are central to the Pastor's intention in the letters. He seems to know of a church-order where a certain 'carelessness' prevails. His advice to bishops, deacons, and widows (cf. Polyc. Phil. 4-6) includes the counsel not to be hasty in the laying on of hands (1 Tim 5.22). On the basis of what we know about the practice of the Marcionites, it seems possible that the author has in mind the latitude of the marcionite church, where 'the ordinations are

---

/57/ Cf. Origen, hom. in Rom. 5.20: '[Marcion] . . . haec fuit causa datae legis ut peccatum, quod ante legem non fuerat, abundaret'. Harnack argues (Neue Studien, 8ff.), 'Ich weiss nicht, wie es noch deutlicher zum Ausdruck gebracht werden kann, dass Marcion alles auf den Glauben stellt, eine innere Umwandlung durch den Glauben bewirkt sieht -- von Sündern zu Guten'.

carelessly administered, capricious and changeable'./58/ The Pastor has
nothing to say of Paul's doctrine of spiritual gifts as the foundation for a
corporate church order (2 Cor 8.14; 1 Cor 12; Rom 12), although it is
virtually certain that the marcionite church followed Paul in this
respect./59/

(b) The remaining clues require two assumptions: first, that the
Pastor, within the general framework of pseudonymous literature of this
kind,/60/ intended to give some hint of the identity of his
opponent — obviously without betraying the underlying anachronism.
Second, that by the time these letters came to be composed, certain
traditions about Marcion had already begun to develop -- though one is aware
of the danger of arguing a case from supposedly 'biographical' hints and then
reading these as proof that the heresy belongs to Marcion. Nevertheless, if
we reckon on a date 'well into the second century' (Marxsen)/61/ as the
likeliest time of composition, then we can imagine that the raw-material

/58/ Tert. Praes. 41. Kelly appears to make an unwarranted separation
between the practice commended by the Pastor and the heresy envisaged
(Pastoral Eps., 107f.); but the question of ordination belongs to the larger
heresiological context. Loisy is correct in acknowledging that 'the
established church hierarchy was largely built up as a defense against
Marcion' (Christian Religion, 46). Campenhausen would argue that 'the
presumed relationships remain much too indefinite' to establish a connection
between the position of these disciples of apostles and a later church office
(Kirchliches Amt und geistliche Vollmacht in den ersten drei Jahrhunderten
[1953], 117). But there is good reason to think that the allusions to the
laying on of hands (1 Tim 5.22; cf. 4.14) refer to a practice already current
in the Pastor's circle. The question of whether this involves an apostolic
succession (cf. Kümmel, 381) by virtue of the ordination of presbyters
cannot be separated from the Pastor's insistence on a succession of right-
teaching received from Paul and transmitted by Timothy (himself ordained,
1 Tim 4.14) and the presbyters to their pupils (1 Tim 1.11; 6.20; 2 Tim 1.14;
2.2). The Marcionites fail both in teaching and in the 'formal' method of
transmitting this teaching. Marxsen's observation is worthwhile: The letters
'are really just the literary expression of the guarantee of right-tradition'
(Introd. NT, 215); the practice of laying on of hands arises specifically in
this connection. Cf. Brockhaus, Charisma und Amt (1975), 21-26.

/59/ Cf. Harnack, Marcion, 212, 146f.; 78*; Barnikol, Entstehung, 1-33;
Bosshardt, Essai sur l'originalité et la probité de Tertullien dans son Traité
contre Marcion (1921), 26; on the catechumenate-practice among the
orthodox, Hippol. Apost. Trad. (Dix's ed.), 28-39.

/60/ Cf. Aland, JTS 12 (1961), 39-49; Torm, Die Psychologie der
Pseudonymität (1932).

/61/ Introd. NT, 215; cf. M. Dibelius, Die Pastoralbriefe, ed. H.
Conzelmann (1955), 5ff.

out of which the Marcion-legend arose had already begun to develop. One such hint is the reference in 1 Tim 1.19, the seafaring metaphor put on Paul's lips: *'Peri tēn pistin enauagēsan'*, i.e., that some have made shipwreck of their faith. Have we reason to suspect that the writer alludes to Marcion's profession and to his erstwhile 'orthodoxy'? On three occasions in the AM, Tertullian refers to Marcion as nauclerus: 'Nos Marcionem nauclerum novimus' (AM 1.18.4; cf. M 4.9.2). In the fifth book, Tertullian uses the metaphor to maximum polemical advantage:

> Quamobrem, Pontice nauclere, si nunquam furtivas merces vel illicitas in acatos tuas recepisti, si nullum omnino onus avertisti vel adulterasti, cautior utique et fidelior in dei rebus, edas velim nobis, quo symbolo susceperis apostolum Paulum, quis illum tituli charactere percusserit, quis transmiserit tibi, quis imposuerit, ut possis eum constanter exponere, ne illius probetur qui omnia apostolatus eius instrumenta protulerit. /62/

In any event the tradition that Marcion was a (wealthy) shipmaster out of Pontus was a polemical convention by Tertullian's day, and does not originate in the adversus Marcionem. While we cannot be sure just how far back this biographical datum goes, it is entirely possible that Tertullian knows of Marcion's profession on the basis of Justin's testimony, which is very early; and Justin may have taken his information from a still earlier source. The tradition relating Marcion to a nautical career was perhaps passed down along with the recollection that he was a Sinopean by birth, and there is no reason to doubt this information. These facts of Marcion's life would not improbably have been known to the writer of these letters. /63/

(c) Unless it is thought that the legend of Marcion's simony originated with Tertullian /64/ (and again, Tertullian seems to point to an earlier source), then the connection between the loss of faith as a consequence of the love of money in 1 Tim 6.10 (cf. Polyc. Phil. 4.1: *'Archē de pantōn*

---

/62/ AM 5.1.2; cf. C. Moreschini, Temi e motivi della polemica antimarcionita di Tertulliano, Studia Classici e orientali 17 (1968), 149-86; Ilona Opelt, 'Marcion', in Die Polemik in der christlichen lateinischen Literatur von Tertullian bis Augustin (Heidelberg 1980), 48ff.; E. Meijering, Contra Marcionem: Gotteslehre in d. Polemik, adv. Marcionem 1-2 (1977); O'Malley, Tertullian and the Bible (1967), 75ff. There is no good reason to doubt the tradition that Marcion was a shipowner.

/63/ Cf. AM 4.4.3, that Marcion's faith once agreed with that held by the orthodox -- which Tertullian also accepts on the basis of tradition; AM 1.1.6; de carne, 2.

/64/ AM 4.4.3; Praes. 30.

*chalepōn philargyria')* may speak directly to the tradition that Marcion had once tried to buy the faith. This conclusion is reinforced by the reference in 1 Tim 6.5, to the effect that the 'men of corrupt mind suppose that gain is godliness'. It is important here to stress the difference between Marcion's and the Pastor's understanding of faith: for the latter, 'faith' is a depositum of received truth and exists as a deliverable commodity to be safeguarded (1 Tim 6.20). For Marcion on the other hand, faith is the acceptance of God's gift of love and mercy. He would not have understood 'buying' the faith, or of 'swerving aside' from right-teaching (1 Tim 1.6) to law-teaching (1.7a) as being synonymous with the loss of faith. Though the legend of Marcion's attempt to buy respectability for his doctrines is obviously very early, the Pastor's concept of faith is later than Marcion's theology and marks a clear revision of the thought of Paul (Rom 3.28f.).

One notes also the conjunction between the legend of Maricon's simony and that of his Sinopean 'predecessor', Diogenes the Cynic. Diogenes Laertius reports that Diogenes was expelled from Sinope 'for adulterating the coinage of the city', and thereafter made his way to Athens, where he became a pupil of Antisthenes./65/ Marcion was widely reckoned to have left Sinope under similar disgraceful circumstances, and to have travelled to Rome where he became Cerdo's pupil. It is obvious that the biographies of the two Sinopeans began to coalesce early on, and that later writers knew almost nothing for certain about Marcion except that he was a shipowner of Sinope. Hippolytus may be thinking of Diogenes' disgrace when he gives as the reason for Marcion's exodus 'a rape committed on a certain virgin'./66/ But Tertullian's story that Marcion presented the church at Rome with two hundred sesterces is just as improbable. However we are to understand these confused reports about Marcion's 'misuse' of the faith, it is important here to recognize that he was understood by his opponents to have erred in this way, and that is enough to explain the Pastor's reference./67/

---

/65/ Diog. Laer. 6.20.

/66/ Ps.-Tert., Omn. haer. 6.

/67/ Kelly points to some not very convincing parallels in Jewish and pagan domestic ethics, on the premise that the theme was a popular one (e.g., Eccles 27.1f.; Philo, Spec. leg. 4.65; Test. XII Patr., Jud. 19); cf. Pastoral Eps., 137ff. But the theme is not otherwise attested in the letters of Paul, and its use here seems to presuppose an entirely different situation.

(d) Most significant for the identification is the reference in 2 Tim 4.11 to the 'companionship' of Luke. We have already noted the existence of a 'companionship-tradition' in the struggle over the entitlement to Paul's teaching. The Marcionites (whether in Marcion's lifetime is uncertain) rejected this tradition, and made the claim that the orthodox version of Luke 'is falsified in respect of its title'./68/ In later heresiological literature, prëeminently in the writings of Irenaeus, 2 Tim 4.11 is the sentence introduced to prove that Luke was specially privy to Paul's teaching -- Luke along with Timothy and Titus forming the official (canonical) phalanx of 'Ephesian' paulinism. Luke is closest of all: *'Loukas estin monos met emou'*. What is as important is that the Pastor makes Luke the last witness to Paul's teaching, since despite the stated intention of Paul to return to Ephesus to fight the heretics himself (1 Tim 4.13), the Pastor must also know that Paul did not in fact return to Ephesus and is required to supply a rationale for this, as well as a sanction for the Ephesian-teaching (2 Tim 1.12ff.; 1 Tim 6.12ff.; cf. 2 Tim 3.14ff.; 4.1, etc.). The rationale is, of course, that Paul died before he could return to the city (2 Tim 4.6-7), and in language designed to repeat Paul's appraisal of his mission (2 Tim 4.7), Timothy is charged to 'fight the good fight' which Paul has been prevented from finishing (1 Tim 6.12). The mention of Luke, importantly, follows immediately on these last words of the Apostle (2 Tim 4.11a), and the assertion that Demas, Crescens, and Titus (!) have forsaken Paul. It is not too much to say that one of the functions of these letters is to establish the pauline succession: Timothy, the guardian of the gospel at Ephesus; Luke the constant companion who is with Paul until the last./69/ In heresiological polemic, this intention was not overlooked. Luke's companionship could be 'proved' by the so-called We-passages in the Acts of the Apostles. Thus for Irenaeus (Haer. 3.14.1-4), Luke is the sectator Pauli who 'was always attached to and inseparable from him': 'as Luke was present at all these occurrences, he carefully noted them down in writing,

---

/68/ AM 4.3.5.

/69/ And in the Acts of Paul, 11.6 (NTA II, 386), also Titus, who is pictured as praying with Luke and Paul after the Apostle's execution. The Acts date from the end of the second century (Quasten, II, 280); cf. Tert. de bapt. 17; Origen, de princ. 1.2.3; Hippol. com. Dan. 3.29 (Sources chrét. 14 [1947], 254); Hennecke, NTA II, 323f.

so that he cannot be convicted of falsehood or boastfulness'./70/ Luke is the orthodox eyewitness 'to the things which happened among us' (Lk 1.1).

In the absence of any independent sources identifying Luke as holding this privileged position,/71/ one is obliged to conclude that the tradition originates in the course of anti-heretical propaganda -- viz., 2 Tim 4.11, and the interpolation at Col 4.14 (the latter being a joint greeting from Luke and Paul to the church in Laodicea!)./72/ In Philemon 24, Luke is mentioned last in a succession of 'fellow-workers' that includes Marcus, Aristarchus, Demas (who deserted Paul?), and Epaphras, the founder of the Colossian church. There is no hint that Luke occupied a secretarial position, or that he had special access to Paul's teaching, and there is no reason to infer such a relationship. It seems likely, in view of Paul's form of greeting, that Lucas was a christian missionary with an apostolate of his own in Asia Minor. Thus, it is the reference in 2 Tim 4.11 that cements the relationship between Paul and Luke and makes Luke the authoritative voice of (orthodox) paulinism.

It is now hardly possible to imagine why Luke, among the minor figures in the NT, should have been chosen for this distinction. Why should a gospel and the first book of church history be ascribed to someone whose authority even Tertullian is at a loss to substantiate?/73/

The reasons for the orthodox response to the marcionite claim are probably inherent to the controversy itself. Could it be, for example, that the Ephesian community knew of orthodox Christians in Laodicea who looked back to Lucas, a co-worker of Paul, as one of the founders of the church there, and have kept themselves separate from the marcionite community in that city? The words put on Paul's lips, 'Only Luke is with me', suggest this, or a similar interpretation -- on what is admittedly very little

---

/70/ Haer. 3.14.1. Cf. W. Eltester, RGG³, III, 891; Haenchen, Acts of the Apostles, 9ff.

/71/ Cf. M. Dibelius, Aufsätze zur Apostelgeschichte (1951), 127ff.; Harnack, TLZ 53 (1928), 126ff.; Wendt, Die Apostelgeschichte (1913), 48.

/72/ But cf. Harnack, Date of the Acts (1911), 28; and Luke the Physician (1900), 12.

/73/ Cf. AM 4.2.4; and cf. Can. Mur., line 5f.; Eus. HE 3.4.6f.; Marcion's text of Col does not witness the epithet agapētos in reference to Luke (cf. Zahn, Forsch., I, 647; II, 528; Harnack, Marcion, 50; 124*). Origen makes Luke (in Luc. hom.) the 'brother' of 2 Cor 8.18.

evidence. But it would be natural for the Ephesian community (for Polycarp?) to assign to this historical Luke (thus to the orthodox segment of Christians in Laodicea) the gospel and history which they produced as counter-polemic to the Urevangelium which they may have shared with the Marcionites. This historical Luke was not the author of the Pastoral Epistles, but a contemporary of Paul. He is an elusive figure known to us only by reputation. At the same time 'Luke' is the authority according to which the Ephesians understand their historical legacy and right to the teaching of Paul. The use of Luke's name, however, was almost certainly not an arbitrary design on the part of the Ephesian litterateurs. The letter to Philemon, valued in orthodox and marcionite circles alike, makes mention of his apostolate. His historicity and his prestige even, or perhaps especially, among the Marcionites, will have to be assumed since his authorship of the gospel and Acts not only survives but establishes itself in the growing demand for apostolicity as a criterion for canonical books./74/ In effect, Luke the 'eyewitness' is introduced to counter the marcionite claim that 'Paul alone knew the truth, because to him the truth of the gospel was made known by revelation': the gospel of Paul had not been corrupted by false apostles, but faithfully transcribed by a true one (Haer. 3.14.1) whose statements both harmonize with and can even be said to be identical with Paul's gospel (Haer. 3.13.3); 'Lucas iste medicus post ascensum Christi, cum eum Paulus quasi adiutorem [?] studiosum secum adsumsisset, nomine suo ex opinione conscripsit'./75/

After Irenaeus, the church knows only the inerrantly transmitted gospel of Luke, sector Pauli, itself the response to the far from secure marcionite claim to possess a gospel deriving from Paul: 'Certe acta apostolorum hunc mihi ordinem Pauli tradiderunt, a te quoque non negandum' (Tert. AM 5.1.6; cf. 4.5.4: 'Nam et Lucae digestum Paulo adscribere solent'). But for Tertullian it remains uncertain why a gospel should have been credited to someone of Luke's stature ('Porro Lucas non apostolus sed apostolicus': AM 4.2.4). Although by the opening decades of the third century we are already too far beyond the controversy to get a

---

/74/ See Enslin, ' "Luke" and "Paul" ', JAOS 58 (1938), 81-91; Haenchen, Acts, 112-116. See Zahn, Forsch. VI, 7, n.2. The so-called Monarchian Prologue and Eus. (HE 3.4.6) described Luke as a Syrian from Antioch. Harnack credits this tradition: Date of the Acts, 29.

/75/ Can. Mur., 4-6.

clear idea of its provenance, it seems far from impossible that the Ephesian church knew of a historical connection between Marcion and Luke's teaching of Paul. This connection, while it may serve to explain why Luke should have been pressed into service in the battle against the paulinist heretics, cannot be historically reconstructed.

The insertion of 2 Tim 4.11 is an affirmation of what the Ephesian community believed to be the case: that they were the rightful heirs to the apostolic tradition <u>about</u> Paul, and possessed a gospel based on eyewitness reports of what had transpired among those who had seen the Lord after the resurrection./76/ On this reckoning, it is possible to agree with Quinn's observation that the gospel assigned to 'Luke', the unnamed history stemming from the same circle, and the epistles to Paul's faithful companions, Timothy and Titus, form a unified body of literature. The unifying element, however, is not Luke's historical situation as Paul's closest ally and companion: the Pastor, after all, assigns to Timothy and not to Luke the distinction of guarding the faith in Ephesus, and it is in Ephesus that the <u>depositum fidei</u> may be said to be localized. It is only in the search for an explanation for Luke's authorship that his proximity to Paul comes into question, and this is settled definitively in the suggestion that Luke was with Paul until the end. By this point, the original controversy between Marcion and the Ephesian circle has been lost sight of. The unnamed gospel of the alien God has become the gospel of the 'beloved' physician.

---

/76/ The Muratorian Canon makes the point that Luke did not see the Lord in the flesh (line 6); but cf. Lk 1.2. B.F. Westcott amended the Latin of the Canon unnecessarily so as to mean that Luke was Paul's journey companion -- a deduction from the Pastorals rather than a correction warranted by the language of the text before him (<u>General Survey of the History of the Canon</u>, 1885). The point urged upon the reader by the canonist, as A.A.T. Ehrhardt has shown (<u>Ostkirchliche Studien</u> [1953], II, 2) is that Luke, 'as an expert in the way of the teaching', was attempting to defend Paul in his writings, the language used by the canonist being taken over from Roman law.

# CONCLUSION

We cannot approach Marcion as a friend. He is not familiar to us in the way that Athanasius and Augustine are familiar. It was the task of the fathers to make him a stranger to the truth, and so he has largely remained: a stranger to the truth and hence a stranger to us. Nearly 2000 years after what NT theologians are accustomed to call the 'Resurrection Event' we are inclined to see his ditheism as a lapse of reason rather than a breach of faith. Men who believe in only one God, or in no God, will find a man who believed in two merely extravagant. Thus Tertullian and Celsus found Marcion, and modern interpreters of his theology have moved only reluctantly beyond the ancient judgment. It has scarcely been recognized that Marcion's belief in two Gods arises not out of an eccentric metaphysical theory, but represents a deduction based on human experience. It has been even less recognized that this deduction is in some respects closer to the gospel of the primitive christian communities, and especially to the Christianity of the synagogue, than was the 'monotheism' of his orthodox opponents.

In the same way, Marcion's 'rejection' of the OT offends modern sensibilities. One of the fruits of the study of christian origins in the last half century has been the rediscovery of Judaism, and a 'relativizing' of the NT: Heilsgeschichte has given way to a deeper understanding of the nascent christian movement within Judaism, and the trajectories that define it. Marcionism was traditionally reckoned to run counter to this movement, i.e., as an essentially anti-Jewish religious philosophy, to be contrasted with the 'orthodox' Christianity which claimed Judaism in the act of superseding it. Marcion broke the bond between the covenants, and would have set Christianity adrift. The Church kept the faith, and made the OT its prophetic witness. That we still know Marcion primarily in these terms -- the heretic who 'rejected the Old Testament root and branch' (Daniélou, II, 221) -- indicates the extent to which the polemic of his opponents has survived even to the present day.

The evidence suggests a different picture: that Marcion was much closer to the Judaism of the diaspora in terms of his biblical exegesis, theological and philosophical innocence, and ethical praxis, than were any of his orthodox opponents. Where Marcionism seems to differ drastically from Jewish thought, namely in its postulation of two Gods, the error remains fundamentally a Jewish heresy, based on the acceptance of two

307

opposing 'sources' of relevation, and without regard to the christian solution: one God in two (or three) dispensations. Marcion's Jewishness consists precisely in his allegiance to the ambiguities of Paul's theology, and his failure to provide a speculative resolution (like the gnostics) for the problems created by his ditheism. Even in this failure -- this emphasis on the givenness of God's revelation and mighty acts -- one reads less of christian heresy than of vestigial Jewish Christianity and an alienated hellenistic Judaism. Such alienation does not consist merely in Marcion's 'nibbling away' at the gospels or in his 'mutilation' of the letters of Paul: despite all efforts to prove the contrary, we cannot be certain that Marcion did either. His rejection of the God of his fathers represents above all a refusal to attribute supremacy to a God who decrees suffering and demands to be worshipped for his power alone -- in short, a God who is less than the God whom Jesus called 'father'. This other and alien God would accomplish not the salvation of Israel alone, but the redemption of mankind from the Creator's justice.

The struggle between Marcion and his opponents was not in the first instance over doctrine, but over rights: namely, the right to the gospel of Paul, and over the 'rightful' interpretation of that gospel. We have no reason to think that Marcion was less interested than (for example) Polycarp or the 'Pastor' in this 'right', or in what terms it was to be defined. Marcion knows nothing of a deposit of faith delivered to the saints and preserved intact by an unbroken succession of teacher-bishops who stand under the shield of the Spirit. He does know a muddled tradition of apostolic preaching, half-hearted acceptance of the gospel, and opposition to the doctrines of Paul. The recognition that Marcion's heresy must be dated considerably earlier than the patristic descriptions in which the traditio apostolica is invoked, and earlier than the canonical redaction of Luke, leads us to conclude that the doctrine of false apostleship is presupposed in and to a significant degree occasions the orthodox doctrine of apostolic authority and the derivative doctrines of paradosis and apostolic authorship of the gospels.

Marcion's appeal was not an appeal 'away from the traditions of men', to use the phrase which his orthodox opponents turned back on him; it was an appeal directly to man's experience of God, and to the divine mystery of revelation made known to Paul, and only to Paul. At the risk of over-simplifying the case, it can be said that for Marcion Paul commands papal authority. He is the sole infallible teacher. Our knowledge of this claim makes it possible to understand how Christianity emerged from the second century with the letters of the Apostle in trust. Had it not been made, it is difficult to imagine that a pauline renaissance, at least of the proportion which Marcion's heresy brought about, would have transpired. We have yet to recognize that Marcion, far from depriving the Church of its 'old' testament, reminded it of its debts to the Apostle who proclaimed himself a member of the Tribe of Benjamin, and preached to the gentiles a God of love who refused to forsake Israel.

# BIBLIOGRAPHY

**A.  Principal Primary Authorities: Editions and Translations**
[Abbreviations, pp. xvii-xxv]

Adamantius, De recta in deum fide, ed. W.H. van de Sande Bakhuyzen.
Leipzig, 1901.

The Apostolic Fathers, ed. and trans. K. Lake. [Loeb Classical Library ed]
2 vols. Cambridge MA, 1975.

Clement of Alexandria, Stromata, 1-6, ed. O. Stählin and L. Fruchtel
(GCS 52/15), Berlin, 1960. Stromata, 7-8, ed. O. Stählin (GCS 17),
Leipzig, 1909.

___ . Stromata, ed. C. Coxe (ANF 2), 1885; rpt. 1979.

Cyprian, Epistles, trans. E. Wallis (ANF 5), 1978.

Ephraem (Syrus), Commentary on the Diatesseron, ed. and trans. R.M.
Tonneau. Dublin, 1963.

____. Prose Refutations of Mani, Marcion, and Bardaisan, ed. C.W.
Mitchell. 2 vols. Oxford, 1912-21.

Epiphanius of Salamis, Panarion Haeresium, ed. K. Höll (GCS 25, 31, 37).
Leipzig, 1915-31.

Eusebius of Caesarea, The Ecclesiastical History, ed. K. Lake, 2 vols.
Cambridge MA, 1926-32 [rpts. GCS text].

____. Historia Ecclesiastica, eds. E. Schwartz (Greek), T. Mommsen
(Latin). GCS 9. 3 vols. Part I (1903), II (1908), [text] III (1909),
[Introd. and indexes].

Eznik de Kolb, De sectis, ed. and trans. (French), L. Maries and C.
Mercier, Patrologia Orientalis. Paris, 1959.

___ . Book IV of the De sectis, trans. N. McClean. Encyclopedia of Religion
and Ethics, ed. James Hastings (Edinburgh, 1915), VIII, 407-09.

Hippolytus, Refutation of All Heresies, trans J. H. MacMahon. (ANF 5),
1978.

Irenaeus of Lugdunum, Adversus Haereses, ed. W.W. Harvey. 2 vols.
Cambridge, 1857 [Sancti Irenaei ep. Lugdunensis libros quinque
adversus haereses].

___ . Against Heresies, ed. C. Coxe. (ANF 1), 1885; rpt. 1979.

___ . Contre Les hérésies, édition critique livre III par Adelin Rousseau et
Louis Doutreleau. (Source chrét. 210, 211), Paris, 1974.

Justin (Martyr), Apologia I & II, ed. J.C.T. Otto. 3 vols. Jena, 1842-48.

___. The Apologies of Justin Martyr, trans. A.W.F. Blunt. Cambridge, 1891.

The Nag Hammadi Library in English, ed. J.M. Robinson, M.W. Meyer, et al. Leiden, 1977.

Origen, On First Principles, ed. G. W. Butterworth. London, 1936.

___. Contra Celsum, ed. H. Chadwick, Cambridge, 1953.

Polycarp of Smyrna, The Two Epistles to the Philippians, ed. and trans. P.N. Harrison. Cambridge, 1936 [includes Greek text].

Pseudo-Tertullianus (Commodianus?), Carmen versus Marcionitas, ed. M. Müller. Ochsenfurt, 1936 [cf. ANF 18, 318-84].

Tertullianus, Opera, ed. E. Dekkers, et al. 2 vols. The Hague [CCSL],

___. Adversus Marcoinem, ed. E. Evans. 2 vols. Oxford [OECT], 1972.

___. De praescriptione haereticorum, ed. E. Kroymann. Vienna [CSEL, 47], 1906.

___. The Treatise Against Praxeas, ed. E. Evans. London, 1948.

___. Tertullian, De Anima, ed. J.H. Waszink. Amsterdam, 1947.

___. Treatise on the Resurrection, ed. E. Evans. London, 1960.

___. Treatise on the Incarnation, ed. E. Evans. London, 1956.

Theodoret of Cyrrhus, Epîtres, ed. Y. Azéma. (Source chrét. 40, 98, 111), Paris 1955-1965.

___. Letters, trans. B. Jackson (ANF 3), 1892; rpt. 1979.

## B. Secondary Literature: Marcion and Marcionism

B. Aland, 'Marcion: Versuch einer neuen Interpretation', ZTK 70 (1973), 420-47.

A. d'Alés, 'Marcion: La réforme chrétienne au II$^e$ siècle', RSR 13 (1922), 137-68.

A. Amann, 'Marcion', art. in DCT 9 (1927), 2009-2332.

J.P. Arendzen, 'Marcionites', art. in The Catholic Encyclopedia. 15 vols. New York, 1910. vol. 9, 645-49.

B.W. Bacon, 'Marcion, Papias, and the Elders', JTS 23 (1922), 134ff.

G. Bardy, 'Marcion', art. in Dictionnaire de la Bible, suppl. 5 (1957), cols. 862-81.

Ernst Barnikol, Die Entstehung der Kirche im zweiten Jahrhundert und die Zeit Marcions. Kiel, 1933.

___. 'Marcions Paulusbriefprologe', TJHC 6 (1938), 15-16.

___. Philippier II: Der marcionitische Ursprung des Mythos Satzes, Phil. 2.6-7. Kiel, 1932.

J. Barr, 'The Old Testament and the Crisis of Authority' [Marcion], Interpretation 25 (1971), 24-40.

U. Bianchi, 'Marcion: Theologien biblique ou docteur gnostique?', VC 21 (1967), 141-42.

A. Bill, Zur Erklärung und Textkritik des 1. Büches Tertullians Adversus Marcionem. TU 3. Leipzig, 1911.

E.C. Blackman, Marcion and His Influence. London, 1948.

E. Bosshardt, Essai sur l'originalité et la probité de Tertullien dans son traité contre Marcion. Thesis, Fribourg, 1921.

F.M. Braun, 'Marcion et la gnose simonienne', Byzantion 5/27 (1955), 631-48.

N. Brox, 'Non huius aevi deus: Zu Tertullian Adversus Marcionem', ZNTW 59 (1968), 259-61.

D. de Bruyne, 'Prologes bibliques d'origine Marcionite', Rev. Bénéd. (1907).

E. Buonaiuti, 'Marcione ed Egesippio', Religio 12 (1936), 401-13.

H. von Campenhausen, 'Marcion et les origines du canon neo-testamentaire', Révue d'histoire et de philosophie réligieuses 46 (1966), 213-26.

P.L. Couchoud, 'Is Marcion's Gospel One of the Synoptics?', Hibbert Jnl. (1936), 265-77.

___. 'La premier édition de saint Paul', RHPhR, Paris (1926).

Nil Dahl, 'The Origins of the Earliest Prologues to the Pauline Letters', Semeia 12 (1978), 233-77.

R. Eisler, The Enigma of the Fourth Gospel [On Marcion as John's amanuensis], London, 1938

V. Ermoni, 'Le Marcionisme', RQH 82 (1910), 5-23.

___. 'Marcion dans la littérature armenienne', RO Chr. I (1896), 461ff.

E. Evans, Tertullian's Commentary on the Marcionite Gospel (TU 73), Berlin, 1959, pp. 699-705 [Papers presented to the International Congress on the Four Gospels held at Christ Church, Oxford, 1957; ed. K. Aland, F.L. Cross, J. Danielou, and H. Riesenfeld].

J.M. Fiey, 'Les Marcionites dans les textes historiques de l'église des péres', Le Museon 13 (1970), 183-88.

W.H.C. Frend, 'Their Word to Our Day: Marcion', ExT 80 (1969), 328-32.

J.G. Gager, 'Marcion and Philosophy', VC 26 (1972), 53-59.

R.M. Grant, 'The Oldest Gospel Prologues', Angl. Theol. Rev. 23 (1941), 231ff.

E. Gutwenger, 'The Anti-marcionite Prologues', TS 7 (1946), 393-409.

A. Hahn, Antitheses Marcionis Gnostici. Königsberg, 1823.

A. Harnack, 'Die ältesten Evangelien Prologe und die Bildung des Neuen Testaments', Sitzungsberichte Berlin Akademie, 1928.

___. Marcion: Das Evangelium vom fremden Gott. Leipzig [TU 45], 1921; 1924; rpt, 1960.

___. 'Der marcionitische Ursprung der ältesten Vulgata Prologe zu den Paulusbriefen', ZNTW (1925).

___. Neue Studien zu Marcion. Leipzig, 1923.

R. Harris, 'Marcion's Book of Contradictions', BJRL 8 (1924).

P.N. Harrison, 'The False Teachers at Philippi', in Polycarp's Two Epistles to the Philippians. Cambridge, 1936, 172-206.

W. Hartke, Vier urchristliche Partein und ihre Vereinigung zur apostolischen Kirche. Berlin, 1961.

A.J.B. Higgins, 'The Latin Text in Marcion and in Tertullian', VC 5 (1951), 1-42.

A. Hilgenfeld, Kritische untersuchungen über die Evangelien Justins, der clementischen Homilies und Marcions. Halle, 1880.

A. Holland, Deux Hérétiques: Marcion et Montan. Paris, 1935.

W.F. Howard, 'The Anti-Marcionite Prologues to the Gospels', ExT 47 (1936), 534-38.

H. Kayser, 'Natur und Gott bei Marcion', ThStKr (1929), 279-96.

___. 'Zur marcionitischen Taufformel', ThStKr 108 (1938), 370-86.

E. Kikuchi, 'The Bible and Marcion' [In Japanese], St. Paul's Rev. of Arts and Letters 30 (1972), 1-20.

H. Kraft, 'Marcion', art. in RGG 4 (1960), 740-42.

J. Knox, Marcion and the New Testament: An Essay on the Early History of the Canon. Chicago, 1942.

___. 'On the Vocabulary of Marcion's Gospel', JBL 58 (1939), 193-201.

G. Krüger, 'Marcion', art. in PRE 12 (1903), 266-77.

J.M. Lagrange, Rev. B. 30 (1921), 602-ll. (Rev. of Harnack).

S.E. Lodovici, 'Sull' interpretazione di alcuni testi della lettura ai Galati in Marcione e in Tertulliano', Aevum 46 (1972), 371-401.

A. Loisy, 'Marcion's Gospel: A Reply' [to Harnack], Hibbert Jnl. (1936), 378-87.

F. Loofs, Theophilus von Antiochien Adversus Marcionem, und die anderen theologischen Quellen bei Irenaeus. Leipzig, 1930.

J. Mahe, 'Tertullien et l'épistula Marcionis', Rev. SR 45 (1971), 338-71.

A. Maillot, 'Eloge de Marcion', Foi Vie 72 (1973), 29-34.

N. McClean, 'Marcion', art. in Enc. of Rel. and Ethics, ed. James Hastings. Edinburgh, 1915, vol. 8, 407-409 [includes ET of Eznik's diatribe v. Marcion].

E.P. Meijering, 'Bemerkungen zu Tertullians Polemik gegen Marcion', VC 30/2 (1976), 81-108.

H. Meyboom, Marcion en de Marcionieten. Leiden, 1888.

C. Moreschini, 'L'Adversus Marcionem: nell' ambito dell' attivita letteraria di Tertullian', Omaggio a E. Frankel. Rome (1968), 113-35.

___. 'Osservazioni sul testo dell' Adversus Marcionem di Tertulliano', Annali della Scula normale superiore di Pisa 39 (1970), 489-513.

___. 'Per una nuova lettura dell' Adversus Marcionem di Tertulliano', Studi classici e orientali (Pisa) 23 (1974), 60-9.

___. 'Prologomena ad una nuova edizione dell' Adversus Marcionem di Tertulliano', ASNSP 36 (1968), 93-102; 149-86.

___. 'Temi e motivi della polemica antimarcionita di Tertulliano', Studi classici e orientali 17 (1968), 149-86.

M. Müller, Untersuchungen zum Carmen Adversus Marcionitas. Würzburg D.Phil.; Oschenfurt, 1936.

W. Mundle, 'Der Herkunft der marcionitischen Prologe zu den paulinischen Briefen', ZNTW, 1925.

C.M. Nielson, 'The Epistle to Diognetus: Its Date and Relationship to Marcion', Angl. Theol. Rev. 52 (1970), 77-91.

G. Ory, Marcion. Paris, 1980.

G. Pelland, 'Marcion', art. in Dictionnaire de spiritualité, ascetique et mystique, doctrine et histoire. Suppl., Paris (1977), 311-320.

G. Quispel, De Bronnen van Tertullianus' Adversus Marcionem. Leiden, 1943.

C. Rambeaux, 'Un locus non desperatus: Carmen adversus Marcionem, 4.105', REA 18 (1972), 43-5.

H. Raschke, 'Der Römerbrief des Marcion nach Epiphanius', Abhandlung und Vorträge der Bremer wissenschaftlichen Gesellschaft, I (Bremen, 1926), 128-201.

J. Regul, 'Die antimarcionitischen Evangelien Prologe', in Geschichte der lateinischen Bibel, vol. 6. Fribourg (1969), 164-77.

W. Richardson, 'Nomos empsychos: Marcion, Clement of Alexandria, and St. Luke's Gospel', Studia Patristica 6, 188-96.

R. Riedingen, 'Zur antimarkionitischen Polemik des Klemens von Alexandreia', VC 29 (1975), 15-32.

M. Rist, 'Pseudepigraphic Refutations of Marcionism', JR 22 (1942), 39-62.

A. Ritschl, Das Evangelium Marcions und das kanonisch Evangelium des Lukas. Tübingen, 1846.

J. Rivière, 'Sur la doctrine marcionite de la rédemption', Rev. SR 5 (1925), 633-45.

___. 'Un exposé marcionite de la rédemption', Rev. SR 1 (1921), 185-207; 297-323 [On Eznik de Kolb].

L. Rougien, 'La critique biblique dans l'antiquité: Marcion et Fauste de Milève', Cahiers du cercle Ernst Renan 18, Paris (1958).

A. Salles, 'Simon le magicien ou Marcion?', VC 12 (1958), 197-224.

G. Salmon, 'Marcion', art. in DCB 3 (1881), 816a-824b.

K. Schäfer, 'Marcion und die ältesten Prologe zu den Paulusbriefen' in Kyriakon: Festschrift J. Quasten, I (Münster, 1970), 135-50.

___. 'Marius Victorinus und die marcionitischen Prologe zu den Paulusbriefen', in ibid., 7-16.

F. Scheidweiler, 'Arnobius und der Marcionitismus', ZNTW 45 (1955), 45-8.

H. Schoeps, Aus frühchristlicher Zeit. Tübingen, 1950, 257ff.

E.U. Schule, 'Der Ursprung des Bösen bei Marcion', ZRGes 16 (1964), 23-42.

F.G. Sirna, 'Arnobia e l'eresia marcionita di Patrizio', VC 18 (1964), 37-50.

H. von Soden, 'Die lateinische Paulus-texte bei Marcion und Tertullian', Festgabe Adolf Jülicher. Tübingen (1927); ZKG 40 (1922), 191ff.

J.C. Thilo, 'Evangelium Marcionis ex auctoritate veterum monumentorum', Codex apocr. Novi Test. I, Leipzig (1832), 401-80.

H. Vogels, 'Der Einfluss Marcions und Tatians auf Text und Kanon des Neuen Testaments', in Synoptische Studien (1953), 289ff.

G. Volckmar, Das Evangelium Marcionis. Leipzig, 1852.

C.H. Wagers, 'Creation and Providence: Marcion', Co.B2 38 (1961), 36-50.

H. Waitz, Das ps.-Tertullianische Gedicht Adversus Marcionitas: Ein Beitrag zur Geschichte der altchristlichen Literatur sowie zur Quellenkritik des Marcionitismus. Darmstadt, 1901.

C.S.C. Williams, 'Eznik's Résumé of Marcion's Doctrine', JTS 45 (1944), 65-73.

R.S. Wilson, Marcion: A study of a Second-Century Heretic. London, 1933.

J. Woltmann, 'Der geschichtliche Hintergrund der Lehre Markions vom fremden Gott', in Festgabe Hermenegild Biedermann (1971), 15-42.

Th. Zahn, Forschungen zur Geschichte des neutestamentlichen Kanons und der altkirchlichen Literatur, I.2, 585-718; II.2, 409-529 ['Marcions Neues Testament'], 1881-1929.

## C.   Studies of Ancient Writers

G.J.D. Aalders, 'Tertullian's Quotations from St. Luke', Mnemosyne 3/5 (1937), 241-82.

A. d'Ales, La théologie de Tertullien. Paris, 1905.

T.D. Barnes, Tertullian: A Historical and Literary Study. Oxford, 1971.

A.A.R. Batiaensen, 'Tertullian's Argumentation in the De praescriptione haereticorum', VC 31 (1977), 35-46.

W. Bauer, Die Briefe des Ignatius von Antioch und der Polykarpbrief. Tübingen, 1920.

C. Becker, Tertullian's Apologeticum: Werden und Leistung. Munich, 1954.

A. Benoit, S. Irénée: Introduction a l'étude de sa théologie. Paris, 1960.

H. v. Campenhausen, 'Irenäus und das Neue Testament', TLZ 20 (1965), 1-8.

___. 'Polykarp von Smyrna und die Pastoralbriefe', in Aus der frühzeit des Christentums.

H. Chadwick and J. Oulton, eds., Alexandrian Christianity. Philadelphia [LCC], 1954.

J. Chapman, 'St. Irenaeus on the Date of the Gospels', JTS 6 (1905), 563-85.

W.L. Duliére, 'Le canon néotestamentaire et les écrits chrétiens approuvés par Irénée, Nuov. Clio 6 (1954), 199-224.

E.R. Goodenough, The Theology of Justin Martyr. Jena, 1923.

F.S. Gutjahr, Die Glaubwertigkeit des irenäischen Zeugnisses über die Abfassung des vierten kanonischen Evangeliums. Graz, 1904.

V. Hahn, 'Schrift, Tradition, und Primat bei Irenaeus', ZTK 70 (1961), 233-43; 292-302.

A. Harnack, Das Alte Testament in den paulinischen Briefen und in den paulinischen Gemeinden. Berlin, 1928.

R. Holte, 'Logos Spermatikos: Christianity and Ancient Philosophy According to St. Justin's Apologies', ST 12 (1958), 106-68.

S.H. Kelley, Auctoritas in Tertullian: The Nature and Order of Authority in His Thought. PhD Emory (1974), 289pp. [Microfilm].

W. Leuthold, Das Wesen der Häresie nach Irenäus. D.Theol. Zürich, 1954.

F. Loofs, Theophilus von Antiochien Adversus Marcionem. Leipzig, 1930.

A. Mehat, Étude sur les Stromates de Clement d'Alexandrie. Paris, 1966.

D. Michaelides, Foi, écritures, et tradition ou les Praescriptiones chez Tertullien. Paris [Theol. fasc. 76], 1969.

T.P. O'Malley, Tertullian and the Bible. Nijmegen. 1967.

P. Perkins, 'Irenaeus and the Gnostics: Rhetoric and Composition in the Adversus Haereses Book I', VC 30 (1976), 193-200.

O. Piper, 'The Nature of the Gospel According to Justin Martyr', JR 41 (1961), 155-68.

P. Prigent, Justin et l'Ancien Testament. Paris, 1964.

F.M. Sagnard, La gnose valentinienne et le témoignage de saint Irénée. Paris, 1947.

W. Schoedel, 'Philosophy and Rhetoric in the Adversus Haereses of Irenaeus', VC 13 (1959), 22-32.

C. de Lisle Shortt, The Influence of Philosophy on the Mind of Tertullian. London, 1933.

J.P. Smith, St. Irenaeus: Proof of the Apostolic Preaching. Westminster MD, 1952.

A.C. Sundberg, 'Dependent Canonicity in Irenaeus and Tertullian', StEv 2 (1964), 403-09.

P.G. Verwejis, Evangelium und neues Gesetz in der ältesten Christenheit bis auf Marcion. Utrecht, 1960.

M. Widmann, 'Irenäus und seine theologischen Väter', ZTK 54 (1957), 156-73.

## D. Orthodoxy and Heresy in Early Christianity

H.D. Altendorf, 'Zum Stichwort: Rechtglaubigkeit und Ketzerei im ältesten Christentum', ZKG 80 (1969), 61-74.

W. Bauer, Rechtglaubigkeit und Ketzerei im ätesten Christentum. Tübingen, 1934. ET: Orthodoxy and Heresy in Earliest Christianity, 1971.

H.D. Betz, 'Orthodoxy and Heresy in Earliest Christianity: Some Critical Remarks on George Strecker's Republication of Walter Bauer's Rechtglaubigkeit und Ketzerei im ältesten Christentum', Interpretation 17 (1965), 299-311.

K. Beyschlag, 'Zur Simon-Magus-Frage', ZTK 68 (1971), 395-426.

H. Dörries, 'Urteil und Verurteilung-Ein Beitrag zum Umgang der alten Kirche mit Häretikern', ZNTW 55 (1964), 78-94.

M. Elze, 'Häresie und Einheit der Kirche im 2. Jahrhundert', ZTK 71 (1974), 389-409.

D.J. Hawkins, 'A Reflective Look at the Recent Debate on Orthodoxy and Heresy in Earliest Christianity', Eglise Th. 7 (1976), 367-78.

A. Hilgenfeld, Die Ketzergeschichte des Urchristentums. Leipzig, 1884.

H. Köster, 'Häretiker im Urchristentum', in RGG 3 (1959), 17-21.

___. 'The Theological Aspects of Primitive Christian Heresy', in The Future of Our Religious Past, ed. J.M. Robinson. New York/London, 1971, 65-83.

___. and James M. Robinson, Trajectories through Early Christianity. Philadelphia, 1971.

R.A. Kraft, 'The Development of the Concept of Orthodoxy in Early Christianity', Current Issues in Biblical and Patristic Interpretation: Studies in Honour of M.C. Tenney and G.F. Hawthorne. New York, 1975, 47-59.

M. Lods, 'Unité de l'Église: Les limites de l'hérésie chez les premiers péres', ETRel. 42 (1967), 81-9.

N.J. McEleney, 'Orthodoxy and Heresy in the New Testament', Proceedings of the Catholic Theological Society of America 25 (1970), 54-77.

M. Meinertz, 'Schisma und hairesis im Neuen Testament', Biblische Zeitschrift 1 (1957), 114-18.

J.M. Robinson, 'Gnosticism in the New Testament', in Gnosis: Festschr. für Hans Jonas, ed. B. Aland. Göttingen (1978) 125-43.

J. Schirr, 'Motive und Methoden Frühchristlicher Ketzerkämpfung', Theol. Lit. 103 (1978), 71-72.

## E. Tradition and Apostolicity in the Early Church

J.N. Bakhuizen van den Brink, 'Traditio im theologischen Sinne', VC 13 (1959), 74-6.

C.K. Barrett, The Signs of an Apostle. London, 1970.

A. Benoit, 'Ecriture et tradition chez Irénée', RHPhR (1960).

F. Bolgiani, 'La tradizione eresiologica sull' encratismo', Atti della Accademia . . . di Torino 96 (1961/62), 537-64.

L. Bouyer, 'Holy Scripture and Tradition as Seen by the Fathers', Early Churches Quarterly (1974), 1-16.

F.F. Bruce and E.G. Rupp, eds. The Holy Book and Holy Tradition. Manchester, 1968.

F.F. Bruce, 'Apostolic Tradition in the New Testament'; 'Tradition and the Gospel'; and 'Tradition in the Canon of Scripture', in Tradition Old and New. London, 1970, 29-38; 39-57; 74-86; 129-50.

___. 'The Appeal to History', Tradition Old and New. London (1970), 172-74.

H.v. Campenhausen, Ecclesiastical Authority and Spiritual Power in the Church of the First Centuries. London, 1965.

___. Tradition and Life in the Church. London, 1968.

Yves Congar, Tradition and Traditions. London, 1966.

O. Cullmann, La Tradition: Probléme exégétique, historique, et théologique. Paris/Neuchatel [Cahiers theol. 33], 1953.

___. 'The Tradition', in The Early Church. London (1965), 59-75.

A. Deneffe, Der Traditionsbegriffe. Münster, 1931.

G. Ebeling, 'Sola Scriptura and the Problem of Tradition', in The Word of God and Tradition: Historical Studies Interpreting the Divisions of Christianity, trans. S. Hooke. Philadelphia, 1968.

D. van den Eynde, Les normes de l'enseignement chrétien dans la littérature patristique des trois premiers siècles. Gembloux/Paris, 1933.

E. Flesseman van Leer, Tradition and Scripture in the Early Church. Assen, 1954.

L. Goppelt, 'Tradition nach Paulus', Kerygma und Dogma 4 (1958), 213-33.

F. Hahn, 'Das Problem Schrift und Tradition im Urchristentum', EvTh 30 (1970), 449-68.

R.P.C. Hanson, 'The Rule of Faith', in Tradition in the Early Church. London (1962), 42ff.

___. Tradition in the Early Church. London, 1962.

G.W.H. Lampe, 'The Early Church', in Scripture and Tradition, ed. F.W. Dillistone. London (1955), 21-52.

J.A. Möhler, Die Einheit in der Kirche, oder das Prinzip des Katholizismus dargestellt im Geiste der Väter der drei ersten Jahrhunderte. Crit. ed., Köln, 1957.

___. Die mündliche Uberlieferung. Beiträge zum Begriff der Tradition, ed. M. Schmaus. Munich, 1957.

K.F. Morrison, Tradition and History in the Western Church. Princeton, 1969, 300-1140.

G.L. Prestige, Fathers and Heretics. London, 1940.

D.B. Reynders, 'Paradosis. Les progrés de l'idée de tradition jusqu'à saint Irénée', Religious and Theological Abs. 5 (1933), 155-91.

___. 'Premières reactions de l'église devant les falsifications du dépôt apostolique', in L'infallibilité de l'Eglise. Chevetogne, 1963, 27-52.

D.J. Theron, Evidence of Tradition. London, 1957.

H.E.W. Turner, The Pattern of Christian Truth. London, 1954.

K. Wengst, 'Der Apostel und die Tradition', ZTK (1972), 145-62.

R.M. Wilken, 'Tertullian and the Early Christian View of Tradition', CTM 38 (1967), 221-33.


**F. Canonicity and Related Subjects**


K. Aland, 'The Problem of Anonymity and Pseudonymity in Christian Literature of the First Two Centuries', JTS 12 (1961), 39-49.

___. 'Das Problem des NT Kanons', in Studien zur Uberlieferung des NT. Berlin (1967), 1-23.

B.W. Bacon, 'The Latin Prologue of John', BLJ 32 (1913), 194ff.

F.F. Bruce, 'New Light on the Origins of the NT Canon', in New Dimensions in New Testament Study, ed. R. Longenecker and M. Tenney. Philadelphia (1974), 3-18.

D. de Bruyne, 'Les plus anciens prologues latins des Evangiles', Rev. Bénéd. 40 (1938), 193-214.

R. Bultmann, The History of the Synoptic Tradition. Oxford/Blackwell, 1963.

F.C. Burkitt, The Gospel History and its Transmission. New York, 1961.

E.C. Caldwell, 'The Meaning of Canonicity', in The Study of the Bible. Chicago (1937), 1-37.

H.v. Campenhausen, Die Entstehung der christlichen Bibel. Tübingen, 1968; ET, J.A. Baker, The Formation of the Christian Bible. London, 1972.

K.L. Carroll, 'The Creation of the Four-fold Gospel', BJRL 37 (1954), 68-77.

___. 'The Earliest New Testament', BJRL 38 (1955/6), 47-57.

___. 'The Expansion of the Pauline Corpus', JBL 72 (1953), 230-37.

H. Clavier, Les varietés de la pensée biblique et le problème de son unité. Suppl. to Nov. Test. 43 (1976).

H. Conzelmann, 'Die Frage der Einheit der neutestamentlichen Schriften', in Modern Exegese und historische Wissenschaft, ed. J. Hollenbach. Trier (1972), 67-76.

O. Cullmann, 'The Plurality of the Gospels as a Theological Problem in Antiquity'; 'The Tradition'; in The Early Church: Historical and Theological Studies. London (1956), 39-54; 75-99.

M. Dibelius, A Fresh Approach to the New Testament and Early Christian Literature. New York, 1936.

___. From Tradition to Gospel. Cambridge (rpt.), 1972.

D.L. Dungan, 'The New Testament Canon in Recent Study', Interpretation 29 (1975), 339-51.

___. 'Reactionary Trends in the Gospel-producing Activity of the Early Church: Marcion, Tatian, Mark', in L'Evangile selon Marc: Tradition et Redaction. Paris (1973), 179-202.

J. Dupont, 'Pour l'histoire de la doxologie finale de l'épître aux Romains', Rev. Bénéd. 58 (1948), 3-22.

E. Flesseman van Leer, 'Prinzipien der Sammlung und Ausscheidung bei der Bildung des Kanons', ZTK 61 (1964), 404-20.

E.J. Goodspeed, The Form of the New Testament. London, 1926.

A.v. Harnack, 'Die ältesten Evangelienprologe und die Bildung des Neuen Testaments', Sitzungsberichte Berlin Akad. Berlin, 1928.

___. Die Entstehung des neuen Testaments und die wichtigsten Folgen der neuen Schöpfung. Leipzig, 1914/New York, 1925.

___. Das Neue Testament um das Jahr 200. Freiburg, 1899.

E. Käsemann, Das Neue Testament als Kanon. Göttingen, 1970.

H. Köster, Synoptische Uberlieferung bei den apostolischen Vätern. Berlin, 1957.

W.G. Kümmel, 'The Origin of the Canon of the New Testament', in Introduction to the New Testament. London (1966), 334-68.

A. Loisy, The Origin of the New Testament. Londonm 1950.

I. Lönning, 'Kanon im Kanon': Zum dogmatischen Grundlagproblem des neutestamentlichen Kanons. Oslo, 1972.

C.F.D. Moule, The Birth of the New Testament. London, 1962.

J. Murray, 'How Did the Church Determine the Canon of Scripture?', Heythrop Jnl. 11 (1970), 115-26.

B. Reicke, 'Einheitlichkeit oder verschiedene Lehrbegriffe in der neutestamentlichen Theologie', ThZ 9 (1953), 401-15.

A.C. Sundberg, 'Towards a Revised History of the New Testament Canon', in StEv 4 (= TU 102), Berlin (1968), 452-461.

A. Souter, The Text and Canon of the New Testament. London/New York, 1954.

H.F.D. Sparks, 'The Idea of a New Testament and the Growth of the NT Canon', in The Formation of the New Testament. London (1952), 144-54.

B.H. Streeter, The Four Gospels: A Study of Origins. London, 1924.

A. Vielhauer, Geschichte der urchristlichen Literatur. New York/Berlin, 1975.

H.P. West, 'A Primitive Version of the New Testament', in NTS 14 (1967), 75-95.

B.F. Westcott, A General Survey of the History of the Canon of the New Testament During the First Four Centuries. Cambridge, 1855.

Th. Zahn, Einige Bemerkungen zu A. v. Harnacks Prufung der Geschichte des neutestamentlichen Kanons. Erlangen, 1899.

____. Forschungen zur Geschichte des neutestamentlichen Kanons und der altkirchlichen Literatur. Leipzig, 1900.

____. Geschichte des neutestamentlichen Kanons. 4 vols. Leipzig, 1888-92.

## G. Gnosticism and Early Christianity

B. Aland, ed., Gnosis: Festschrift für Hans Jonas. Göttingen, 1978.

R. Ambelain, La notion gnostique du démiurge dans les Ecritures et les traditions judéo-chrétiennes. Paris, 1959.

F.C. Baur, Die christliche Gnosis. Tübingen, 1835.

324/Bibliography

U. Bianchi, ed., Le origini dello Gnosticismo. Leiden, 1967.

W. Bousset, Hauptprobleme der Gnosis. Göttingen, 1907.

R. Bultmann, 'Gnosis', in G. Kittel, TWNT 5. London (1952).

F.C. Burkitt, Church and Gnosis. Cambridge, 1932.

E. Butler, The Myth of the Magus. Cambridge, 1948.

L. Cerfaux, 'La gnose simoniènne', RSR 15 (1925), 489ff.; (1926), 5ff.; 265ff.; 285ff.

C.E. Colpe, E. Haenchen, 'Gnosis', in RGG 3 (1958), 1648-61.

___. Die religionsgeschichtliche Schule: Darstellung und Kritik ihres Bildes vom gnostischen Erlösermythus. Göttingen, 1961.

F.L. Cross, ed., The Jung Codex: Three Studies [essays by Puech, Quispel, and Unnik]. London, 1955.

O. Cullmann, 'Salvation History and the Significance of the Anti-Gnostic Debate in the Second Century', in Salvation in History. London (1967), 24-8.

M. Friedländer, Der vorchristliche jüdische Gnostizismus. Göttingen, 1898.

S. Giversen, 'Nag Hammadi Bibliography, 1948-1963', StTh 17 (1963), 139-87.

R.M. Grant, Gnosticism: An Anthology. London/New York, 1961.

___. Gnosticism and Early Christianity. New York, 1959.

___. 'Notes on Gnosis', VC 11 (1957), 145-51.

G. van Groningen, First-Century Gnosticism: Its Origins and Motifs. Leiden, 1967.

A. Guillaumont, et al., The Gospel According to Thomas. Coptic Text and English Translation. Leiden/New York, 1959. Cf. H. Köster, infra, The Nag Hammadi Library, 117-30.

J.J. Gunther, 'Syrian Christian Dualism', VC 25 (1971), 81-93.

R. Haardt, Die Gnosis: Wesen und Zeugnisse. Salzburg, 1967.

___. Gnosis: Character and Testimony, trans. J. Hendry. Leiden, 1971.

___. 'Gnosis' and 'Gnosticism', arts. in Sacramentum Mundi II (New York, 1968), 374-79; 379-81.

___. 'Zwanzig Jahre der Erforschung der koptisch-gnostischen Schriften von Nag Hammadi', Theologie und Philosophie 42 (1967), 390-401.

H. Jonas, Gnosis und spätantiker Geist. 2 vols. Göttingen, 1934/5.

M. Krause, Gnosis and Gnosticism. Leiden, 1977.

G.W. MacRae, 'Gnosis' and 'Gnosticism', arts. in the New Catholic Encyclopedia. VII (New York, 1967), 522-23; 523-28.

R.A. Markus, 'Pleroma and Fulfillment', VC 8 (1954), 193-208.

E. Norden, Agnostos Theos. Leipzig, 1913.

N. Brox, Offenbarung, Gnosis, und gnostischer Mythos bei Irenaeus von Lyon. Munich, 1966.

E. Pagels, The Gnostic Gospels. New York, 1979.

_____. The Gnostic Paul: Gnostic Exegesis of the Pauline Letters. Philadelphia, 1975.

B. Pearson, 'Biblical Exegesis in Gnostic Literature', Armenian and Biblical Studies, ed. Michael Stone. Jerusalem (1976), 70-80.

H.-Ch. Puech, 'Gnostic Gospels and Related Documents', in Hennecke-Schneemelcher, New Testament Apocrypha I, 231-62.

G. Quispel, 'Christliche Gnosis und jüdische Heterodoxie', EvTh 14 (1954), 474-84.

J.M. Robinson, 'The Coptic-Gnostic Library Today', NTS 14 (1967/68), 356-401; updated in NTS 16 (1969/70), 185-90 seqq.

K. Rudolph, 'Gnosis and Gnostizismus, ein Forschungbericht', Th.Rund. 34 (1969), 121-175; 181-231; 358-361.

H.J. Schoeps, Aus frühchristlicher Zeit. Tübingen, 1950.

D.M. Scholer, Nag Hammadi Bibliography. Nag Hammadi Monograph Series, vol I. Leiden, 1971 seqq. Updated annually in Novum Testamentum.

W. Speyer, 'Genealogy im Gnostizismus', RAC VIII. Stuttgart (1950).

W.C.v.Unnik, 'Die jüdische Komponente in der Entstehung der Gnosis', Numen 15 (1961), 65-82.

H.F. Weiss, 'Paulus und die Häretiker', in Christentum und Gnosis, ed. W. Eltester. Berlin (1969); ZNTW 37, 116-28.

R.McL. Wilson, Gnosis and the New Testament. Oxford/Blackwell's, 1968.

_____. The Gnostic Problem. London, 1964.

F. Wisse, 'The Nag Hammadi Library and the Heresiologists', VC 25 (1971), 205-23.

E.M. Yamauchi, Pre-Christian Gnosticism: A Survey of the Proposed Evidences. London, 1973.

## H. Paul and Paulinism [See further, 'J']

C.K. Barrett, From the First Adam to the Last: A Study in Pauline Theology. London, 1962.

___. 'Pauline Controversies in the Post-Pauline Period', NTS 20 (1973/4), 229-45.

J.H. Bernard, The Pastoral Epistles. Cambridge, 1899.

G. Bornkamm, Paul. New York, 1971.

N. Brox, 'Lukas als Verfasser der Pastoralbriefe', JAC 13 (1970), 62-77.

F.F. Bruce, Paul and Jesus. London, 1974.

C.H. Buck and G. Taylor, St. Paul: A Study in the Development of His Thought. New York, 1969.

R. Bultmann, 'The Significance of the Historical Jesus for the Theology of Paul', in Faith and Understanding: Collected Essays. London (1969), 220-46.

H. Conzelmann, 'Current Problems in Pauline Research', in New Testament Issues, ed. R. Batey. London (1970).

___. ed. M. Dibelius, Die Pastoralbriefe, Tübingen, 1955.

___. 'Paulus und die Weisheit', NTS 12 (1966), 231-44.

W.D. Davies, Paul and Rabbinic Judaism. London, 1955.

B.S. Easton, The Pastoral Epistles. London, 1948.

R. Falconer, The Pastoral Epistles. Oxford, 1937.

L. Goppelt, 'Tradition nach Paulus', Kerygma und Dogma 4 (1958), 213-33.

A.T. Hanson, Studies in the Pastoral Epistles. London, 1968.

___. Studies in Paul's Technique and Theology. London, 1974.

A.v. Harnack, Die Apokryphen Briefe des Paulus an die Laodicinen und Korinther. Bonn, 1905.

P.N. Harrison, The Problem of the Pastoral Epistles. London, 1921.

E. Käsemann, Perspectives on Paul. Philadelphia, 1977.

J.N.D. Kelly, The Pastoral Epistles. London, 1963.

O. Küss, 'Die Rolle des Apostels Paulus in der theologischen Entwicklung der Urkirche', Münchener theologische Zeitschrift 14 (1963), 1-59; 109-87.

B. Metzger, 'A Reconsideration of Certain Arguments Against the Pauline Authorship of the Pastoral Epistles', ExT (1958/9), 91-94.

O. Michel, Paulus und seine Bibel. Gütersloh, 1929.

C.G. Montefiore, Judaism and St. Paul. London, 1973.

C.F.D. Moule, 'The Problem of the Pastoral Epistles: A Reappraisal', BJRL 47 (1965), 430-62.

W. Pauck, Der Herkunft des Verfassers der Pastoralbriefe. D.Theol., Göttingen, 1962.

E.P.Sanders, Paul and Palestinian Judaism. London, 1977.

W. Schmitals, Paul and the Gnostics. New York, 1972.

H.J. Schoeps, Paul: The Theology of the Apostle in the Light of Jewish Religious History. London, 1961.

T. Spicq, S. Paul: Les Epîtres pastorales. Paris, 1967.

J. Wagemann, Die Stellung des Paulus neben den Zwölf. Giessen, 1926.

D. Whiteley, The Theology of St. Paul. Oxford, 1964.

S. Wilson, Luke and the Pastoral Epistles. London, 1979.

H. Windisch, 'Zur Christologie der Pastoralbriefe', ZNTW 34 (1935), 213ff.

## I.  Luke and Urlukas

C.K. Barrett, Luke the Historian in Recent Study. Philadelphia, 1970.

A. Ehrhardt, 'The Construction and Purpose of the Acts of the Apostles', StTh 12 (1958), 45-79.

W. Eltester, 'Lukas und Paulus', Eranion (1961), 1-28.

M.S. Enslin, 'Luke and Paul', Jnl. of the American Oriental Society, 1958.

W.W. Gasque, A History of the Criticism of the Acts of the Apostles. Tübingen, 1975.

E. Haenchen, The Acts of the Apostles. Oxford, 1971.

A.v. Harnack, The Date of Acts, trans. J. Wilkinson. London, 1911.

M. Hengel, Acts and the History of Earliest Christianity. London, 1979.

J. Jervell, Luke and the People of God. Minneapolis, 1972.

L.E. Keck and J.L. Martin, Studies in Luke-Acts. New York, 1968 [includes Vielhauer, 'On the Paulinism of Acts', 33ff.; Bornkamm, 'The Missionary Stance of Paul in 1 Cor 9 and in Acts', 194ff.; Haenchen, 'The Book of Acts as Source Material for the History of Early Christianity', 258ff.; Knox, 'Acts and the Pauline Letter Corpus', 279ff.; Käsemann, 'Ephesians and Acts', 288ff.].

J.C. O'Neill, The Theology of Acts in its Historical Setting. London, 1961.

C.H. Talbert, Luke and the Gnostics. New York, 1966.

V.E. Wilshire, 'Was Canonical Luke Written During the Second Century?' NTS 20 (1974), 246-53.

S.G. Wilson, Luke and the Pastoral Epistles. London, 1979.

## J. Pauline and Post-Pauline Controversies: Apostolic Legitimacy

C.K. Barrett, A Commentary on the Second Epistle to the Corinthians. London, 1973.

___. Essays on Paul. London, 1982 [contains the essays 'Christianity at Corinth', 1ff.; 'Cephas and Corinth', 28ff.; 'Paul's Opponents in 2 Cor', 60ff.; 'Pseudapostoloi', 87ff.; 'The Allegory of Abraham, Sarah and Hagar in the Argument of Galatians', 154ff.].

___. 'Pauline Controversies in the Post-Pauline Period', NTS 20 (1973-1974), 229-45.

___. The Signs of an Apostle. London, 1970.

G. Bornkamm, 'Die Vorgeschichte des sogennanten Zweiten Korintherbriefes', Sb. der Heidelberger Akad. der Wissenschaft, 2 (1961).

R. Bultmann, Exegetische Probleme des Zweiten Korintherbriefes. Upsala, 1947.

C. Burchard, 'Paulus in der Apostelgeschichte', TLZ 100 (1975), 881-95.

C. Franklin, Paul and the Early Christians. Dublin, Indiana, 1978.

G. Friedrich, 'Die Gegner des Paulus im 2. Korintherbrief', in Abraham unser Vater, ed. Betz, et al. (1963), 181-215.

D. Georgi, Die Gegner des Paulus im 2. Korintherbrief. Heidelberg, 1964.

B. Holmberg, Paul and Power: The Structure of Authority in the Primitive Church as Reflected in the Pauline Epistles. London, 1978.

R.J. Karris, 'The Background and Significance of the Polemic of the Pastoral Epistles', JBL 92 (1973), 549-64.

E. Käsemann, 'Die Legitimität des Apostels', ZNTW 41 (1942), 33-71.

____. 'Paul and Early Catholicism', in NT Questions of Today. (London, 1969), 236-251.

____. Perspectives on Paul, trans. M. Kohl. Philadelphia, 1971.

J. Kirk, 'Apostleship since Rengstorf: Towards a Synthesis', NTS 21 (1974-1975), 249-64.

A. Lindemann, Paulus im ältesten Christentum: Das Bild des Apostels und die Rezeption der paulinischen Theologie in der frühchristlichen Literatur bis Marcion. Tübingen, 1979.

J. Quinn, 'P$^{46}$ -- The Pauline Canon?', CBQ 36 (1974), 379-85.

K.H. Rengstorf, ed. Das Paulusbild in der neueren deutschen Forschung. Darmstadt, 1956 [includes, Schlatter, 'Paulus', 200ff.; Reitzenstein, 'Paulus als Pneumatiker', 246ff.; Bultmann, 'Zur Geschichte der Paulus-Forschung', 304ff.; Lietzmann, 'Paulus', 380ff.; Käsemann, 'Legitimität', 475ff. (see above); Rengstorf, 'Über das paulinische Christentum', 613ff.].

S. Sandmel, The First Christian Century in Judaism and Christianity: Certainties and Uncertainties. New York, 1969.

W. Schmithals, The Office of the Apostle in the Early Church. Nashville, 1969.

H.M. Schenke, 'Das Weiterwirken des Paulus und die Pflege seines Erbes durch die Paulus-Schule', NTS 21 (1974-1975), 505-18.

J.H. Schütz, Paul and the Anatomy of Apostolic Authority. Cambridge, 1975.

E.M. Sidebottom James, Jude, and 2 Peter. London, 1967.